As one of the world's longest established
and best-known travel brands,
Thomas Cook are the experts in travel.

For more than 135 years our
guidebooks have unlocked the secrets
of destinations around the world,
sharing with travellers a wealth of
experience and a passion for travel.

**Rely on Thomas Cook as your
travelling companion on your next trip
and benefit from our unique heritage.**

Thomas Cook **driving** guides

NEW ENGLAND

**Tom Bross, Patricia Harris, David Lyon, Stephen H Morgan,
Barbara Radcliffe Rogers and Stillman D Rogers**

Your travelling companion since 1873

Thomas
Cook

Written and updated by Tom Bross, Patricia Harris, David Lyon, Stephen H Morgan, Barbara Radcliffe Rogers and Stillman D Rogers

Published by Thomas Cook Publishing,
A division of Thomas Cook Tour Operations Limited.
Company registration no. 3772199 England
The Thomas Cook Business Park, Unit 9, Coningsby Road,
Peterborough PE3 8SB, United Kingdom
E-mail: books@thomascook.com, Tel: + 44 (0) 1733 416477
www.thomascookpublishing.com

Produced by Cambridge Publishing Management Limited
Burr Elm Court, Main Street, Caldecote CB23 7NU

ISBN: 978-1-84848-208-1

Series Editor: Adam Royal
Production/DTP: Steven Collins

Printed and bound in India by Ajanta Offset & Packaging Ltd

Cover photography: Front: © 4CR, Franco Cogoli

About the authors

Tom Bross, a long-time resident of Boston, has been a freelance travel writer/photographer since the mid-1970s. In that capacity, he is a frequent visitor to central Europe – especially Germany – as well as eastern Canada, northern California and the US's six-state New England region. He has contributed Canadian and New England chapters to previous Thomas Cook guidebooks. For this current driving guides volume, he contributed chapters covering Providence, Newport and their respective vicinities in Rhode Island and southwestern Massachusetts, plus all of the chapters focused on cities and regions in Connecticut. Tom would like to thank Evan Smith of the Newport County (RI) Convention & Visitors' Bureau, Anne Lee and Diane Moore of the Greater Hartford Convention and Visitors' Bureau, and Tom Silvia of the Providence/Warwick Convention & Visitors' Bureau for help given while researching these chapters.

Patricia Harris and David Lyon write about travel, food and art from their base in Cambridge, Massachusetts. They contributed to *driving guides Washington DC, Virginia, Maryland & Delaware* and are authors of *Drive Around Andalucia and the Costa del Sol*, as well as several other titles. For this guide, they contributed the chapters covering West of Boston, Massachusetts North Shore, Cape Cod, the Berkshires, Maine's North Woods, New Hampshire and the Southern Maine Coast, Portland, Midcoast Maine, Penobscot Bay and Mount Desert Island.

Stephen H Morgan is a Boston-based travel writer and staff editor at *The Boston Globe*. He edited the Thomas Cook *On the Road Around New England* and *Touring Eastern Canada* guides, and his stories have appeared in a number of US newspapers and magazines. For this guide, Stephen contributed the Boston chapter and Travel Facts section.

Barbara Radcliffe Rogers and Stillman D Rogers belong to a prolific family team of writers and photographers. They specialise in writing about Canada and New England for guidebooks, magazines and websites. They are the authors of three books on Vermont, one on New Hampshire and one on Massachusetts. They also contributed to the Thomas Cook *Touring Eastern Canada* guide. For this guide they contributed chapters on Pioneer Valley, the Southern Green Mountains, Lake Champlain and the Northern Green Mountains, the Northeast Kingdom, the Upper Connecticut Valley, the New Hampshire Lakes and the White Mountains. They would like to thank Glenn Faria and William DeSousa for help given during the research for these chapters.

Contents

About driving guides

Thomas Cook's driving guides are designed to provide you with a comprehensive but flexible reference source to guide you as you tour a country or region by car. This guide divides New England into touring areas – one per chapter. Major cultural centres or cities form chapters in their own right. Each chapter contains enough attractions to provide at least a day's worth of activities – often more.

Above
Wagon ride at Maple Sugar
Shack, Canterbury

Symbol Key

❶ Tourist Information Centre

❷ Advice on arriving or departing

❿ Parking locations

❒ Advice on getting around

❸ Directions

❻ Sights and attractions

❍ Accommodation

❾ Eating

◯ Shopping

❾ Sport

◯ Entertainment

Ratings
To make it easier for you to plan your time and decide what to see, every area is rated according to its attractions in categories such as Architecture, Entertainment and Children.

Chapter contents
Every chapter has an introduction summing up the main attractions of the area, and a ratings box, which will highlight the area's strengths and weaknesses – some areas may be more attractive to families travelling with children, others to wine-lovers visiting vineyards, and others to people interested in finding historic sites, nature reserves or good beaches.

Each chapter is then divided into an alphabetical gazetteer and a suggested tour. You can select whether you just want to visit a particular sight or attraction, choosing from those described in the gazetteer, or whether you want to tour the area comprehensively. If the latter, you can construct your own itinerary, or follow the author's suggested tour, which comes at the end of every area chapter.

The gazetteer
The gazetteer section describes all the major attractions in the area – the villages, towns, historic sites, nature reserves, parks or museums that you are most likely to want to see. Maps of the area highlight all the places mentioned in the text. Using this comprehensive overview of the area, you may choose just to visit one or two sights.

One way to use the guide is simply to find individual sights that interest you, using the index or overview map, and read what our authors have to say about them. This will help you decide whether to visit the sight. If you do, you will find plenty of practical information,

Practical information

The practical information in the margin or sidebar will help you locate the services you need as an independent traveller – including tourist information centres, car parks and public transport facilities. You will also find the opening times of sights, museums, churches and other attractions, as well as useful tips on shopping, market days, cultural events, entertainment, festivals and sports facilities.

such as the street address, the telephone number for enquiries and opening times.

Alternatively, you can choose a hotel, perhaps with the help of the accommodation recommendations contained in this guide. You can then turn to the overall map on page 10 to help you work out which chapters in the book describe those cities and regions that lie closest to your chosen touring base.

Driving tours

The suggested tour is just that – a suggestion, with plenty of optional detours and one or two ideas for making your own discoveries, under the heading *Also worth exploring*. The routes are designed to link the attractions described in the gazetteer section, and to cover outstandingly scenic coastal, mountain and rural landscapes. The total distance is given for each tour, as is the time it will take you to drive the complete route, but bear in mind that this indication is just for the driving time: you will need to add on extra time for visiting attractions along the way.

Many of the routes are circular, so that you can join them at any point. Where the nature of the terrain dictates that the route has to be linear, the route can either be followed out and back, or you can use it as a link route, to get from one area in the book to another.

As you follow the route descriptions, you will find names picked out in bold capital letters – this means that the place is described fully in the gazetteer. Other names picked out in bold indicate additional villages or attractions worth a brief stop along the route.

Accommodation and food

In every chapter you will find lodging and eating recommendations for individual towns, or for the area as a whole. These are designed to cover a range of price brackets and concentrate on more characterful small or individualistic hotels and restaurants. In addition, you will find information in the *Travel facts* chapter on chain hotels, with an address to which you can write for a guide, map or directory. The price indications used in the guide have the following meanings:

$ budget level
$$ typical/average prices
$$$ de luxe.

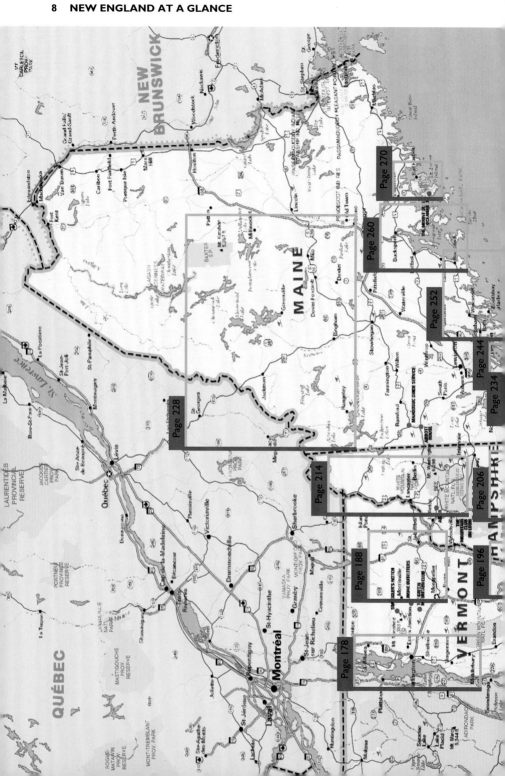

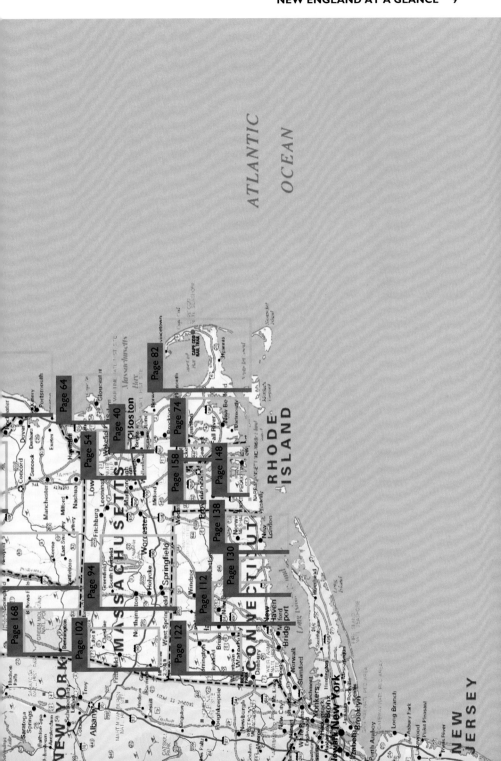

Introduction

Above
Trees showing a beautiful autumnal hue

The best thing about New England is that every road to nowhere actually ends up somewhere, and apart from the northern reaches of Maine, the trip is usually short. By New World standards, New England is a compact region studded with attractions and dense with history. Generations of landscape painters have lined its rocky shores and sandy strands, and some of America's leading poets have been spurred to rhetorical heights by the inland mountain ranges, lakes and woodlands. But the most inspired of all have been the holidaymakers touring the New England landscape in their family cars, bent on discovering whatever lies around the next bend in the road.

While New England is one of America's more densely populated regions, civilisation always sits in the midst of a natural world. It is a simple matter to park the car and strike out on a hiking trail through a nature reserve, glide through bird-filled marshes in a canoe, or simply stroll along a sandy beach picking up shells. All along the New England coast, from Cape Cod northwards, small boats speed to the offshore shoals to observe the great whales – finback, humpback, even the endangered right – that come to New England to feed. More intense natural experiences are also available, such as a week of hiking along the mountainous Long Trail in Vermont, ten days of traversing the Allagash Wilderness in a canoe, or single days spent in a sea kayak exploring Nantucket's shores or the small islands between Stonington, Maine and Isle au Haut.

Beauties wrought by human hands abound as well: the skyscrapers of Boston, the artful overpass bridges of the Merritt Parkway, the lovely green ribbon of Boston's Emerald Necklace parks, the sculpted grace of Augustus Saint-Gaudens' retreat in Cornish, New Hampshire. The engineering feats of the Cape Cod Canal and the long, graceful arc of the Jamestown Bridge between Conanicut and Aquidneck Islands actually complement the startling landscapes they conquer.

World-class art museums grace Hartford and Boston, two cities joined by Portland, Maine, and Providence, Rhode Island, as regional centres for theatre, dance, art and music. New England's long history is recounted in innumerable historic houses, with Portsmouth, New Hampshire, offering perhaps the largest concentration (the wonderful colonial houses of Deerfield, Massachusetts, largely function as decorative arts museums). Domestic history buffs will discover that virtually any town large enough to have a traffic light also has an historic house open to tours when volunteer guides are available. The region's romance with the sea is served at the whaling museums of Nantucket and New Bedford, by the astonishing China Trade collections of Salem's Peabody Essex Museum, by the delightful

Penobscot Marine Museum in the village of Searsport, Maine, and through a complex of wharves and sailing ships at Mystic Seaport in Connecticut. So-called 'living history' museums staffed by costumed interpreters enliven the Pilgrim past at Plymouth, Massachusetts, and the rural countryside circa 1840 at Sturbridge, Massachusetts.

New England travellers need never fear they will go hungry, as the tastes of the region are every bit a match for the sights. Even the thin soils of eastern Maine spout a kind of gastronomic poetry in their delicate fiddlehead ferns of spring and their tart blueberries of summer. The Maine coast is renowned for its lobster – *Homarus americanus* – which may be consumed cold in a salad with grapefruit in a smart Portland restaurant or simply enjoyed 'in the rough' at a dockside picnic table on the Pemaquid Peninsula. Portland, Boston and Providence can claim some of the finest chefs in North America, and the chic dining scene in all three cities is unequalled. But linen tablecloths and an array of wineglasses are not essential to good eating. One might experience a gourmet epiphany over the local maple syrup in a New Hampshire pancake house, a clam and oyster raw bar on Cape Cod, or from a fine local cheese, fresh sourdough bread and pint of ale in a Vermont brew-pub.

Right
Landing stage at Canterbury, in the New Hampshire lakes region

Travel facts

Accommodation

New England offers accommodation of every style and price level, from five-star hotels and posh inns to budget motels and campsites. Local tourist offices provide lodging lists and telephone numbers, but cannot make bookings.

$$$	de luxe
$$	average
$	budget

At chain hotels and motels, even with budget prices, expect a clean, comfortable, relatively spacious room with either one or two double or queen-sized beds and a private bathroom. Some independent hotels and motels provide a lower standard, but others have good quality facilities plus charm and character. Motels often line major auto routes and advertise availability with 'vacancy' signs. Most chains have freephone reservation telephone numbers that can be reached from anywhere in North America.

Bed and breakfasts can be a less impersonal alternative to homogenous hotels, but they are seldom a bargain in New England. In Boston, a B&B might consist of an entire apartment or condominium; in rural areas, it could offer a tidy room with antique furnishings and handmade quilts in a restored 19th-century home. Bath facilities may be shared but will most likely be private.

Country inns offer charm and personal attention. A small inn might have the look and feel of a B&B, but it will usually offer more rooms and breakfast choices. Bigger inns typically include a full restaurant with hearthside dining, a wide porch with rocking chairs for relaxing, and high prices to boot.

Camping means a tent or a recreational vehicle (RV) in a rural campsite. Those in state or national parks and forests are the quietest and most primitive, with firewood available but facilities sometimes limited to pit toilets and cold showers. Private sites usually offer more facilities but may be crowded with RVs.

Accommodation may be hard to find in major tourist destinations during high season – Memorial Day (end of May) to Labor Day (early September). The hardest time to find a room is foliage season (mid-September–mid-October, *see page 38*) in Maine, Vermont, New Hampshire and Western Massachusetts; many inns and hotels are fully booked in advance by return clients.

Thomas Cook or any other good travel agent can handle room bookings when purchasing air tickets and local transportation. Advance bookings require a voucher or credit card number to

Before you go

Ensure that you have the full address (including zip code) of where you are staying on your first night in the US – the Visa Waiver Program requires this information to be entered on the ESTA form, which you must complete online before travelling (*https://esta.cbp.dhs.gov*).

Children

New England offers many child-friendly attractions. From museums to transport, check for children's rates, often segmented by age, for example, under 3 free, 6–12 years $3, 12–18 years $4.

A few inns are reluctant to host children (and will say so if asked directly), but most driving destinations welcome them and are equipped for children of all ages, from nappies to video games. Most chains allow children under 12, 14, sometimes 18, to stay free in their parents' rooms. Hotels and motels can often arrange for (expensive) babysitters; a rollaway child's bed or cot usually comes free or at low cost.

guarantee the booking. Ask for discounts if you're disabled, a senior citizen, a motoring club member or travelling off-season.

Airports

International travellers arrive at Boston's Logan International Airport, New York's John F Kennedy Airport and Newark International Airport in New Jersey. Connecting flights bring travellers into smaller cities such as Providence, Hartford, Manchester (New Hampshire) and Portland. All international airports have foreign exchange and banking services, car-hire facilities and public transport to the nearest city. Information booths help travellers with transport, lodging or tourism questions, but cannot make bookings and usually have limited staff hours.

Climate

New England's weather is known more for changeability than for extremes. In general, expect cold and snow from December to March, warm days and cool nights from June to September.

Depending on locale, daytime temperatures in summer are in the 20s or 30s°C; July and August usually bring short spells of uncomfortably humid weather with temperatures above 30°C. Winter snows are heaviest in the ski country of Maine, New Hampshire and Vermont. Snowfall is generally light in southern New England, except for occasional big storms; sub-zero temperatures. September and October can be the most pleasant months, with daytime temperatures from 1 to 2°C, and leaves turning colour dramatically.

Currency

US dollars are the only currency accepted. Bill denominations are $1, $2, $5, $10, $20, $50 and $100. There are 100 cents to the dollar: coins are the 1-cent penny, 5-cent nickel, 10-cent dime, 25-cent quarter, 50-cent half-dollar and the rarely seen Sacagawea dollar.

Few banks are equipped to exchange foreign currency or traveller's cheques. However, traveller's cheques in US dollars, from well-known issuers, such as Thomas Cook, are acceptable at banks everywhere and by some larger hotels and shops.

Avoid carrying large amounts of cash. The safest forms of money are US dollar traveller's cheques and credit or debit cards. Car-hire companies, hotels and motels require a credit card imprint, even if the reservation has been fully prepaid. Automated teller machines (ATMs) are a ubiquitous source of cash through withdrawals or cash advances authorised by debit or credit card. Check terms and availability with the card issuer before leaving home.

Food

New England is especially known for its fresh seafood, which is served fried (in batter), broiled (grilled), or sometimes baked, and includes locally caught cod and haddock (called 'scrod' or 'schrod'), bluefish, tuna and salmon. Shellfish appearing on menus include clams (fried whole or as 'strips'), steamers (clams steamed in the shell), quahogs (a round-shell clam), mussels, oysters, scallops and shrimp. New England's greatest treat is the lobster, which turns bright red after immersion (live) into boiling water. It is served whole (a challenge to eat without making a mess), in parts (tails and claws) or picked out of the shell for salads or 'lobster roll' sandwiches.

Toilets

'Restroom' or 'bathroom' are the common terms; 'toilet' or 'washroom' are acceptable; few people recognise WC.

Most businesses, including bars and restaurants, reserve restrooms for clients. Petrol stations provide keys for customers to access restrooms. Public toilets are not common along city streets, but roadside rest stops often have them. Hotels, museums and other tourist attractions do too, of course.

Right
Lobster boats in Mackerel Cove, Maine

Left
Lobster buoys hanging on a wooden building in Kennebunkport, Maine

Customs regulations

Personal duty-free allowances for visitors entering the USA are 1 US quart (approximately 0.9 litres) of spirits or wine, 300 cigarettes or 50 (non-Cuban) cigars and up to $100-worth of gifts. On your return home you will be allowed to take:

- **Australia:** AU$400 in goods (AU$200 under age 18) plus 250 cigarettes or 250g tobacco and 1 litre alcohol.
- **Canada:** C$300 in goods (provided you have been away for over a week) per year; also 50 cigars plus 200 cigarettes and 1kg tobacco (if over 16) and 40oz/1 litre alcohol.
- **New Zealand:** NZ$700 in goods. Anyone over age 17 may also take 200 cigarettes or 250g tobacco or 50 cigars or a combination of tobacco products not exceeding 250g in all, plus 4.5 litres beer or wine and 1.125 litres spirits.
- **UK:** allowances for goods bought outside the EU and/or in EU duty-free shops: 200 cigarettes or 50 cigars or 100 cigarillos or 250g tobacco plus 2 litres still table wine plus 1 litre spirits or 2 litres sparkling wine plus 60cc perfume plus 250cc eau de toilette.

Drinking

Bottled water is popular, but rarely necessary for health reasons. However, water from streams and ponds in natural areas should be considered contaminated and avoided due to *giardia* or other parasites. Soft drinks (called soda or, in Boston, tonic) and fruit juices are available

Above
Patron saint festival in Boston

Festivals

Fourth of July
(Independence Day) is
celebrated in every city
and town with cookouts,
concerts and fireworks.
Memorial Day (30 May)
and St Patrick's Day (17
March) are occasions for
parades. See route
chapters for local festivals.

From late August into
October, small towns
throughout New England
hold town or county fairs
– a custom held over from
agrarian times – with
animal husbandry
competitions, games and
thrill rides. The Big E
(Eastern States Exposition)
in West Springfield, Mass.,
is the biggest of these.

in stunning variety. American coffee is customarily weak, but cafés and gourmet coffee shops offer flavourful alternatives. Tea usually means a cup of hot water with a tea bag.

You must be 21 years old to purchase or to drink alcohol. State and local laws govern hours at licensed establishments, which are generally from morning until 2400, 0100 or 0200. Spirits are sold in state-owned liquor stores in New Hampshire, Maine and Vermont, beer and wine in grocery stores. Elsewhere, privately-owned liquor (or 'package') stores sell beer, wine and spirits; some supermarkets sell beer and wine only. Microbreweries throughout the region are making interesting local beers these days.

Eating out

American meal portions can be large, beginning at breakfast, which may include bacon and eggs cooked to order with fried potatoes, toast and endless refills of coffee. Midday lunch offerings include soups, salads and sandwiches. Evening dinner menus offer appetisers (starters), salads, soups, pastas, entrées (main courses) and desserts.

New England is best known for its seafood (*see Food, page 15*), but a wide variety of cuisine is available, including steak houses, Italian, Mexican, Chinese, Japanese and Thai. In major cities, the melting-pot of cuisine includes Brazilian, Cambodian, Caribbean, Greek, Indian, Middle Eastern, Portuguese, Vietnamese and regional American (such as Dixie-style ribs and barbecue).

Fast-food joints are popular and cheap (McDonalds, KFC, Burger King, Wendy's, Pizza Hut and Taco Bell). Higher on the price and quality ladder are chain restaurants such as Friendly's (ice cream, sandwiches and simple meals), Bertucci's (Italian), Boston Market (roasted chicken) and International House of Pancakes (IHoP), which serves all-day breakfast plus safe, unexciting lunch and dinner choices.

Expect to pay $5–8 for breakfast (much more at hotels), $5–12 for lunch, $15–25 for dinner (plus drinks). Service charges are rarely added to bills, and tipping is expected – at least 15 per cent of the bill before taxes are added in.

Entry formalities

For travellers from British Commonwealth countries, border inspections are generally routine; have your passport, visa or visa waiver, proof of support if necessary and return ticket in order. Before travelling you must also have completed an ESTA form online at *https://esta.cbp.dhs.gov*. There is also an extra check when you arrive at a US airport – a photo plus fingerprinting. Brief crossings into and out of Canada are generally permitted, but they can be time-consuming if an official targets you for a car search. If you're not carrying illegal drugs, alcohol, firearms or agricultural products, and if your documents are in order, you should have no difficulty.

Maps

Good state, regional and city maps are produced by the **American Automobile Association**, known as AAA ('Triple A'), and distributed free at AAA offices, but only to members. Most automobile clubs worldwide have reciprocal agreements with AAA to provide maps and other member services. Be prepared to show a membership card.

The most detailed road maps are produced by **American Map Inc** *www.americanmap.com*. These wire-bound and folding maps are sold at booksellers, news-stands, souvenir shops and airports. Detailed up-country maps are available from **DeLorme Map Co** 2 *DeLorme Dr, PO Box 298, Yarmouth, ME 04096; tel: (207) 864-7000; www. delorme.com*

For back-country travel, US Geological Survey topographic maps show terrain reliably; they can be purchased in Cambridge, MA at the **Globe Corner Bookstore** (see *Reading, page 20*). For hiking in the White Mountains or along the Appalachian Trail, maps and guidebooks from **The Appalachian Mountain Club** 5 *Joy St, Boston, MA 02108; tel: (617) 523-0636; www. outdoors.org*, are indispensable.

Health

Hospital emergency rooms are the place to go in the event of life-threatening medical problems. If a life is at risk, treatment will be swift and top-notch, with payment problems sorted out later. For mundane problems, doctors' offices or health clinics can provide care.

Non-US national health plans are not accepted by US medical providers, so some form of health insurance coverage is mandatory – at least $1 million of cover is essential.

Bring enough prescription medication to last the entire trip and carry a copy of the prescription in generic language in case of emergency. No inoculations are required, and New England is basically a healthy place to visit. However, when visiting state and national parks or other natural areas, take note of posted warnings about rabies, Lyme disease or other local health risks.

Information

In the USA, each state is responsible for its own tourism promotion.

- **Connecticut Commission on Culture & Tourism** *1 Constitution Plaza, 2nd Floor, Hartford, CT 06103; tel: (860) 256-2800, (to order brochures, within North America) 888-288-4748; fax: (860) 270-8077; www.ctvisit.com*
- **Maine Office for Tourism** *Hallowell, ME 04347-2300; tel: (207) 623-0363; www.mainetourism.com.* **Maine Office of Tourism** *59 State House Station, Augusta, ME 04330; tel: (207) 287-5711 or (888) 624-6345; www.visitmaine.com*
- **Massachusetts Office of Travel and Tourism** *10 Park Plaza, Suite 4510, Boston, MA 02116; tel: (617) 973-8500, (800) 227-MASS; www.mass-vacation.com*
- **New Hampshire Division of Travel and Tourism Development** *PO Box 1856, Concord, NH 03302; tel: (603) 271-2665; fax: (603) 271-6870; www.visitnh.gov*
- **Rhode Island Tourism Division** *315 Iron Horse Way, Suite 101, Providence, RI 02908; tel: (800) 250-7384; fax: (401) 273-8270; www.visitrhodeisland.com*
- **Vermont Bureau of Tourism** *National Life Building, 6th floor, Montpelier, VT 05620; tel: (802) 828-3237; www.travel-vermont.com*

Information, brochures, maps and itinerary planning are also available from: **Discover New England** *Beth Cooper Public Relations, Hatchlands Park, East Wing, East Clandon, Surrey GU4 7RT; tel: (0148) 322 2676; fax: (0148) 321 2947.* In the USA, the address is *Box 3809, Stowe, VT 05672; tel: (802) 253-2500; fax: (802) 253-9064; www.discovernewengland.org*

Insurance

Experienced travellers carry insurance that covers their belongings, holiday investment (including provision for cancelled or delayed

Public holidays

The following holidays are celebrated nationally: New Year's Day (1 Jan); Martin Luther King Jr Day (third Mon in Jan); Presidents' Day (third Mon in Feb); Memorial Day (last Mon in May); Independence Day (4 Jul); Labor Day (first Mon in Sept); Columbus Day (second Mon in Oct); Veterans Day (11 Nov); Thanksgiving Day (fourth Thur in Nov); and Christmas (25 Dec).

Post offices and government offices close, as do many businesses and shops. Large department stores stay open and hold huge sales. Convenience stores, supermarkets, liquor stores and petrol stations generally remain open (sometimes with curtailed hours). Nearly everything closes on New Year's Day, Thanksgiving Day and Christmas Day.

Electricity

The USA uses 110V 60Hz current. Two- or three-pin electrical plugs are standard. Electrical gadgets from outside North America require plug and power converters. Both are difficult to obtain in the USA. Beware of buying electrical appliances in the USA: few gadgets on the US market can run on 220V 50Hz power. Exceptions are battery-operated equipment such as radios, cameras and portable computers – or dual-voltage shavers and hair dryers.

Left
Mount Monadnock in New Hampshire

flights and weather problems) and health (including immediate evacuation home in case of medical emergency). Many hospitals refuse treatment without proof of insurance. Thomas Cook and other travel agencies offer comprehensive policies. Medical coverage should be high – at least $1 million.

Museums

Many major museums open seven days a week all year. Others close Mondays, and all close for New Year's Day, Christmas and Thanksgiving. Hours are generally 0900 or 1000 to 1700 or 1800, with seasonal variations; some stay open one evening per week. Smaller museums, particularly in less touristy areas, may have limited hours or days of opening and may close in winter.

National parks

The National Park Service administers Acadia National Park in Maine, the Cape Cod National Seashore, historical parks in Boston, Lexington and Concord, Lowell and Salem, Mass., and a variety of smaller historical parks, monuments and sites around the region; for details see the appropriate chapters in this book. For general information, contact **National Park Service** *Charlestown Navy Yard, Boston, MA 02129; tel: (617) 242-5642; www.nps.gov*
Some sites charge an entry fee. Senior and disabled persons should ask if discounts apply. The 'America the Beautiful' pass ($80) covers entry to all federal recreation areas and National Parks for one year. The pass admits four.

Opening times

Office hours are generally Monday–Friday 0900–1700, although a few tourist offices also keep short Saturday hours all year, and weekend hours in summer. Many banks open from 0900 or 1000 to 1500 or 1600; a few stay open Thursday to 1900 and Saturday 0900–1300. Petrol stations open from early until late; a few stay open 24 hours on major routes. In cities, the big stores and shopping centres open at 0900 or 1000 Monday–Saturday and close at 2000 or 2100, occasionally with shorter hours on Sunday.

Packing

Everything you could ever need is available, so don't worry if you've left anything behind – in fact, most US prices will seem low. Carry all medicines, glasses and contraceptives with you, and keep duplicate prescriptions to verify your need for a medicine.

Safety and security

Despite well-publicised incidents of street violence, millions of people travel (and live) in perfect safety each year in the USA. So can you if you follow common-sense precautions.

Never publicly discuss travel plans or money or valuables you are carrying; keep to well-lit areas; do not wear or carry expensive jewellery or flash rolls of banknotes. Use a hidden moneybelt for your valuables, travel documents and spare cash. In the unlikely event you are mugged, don't resist.

If you do encounter trouble, dial 911 on any telephone for free emergency assistance from police, fire and medical authorities.

Smoking

All states in this guide have legal bans on indoor smoking in public places, although some communities may make exceptions for bars and casinos. As non-smoking becomes the norm in the USA, many hotels and almost all B&Bs ban smoking in their rooms.

Time

New England clocks are set to GMT minus 5 hours, called Eastern Standard Time (EST). From the second Sunday in March until the first Sunday in November, clocks go forward 1 hour to Eastern Daylight Time (EDT).

Postal services

Almost every town has at least one post office. Hours vary, although all are open Monday–Friday, morning and afternoon. Major US Postal Service branches are open Saturday, only a select few on Sunday. Stamps may be purchased from machines in some pharmacies and convenience stores. Letters and cards with correct postage may be dropped in blue boxes outside postal branches or on street corners; parcels weighing more than 1lb must be handed to a postal clerk for security reasons. Mail everything going overseas as Air Mail (surface mail takes weeks or even months). All US mail must include the five-digit zip code (also use the four-digit suffix if you know it).

Public transport

Train travel is sparse in the USA. **Amtrak** *tel: (800) 872-7245; www.amtrak.com*, handles passenger services nationwide. The main New England route runs from Boston to New York City, with stops at Providence and points along the Connecticut shore – a 5-hour ride, 3¹/₂ hours via Acela Express trains. Prices vary according to the day and time of travel, but they are usually cheaper than air travel, which takes only about one hour from Boston to New York.

Bus (coach) lines serve more destinations, with prices similar to train fares. **Greyhound Bus Lines** *tel: 214-849-8100 (0500–0100 Central time zone), 800-231-2222; www.greyhound.com*, provides long-distance bus services nationwide between major cities, including Boston. Peter Pan, Bonanza and other local lines carry passengers between cities and towns in New England. The bi-monthly *Thomas Cook Overseas Timetable* contains timetables for rail and bus travel; buy online at *www.thomascookpublishing.com* or *tel: (0)1733 416477*.

Reading

Comprehensive guides to areas covered in this book as well as maps and more specialised books on New England history, culture and lore may be purchased at **The Globe Corner Bookstore** *90 Mount Auburn St, Cambridge, MA 02138; tel: (617) 497-6277; www.globecorner.com*, and many other bookshops. Specialised guides include *Off the Beaten Path* guides to each state (Globe Pequot Press) and the *AMC White Mountain Guide* (Appalachian Mountain Club, Boston), strictly for hikers.

Stores

Large department stores found throughout New England include Macy's and several discount chains. National chains such as Lord &

Shopping

Clothing can be a bargain, particularly at discount stores or factory outlets, as can cameras and other photo equipment, but do your homework on prices before you go, and shop around. New England prices for alcohol, tobacco and perfume beat most duty-free shops.

New England souvenirs include Vermont maple syrup, live Maine lobsters packed for the flight home, 'Boston Harbor tea', Cape Cod saltwater taffy, hand-made patchwork quilts and the ubiquitous T-shirts.

There is no Valued Added Tax in the USA. Each state imposes its own tax on sales of products, meals and lodgings, ranging from 5 to 10 per cent. Clothing, baby products and grocery items are tax-free in some states.

Sport

Boston is home to several professional sports teams. The Boston Red Sox play baseball at Fenway Park from April to September, the Boston Bruins (hockey) and Boston Celtics (basketball) compete at the TD Banknorth Garden from autumn to spring. The New England Patriots (American football) are based in Foxborough (a Boston suburb), as are the New England Revolution, a pro team in soccer (football), which has a small following in the USA.

Taylor (clothing), L L Bean (sportswear and equipment), The Gap (clothing), J C Penney (clothing, housewares, furniture, etc) and Sears (clothing, hardware and appliances) are well represented.

For good prices and reasonable quality, follow the locals into discount stores such as Marshalls, Target and others. In Maine, look for Renny's stores. In some locales, factory outlet stores cluster together as a magnet for shoppers.

Telephones

Dialling instructions are in the local white pages telephone directory. Phone numbers are always 7 digits, preceded by a 3-digit area code when calling outside the local area (in Eastern Massachusetts, always dial all 10 digits). For long-distance calls, precede the area code with a 1.

Payphones take coins and are located on street corners or inside restaurants, hotels and other public buildings. A local call usually costs $0.50; a computer voice will come on-line to ask for additional coins when needed. Prepaid phone cards are popular and may be purchased at pharmacies, news-stands and convenience stores. Many hotels and motels add a stiff surcharge to the cost of a call from a room.

In emergencies, dial 911 for police, medical or fire brigade response. Dial 0 for an operator. For information, dial 411. There will be a charge for information calls. Most phone numbers with the 800, 877 or 888 area code are toll-free (freephone). Those with the 900 area code charge the caller for information or other services, often at high per-minute rates.

For international dialling, dial 011–country code–city code (omitting the first 0 if there is one)–local number; eg, to call Great Britain, Inner London, dial: 011-44-20-local number. Some country codes: Australia 61, New Zealand 64, Republic of Ireland 353, South Africa 27, United Kingdom 44.

Travellers with disabilities

State and federal laws, particularly the Americans with Disabilities Act (ADA), require that all businesses, buildings and services used by the public be accessible by handicapped persons, including those using wheelchairs, ie they must have access ramps and toilets designed for wheelchairs. Most cities and towns have ramps built into street crossings, and most city buses have some provision for wheelchair passengers. However, many older facilities do not yet comply with the standards. Special controls for disabled drivers are seldom an option on hired vehicles. For more information, contact: SATH (Society for Accessible Travel & Hospitality), *347 Fifth Ave, Suite 610, New York, NY 10016; tel: (212) 447-7284; www.sath.org,* or RADAR, *12 City Forum, 250 City Rd, London, EC1V 8AF; tel: (020) 7250-3222; www.radar.org.uk*

Driver's guide

Accidents

In the event of a collision, always stop (penalties for failing to stop can include imprisonment). If either vehicle or any person is injured, immediately report the accident to state police if it occurred on a state or interstate road, or to local police. Everyone involved should exchange numbers of drivers' licences, car registration, insurance coverage information and addresses and telephone numbers for further contact. This same information will generally be provided to the police as well. Collisions with property or personal damage must also be reported to your car-hire company and to the state department of motor vehicles in every state except Connecticut. Although the grace period for reporting to the state varies, doing so within 48 hours ensures legal compliance.

Breakdowns

Should a breakdown occur, pull to the side of the road where you will be visible but out of the way of traffic. Switch on hazard lights and, if it is safe to do so, raise the bonnet and trunk lids. Change a tyre only if you're out of the flow of traffic.

Dial 911 from any telephone to summon emergency assistance. Report your telephone number, problem, location and any need for medical assistance. Emergency phone boxes are usually placed at frequent intervals along Interstate Highways. If one is not visible, stay with the vehicle and wait for a patrol car to stop to render assistance.

Car hire

Hiring a vehicle provides you with freedom to travel as you please with a vehicle you can leave behind when you depart. Whether booking a fly-drive package or making independent arrangements, plan well in advance to ensure getting the type and size of vehicle you desire. Unlimited mileage is standard on most car-hire contracts, but not on recreational vehicles (RVs). Most US rental cars come with either two or four doors, an automatic transmission and air conditioning.

Most rental companies require that the driver be at least 21 years old (some specify age 25), hold a valid driver's licence and use a credit card to secure the value of the vehicle. Before leaving the hire agency,

Documents

A valid driver's home country licence should be carried on your person at all times. Vehicle registration and, where applicable, a valid car-hire contract must be in the vehicle when it is under way. Proof of liability insurance must also be supplied in the event of an accident. Minimum driving age in New England is 16 but drivers under 18 may have rules limiting the privilege.

Drinking and driving laws

Driving under the influence of alcohol or other drugs is illegal throughout New England. Intoxication is defined as 0.08 per cent blood alcohol in most states (and zero tolerance for under 21s). If a police officer stops you and suspects you may be impaired, you may be asked to take an instant breathalyser test that estimates blood alcohol from alcohol in your breath. You are permitted to refuse the test, but doing so means automatic suspension of your driver's licence.

Essentials

You should travel with three red reflective warning triangles, road flares, a torch, a first aid kit and a jack for tyre repair. If the vehicle has a spare tyre, make sure that it is properly inflated.

be certain that you have the car registration and all rental documentation. Also be sure you know how to operate the vehicle (there's nothing more maddening than running low on petrol and being unable to find the fuel tank release).

Caravans and camper vans (Trailers and RVs)

Convenient as it may be to drive around in one's lodging, caravans and camper vans can pose some difficulties. Most New England communities require that they be parked in a proper campsite before using them as a place to sleep, and some communities prohibit roadside parking, especially after dark. Some urban car parks lack the overhead clearance to accommodate caravans. Nantucket bans caravans from the island altogether. Very large caravans must follow posted road regulations for trucks (lorries), which generally ban them from high-speed or passing lanes.

Driving in New England

Below
Barn at Freeman Farm, Old Sturbridge Village

The worst driving conditions in New England involve snow in the winter, or heavy rains or dense fog at any time of year. Driving with low-beam headlights at all times is a recommended safety precaution. Avoid using high beams in snow, rain or fog to avoid blinding other drivers (or yourself with reflected glare). If visibility is poor, pull over and wait for the storm to pass. The danger of aquaplaning arises during sudden heavy rains, particularly at speeds above 35mph.

Driving on snow takes skill, and if you are unfamiliar with stopping, turning and negotiating skids on snow, practise in a vacant car park before venturing out on the road. Better yet, stay off the road. Apply brakes lightly and steadily to stop on snow. Hired cars are generally equipped with all-season tyres, which are not particularly effective at gripping snow. During winter driving, keep the petrol tank topped up in case you are stuck in a snow drift awaiting help. If you do become stuck in a snowstorm, stay in the vehicle, place a red flag on the antenna or door handle, try to keep warm with blankets, and do not run the engine any more than necessary. Make sure the exhaust pipe is not clogged with snow. Useful winter driving gear includes a blanket, a windscreen ice scraper, a small shovel and a bucket or bag of sand. In all but remote areas of New England, snow is cleared promptly from streets and roads and a mixture of sand and salt is applied to reduce icing.

Driving rules

Below
Camden Baptist Church,
Penobscot Bay

Traffic drives on the right in the United States. Where streets meet and vehicles arrive at close to the same time, priority belongs to the vehicle on the right. Traffic already on a roundabout (traffic circle or rotary) has the right-of-way, and those waiting launch into the curve whenever they can. Unless otherwise posted, a vehicle can turn right from the right-hand lane after coming to a complete stop. Before turning, the driver signals the direction of the intended turn, although in practice, many drivers don't bother. When turning left, a green arrow gives right of way; a green light means you may turn but oncoming traffic has the right of way. Flashing amber lights indicate proceed, but with caution; flashing red lights mean stop and then proceed cautiously once the green light reappears. Horns are seldom used.

Interstate Highways and highway entrances are clearly marked with green and white signs. On city streets and occasionally on country roads, bicycle paths are marked as a separate lane on the right where bikes have the right-of-way. A school bus stopped with flashing lights or signal lights at a railway crossing requires all traffic to stop as long as lights flash, and violations are serious.

Road information

Many non-North American auto clubs have reciprocal privileges with the American Automobile Association (AAA), including touring books, road maps, discounts at hotels and motels and some roadside assistance. Emergency towing is not always included. For information on services, ask your own club or request Office to Serve You Abroad, American Automobile Association, 1000 AAA Drive, Heathrow, FL 32756-5063; tel: (407) 444-7700. On Interstate Highways, look for posted radio frequencies that give weather and road conditions.

Tolls

Every New England state has some toll roads, which may include stretches of Interstate Highway. On short toll roads, drivers are expected to pay cash at the toll booths (a good supply of quarters, also useful for parking meters, comes in handy). On longer toll roads, drivers pick up a toll card when entering the highway and pay a variable rate based on mileage when exiting.

Roadways are marked with a solid white line for 'do not pass', and with a broken line where passing another vehicle is permitted. Blind curves are not infrequent, dictating slower speeds. Police use radar, lasers and aeroplanes to track and stop speeding drivers. Pedestrians have the right-of-way at crossings and intersections.

Fuel

Petrol stations are plentiful on all but the most remote roads. A few are open around the clock with pumps equipped with credit card machines enabling payment to be made at the pump. Petrol stations generally accept cash, credit cards and debit cards. Due to counterfeiting and safety concerns, petrol station clerks will not accept $50 or $100 bills. Petrol (and diesel) is sold at petrol stations in US gallons (about 3.5 litres per gallon). Most vehicles take unleaded petrol that comes in regular, premium and super grades. Buy regular unless the car rental company or the vehicle operation manual specifies otherwise. Most stations are self-service, although some offer a higher-priced full-service alternative. Pump prices include all taxes. Fuel prices can vary wildly, so watch prices and refill when you see the lowest ones. The cost per gallon is always shown with .9 at the end, as in 299.9.

Parking

In cities, public car parks are generally indicated with a blue sign, carrying the letter 'P' and a directional arrow. Rates are posted at the entrance. Urban garages are often expensive but may give discounts to shoppers or theatregoers who have their timecards stamped with a validation sticker. Coin-operated parking meters are in effect in most areas, with rates ranging from $1 per hour in urban areas to as little as 25 cents per hour in small towns. Parking near a fire hydrant, a red or yellow kerb or in front of a wheelchair access ramp is forbidden. In urban areas, kerbside parking may be banned during morning and evening commuting hours. If you violate parking regulations or let a meter expire, expect to be issued a citation. If you do not pay it, the car-hire company may charge the fine to your credit card along with a substantial penalty.

Police

Police cars signal drivers with flashing blue or blue and red lights and sometimes with a siren. While most police vehicles are marked, some highways are patrolled by unmarked cars. When signalled, pull over to the side and have your driver's licence and vehicle registration ready for inspection. Roll down the window but do not leave the vehicle unless requested. You have the right to ask an officer for identification.

Above
Autumn colours in New England

Seatbelts

All New England states require the driver and front seat passenger to wear seatbelts. Rear seatbelts should be worn where fitted.

Security

Lock your car. Lock it when you are inside and when you leave it. Do not leave maps, guidebooks or other tourist paraphernalia in clear sight. In cities try always to park in well-lit areas.

Speed limits

Official highway speed limits are 65mph in rural areas, 55mph in urban areas. Many New England drivers take these as suggestions rather than law. You are safest when moving with the flow of traffic, neither faster nor significantly slower. Note that most Interstate Highways also have minimum speed limits. Expect to be overtaken and passed on both sides if you are moving slower than the rest of the traffic. This can be disconcerting but is perfectly legal in most states. On secondary roads, speed limits are much lower. When no limit is posted, assume the limit is 30mph in residential areas, 20mph near schools and hospitals.

Road signs

International symbols are used for many road signs in New England; all language signs are in English. Signs may be white, yellow, green, brown or blue. Stop, Yield, Do Not Enter and Wrong Way signs are usually red and white. Warning or direction indicators are generally yellow. Roadwork and temporary detour signs are generally reflective orange. Green indicates highway directions, blue denotes non-driving information (parking, informational radio frequencies). Brown signs are usually reserved to indicate parks, campsites and attractions.

Traffic lights are red (stop), green (go) and yellow (caution). Simultaneous red and yellow lights indicate a pedestrian crossing. Unless otherwise posted, it is legal to make a right-hand turn at a red light if there is no traffic and no pedestrian crossing light is lit. Motorists are expected to yield the right of way to pedestrians at all zebra crossings or 'crosswalks', although the law is observed more in the breach than in the practice so be careful when crossing on one.

Typical road signs in New England

INSTRUCTIONS

Stop

Give way

Wrong way - often together
with 'No entry' sign

No right turn

No U-turn

One-way
traffic

Two-way left
turn lanes

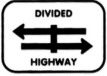

Divided highway
(dual carriageway)
at junction ahead

Speed limit
signs: maximum
and maximum/
minimum limits

WARNINGS

Crossroads

Junction

Curve (bend)

Winding road

Stop ahead

Two-way traffic

Divided highway
(dual carriageway)

Road narrows
on right

Roadworks
ahead

Railway
crossing

No-overtaking
zone

Getting to New England

Above
Mount Washington cog railway

Driving into Boston from Logan Airport

The 3-mile drive into Boston is frequently complicated by construction projects, resulting in frequent changes in routing and signs.

From the airport loop, follow signs to 'Airport Exit' then 'Route 1A South to 93/Sumner Tunnel/Boston' or 'Ted Williams Tunnel/Boston'. Be prepared for confusing signage and quick lane changes at the tunnel's end. Then do the following.
• To Back Bay/Boston Common area: follow signs to Routes 3 and 93 *North*, then signs onto 'Storrow Drive'.

(continued on page 29)

By air

International travellers to New England arrive at Boston's Logan International Airport (BOS), New York's John F Kennedy International Airport (JFK) or Newark International Airport (EWR) in New Jersey. After clearing Customs and Immigration and re-checking baggage, passengers transfer to flights into Providence, Hartford/Springfield, Manchester, Portland, Burlington or smaller cities. There are car-hire facilities at any airport (always reserve in advance) and public transport of some type (train, bus, limousine, taxi) into the nearest city.

Unless you have a reason to be in New York, arrival and departure are generally easier at Boston. It is much smaller, easier to get in and out of, less expensive and closer to most places in New England. British Airways, Virgin Atlantic, American Airlines and Aer Lingus all offer direct flights into Boston, and any airline can book connecting flights from JFK or Newark. If you do fly into New York, keep in mind that Newark Airport is smaller, less crowded and slightly closer to Manhattan than JFK, and is connected to the city and to New England's major cities by direct Amtrak trains.

It is always a good idea to book your first night's room in advance, but in Boston and New York it is absolutely essential because rooms can be hard to find.

Consider going without a car if you stay in downtown Boston – after all, public transport into and within Boston is quick and simple, while parking places are scarce and expensive. If you must pick up your hire car on arrival at Logan Airport, arrange parking in advance with your Boston hotel. However, if you stay outside Boston proper, a car is usually a necessity and parking might well be free.

Travellers arriving at New York face a similar choice: a hire car can be a liability in Manhattan but a necessity in the suburbs. If you don't plan to stay in New York, just pick up a hire car and go. You can be well on your way into Connecticut within an hour's driving time from JFK or Newark.

Domestic US air service is extensive: there are shuttle flights into Boston every hour from New York's LaGuardia Airport and from Washington, DC, plus regularly scheduled flights into Boston, Hartford, Portland, Providence and some smaller New England cities from cities all over the USA and Canada. Manchester, in New Hampshire, is the gateway to the White Mountains.

By train and bus

Driving into Boston from Logan Airport
(continued from page 28)

• To South Station or Massachusetts Turnpike: follow signs onto Routes 3 and 93 *South*.
• To Faneuil Hall area: follow signs to 'North End', 'Haymarket' or 'N. Washington St'.

For precise, current driving directions to your destination, be sure to get a map and ask the agent for help when picking up your hire-car at the airport. Your hotel can give you exact instructions.

Amtrak, the US passenger rail system, offers frequent but limited services into and within New England. The main route is from New York's Pennsylvania Station to South Station in Boston, with stops along the Connecticut shore and in Providence. New York–Boston is a pleasant ride but slow. It takes 5 hours by train, 3½ hours on Acela Express runs, less than an hour by air. The Amtrak train service continues north to Portland, Maine.

Another Amtrak route goes north from New Haven to Hartford, Connecticut, and on to Springfield, Massachusetts. A special train on this line, the *Montrealer*, continues into Vermont, then transfers passengers on to buses across the Canadian border to Montreal. There's also the Boston–Chicago service (continuing to California) via Springfield, but trains run infrequently. Most Amtrak passengers heading to New England travel through New York.

Bus (coach) lines (Greyhound nationwide; Bonanza, Peter Pan, Vermont Transit and other lines locally) serve many more destinations within New England and in neighbouring regions than rail does. The Boston–New York bus trip, along major highways, is comparable to the train in duration but is at a lower price.

By car

The extensive US Interstate Highway system brings car traffic smoothly into and around New England from neighbouring areas. The best of US roads, these are dual carriageway, limited-access highways carrying two, three, four or more lanes of traffic in each direction.

The main routes into New England are I-95 (a north–south route from Florida to Maine) and I-90 (an east–west route from Seattle to Boston). I-95 enters New England from New York City and follows the Connecticut shore to Providence, Boston, Portland and northwards. I-

Below
Sandwich, New Hampshire

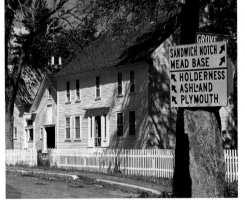

90, which begins (or ends) in Boston, is a toll road where it crosses Massachusetts and upper New York State. Other interstate routes criss-cross the region. Driving New York–Boston takes four hours or more, depending on traffic.

Interstates are the quickest, most direct routes but, except in New Hampshire and Vermont, offer little to see. Petrol stations, restaurants and motels generally cluster at exits, off the highway; rest stops between some exits offer parking and toilet facilities and often food. Rest stops along toll roads (Massachusetts Turnpike and New York State Thruway) offer petrol and food as well.

Setting the scene

Above
'Living history' at Old
Sturbridge Village

The place

New England is geographically a small segment of the United States. The six northeastern states of Connecticut, Rhode Island, Massachusetts, Vermont, New Hampshire and Maine cover 66,672 square miles, making the region about three-quarters of the area of Great Britain. But New England delivers a great deal of cultural and natural diversity in its compact package.

The New England landscape is extremely varied, its drama deriving from some of the most complex geology in the world. Bits and pieces of three primordial continents adhere to its shoreline and three distinct ranges of ancient mountains, now worn down to their hardest rocks, buckle up along its width. But the most prominent geological features of New England were created by the mile-thick Laurentian ice sheet, which began its retreat about 11,000 years ago. As the glacier's southern edge melted, huge dumps of sand and gravel were left behind to become the islands and sand beaches of the southern New England coast, including Nantucket, Martha's Vineyard and Cape Cod. The coast of northern New England, on the other hand, pre-dates the glaciers by hundreds of millions of years, representing the continental face shattered by separation from northern Europe aeons ago. Maine's rocky coast bears a striking resemblance to the Hebrides and to Scandinavia for good reason, as they once fitted together like puzzle pieces.

But even the Maine coast was altered by the great ice sheet, which etched the entire New England landscape in a north–south pattern, scraping the mountain ranges to their backbones of quartzite and granite. As a result, the river valleys of New England follow the same north–south track as the glaciers, and the mountains, while perhaps lacking the soaring heights of the limestone Alps and Rockies, rise with startling rapidity.

The largest of New England's rivers is the Connecticut, an ancient split in the planetary crust extending from northern New England to Long Island Sound. At various periods a lake bed, a swampland or a river, the Connecticut Valley was home during the Jurassic period to many species of dinosaurs, whose tracks lie preserved in the ancient sediments. New England's other major rivers are younger by far, and are all found in the north, where they drain the flanks of the White Mountains and Maine's less-known Longfellow Range. Thousands of smaller streams and rivers flow off New England's central highlands to the sea, providing the water power for mill works in virtually every hamlet. While few of those mills continue to grind corn or to power

Native names

Almost all the pre-European inhabitants of New England spoke variants of the Algonquian (sometimes spelled Algonkian) language. While only a handful of New Englanders still speak these tongues – and almost none speak them as a primary language – fragments of the languages remain as place and river names throughout the region.

Kennebec long, quiet water

Mashpee land near the great cove or pond

Monadnock place of the surpassing mountain

Pawtucket at the falls in the river

Penobscot at the descending rocks

Winnipesaukee lake in a high place

Chargoggagoggman-chauggagoggchaubun-agungamaugg Englishman at Manchaug at the fishing place at the boundary (the longest, most complex name in US geography).

spinning machinery, almost every village in interior New England has a mill dam and a mill building, more often than not occupied by a dealer in antiques.

Farming is still a way of life in the Lake Champlain valley and the fertile floodplains of the Housatonic and Connecticut rivers. But most of New England is cursed with stony glacial soils – evident in stone walls throughout the region – and agriculture declined in New England as soon as other alternatives became available. The opening of fertile land in Ohio in the 1830s came on the heels of several disastrous crop years, and many New England farms were abandoned and allowed to return to forest by 1845. Much of the farming today is in speciality crops such as herbs and flowers in eastern Massachusetts, maple syrup groves in the northern states and 'wild' blueberries in Maine. Dairy farming, while always threatened, maintains a strong presence in Vermont, given a boost by the popularity of Ben & Jerry's ice cream and the elevation of the Holstein cow to pop culture icon, as well as thriving cheese production.

The past

Apparently New England has always attracted hardy souls. Native peoples were scattered throughout the region, mostly on now-submerged coastline, even before the glaciers retreated. By 1600 at least nine distinct tribal divisions of the Algonquian linguistic group inhabited the region, living mostly along the coast and riverbanks where they augmented hunting and gathering with agriculture. Slash-and-burn farming was based on the triad of maize, beans and squash that first took hold in the Mexican highlands and spread to New England in around AD 900. Contrary to many early anthropological characterisations, these 'Indians' lived in relatively stable communities. Shell middens at the mouth of the Damariscotta River in Maine, for example, indicate more than 2000 years of continuous inhabitation at that oyster-rich site. The shells were so extensive that they were mined commercially for agricultural limestone from 1650 into the beginning of the 20th century.

Portuguese, Spanish and perhaps Irish fishermen knew New England waters well in the century immediately prior to the 'official' discovery of the New World. But colonisation of New England began with the conjunction of two significant historical circumstances. The pre-colonial population of the region crested in the 1590s at around 90,000 souls, but crashed to fewer than 30,000 by 1619 as a result of successive plagues of European diseases. Many of the most desirable settlement sites were abandoned and burned just before the English sailed over the horizon looking for homesteads. At the same time, English political tensions swelled the ranks of religious separatists and dissenters ready to flee a repressive regime to build a New Jerusalem in the wilderness. As a result, the first substantive towns in New England – Plymouth, Salem and Boston of the Massachusetts Bay Colony –

were settled by unusually well-educated ideologues. The tall spires of white Congregational churches found on virtually every New England town green have been one of their most enduring legacies. Another has been their dedication to education, of which Harvard College was the first fruit.

Intellect, however, does not necessarily imply tolerance. The Massachusetts Bay Colony expelled anyone who disagreed with Puritan orthodoxy, leading Roger Williams (a Baptist at the time) and Anne Hutchinson (a Quaker) to found Rhode Island. Quakers also settled throughout southern New England, and in the 17th century they constituted a majority in much of Rhode Island and on the islands of Martha's Vineyard and Nantucket. The austere Quaker architecture of Nantucket remains one of the island's hallmarks. Connecticut and western Massachusetts became Puritan strongholds, as their richest river bottomlands were settled by land-hungry immigrants who pressed westwards from Boston and Salem.

Northern New England remained largely unsettled until the 1760s, despite the planting of a few coastal trading posts in the mid-17th century. The deep forested interior was inhabited, if at all, by Native Americans and French trappers. The French had laid claim to much of New England well before the English arrived, and continuing French claims put a damper on settlement of the interior.

Settlement of the coastal region continued apace, however, and once-cordial relations between the English and the Native tribes deteriorated. Finally, in 1675 the Wampanoag chieftain Metacom (called King Philip by the English) united many of the coastal tribes in a scorched-earth war intended to drive the English off the continent. The fighting lasted for nearly two years, and historians argue that Philip might have succeeded with a few good breaks. He and his troops truly savaged the English villages, killing one colonist in ten and putting their buildings and crops to the torch. But the Natives fared even worse. Entire communities were destroyed; their survivors either fled to Canada or were sold into slavery in the Caribbean. Once King Philip's war ended in 1676, the colonists enjoyed only the briefest period of peace. By the 1690s, they were drawn into a frontier echo of the European wars between the French and English, doing battle repeatedly with French colonists and their Native allies in what North Americans call the French and Indian wars.

In an almost Nietzschean fashion ('what does not kill me makes me stronger'), the French and Indian wars forged great strengths in the New England colonies. By the time France withdrew from North America in 1763, the colonies had two generations of battle-hardened militia men who would make up the corps of American troops in the Revolution. Barred from expansion into the interior, New England had grown rich from the sea, exploiting its cod fisheries and perfecting the 'triangle trade' of African slaves, Caribbean molasses and New England rum. When the wars did end, a cash-strapped Crown paid off many of

History in your pocket

A series of 25-cent coins (usually called 'quarters') has slowly been minted by the US government. Each state selected its own image to appear on the reverse side, which also notes the year that the state entered the union, and the coins were issued in the order that states joined the new nation. The Connecticut quarter, for example, features its Charter Oak, New Hampshire's quarter shows the Old Man of the Mountain, and Massachusetts' quarter depicts a Minuteman, musket in hand.

Above
Plymouth Rock memorial

its soldiers with land grants to the interior of New England, salting the region with independent spirits who knew how to use a gun.

Given New England's dependence on seaborne trade, it is little wonder that New Englanders bridled at the imposition of British trading rules and cargo taxes to pay for the colonial wars. Boston, in particular, was a hotbed of rebellion, and hostilities began following the 1770 Boston Massacre in which a squad of British soldiers fired on a hostile crowd pelting them with snowballs, killing five civilians and wounding several others. In 1773, patriots dressed as Indians tossed a valuable shipment of British tea into the harbour as a protest against the Stamp Tax, and in 1775 armed troops finally clashed in Lexington and Concord, Massachusetts, considered the first battles of the Revolution. Throughout the war, the British Navy ravaged the New England coast, which is why most coastal towns have no pre-1780 buildings. Field warfare was limited to the Boston area and to New England's western flank, where the Bennington Monument marks the successful American defence of the Lake Champlain valley.

The Revolution dragged on into the 1780s, but New England swiftly rebuilt its merchant navy after Independence. Shut out of British ports (indeed, out of much of Europe), New England traders led the way in opening Japan, China and Korea to world trade. During this same period, Massachusetts whalers from Nantucket and (after 1820) from

New Bedford dominated the worldwide whaling industry until the discovery of petroleum in the 1850s. Salem, Massachusetts, led world trade in the 1790s, but all up and down New England's northern coast, the tall timber of the newly inhabited interior was sent downriver to be transformed into sailing vessels. Much of the wealth still visible in northern New England's shore towns dates from the period 1790–1890, when every port town bristled with shipyards and most of America's overseas trade sailed on vessels under the command of New England captains. The heritage of those years has been surprisingly well preserved in the whaling museums of New Bedford and Nantucket, the art and history museums of Salem, and the maritime museums of Salem and Searsport, Maine.

A young America grew rich on trade, and New England grew richest in the years leading up to the American Civil War. New England merchants visiting Britain observed early textile machinery with great interest. They returned home with sufficiently accurate drawings to place New England in the thick of the Industrial Revolution by the 1830s. As the region's farmers migrated westwards to better land, the population that stayed behind flocked to the new mill towns as the first generations of industrial workers. New England was transformed from a rural to an industrial economy in the space of a single generation – a transformation visible today in the sites of Old Sturbridge Village and the Lowell National Historical Park.

Architecture

The wealth that rapidly accumulated during the industrial revolution in the 19th century found architectural expression first in the Federal style, which harked back to Greek and Roman neo-classical models – styles appropriate to the ideals of a fledgling democracy. The Massachusetts State House, the quintessential Federal-style building designed in 1795 by Charles Bulfinch, so seized the American imagination that it was imitated in the US Capitol and subsequently in half the state capitols across the country. Domestic architecture, especially after 1830, favoured a style known in the US as Greek Revival – a grandiose boxiness with a blend of Greek capitals on massive columned façades. Only in the second generation of wealth, as Americans began to travel in Europe, did the 'Italianate' style begin to compete, with its square turrets and long hip roofs. A growing cosmopolitanism also found expression at the end of the 19th century in several forms of Romanesque Revival architecture, notably the work of Boston-based H H Richardson and his followers. Richardson's Trinity Church in Boston is considered the high-water mark of the movement.

Ironically, the turn of the 20th century sent Americans in general and New Englanders in particular into a frenzy of rediscovering their English colonial roots. The architectural spawn of this social phenomenon was an eclectic style called Colonial Revival, notable chiefly for grafting large columned porches on to vaguely Georgian houses, then painting them stark white with either black or green wooden shutters. A mid-20th-century version of this architectural nostalgia is reflected in the proliferation of 'Cape Cod' houses throughout New England – modern versions of the 1½-storey 18th-century homes of Cape Cod, America's first indigenous domestic architecture.

Seeing the sights

Even today, travellers criss-crossing New England are driving on roads that parallel the old railroad beds. Although some hardy coach travellers came looking for 'sublime' nature in the New England mountains early in the 19th century, it took the railroad to open up the region to pleasure travel. Initially the railway lines followed the major north–south river valleys. When the Grand Trunk Railroad cut across the mountains in the 1850s, rail travel opened up the coast of Maine to the wealthy denizens of Montreal and gave Bostonians access to the wilderness lakes and woods of northern New England. By 1870, a traveller could board a train in Boston and ride all the way to the summit of Mount Washington with only a few miles of carriage ride connecting the trains.

Many spots in New England developed an early cachet. Families who acquired great industrial fortunes at the end of the 19th century created a new social set that shuttled from one mammoth 'cottage' to another in Newport, the Berkshires of western Massachusetts, and Mount Desert Island on the Maine coast. Today the surviving cottages are often tourist attractions in themselves, and a few, such as Wheatleigh in the Berkshires, have become luxury resorts. During the same period, sometimes called the Gilded Age, hunting and fishing became the vogue for some of America's richest men, leading to the development of the 'sporting camp' where robber barons would retreat to smoke cigars, drink brandy and kill trout. Many such camps survive, albeit with less well-heeled clientele, in the north woods of Maine and New Hampshire. The working man's equivalent, the modest private cabins often called 'camps', are found along the shores of the more accessible lakes throughout New England.

Resort hotels flourished both in the mountainous areas of New Hampshire and Vermont and at coastal beaches from Connecticut to Maine. While the structures have largely disappeared (with a few delightful exceptions such as the Balsams, Wentworth-by-the-Sea and the Mount Washington Hotel, all in New Hampshire), the resort ambience lingers on from Watch Hill, Rhode Island, to Old Orchard Beach, Maine. The ultimate democratisation of tourism in New England began with the automobile. Auto touring spawned the roadside diner (still visible throughout New England), strings of cabins and classic motel architecture. Route 1 in coastal Maine has particularly well-preserved examples of 'motor hotels' ranging from homespun individual cabins to streamlined structures that echo the tail fins of the first automobiles that stopped at them.

Pleasure travel in New England has not changed dramatically from that golden age of auto touring other than the rise of the B&B and the country inn in the last 20 years. In-town hotels are so unusual outside major urban centres that they are often advertised as 'classic' or 'heritage' properties. Virtually every hamlet large enough to appear on a map has at least one house where the family takes in guests for the night and serves them breakfast before they hit the road in the morning. Ironically, such facilities began as a low-cost alternative to motels, but now often cost 10–40 per cent more. If you plan to make extensive use of B&Bs and country inns, be prepared for gregarious hosts – a liability or an asset, depending on personal taste.

The seasons

New England's busiest travel season begins unofficially on Memorial Day weekend (usually the weekend that includes the last Sunday in May) and concludes with Labor Day weekend (the weekend that includes the first Monday of September). In practice, the high season is July and August, when the ocean and inland waters are warm enough for swimming and the weather is shirtsleeve balmy.

The second season for travel in New England is autumn (fall), especially during the fall foliage period. The foliage season is unpredictable from year to year, but generally peaks in northern New England during the third week of September and in southern New England during the second week of October. The original forests encountered by Puritan settlers have long since been cleared, but the forests that have grown up since farms were abandoned in the 19th century contain a much higher percentage of deciduous trees

Right
Portland harbour

than the primeval forest. Moreover, they are composed of a greater percentage of maple trees than hardwood forests anywhere else on the planet. And several strains of maples found only in New England produce greater quantities of red pigments in autumn than maples elsewhere. Although spring travel in New England is slight, the region enjoys a reverse of the fall foliage displays as spring blooms begin in southern New England in March and spread to northern New England by early June.

Most overseas travellers tend to overlook New England's winter season, when the cities of Boston, Hartford and Providence become lively centres of performing arts and the north country is transformed into some of the world's finest ski terrain. Alpine skiing in the United States began in New Hampshire and Vermont, and together with Maine, they have made northern New England a major ski destination. Ski resorts offer state-of-the-art lifts and trail grooming, beautiful new trailside lodgings, warm and inviting country inns and even newly-winterised grand hotels, in addition to a lively après-ski scene. A wide variety of other winter sports and activities – cross-country (Nordic) skiing, snowshoeing, sledding, dog-sledding, sleigh rides and ice skating – make these resorts appealing to skiers and non-skiers as well. Most of these are four-season resorts, with golf, tennis, swimming and other activities on offer.

Three itineraries

These three itineraries capture different aspects of the New England experience. Because so many travellers enter New England through Boston, all routes circle from here.

Rocky coast and high peaks

This itinerary takes advantage of the proximity of New England's wildest coastline and its most rugged mountains. While the route can be appreciated through the windscreen, it is more rewarding for travellers who enjoy outdoor activities.

From Boston, drive north on Rte 1 to Salem, following the Massachusetts North Shore route (*see page 64*). Continue north on Rte 1 to the route suggested in New Hampshire and the Southern Maine Coast (*see page 234*) to take in the sandy beaches en route to Portland (*see page 244*) on Casco Bay. The 'rocky coast of Maine' begins here heading north on Rte 1 with detours down the rocky peninsulas of Midcoast Maine (*see page 252*) into the ocean-overlook highlands of Penobscot Bay (*see page 260*). From Blue Hill, follow Rte 172 to Ellsworth, then Rte 3 to Mount Desert Island (*see page 270*) to experience the jaw-dropping scenery of Acadia National Park. To move quickly to the high country, backtrack on Rte 3 through Belfast. Follow Rte 3 west 45 miles to the Maine Turnpike (I-95) and drive south 32 miles to exit 11 on to Rte 202 west. In 3 miles, turn right on to Rte 302 west through the Sebago Lakes region to Conway, New Hampshire, in the White Mountains (*see page 214*). At Conway, the Kancamagus Highway (Rte 112) cuts through the heart of the White Mountain National Forest, concluding in Lincoln at I-93, which leads due south to Boston.

The grand foliage circuit

Many 'scenic roads' become so gridlocked during the foliage season that traffic obscures the leaves. This itinerary skips famous leaf-peeper routes in favour of small towns and forested northern interiors where the foliage is equally fine and the traffic is lighter.

From Boston, drive west on Rte 2 through Lexington and Concord (West of Boston, *see page 54*), continuing 42 miles west to the junction with Rte 202 (exit 19). Drive north on Rte 202 through the arts colony region of Jaffrey and Peterborough, New Hampshire. Seven miles north of Peterborough, follow the left fork on to Rte 123, which winds 34 leafy miles west through tiny villages to Alstead. At Alstead, turn on to Rte 12A to connect with Rte 12 in South Charlestown. Rte 12

Fall foliage

The deciduous trees of New England exhibit some of the most diverse and intense foliage in the world. Birches, beeches, aspens and willows provide a range of golden tones while maples, oaks, sumacs and sassafras glow in a spectrum of red, orange and even purple hues – often with more than one colour appearing on a single tree. When leaves begin to die at the end of the growing season, their green chlorophyll is no longer renewed and the underlying pigments become visible. Intensity of leaf colour is enhanced by bright autumn days followed by freezing or near-freezing nights – the dominant meteorological conditions during New England autumns.

and Rte 12A continue north through the area described in The Upper Connecticut Valley (*see page 196*) until they connect with I-89 in West Lebanon. Follow I-89 west to cross into Vermont and take the first exit for Rte 4 west to follow the Quechee River stream bed through stunning little Woodstock and on to Killington, one of the more striking skiing centres in the Green Mountains (*see page 168*). At Sherburne Pass, turn right on to Rte 100 north to follow the eastern ridges of the Green Mountains through Warren and Waitsfield, the ski village of Stowe, and on to Newport (Vermont) at the southern tip of Lake Memphremagog in The Northeast Kingdom (*see page 188*). East of town, connect with I-91 south for a strikingly scenic drive to St Johnsbury, Vermont, where I-93 crosses the Connecticut River and descends through Franconia Notch in the White Mountains (*see page 214*) to return to Boston.

New England roots

This itinerary encompasses some of the early settlements and boom towns while visiting the region's three great 'living history' museums. The swiftest of the three, it is a good choice if you have limited time.

Tour the Freedom Trail in Boston (*see page 46*) before driving west on Rte 2 through Cambridge, Lexington and Concord, detailed in West of Boston (*see page 54*). Backtrack on Rte 2 to I-95 south to Rte 3 in Quincy, following Rte 3 south to Plymouth to visit Plimoth Plantation, detailed in Southeastern Massachusetts (*see page 74*). Continue south to exit 5, following the Myles Standish State Forest road to I-195 to New Bedford and Fall River. Turn south on Rte 24 to Rte 114 into Newport, Rhode Island, the yachting capital of New England (*see page 148*). Continue west on Rte 138 to Rte 1 south along the Rhode Island coast into Connecticut's Southeastern Corner (*see page 138*) to visit the sail-era museum of Mystic Seaport. Eight miles west in New London, follow Rte 32 north to I-395 north through eastern Connecticut over the border into Massachusetts. At exit 6, drive 12 miles west on Rte 20 to visit Old Sturbridge Village, detailed in Pioneer Valley (*see page 94*). The Massachusetts Turnpike, I-90, returns to Boston.

Above
Harvest-time pumpkin sale

Boston

Ratings

Arts and culture	●●●●●
History	●●●●●
Museums	●●●●●
Children	●●●●○
Shopping	●●●●○
Food and drink	●●●○○
Beaches	●○○○○
Scenery	●○○○○

B oston is 'The Hub' – a name bestowed in 1858 by Oliver Wendell Holmes, who wrote that Bostonians considered their city 'the Hub of the Universe'. Learning and culture rank high in this Athens of America, where the first school was built in 1636 and 25-odd colleges and universities thrive today. The oldest US city, founded in 1630, Boston was once a Brahmin town – 'the home of the bean and the cod, where the Lowells speak only to Cabots, and the Cabots speak only to God'. There's still a Yankee establishment, but it's matched by an Irish one, and ethnic diversity is on the rise. The compact size of Boston's centre surprises visitors, who find they can get nearly everywhere on foot.

Getting there and getting around

ⓘ Greater Boston Convention and Visitors Bureau (GBCVB) 2 Copley Pl, Suite 105; tel: (888) 733-2678; www.bostonusa.com, operates visitor information centres on Boston Common and in the Prudential Center. Along the Freedom Trail is the **National Park Service Visitor Center** 15 State St; tel: (617) 242-5642; www.nps.gov

Arriving and departing

Logan International Airport is in East Boston, directly across the harbour from downtown, 20–30 minutes by public transport. A free shuttle connects the international terminal (E) to domestic terminals (A–D) and the airport subway station. By car, downtown is 3 miles away via toll tunnel. A free shuttle to car-hire locations, taxis and hotel shuttles is available; for suburban express buses, tel: (617) 23-LOGAN or visit www.massport.com/logan

Amtrak (tel: (800) 872-7245; www.amtrak.com) has train services from South Station (www.south-station.net), at the corner of Summer St at Atlantic Ave. Also at South Station is the Bus Terminal serving Greyhound (tel: (800) 229-9424;

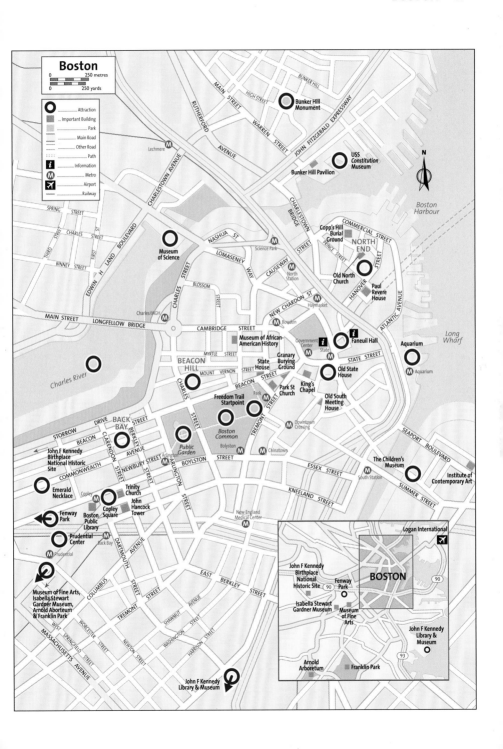

See page 28 for detailed directions into the city from Logan Airport.

Public parking is limited and pricey downtown; metered street parking is especially scarce. If you absolutely must bring a car, leave it in your hotel car park or a multistorey public car park and see the city by foot and public transport.

New England Aquarium $$
Central Wharf (T: Aquarium); tel: (617) 973-5200; www. neaq.org. Open Jul–Labor Day daily 0900–1800, Wed and Thur to 2000, weekends and holidays to 1900; rest of year daily 0900–1700, weekends and holidays to 1800.

Adjacent to the Aquarium is **Simons IMAX 3D Theatre** $ tel: (617) 973-5206. Open Sun–Wed 0930–2130, Thur–Sat 0930–2230.

State House Beacon St (T: Park St); tel: (617) 727-3676. Tours weekdays 1000–1600. Free admission.

Museum of African-American History
46 Joy St (T: Park St); tel: (617) 725-0022; www.afroammuseum.org. Open Mon–Sat 1000–1600, daily in summer. Free admission.

Left
Old State House

www.greyhound.com) and other intercity coach services. The **Massachusetts Bay Transportation Authority** (the 'T') operates a Commuter Rail service to suburbs and nearby cities from North Station, Causeway St and Back Bay Station, tel: (617) 722-3200 or (800) 392-6100; www.mbta.com. Tickets can be purchased at machines in station lobbies; coins or small notes may be used, or tickets can be charged to credit cards.

Getting around
Boston is America's most walkable city and among the worst to drive in because of traffic congestion and a confusing street pattern. Most major tourist attractions are within a compact, walkable area downtown or a short distance from public transport.

Massachusetts Bay Transportation Authority (see above) operates buses, streetcars (trams) and subways in Boston and nearby suburbs. Subway tickets are sold at all T stations; buses and streetcars take tickets or exact change. Information, schedules and multi-day Boston Visitor Passes are available at major T stations, Bostix booths and some hotels. You can also obtain a Charlie Card that you pre-load with money and wave in front of the barrier as you enter a station. This works out slightly cheaper compared to normal tickets.

Sights

Aquarium
On the waterfront near **Faneuil Hall**, the New England Aquarium is Boston's biggest attraction for children of all ages. The main feature is a four-storey glass ocean tank, encircled by a winding walkway, from which you can watch sea life swimming in and out of a coral reef. There's an open-air penguin rookery, a sea lion show and exhibits of exotic ocean life. Avoid school holiday weeks and rainy weekends, when the din of squealing children peaks. From adjacent Long Wharf, tour boats depart for Boston harbour cruises – the best way to see the waterfront, which otherwise offers little public access.

Back Bay
Originally a foul-smelling mudflat, Back Bay was filled in during the late 1800s and laid with a grid of parallel streets, an oddity in Boston. Alphabetically named (from Arlington to Hereford), those streets are now lined with smart town houses, many occupied by schools, consulates and condominiums, making it an interesting place to wander from the shops and restaurants along Newbury St. Also here is Boston's prettiest promenade: tree-lined Commonwealth Ave, which shows its finest colours in May with cherry, apple and magnolia blossoms.

Beacon Hill
Early Boston was a tiny peninsula on which stood three prominent hills. Two were razed and used as landfill, but atop the tallest, early

The Big Dig

With construction commencing in 1991 and completed 15 years later, the officially designated Central Artery/Tunnel Project (CA/T) was instantly nicknamed the Big Dig. During this most ambitious public-works effort in American history, an ugly and antiquated elevated highway that had separated downtown Boston from its waterfront neighbourhoods and parks was dismantled – since replaced by a pair of northbound and southbound tunnels. Upon completion of 'Big Dig digging', over-budget costs amounted to $14.6 billion.

On a positive note, the sleek tunnels (including a branch that connects the busy financial and shopping districts with Logan International Airport), have noticeably reduced traffic slowdowns during peak rush-hour commuting periods. Central Boston is now reconnected to its historic harbourfront. Furthermore, removal of the elevated behemoth has brought urban-landscape acreage out of its long-time shadows. Work on a three-mile stretch of interconnected greenways, curving through the three-century-old heart of Boston, is nearing completion. Traffic is also moving smoothly between downtown and northerly Charlestown by way of a new, strikingly modernistic, high-level suspension bridge.

colonists erected a signal beacon. On that site today is the gold-domed 1797 **State House**, the seat of the Massachusetts Legislature, an architectural treasure designed by Charles Bulfinch. Bordered by **Boston Common** and antiques-shop-lined Charles St, Beacon Hill is one of the oldest parts of the city, a European-looking warren of narrow streets and brick town houses.

Rambling through it is the **Black Heritage Trail**, a 1½-mile walking tour that includes several stops on the Underground Railroad, which shepherded runaway slaves from the Southern United States to Canada. Pick up a map at the Boston Common Visitor Center or the **Museum of African-American History**. The trail starts at **The Robert Gould Shaw and 54th Regiment Memorial**, on Boston Common opposite the State House, depicting the first black regiment of the US Civil War.

Boston Children's Museum

This museum was a pioneer in the concept of interactive exhibitions. It is completely designed to entertain and educate kids, and includes a playspace for the littlest ones.

Boston Common and Public Garden

America's first public park, 50-acre Boston Common was laid out in 1634 as a common pasture area for colonists' cows. They also used it for public hangings of criminals, including those whom today we might call victims of religious persecution. On the other side of Charles St is the Public Garden, the first US botanical garden (1837), where swan boat rides have soothed summer afternoons since 1877.

Bunker Hill

After the opening shots of the American Revolution at Lexington and Concord on 19 April 1775, British forces tried to lift a rebel siege of Boston. The misnamed Battle of Bunker Hill (it actually took place on Breed's Hill) on 17 June 1775 was a victory for Britain, though a costly one, and British troops evacuated Boston for good the following March. Marking the battleground is a 221ft obelisk, the **Bunker Hill Monument** in Charlestown. **Bunker Hill Pavilion** at nearby Charlestown Navy Yard has a multimedia show about the battle, in which the American commander told his Minutemen, 'Don't fire until you see the whites of their eyes!'

Charles River

The Esplanade, a greenbelt along the Boston side of the Charles River Basin, is where Bostonians go to stroll, sunbathe, rollerblade, bicycle and hang out on Sunday afternoons. The Hatch Shell hosts summer concert series. A pathway for pedestrians and cyclists continues for

Boston Children's Museum $$ *300 Congress St, Museum Wharf (T: South Station); tel: (617) 426-6500; www.bostonkids. org. Open Mon–Sun 1000– 1700, Fri 1000–2100.*

Bunker Hill Monument *Monument Sq, Charlestown (T: Community College); tel: (617) 242-5641.*

Bunker Hill Pavilion $ *55 Constitution Rd, Charlestown; tel: (617) 241- 7575.*

Arnold Arboretum *main entrance 125 Arborway, Jamaica Plain (T: Forest Hills); tel: (617) 524-1718; www.arboretum.harvard.edu. Open dawn to dusk. Free admission.*

Faneuil Hall *Faneuil Hall Marketplace (T: Haymarket, State St or Government Center); tel: (617) 523-1300. Open daily 0900–1700. Free admission.*

Above
Faneuil Hall
Left
Charles River promenade

several miles along the Boston shore and across the bridges to Cambridge, where the best views of sailing boats and Boston's skyline can be had.

Copley Square
One of Boston's main plazas, Copley Square is where shoppers rest their feet, office workers munch sandwiches at noon and skateboarders test their skills. Two architectural treasures face each other across the square: the 1877 **Trinity Church**, the brownstone Romanesque Revival masterpiece of architect Henry Hobson Richardson, and the 1895 **Boston Public Library**, worth a peek inside for its marble main staircase and quiet central courtyard. At one corner of the square is the 60-storey **John Hancock Tower**, whose mirror-glass panels reflect Trinity Church's rusticated roofs and walls; at another is an entrance to the Copley Place mall. The other two corners lead to shopping along Boylston and Newbury Sts.

Emerald Necklace
Between 1884 and 1896 Frederick Law Olmsted designed a system of nine parks as an 'Emerald Necklace' around the city; they still form a greenbelt for walking or cycling through Boston. The system begins downtown with **Boston Common** and the adjacent **Public Garden** and continues down Commonwealth Ave out to 527-acre Franklin Park, which has a small zoo, mostly of local interest. The greatest draw for visitors is **Arnold Arboretum**, whose 265 acres include gardens with 7000 varieties of trees, shrubs and flowers, all labelled: a gardener's delight. The quiet paths and rolling hills are perfect for a relaxing stroll.

🅵 Museum of Fine Arts $$ 465 Huntington Ave (T: Museum); tel: (617) 267-9300, Box Office (617) 278-5156; www.mfa.org. Open daily from 1000.

Isabella Stewart Gardner Museum $$ 280 The Fenway; tel: (617) 566-1401; www.gardnermuseum.org. Open Tue–Sun 1100–1700.

Institute of Contemporary Art $ 100 Northern Ave; tel: (617) 478-3100, Box Office (617) 478-3103; www.icaboston.org. Open Tue, Wed & Fri 1200–1700, Thur 1200–2100, Sat and Sun 1100–1700, Thur free 1700–2100.

Park St Church / Park St (T: Park St); tel: (617) 523-3383; www.parkstreet.org

Granary Burying Ground Tremont St. Gate open 0900–1700, winter 0900–1500.

Faneuil Hall

At Faneuil Hall, firebrands such as Samuel Adams once aired ideas that led to the American Revolution, earning this historic 1742 meetinghouse-atop-a-marketplace its title as the Cradle of Liberty. Today it is still a meetinghouse, hosting public debates, lectures and political rallies. It is also a stop on the **Freedom Trail**, and Park Service rangers explain its history every half-hour. Beside it is popular Faneuil Hall Marketplace.

Fenway Park

A true Bostonian landmark and a throwback to classic old-time baseball stadiums, Fenway Park – walkably close to Kenmore Square and the artsy Fenway neighbourhood – is the home playing field of the American League's Boston Red Sox, where baseball is played from early April to early October. The Sox were wildly celebrated for winning the sport's World Series in 2007. New team owners have greatly refurbished and expanded the antique, intimate ballpark, which opened in 1912, all to the delight of fans who regard it as hallowed ground.

Fine arts museums

Boston has a trio of top-notch art museums. For paintings, prints, sculpture and other artworks from a wide range of periods, there's the **Museum of Fine Arts**. Of special note is its Asiatic art. A short walk from the MFA is the unique **Isabella Stewart Gardner Museum**, showing works by Rembrandt, Botticelli and Titian, along with tapestries and Graeco-Roman statuary – the eclectic collection of a 19th-century socialite inside a re-created 15th-century Venetian palazzo. Its rooms overlook an ornate courtyard of trees, flowering plants and artworks. Located on the South Boston waterfront is the smaller **Institute of Contemporary Art**, with changing exhibitions of photography, painting, sculpture and performance art.

King's Chapel *58*
*Tremont St; tel: (617)
227-2155; www.kings-
chapel.org. Open daily at
irregular hours; not open for
touring during services. Free
admission.*

**Old South Meeting
House $**
*Washington and Milk Sts;
tel: (617) 482-6439; www.
oldsouthmeetinghouse.org.
Open Apr–Oct 0930–1700;
Nov–Mar 1000–1600.*

**John F Kennedy Library
and Museum $$**
*Columbia Point, Dorchester
(T: JFK/UMass); tel: (617)
514-1600; www.jfklibrary.org.
Open 0900–1700.*

**John F Kennedy
Birthplace National
Historic Site**
*83 Beals St, Brookline
(T: Coolridge Corner);
tel: (617) 566-7937. Tours
Apr–Nov Wed–Sun
1000–1630. Free
admission.*

Museum of Science $$
*1 Science Park (T: Science
Park); tel: (617) 723-2500;
www.mos.org. Open early
Sept–4 Jul Sat–Thur
0900–1700 (rest of
year 0900–1900),
Fri 0900–2100 (all year).*

Opposite
The Isabella Stewart Gardner
Museum

Freedom Trail

The 2½-mile Freedom Trail, marked with a red line along the sidewalk, leads visitors to 16 sites in the heart of downtown Boston, covering 350 years of history. The trail begins at Boston Common Visitor Center, where you can pick up a map. Halfway along is the National Park Service office, with a better map, public toilets and rangers who know the history.

From Boston Common and the State House, the trail leads on to **Park St Church** (*limited tours Jul and Aug*), where abolitionist William Lloyd Garrison first spoke out against slavery (1829) and the hymn *America* was first sung (1831). A few steps away on Tremont St, the 17th-century **Granary Burying Ground** holds the graves of revolutionary leaders John Hancock and Samuel Adams and Patriot Paul Revere. The 1754 **King's Chapel** was Boston's first Anglican church (in 1785 it became Unitarian); beside it is **Boston's oldest burial ground**, where Puritan Governor John Winthrop is buried. Around the corner on School St is the site of Boston's first Public School and the 1862 Old City Hall. The Old Corner Bookstore, School and Washington Sts, was a gathering place for writers of the early 1800s who made Boston the 'Athens of America'.

Next, the 1729 Georgian-style **Old South Meeting House**, Washington and Milk Sts, is a colonial church where the Boston Tea Party was launched. The **Old State House** and **Faneuil Hall** lead on to the Blackstone Block, the only part of Boston that approximates to the look of the 1700s. The trail continues into the **North End**, with **Paul Revere House**, **Old North Church** and **Copp's Hill Burial Ground**, then to Charlestown for **Old Ironsides** and **Bunker Hill**.

John F Kennedy Library and Museum

The 35th US president started in politics by running for a seat in Congress representing parts of Boston, Cambridge and Charlestown. His grandfather, John F 'Honey Fitz' Fitzgerald, was one of Boston's early Irish mayors. The story of his brief presidency is told here at the John F Kennedy Library and Museum, Columbia Point, south of the city centre on a dramatic point of land with a sweeping view of Boston harbour and Dorchester Bay. Just outside Boston, but not near the museum, is the modest Brookline home where he was born, now administered by the National Park Service as the **John F Kennedy Birthplace National Historic Site**.

Museum of Science

A site with kids in mind is the Museum of Science, which reveals the secrets of everything from anthropology to space exploration, with many hands-on exhibits. It incorporates some exhibits from the former Computer Museum. Separate admissions get you into the Charles Hayden Planetarium show and the giant-screen 70mm films shown in the Mugar Omni Theater. The modernistic complex was built on a dam at the mouth of the **Charles River**.

Paul Revere House
$ 19 North Sq; tel:
(617) 523-2338;
www.paulreverehouse.org.
Open Nov–mid-Apr
0930–1615; mid-Apr–Oct
0930–1715; closed Mon in
winter.

**Old State House
Museum** $ 206
Washington St (T: State St);
tel: (617) 720-1713;
www.bostonhistory.org. Open
daily Feb–Jun & Sept–Dec
0900–1700; Jan
0900–1600; Jul–Aug
0900–1800.

Old North Church
193 Salem St;
tel: (617) 523-6676. Open
Mar–Dec daily 0900–1700;
Jan–Feb Tue–Sun
0900–1700; longer hours
Jul–Aug.

**Prudential Skywalk
Observation Deck** $
Prudential Tower, 800
Boylston St; tel: (617) 859-
0648. Open winter
1000–2000; summer
1000–2200; last lift 30 mins
before closing.

North End

Boston's Italian neighbourhood is a maze of narrow streets lined with restaurants, cafés and apartment houses. Zigzagging through it, a portion of the **Freedom Trail** leads to some of the city's best-known sites, including circa-1680 **Paul Revere House**, Boston's only remaining 17th-century house. It was home to silversmith Paul Revere, famed for his midnight ride of 18 April 1775 to warn patriot leaders at Lexington and Concord of British troop movements. On nearby Hanover St is a landmark statue of Revere on horseback, and a small park leads to the 1723 **Old North Church** (Christ Church), from whose steeple two lanterns were hung as a signal ('one if by land, two if by sea') on the night of Revere's ride. Uphill from the church, between tenements, is **Copp's Hill Burial Ground**, where Cotton Mather and other Puritans were laid to rest in the 1600s (*open daily*).

Old State House

Surrounded now by tall buildings, the 1713 Old State House was the seat of British government between 1713 and 1776 (its eastern end still bears the royal lion and unicorn) and later of the Massachusetts Legislature. Inside is a museum of colonial and maritime memorabilia. Outside is a circle of cobblestones marking the site of the 1770 Boston Massacre, in which British sentries fired on a mob protesting against taxes and killed five colonists (who now lie in the nearby Granary Burying Ground).

Prudential Center

Boston's first tall building and possibly its ugliest landmark, the Prudential Center has a 50th-storey **Skywalk Observation Deck** offering high-altitude views of Boston, the harbour and surrounding terrain. The Greater Boston Convention and Visitors Bureau (GBCVB) staffs an information booth in the lobby level, amid mall shops and restaurants. On Boylston St in front of the 'Pru', **Boston Duck Tours**

The Boston Tea Party

In the 1760s, Britain tried to defray the costs of defeating France in the Seven Years' War with new taxes on colonists in North America. Some were repealed after boycotts, but an import duty on tea stood. In 1773 Parliament agreed to let the East India Company dispose of its tea surplus here and to refund the duty in order to break the boycott.

When the *Dartmouth*, *Eleanor* and *Beaver* arrived in Boston harbour, patriot leaders were determined to stop their cargo of tea from unloading. After a rally at Old South Meeting House on 16 December 1773, 50 to 100 men dressed up as Mohawk Indians and boarded the three ships at Griffin's Wharf. They tore open the 342 chests of tea and dumped them into the harbour. Similar acts followed in other ports, and Parliament punished the colonies harshly, setting the stage for revolution.

The original site is now on dry land, but a replica ship *Beaver II* and a small waterfront museum recount the history.

USS *Constitution* Museum
Building 22, Charlestown Navy Yard, Charlestown; tel: (617) 426-1812. Open daily Apr–Oct 0900–1800; Nov–Mar 1000–1600. Free admission. The ship 'Old Ironsides' tours daily 0930–1600.

(tel: (800) 226-7442 or *(617) 723-3825; www.bostonducktours.com)* and several trolley tour companies sell tickets and board passengers.

USS *Constitution* ('Old Ironsides')
Permanently docked at Pier 1 in Charlestown is the 52-gun frigate USS *Constitution*, the world's oldest commissioned warship (still part of the US Navy), whose solid oak hull caused enemy cannonballs to bounce off during the war of 1812 with Britain, earning it the nickname 'Old Ironsides'. The ship's history is told in the nearby USS *Constitution* Museum.

Entertainment

The Calendar section in Thursday's *Boston Globe*, Scene in Friday's *Boston Herald* and the weekly *Boston Phoenix* have listings of what's happening.

The theatre district around Tremont and Boylston Sts hosts mostly blockbuster shows at the cavernous Wang Center, the classy Colonial, the more intimate Wilbur and Emerson Majestic and the tiny Charles Playhouse. There's a thriving small-theatre scene, and classic and contemporary drama are performed at the Lyric Stage, *140 Clarendon St; tel: (617) 585-5678; http://lyricstage.com,* and Huntington Theater Company, *264 Huntington Ave; tel: (617) 266-0800; www.huntingtontheatre.org.* Half-price same-day tickets are sold, cash only, at Bostix booths at Faneuil Hall and Copley Sq; no phone.

Musical offerings include the Boston Symphony Orchestra at the venerable 2600-seat Symphony Hall, *301 Massachusetts Ave; tel: (617) 266-1492 (information) or 266-1200/(888) 226-1200 (tickets); www.bso.org,* from early Oct to mid-Apr. The Boston Pops, a smaller group of BSO musicians, plays in summer at Symphony Hall and gives free concerts at the Hatch Shell on the Esplanade in early July. There's also the Boston Ballet at the Wang Center, Boston Lyric Opera at Emerson Majestic Theater, and the Handel & Haydn Society, the oldest continuing US arts organisation, at Jordan Hall and other venues.

Boston also has a lively rock, jazz and folk scene at clubs in Kenmore Sq, Allston and elsewhere. Don't overlook Boston's public lecture series, especially the renowned Ford Hall Forum, plus poetry and prose readings. See local media for listings.

The Boston Marathon draws runners from around the world on Patriots Day (*19 April or the closest Monday*), a celebration of the Revolutionary War battles of Lexington and Concord; fans turn Back Bay into a giant party. The weekend-long Boston Harborfest culminates in fireworks at the giant Fourth of July Concert (attendance: 500,000 or more) given by the Boston Pops on the Charles River Esplanade.

Accommodation and food

As Boston is a popular tourist, convention, business and academic city, hotels are always heavily booked. Moderate rooms are scarce, budget rooms almost non-existent.

The GBCVB offers lodging information by mail and on its website, but cannot make bookings. Instead, try **Bed & Breakfast Agency of Boston**, *47 Commercial Wharf; tel: (617) 720-3540 or (800) 248-9262 (US and Canada), 0800 895 128 (from the UK); www.boston-bnbagency.com,* for rooms in local homes, including waterfront lofts, and **Citywide**

Below
Boston Harbor waterfront

● Boston's main shopping district is **Downtown Crossing**, a crowded pedestrian mall centred on Washington and Winter Sts, where the big department store Macy's and many smaller shops are located.

Back Bay's **Newbury St** is a people-watcher's paradise amid galleries, cafés and boutiques, ranging from posh to funky. Paralleling it is a mile-long indoor concourse with moderate to pricey shops and restaurants. The 70-shop Prudential Center mall connects via walkway to 100-shop Copley Place.

Faneuil Hall Marketplace, packed with tourists and local people day and night, is a group of three renovated 1825 market buildings, supplemented by newer structures, that house 125 shops, restaurants, food stalls and pubs.

Reservation Services, *25 Huntington Ave, Suite 500; tel: (617) 267-7424 or (800) 468-3593; http://cityinsights.com*

At the table, Boston is still best known for fresh, simply prepared seafood. There's also no shortage of traditional Irish, Italian and Yankee fare, such as pot roast, baked beans and Indian pudding. But these are now complemented by a whole world of ethnic cuisine, plus trendy restaurants offering nouveau variations on American and other dishes. Browse through Hanover and Salem Sts in the North End and take your pick of Italian eateries; do the same on Beach St in Chinatown for Chinese.

Beacon Inn $ *1087 Beacon St, Brookline; tel: (617) 566-0088 or (888) 575-0088; www.beaconinn.com.* Just out of Boston on a streetcar line, 25-room Victorian-style guesthouse.

Faneuil Hall Marketplace $–$$$ *www.faneuilhallmarketplace.com.* Restaurants and food stalls offering everything from pizza and hot dogs to Greek and Chinese.

Copley Square Hotel $$ *47 Huntington Ave; tel: (617) 536-9000 or (800) 225-7062; www.copleysquarehotel.com.* This Boston landmark has packages that include coveted Red Sox tickets.

Dolce Vita $$ *22 Hanover St; tel: (617) 720-0422; www.dolcevitaristorante.com.* A North End favourite for huge portions of Italian food.

Durgin-Park $$ *340 Faneuil Hall Marketplace; tel: (617) 227-2038; www.durgin-park.com.* Taste of old Boston, with hearty New England fare.

Legal Sea Foods $$ *27 Columbus Ave, and at Central Wharf, Copley Place, Prudential Center, Kendall Sq in Cambridge, Chestnut Hill, Logan Airport and Legal Test Kitchen at the Seaport; tel: (617) 426-5566.* Casual, crowded, noisy local chain.

Shawmut Inn $$ *280 Friend St; tel: (617) 720-5544.* Very basic rooms with kitchenettes, on the upper floors of a building near North Station.

Sonsie $$ *327 Newbury St; tel: (617) 351-2500; http://sonsieboston.com.* Informal and trendy, with eclectic, creative cuisine.

Fairmont Battery Park $$$ *3 Battery Wharf; tel: (617) 994-9000, US & Canada (800) 257-7544, international (800) 0441 1414; www.fairmont.com/batterywharf.* Boston's newest luxury hotel, on the waterfront with harbour views from all rooms and impeccable service.

Fairmont Copley Plaza $$$ *138 St James Ave; tel: (617) 267-5300 or US and Canada (800) 257-7544, international (800) 0441 1414; www.fairmont.com/copleyplaza.* Commands a grand view of Copley Sq.

Above
'Ben Franklin' greets Boston
shoppers

Four Seasons $$$ *200 Boylston St; tel: (617) 338-4400 or US and Canada (800) 819-5053, Europe (00 800) 6488 6488; www.fourseasons.com/ boston.* Modern, posh and facing the Public Garden.

Omni Parker House $$$ *60 School St; tel: (617) 227-8600 or US only (888) 444-6664; www.omnihotels.com.* Right on the Freedom Trail and steeped in Boston history.

Suggested tour

Total distance: 2¹/₂ miles for the **Freedom Trail**, plus diversions for special interests.

Time: All day if you enter all the **Freedom Trail** sites. Casually walking it to catch the city's flavour takes a couple of hours.

Route: Park your car in the garage under **BOSTON COMMON ❶** (entrance on Charles St) and forget about it; one-way streets and difficult parking render it too frustrating to use for sightseeing. Cross the Common and pick up a map at the GBCVB visitor centre (near Park and Tremont Sts) to begin the **FREEDOM TRAIL ❷** .

Alternatively, you could cross Charles St into the **PUBLIC GARDEN ❸** , then stroll down Newbury St for shopping. Off Newbury St one block left are **COPLEY SQUARE ❹** and the **PRUDENTIAL CENTER ❺** ; to the right are **BACK BAY ❻** streets heading towards the **Charles River** Esplanade **❼** . From there, veer right again to wander into the **BEACON HILL** area **❽** and back to Boston Common. Carry a map and you can't get lost – it's a small area.

From Park St Station in the corner of Boston Common, you could also take a Green Line train to Copley Square, the Prudential Center or along Huntington Ave to the Museum of Fine Arts; or take a Red Line subway train to South Station for **THE CHILDREN'S MUSEUM ❾** or JFK/UMass for the **JFK LIBRARY ❿** .

Freedom Trail directions are easy: just follow the red line along the sidewalk (pavement). Or make your own tour by wandering on and off the Trail. The red line leads up to the State House on Beacon Hill (where it intersects the **Black Heritage Trail ⓫**), then doubles back to Tremont St and down School St to Washington St. Here, you are only a few minutes from Downtown Crossing shops or the city's financial district. **Faneuil Hall Marketplace ⓬** is a convenient stop for lunch and more shopping, and you also have the choice of diverting to the New England **AQUARIUM ⓭** , then further along the waterfront to Museum Wharf. Staying instead on the **Freedom Trail** leads you through the **NORTH END ⓮**'s intriguing lanes, then it's a hike over the Charlestown Bridge to the **USS *CONSTITUTION* ⓯** site and up to **Bunker Hill Monument ⓰** . The easiest way back downtown is by taxi.

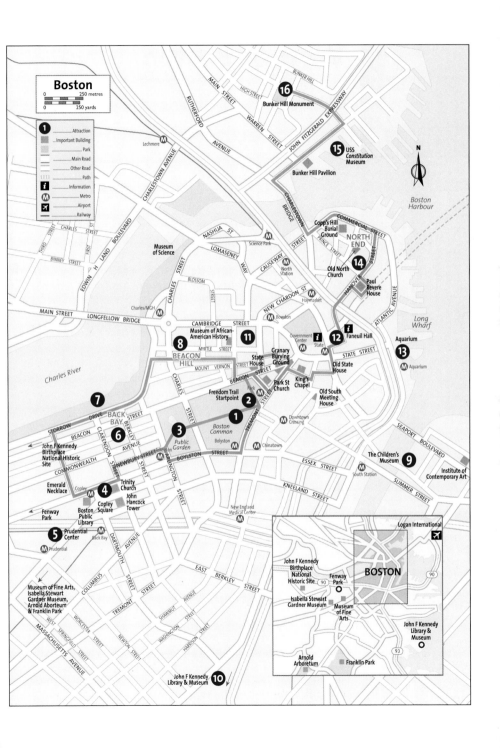

Boston

0 _____ 250 metres
0 _____ 250 yards

1 .... Attraction
...Important Building
.... Park
.... Main Road
.... Other Road
.... Path
i .... Information
M .... Metro
✈ .... Airport
.... Railway

16 Bunker Hill Monument

15 USS Constitution Museum

Bunker Hill Pavilion

N

Boston Harbour

Copp's Hill Burial Ground

NORTH END

14 Old North Church

Paul Revere House

Museum of Science

Long Wharf

Museum of African-American History

11

12 Faneuil Hall

Aquarium

13

8 BEACON HILL

State House

Granary Burying Ground

Old State House

STATE STREET

Charles River

Freedom Trail Startpoint

Park St Church

King's Chapel

Old South Meeting House

7 BACK BAY

1 Boston Common

3 Public Garden

2

SEAPORT BOULEVARD

John F Kennedy Birthplace National Historic Site

6

Emerald Necklace

4 Trinity Church

John Hancock Tower

The Children's Museum

9

Institute of Contemporary Art

Fenway Park

Copley Square

Boston Public Library

5 Prudential Center

Museum of Fine Arts, Isabella Stewart Gardner Museum, Arnold Aborteum & Franklin Park

Logan International

✈

John F Kennedy Birthplace National Historic Site

Fenway Park

BOSTON

Isabella Stewart Gardner Museum

Museum of Fine Arts

John F Kennedy Library & Museum

Arnold Arboretum

Franklin Park

10 John F Kennedy Library & Museum

West of Boston

Ratings

Arts and culture	●●●●●
History	●●●●●
Food and drink	●●●●○
Museums	●●●●○
Shopping	●●●○○
Children	●●○○○
Nature/scenery	●●○○○
Beaches	●○○○○

One could say that America came of age in the communities just west of the circumscribed confines of Boston, where revolutionary thought and action neither began nor ended with America's War of Independence. Anchored by Harvard University, Cambridge is a leader in American intellectual thought and popular culture trends. The first shots of the American Revolution rang out in the more bucolic towns of Lexington and Concord, and, half a century later, Concord's authors launched a revolution of their own in 19th-century American letters. Battle sites alternate with authors' homes as attractions. On the banks of the Merrimack River, Lowell sprang up as the birthplace of the American version of the Industrial Revolution. An impressive historical park in the city preserves and interprets the mechanical ingenuity of the era as well as American industrial labour history.

CAMBRIDGE

 **Cambridge Office for Tourism** 4 Brattle St; tel: (617) 441-2884; www.cambridge-usa.org. Harvard Square info kiosk open daily 1000–1700.

Harvard Information Center Holyoke 1350 Massachusetts Ave; tel: (617) 495-1573; www.harvard.edu. Harvard Yard tours (free) Sept–May Mon–Fri 1000 & 1400, Sat 1400; mid-Jun–mid-Aug Mon–Sat 1000, 1115, 1400 & 1515.

Harvard University and the city of Cambridge are forever locked in a symbiotic embrace, and only the historical record makes clear which was the chicken and which the egg. The oldest (1631) part of the city is **Harvard Square**, just outside the college walls, where street layouts have barely changed since the 1660s but where the passing scene changes almost daily in anticipation of the next fad in dress style, music or pose. The square's most enduring charm is one of the world's densest concentrations of bookstores. A bustling café scene and a veritable frenzy of street performers give the square a lively air throughout the year.

'Other American colleges have campuses' wrote poet David McCord, 'but Harvard has always had and always will have her Yard of grass and trees and youth and old familiar ghosts.' Surrounded by brick walls, the inner sanctum of **Harvard Yard** is haunted by many spirits,

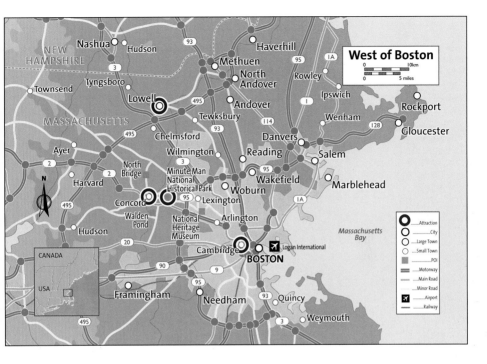

Harvard University Art Museums $$

Sackler Museum, 485 Broadway; tel: (617) 495-9400; www.artmuseums. harvard.edu, www. harvardartmuseum.org. Open Mon–Sat 1000–1700, Sun 1300–1700. Fogg Art Museum and Busch-Reisinger Museum, 32 Quincy St; closed for renovations until 2013.

Harvard Museum of Natural History $$
24–26 Oxford St; tel: (617) 495-3045; www.hmnh.harvard.edu. Open daily 0900–1700.

Longfellow National Historic Site $ *105 Brattle St; tel: (617) 876-4491; www.nps.gov/long. Open Jun–Oct Wed–Sun 1000–1630.*

including the young cleric John Harvard, who left half his money and all his books to the fledgling college when he died in 1638, two years after it was founded. Student-led tours hit the highlights, pointing out splendid buildings whose creators read like an honour roll of America's leading architects.

The **Sackler Museum** takes centre stage with exhibitions of selections from all of the Harvard Art Museums while the **Fogg Art Museum** and the **Busch-Reisinger Museum** undergo renovations until at least 2013. The Fogg holdings are a virtual survey of Western European art, while the Busch-Reisinger's strength lies in German Expressionism. The Sackler collections have a wide range of classical, Chinese, Islamic, Japanese, Indian and other Asian art.

Brattle St north of Harvard Sq is called Tory Row, after the fine houses built by rich merchants who fled during the American Revolution. The **Longfellow National Historic Site** was confiscated and served as headquarters for General George Washington during the siege of Boston. Later it was the home of poet Henry Wadsworth Longfellow and depicts the family's comfortable mid-19th-century lifestyle.

P Parking in or near Harvard Sq is very limited. Metered spaces on the streets cost only $1 per hour. Rates at more expensive car parks on Eliot and Church Sts vary with hour and day.

★ American Repertory Theatre 64 Brattle St; tel: (617) 547-8300; www.amrep.org. One of America's leading avant-garde theatres.

Head of the Charles Regatta Tel: (617) 868-6200; www.hocr.org. The largest two-day rowing event in the world is held during the height of the mid-October foliage season.

Club Passim 47 Palmer St; tel: (617) 492-7679. Legendary singer-songwriter venue has launched careers of the likes of Joan Baez and Patty Larkin.

Ryles Jazz Club 212 Hampshire St; tel: (617) 876-9330. Touring headliners and grassroots local talent might top the bill any given night. Ballroom, Latin and swing dancing upstairs.

Regatta Bar Charles Hotel, 1 Bennett St; tel: (617) 395-7757; www.regattabarjazz.com. Top local, national and international jazz artists.

Accommodation and food in Cambridge

Toscanini $ *899 Main St; tel: (617) 491-5877.* There are many who happily make a meal of the home-made burnt caramel, saffron or green tea ice cream.

A Friendly Inn at Harvard Square $$ *1673 Cambridge St; tel: (617) 547-7851; www.afinow.com.* Overseas visitors favour this casual B&B about a five-minute walk from Harvard Sq.

Isaac Harding House $$ *288 Harvard St; tel: (617) 876-2888 or (877) 489-2888; www.cambridgeinns.com.* Historic home about a ten-minute walk from Harvard Square with large, elegant rooms.

Casablanca $$–$$$ *40 Brattle St; tel: (617) 876-0999; open for lunch and dinner.* The bar with Bogart murals on the walls is a favourite hangout of local celebrities and the dining room serves delicious bistro food with a North African flavour.

Charles Hotel in Harvard Square $$–$$$ *1 Bennett St; tel: (800) 882-1818 or (617) 864-1200; www.charleshotel.com.* Modern hotel in the heart of Harvard Sq offering many packages. The swanky Rialto ($$$) restaurant is among the best in the Boston area.

Sandrine's Bistro $$–$$$ *8 Holyoke St; tel: (617) 497-5300; open for lunch and dinner.* Outstanding Alsatian bistro with good *choucroute* and hearth-baked *Flammkuchen*, a pizza-like bread with toppings – a fine bar snack with a glass of bone-dry Riesling.

Craigie on Main $$$ *853 Main St; tel: (617) 497-5511; www.craigieonmain.com.* The menu is outstanding anytime, but on Tuesday to Thursday after 2100 the 'Chef's Whim' brings either four or six courses to your table – spontaneous and

The statue of three lies

The university's favourite photo opportunity, the statue of John Harvard in Harvard Yard (*above*) is widely known as the 'statue of three lies'. It is inscribed, 'John Harvard, Founder, 1638'. The college was founded in 1636 while Harvard was still in England. The young minister was the college's benefactor, not its founder. And since no likeness of the man survived, Daniel Chester French modelled the sculpture's features on a popular student of the class of 1882.

Above
Harvard University's 17th-century elegance

creative dishes that might not be on the regular menu, and at lower-than-menu prices.

UpStairs on the Square $$$ *91 Winthrop St; tel: (617) 864-1933; open for lunch and dinner.* Two dining rooms give choice of casual or gourmet interpretations of New American cuisine.

CONCORD

ⓘ Concord Chamber of Commerce
58 Main St; tel: (978) 369-3120; www.concordchamber ofcommerce.org. Open Mon–Fri 0900–1700.

ⓝ Emerson House $
28 Cambridge Turnpike, tel: (978) 369-2236. Open mid-Apr–Oct Thur–Sat 1000–1630, Sun 1300–1630.

This Boston dormitory community was the scene of an extraordinary blossoming of American letters in the mid-19th century, when writers seized on Ralph Waldo Emerson's philosophy and created a self-consciously national literature. The **Emerson House**, where the 'sage of Concord' lived between 1835 and 1882, has been maintained largely as he left it, complete with books, personal belongings and furniture. The **Orchard House**, which Louisa May Alcott described in loving detail in *Little Women*, captures the Alcott family experience of rich emotions amid modest circumstances. Displays in the attached barn give the general outlines of Concord's literary blossoming. Many Concord literati rest in peace on 'Author's Ridge' in **Sleepy Hollow Cemetery**, including Ralph Waldo Emerson, Henry David Thoreau, Nathaniel Hawthorne and Louisa May Alcott. Pilgrims to this low-key cemetery frequently leave tokens of their admiration. Thoreau's beloved **Walden Pond** is a popular place for swimming, boating and

Right
Concord in the fall

Orchard House $$
*399 Lexington Rd;
tel: (978) 369-4118;
www.louisamayalcott.org.
Open Apr–Oct Mon–Sat
1000–1630, Sun 1300–
1630; Nov–Mar Mon–Fri
1100–1500, Sat 1000–
1630, Sun 1300–1630.
Closed Jan 1–15.*

**Sleepy Hollow
Cemetery**
*Bedford St (Rte 62); no tel.
Open daily dawn–dusk.*

Walden Pond $
*Rte 126; tel: (978) 369-
3254. Open daily
0800–dusk*

fishing. A model of Thoreau's cabin in the car park reminds visitors of the writer's somewhat loftier concerns about the place. Rangers can provide directions to the site of the original cabin, still marked by the crumbled chimney hearth.

Accommodation and food in Concord

Walden Grille $$ *24 Walden St; tel: (978) 371-2233.* Convenient downtown location for creative American food.

Colonial Inn $$–$$$ *48 Monument Sq; tel: (978) 369-9200 or (800) 370-9200; www.concordscolonialinn.com.* Original section of inn dates from early 1700s; additions from each century since. Dining room ($$) features traditional New England fare.

LOWELL

**Greater
Merrimack Valley
Convention & Visitors
Bureau**
*9 Central St, Suite 201;
tel: (800) 443-3332 or
(978) 459-6150;
www.merrimackvalley.org.
Open Mon–Fri 0900–1700.*

Native son Jack Kerouac once described Lowell as 'the textile factories built in brick, primly towered, solid, all ranged along the river and the canals, and all night the industries hum and shuttle'. By 1950, when he wrote this nostalgic sketch, Lowell's textile industry was on its deathbed. But the mills were revolutionary in the 1830s, when they brought all the processes of textile manufacture under a single roof and transformed an agricultural economy into an industrial one. Using the structures and canals of the mill city, **Lowell National Historical Park** conveys the entrepreneurial excitement of the era while also paying due respect to the workers. Park rangers offer

P On-street parking is limited; follow signs to free Dutton St car park behind the National Historical Park's Visitor Center.

Q During Mar–Oct, a free electric trolley, modelled on a 1901 streetcar, connects several sites within Lowell National Historic Park.

B Lowell National Historical Park Visitor Center
246 Market St; tel: (978) 970-5000; www.nps.gov/lowe. Open Mar–Oct daily 0900–1700; Nov–Feb Mon–Sat 0900–1630, Sun 1000–1700. Free admission.

Boott Cotton Mills $$
115 John St; tel: (978) 454-9033. Open late May–Oct daily 0930–1630; call for off-season hours.

Boarding House *40 French St; tel: (978) 970-5000. Open daily 1330–1630. Free admission.*

American Textile History Museum $$
491 Dutton St; tel: (978) 441-0400; www.athm.org. Open Wed–Sun 1000–1700.

New England Quilt Museum $
18 Shattuck St; tel: (978) 452-4207; www.nequiltmuseum.org. Open Tue–Sat 1000–1600; May–Dec also open Sun 1200–1600.

informative free tours. Canal tours by boat ($$ late May–Oct) provide another perspective on the layout of the industrial city. **Boott Cotton Mills** is one of the best surviving examples of early mill architecture in Lowell. Although fewer than a dozen of the 88 first-floor power looms are shown in operation, the din is deafening, even through the ear plugs supplied to visitors. The mill owners initially hired the daughters of New England farmers as their labour force. As a trade-off for the demands of the job, the young women gained a social freedom unusual in their day. Even after working 13 to 14 hours a day Monday to Friday and 8 hours on Saturday, they attended lectures, created pottery (now much sought by collectors) and even organised the first labour strikes in the US. Their story, as well as that of later immigrant workers, is the focus of the **Boarding House** adjacent to Boott Mills.

Two additional Lowell museums augment the picture presented by the National Historic Park. **The American Textile History Museum** traces cloth-making in America from hand-spinning and weaving to computer-controlled looms. A new facility emphasises the role of textiles in modern daily life, from fibres that wick moisture from the skin to anti-bacterial cloth. The many interactive exhibits include a weaving simulator and a family craft area. The **New England Quilt Museum** has a select permanent collection of historic and contemporary quilts and mounts several temporary exhibitions each year. Its galleries are among the best places to see new quilt design, and the museum shop is an excellent resource for books and other quilt-related items.

Right
Antique trolleys carry visitors round Lowell National Historical Park

Lowell Celebrates Kerouac *www. lowellcelebrateskerouac.org.* Early October event celebrates native son, poet and novelist Jack Kerouac, with music, poetry readings and tours of his haunts.

Lowell Folk Festival *Tel: (978) 970-5000; www.lowellfolkfestival.org.* With a large and diverse ethnic population, Lowell is a fitting place for the largest free folk festival in the US, held in late July.

Accommodation and food in Lowell

Four Sisters Owl Diner $ *244 Appleton St; tel: (978) 453-8321.* Open only for breakfast and lunch, this diner used to serve mill workers and offers 'one of the best breakfasts in the Northeast'.

Old Worthen House $ *141 Worthen St; tel: (978) 459-0300; weekday lunch only.* The pub grub is unremarkable, but half the patrons come to look for the table where Jack Kerouac carved his name.

Southeast Asian Restaurant $–$$ *343 Market St; tel: (978) 452-3182; open for lunch and dinner.* Large Cambodian and Vietnamese populations have brought a cosmopolitan quality to Lowell's dining scene. The weekday lunch buffet is a good deal.

Courtyard by Marriott $$ *30 Industrial Ave E; tel: (800) 321-2211 or (978) 458-7575; www.marriott.com.* Although a short drive from the historic district, this 120-room motel is a good base for exploring the city.

Doubletree Hotel Lowell $$–$$$ *50 Warren St; tel: (800) 222-8733 or (978) 452-1200; www.doubletree.com.* The lobby of this 259-room hotel looks out on Pawtucket Canal in the middle of Lowell National Historical Park.

La Boniche $$–$$$ *143 Merrimack St; tel: (978) 458-9473; open Tue–Fri for lunch, Tue–Sat for dinner.* Bistro fare in a stately Beaux-arts-style building – Lowell's best fine-dining choice.

MINUTE MAN NATIONAL HISTORICAL PARK

Lexington Chamber of Commerce Visitor Center *1875 Massachusetts Ave; tel: (781) 862-2480; www.lexingtonchamber.org. Open Apr–Nov daily 0900–1700; Dec–Mar daily 1000–1600.*

Minute Man Bikeway, a 10½-mile paved trail on a former rail bed follows the route of the British retreat to Boston after the Battle of North Bridge in Concord.

Right An engraving showing the Battle of Lexington

This park commemorates the events of 19 April 1775, when British troops making a show of force in Lexington and Concord were met by such intense armed resistance that they were driven to retreat. Most of the park follows Rte 2A along that retreat path, called 'Battle Road'. The **Minute Man Visitor Center** presents an excellent video encapsulating the events that are widely credited as the first volleys of the American Revolution. A diorama traces the first 4 miles of the British retreat along Battle Road. **Lexington Green**, site of the dawn skirmish, is surrounded by white-spired churches and the yellow clapboard Buckman Tavern,

Minute Man Visitor Center *Rte 2A, Lexington; tel: (781) 674-1920; www.nps.gov/mima. Open mid-Mar–mid-Nov daily 0900–1700. Free admission.*

North Bridge Visitor Center *Minute Man National Historical Park, 174 Liberty St, Concord; tel: (978) 369-6993. Open mid-Mar–Oct daily 0900–1700; call for winter hours. Free admission.*

National Heritage Museum *33 Marrett Rd (Rte 2A), Lexington; tel: (781) 861-6559. Open Mon–Sat 1000–1700, Sun 1200–1700. Free admission.*

Patriots Day *Tel: (781) 674-1920.* Each year on or near 19 April, costumed re-enactors play out the battles of Lexington Green and North Bridge.

where militiamen – known as minutemen because they undertook to be ready at a minute's notice – assembled overnight, only to be routed by the British. **North Bridge** in Concord was the next major battle site, and disciplined colonials turned the tables and sent the Redcoats packing. Both sides are memorialised here, with the Minute Man Statue by Daniel Chester French and a plaque on the opposite side of the bridge remembering British soldiers who died far from home. Costumed re-enactments of both battles are held each April.

Although separate from the National Historic Park, the **National Heritage Museum** in Lexington displays the original 'Lexington Alarm', a call to arms penned on 19 April 1775 that successfully rallied the other American colonies to revolution. Most of the museum is dedicated to an often fascinating exploration of American popular culture.

Right
Minute Man statue in Lexington

Above
Concord's Wayside Inn, former home of the Alcott family and Nathaniel Hawthorne

Name that tree

The *National Audubon Society Field Guide to New England* by Peter Alden and Brian Cassie (New York, Knopf, 1999) should be in your glovebox as you drive around New England. A slim and beautiful guide, it supplies instant identification for birds, trees and even foliage.

Suggested tour

Total distance: 38 miles; 40 miles with detours.

Time: 2 hours' driving. Allow 2–3 days.

Links: Connects via city streets to Boston (*see pages 40–53*).

Route: Much of this route follows urban streets with frequent traffic lights. Begin at Harvard Sq and follow Massachusetts Ave (Rte 2A) north and west for 4 miles into the shopping centre of **Arlington ❶**, a pleasant residential community with many inexpensive restaurants. Continue northwest on Rte 2A another 5 miles to the outskirts of **Lexington ❷** and the **National Heritage Museum ❸**. Leaving the museum, turn left on to Massachusetts Ave and drive 1¹⁄₂ miles to **Lexington Green**. Continue on Massachusetts Ave towards CONCORD ❹, rejoining Rte 2A as Marrett Rd in 1¹⁄₂ miles. In 2¹⁄₂ miles, veer right on to Lexington Rd, following it past several historic sites for less than 2 miles to **Concord** centre and the **Emerson House ❺**. In the village centre, Bedford Rd leads northeast half a mile to **Sleepy Hollow Cemetery ❻**; Monument St leads half a mile north to the **North Bridge battle site ❼**. Walden St leads south from the centre of Concord 2 miles to **Walden Pond ❽** and the associated state recreation area.

⊕ Great Meadows National Wildlife Refuge *Weir Hill Rd, Sudbury; tel: (978) 443-4661; www.fws.gov/northeast/ greatmeadows. Open dawn to dusk. Free admission.*

From Walden Pond, drive east on Rte 2 for 2 miles to I-95 and Rte 128. Follow them north for three exits (2 miles) to Rte 3, the Middlesex Turnpike. This old Lowell–Cambridge highway parallels a former shipping canal and cuts through beautiful farmland, a seeming anomaly so close to urban centres. In 11 miles, the Lowell Connector splits to the right. Follow it, taking exit 5N ('Thorndike St') into **LOWELL ❾**. Follow signs leading to 'Lowell National and State Park Visitor Parking' at the Dutton St car park.

Also worth exploring

The best inland birdwatching in New England is found in the **Great Meadows National Wildlife Refuge**, a wetlands preserve set aside to provide habitat to migrating birds. Tens of thousands of waterfowl stop during annual migrations, and resident birds include many raptors, herons and sandpipers. A checklist of 231 species identified here is available from the visitor centre. The refuge consists of two units, one south of Concord along the Sudbury River, the other north of Concord centre on the Concord River. Diked impoundments in the Concord unit abound with American lotus.

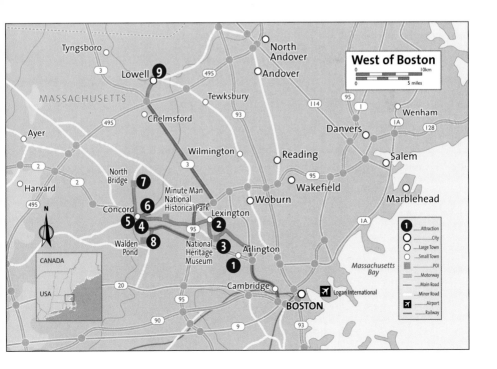

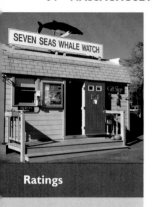

Massachusetts North Shore

Ratings

History	●●●●●
Nature/ scenery	●●●●●
Arts and culture	●●●●○
Beaches	●●●○○
Museums	●●●○○
Children	●●○○○
Food and drink	●●○○○
Shopping	●●○○○

The shore towns north of Boston concentrate New England's chief appeals: an overlay of history, long ocean beaches, dramatic coastal scenery and even a local food speciality. Founded as religious refugee colonies, these communities once dominated the world's cod fisheries and trade with the Far East, before settling into a genteel old age. Today, yachts and pleasure craft far outnumber fishing boats, and the glories of the China Trade are more evident in antiques shops and museums than on the wharves. Landscape painters are more common than overseas traders, and art galleries overshadow chandlers.

Although highways link the North Shore to Boston, smaller roads are less congested, more direct and more interesting. Moreover, the compact area allows for more time on foot and less behind the wheel.

GLOUCESTER

ⓘ **Cape Ann Chamber of Commerce Information Center** *33 Commercial St; tel: (800) 321-0133 or (978) 283-1601; www.capeannvacations.com. Open Mon–Fri 0800–1700.*

Gloucester Visitors Welcoming Center
Stage Fort Park, Hough Ave; tel: (978)281-8865; www. gloucesterma.com. Open late May–Oct daily 0900–1800.

Gloucester fishermen have gone to sea since 1623 and maritime painters have made the port their base for more than 150 years. The interplay of arts and fishing is epitomised at the **Cape Ann Historical Museum**, where exhibitions trace the fishing and boatbuilding heritage (Gloucester shipwrights invented the three-masted schooner). But the museum's glories are its magnificent paintings by native son Fitz Henry Lane, America's

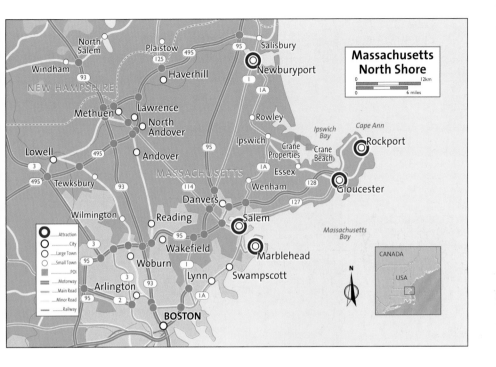

Massachusetts
North Shore

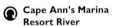

**Cape Ann's Marina
Resort River
Cruises $$** *75 Essex Ave;
tel: (978) 283-2116;
www.capeannmarina.com.*
Sunset and afternoon tours
on Annisquam River,
July–September.

**Whale Watch Cruises
$$$** These operators carry
naturalists on board and
sometimes gather research
data during cruises.
Apr–Oct. **Yankee Fleet
Whale Watch** *37
Commercial St; tel: (978)
283-0313.* **Cape Ann
Whale Watch** *Rose's
Wharf (near Rte 128); tel:
(978) 283-5110.* **Captain
Bill & Sons Whale
Watch** *Harbor Loop (off
Rogers St); tel: (978) 283-
6995.*

premier maritime painter. Lane built his granite house and studio on a
stone outcrop with a commanding view of the harbour, now the
centrepiece of **Fitz Henry Lane Park** on Rogers St. The house is closed
to visitors but a striking statue of Lane at work reclines outside.

Rocky Neck art colony, arguably the oldest working artists' colony
in the US, sits directly across the harbour on a knob of land with a
nearly 360-degree view of sky and water. Today's artists are less
indigent than those of years past, but the Neck retains a bohemian,
improvisational quality, and painters working on their decks or along
narrow streets encourage curious visitors.

Gloucester's dramatic seascape also attracted millionaires. Inspired
by his European journeys, inventor John Hays Hammond Jr built
Hammond Castle Museum, a medieval-style castle, to house the
collection of early Roman, medieval and Renaissance artefacts that
constituted his vision of more romantic days. **Beauport**, also known
as the Sleeper-McCann House, is another fantasy house, where a
theme from literature or history defines the décor in each of the 26
rooms open to tour.

Because Gloucester lies just 15 miles from important whale feeding
grounds, it is one of New England's best places for **whale watching**
cruises. Most operators guarantee rare sightings of humpbacks and
finbacks, and occasionally of northern right whales.

Cape Ann Historical Museum

$$ *27 Pleasant St; tel: (978) 283-0455; www. capeannhistoricalmuseum.org. Open Tue–Sat 1000–1700, Sun 1300–1600.*

Hammond Castle Museum $$ *80 Hesperus Ave; tel: (978) 283-7673; www.hammondcastle.org. Open May–mid-Jun Sat–Sun 1000–1600; mid-Jun–early Sept daily 1000–1600.*

Beauport (Sleeper-McCann House) $$
75 Eastern Pt Blvd; tel: (978) 283-0800; www.historicnewengland.org. Open Jun–mid-Oct Tue–Sat 1000–1600.

Halibut Point $$
289 Main St; tel: (978) 281-1900. When fishermen make port, they come here for grilled haddock and cheese and a pint of local red ale.

Ocean View Inn & Resort $$–$$$
171 Atlantic Rd, tel: (800) 315-7557 or (978) 283-6200; www. oceanviewinnandresort.com. Eight buildings on landscaped grounds looking out to the ocean.

Saint Peter's Fiesta
Tel: (978) 283-1601. Four-day festival in late June honours the patron saint of fishermen.

Schooner Festival
Tel: (978) 283-1601. Large and small schooners compete in three-day early September regatta.

Clam confusion

New England has mussels, but its cockles are scallops, and most restaurants serve only the hinge muscle of tiny ('bay') and large ('ocean') scallops. Two types of clam are harvested in New England: the soft-shelled clam, also known as the 'steamer clam', and the quahog (an Indian name). Small quahogs called 'cherrystones' are often eaten raw. Medium-sized quahogs called 'littlenecks' are generally fried. Large quahogs are usually baked and filled with a cracker stuffing.

MARBLEHEAD

ℹ Chamber of Commerce Information Booth
62 Pleasant St in Masonic Hall; tel: (781) 631-2868; www.marbleheadchamber.org. Open Mon–Fri 0900–1700.

🏛 Abbot Hall
Washington Sq; tel: (781) 631-0000. Open Mon–Thur 0800–1700, Fri 0800–1300; call for summer weekend hours. Free admission.

Marblehead Historical Society *170 Washington St; tel: (781) 631-1768. Open Jun–Oct Tue–Sat 1000–1600; Nov–May closed Sat. Free admission.*

Colonel Jeremiah Lee Mansion $ *161 Washington St; tel: (781) 631-1768. Open Jun–Oct Tue–Sat 1000–1600.*

King Hooper Mansion *8 Hooper St; tel: (781) 631-2608. Open Tue–Sat 1200–1600, Sun 1300–1700. Free admission.*

Marblehead is the best preserved of the early North Shore communities. Some 250 structures predating the American Revolution dot the historic district of Waldron Ct and Essex, Elm, Pond and Norman Sts.

Abbot Hall on Washington Sq houses town government and many community treasures, including the massive painting *The Spirit of '76*, an American patriotic icon. Far more interesting are the naïve artworks of John Orne Johnson Frost at the nearby **Marblehead Historical Society**. Frost's art depicts the hard life of a fisherman and captures Marblehead's past with rough charm.

The **Colonel Jeremiah Lee Mansion** counters Frost's workingman's vision with trader's wealth in a Georgian-style mansion built in 1768. Lee's widow entertained new president George Washington in 1789, perhaps to show off the hand-painted wallpaper and grand public rooms.

Once a town of overseas traders, Marblehead now has more artists than sea captains. The Marblehead Arts Association makes its headquarters in the **King Hooper Mansion**, a handsome 1745 manse filled with members' works for sale.

British soldiers built the simple earth embankment of **Fort Sewall** in 1742 to protect Marblehead harbour from French marauders, only to find colonists aiming the cannons at British ships during the Revolution. The surrounding park off Front St has excellent views of sailing regattas in this yachting capital.

Accommodation and food in Marblehead

Foodie's Feast $–$$ *114 Washington St; tel: (781) 639-1104; open for breakfast and lunch.* Casual café and deli sells takeaway sandwiches and elegant ready-to-cook meals for self-catering.

Oceanwatch $$ *8 Fort Sewall Ln; tel: (781) 639-8660.* Three guest rooms in a Victorian-era home share a superb harbour view with adjacent Fort Sewall.

The Landing Restaurant $$–$$$ *81 Front St; tel: (781) 639-1266; open for lunch and dinner.* Diners have their choice of preparations for fresh seafood.

Previous page
Fisherman's memorial, Gloucester harbour

Above left
Marblehead Cove

Right
Sailing schooner off the coast of New England's yachting capital

NEWBURYPORT

❶ Newburyport Chamber of Commerce *38R Merrimac St; tel: (978) 462-6680; www. newburyportchamber.org. Open Mon–Fri 0900–1700.*

❶ Custom House Maritime Museum $ *25 Water St; tel: (978) 462-8681; www. customhousemaritimemuseum. org. Open May–Dec Thur–Sat 1100–1600, Sun 1200–1600.*

Parker River Wildlife Refuge $ *Plum Island Turnpike; tel: (978) 465-5753. Open daily dawn–dusk. Some beaches close April–July to protect nesting endangered piping plovers.*

The three-storey mansions in the **High St**, crowned with hip roofs and cupolas, attest to the wealth of Newburyport's 18th-century ship owners. Elegant cornices, doorways and windows carved by ships' carpenters place this district among the nation's finest examples of Federal architecture.

An 1811 fire destroyed the commercial sector, so downtown Newburyport was rebuilt in red brick that came as ballast in ships from Asia. Newburyport shifted to European trade in the 19th century, and those ships registered cargo at the granite temple of commerce now converted to the **Custom House Maritime Museum**, where exhibitions evoke the town's overseas trade days. Merrimac, Water and State Sts have developed as a district of boutiques and antiques shops. At the foot of the commercial district, **Waterfront Park** is the site of summer concerts and fireworks and celebrations during the Christmas shopping season.

Newburyport is the gateway to **Plum Island**, dominated by **Parker River National Wildlife Refuge**. The 4662 acres of sand beach and dunes, bogs and tidal marshes support more than 800 species of birds, plants and animals. Plum Island ranks among North America's top ten birdwatching sanctuaries.

Yankee Homecoming
Tel: (978) 462-6680. Nine-day event begins late July and includes parade, concerts, fireworks, crafts, food and races.

Nutcracker Bakery
50 Water St; tel: (978) 465-8482. A good stop for coffee and a cookie or pastry.

Accommodation and food in Newburyport

Clark Currier Inn $$ *45 Green St; tel: (978) 465-8363; www.clarkcurrierinn.com.* Eight antique-filled guest rooms retain the period architectural detail of a shipwright-built 1803 'square house'.

Blu Water Cafe $$–$$$ *140 High St; tel: (978) 462-1088; open for dinner.* Locals head to this friendly, cosy restaurant a few blocks from the main tourist district for well-executed American bistro fare.

Glenn's Restaurant $$–$$$ *44 Merrimac St; tel: (978) 465-3811; open for dinner.* Contemporary bistro favours fresh fish and has a lively bar scene.

Garrison Inn $$$ *11 Brown Sq; tel: (978) 499-8500; www.garrisoninn.com.* This central, brick Federal structure from 1809 is a boutique hotel with a choice of simple rooms or luxurious suites.

ROCKPORT

Cape Ann Chamber of Commerce 33 Commercial St, Gloucester; tel: (800) 321-0133 or (978) 283-1601. Open Mon–Fri 0800–1700.

Rockport Art Association 12 Main St; tel: (978) 546-6604; www.rockportartassn.org. Open mid-May–Dec Mon–Sat 1000–1700, Sun 1200–1700; Feb–Apr, call for hours. Free admission.

Halibut Point State Park $ Rte 127 & Gott Ave; tel: (978) 546-2997. Open late May–early Sept daily 0800–2000; Sept–May dawn–dusk.

Picturesque Rockport is an artists' town and every painter seems to have made at least one canvas of the dusky red 1½-storey fishing shack at the end of Bradley Wharf, **Motif No 1**. The densest concentration of galleries, boutiques, eateries and souvenir shops is found on **Bearskin Neck**, a rocky peninsula that forms the north side of Rockport harbour. Best of the galleries is the **Rockport Art Association**, housed in a mid-1700s tavern and barn.

Located at the tip of the granite peninsula of Cape Ann, Rockport once supplied stone for major buildings up and down the Atlantic seaboard. **Halibut Point State Park**, a 54-acre reserve at the northern tip of the cape, has picnic areas and walking trails through woodlands and along the ocean. The most interesting trail explores a quarry last excavated in 1929. The stunning view over the water-filled quarry to Ipswich Bay is best at sunset, which unfortunately occurs after the park closes in July and August.

Accommodation and food in Rockport

Lobster Pool $–$$ *329 Granite St (Rte 127); tel: (978) 546-7808.* Classic casual seafood is this restaurant's forte – and it is a prime spot to watch the sun set over Folly Cove.

Bearskin Neck Motor Lodge $$ *64 Bearskin Neck; tel: (978) 546-6677 or (toll-free) (877) 507-6272.* Modest eight-room motel occupying ideal location near shops and restaurants, with fine ocean views.

The Inn on Cove Hill $$ *37 Mount Pleasant St; tel: (888) 546-2701 or (978) 546-2701; www.innoncovehill.com.* Built circa 1771, the Caleb

Left
Motif No 1, Rockport

Norwood Jr. house has been converted to a seven-room lodging close to Front Beach and Bearskin Neck.

Yankee Clipper Inn $$–$$$ *127 Granite St; tel: (800) 545-3699 or (978) 546-3407; www.yankeeclipperinn.com.* Located between downtown Rockport and Halibut Point, the property offers 16 rooms in two oceanside buildings.

SALEM

Salem Maritime National Historic Site Visitors Center
193 Derby St; tel: (978) 740-1660; www.nps.gov/ sama. Open May–Oct 0900–1700; call for winter hours. Guided tours $.

Peabody Essex Museum $$$ East India Sq and East India Marine Hall at 162 Essex St; tel: (978) 745-9500; www.pem.org. Open Tue–Sun 1000–1700.

House of Seven Gables $$$ 54 Turner St; tel: (978) 744-0991; www.7gables.org. Open daily Nov–Jun 1000–1700, Jul–Oct 1000–1900. Closed first 3 weeks of Jan.

Haunted Happenings
Tel: (877) 725-3662; www.salem.org. Salem celebrates Halloween throughout October with candlelit tours, haunted houses, psychic fairs and other events.

Above
The Salem Witch Museum

Far right
The House of Seven Gables

Salem remains notorious for executing 20 'witches' in the 1690s, but is prouder of its status as the 'Venice of America' from 1790–1830. Guided tours by rangers of the **Salem Maritime National Historic Site** bring to life the era when the riches of the Orient spilled on to Salem's wharves.

With an extensive new wing by Moshe Safdie, the **Peabody Essex Museum** focuses its exhibitions on the world's largest collection of Asian export art, as well as on art of the Pacific Rim and of North America's indigenous peoples. A complete Qing Dynasty merchants' house is also within the museum (extra fee). The American Decorative Art gallery features 17th- and 18th-century Salem cabinetmaking, some of America's finest. Three house museums on the grounds represent Salem's expanding domestic wealth between 1684 and 1805.

A few blocks northeast of the Peabody Essex Museum, the 9-acre **Salem Common** rivals any in New England with its central bandstand, 19th-century cast-iron fence and leafy arcade. The houses at 74, 82 and 92 Washington St E are associated with Samuel McIntire, Salem's self-taught master architect of the early 19th century. Architecture buffs may also wish to stroll **Chestnut St**, lined with merchants' and sea captains' Federal mansions, designed or inspired by McIntire. The street begins three blocks west of Old Town Hall.

Salem Witch Museum $$
Washington Sq; tel: (978) 744-1692; www.salemwitch museum.com. Open daily Jul and Aug 1000–1900; Sept–Jun 1000–1700. Closed two weeks in Jan Mon–Fri.

Witch Dungeon Museum $$ *16 Lynde St; tel: (978) 741-3570; www. witchdungeon.com. Open Apr–Nov daily 1000–1700.*

In a less grand harbour neighbourhood stands the **House of Seven Gables**, inspiration for Nathaniel Hawthorne's second major novel. The grounds include striking seaside gardens and the modest home where the author was born.

The witch trials may have been Salem's most shameful period, but they are still a lucrative tourist draw. The **Salem Witch Museum** features histrionic narration in darkness punctuated by suddenly lit dioramas. The **Witch Dungeon Museum** dramatises transcripts from the trial of Sarah Good and has a re-created dungeon in the basement. The tasteful and reflective **Salem Witch Trial Memorial** was erected in 1992 on New Liberty St next to the old cemetery.

Droll Designs
50 Grove St; tel: (978) 741-3231. Factory outlet offers discounts on highly popular hand-painted ceramics.

Inn at Castle Hill
$$–$$$ *280 Argilla Rd, Ipswich; tel: (978) 412-2555; www. theinnatcastlehill.com.* Luxury lodging on Crane Estate features 10 rooms and expansive views from front porch.

Accommodation and food in Salem

Salem Beer Works $–$$ *278 Derby St; tel: (978) 745-2337; open for lunch and dinner.* The barbecue plates are a good match for ales brewed on the premises. Big TVs feature sporting events.

The Hawthorne Hotel $$ *On the Common; tel: (800) SAY-STAY or (978) 744-4080; email: info@hawthornehotel.com; www.hawthornehotel.com.* Built in 1925, this red-brick member of Historic Hotels of America is well situated for touring.

Lyceum Bar & Grill $$ *43 Church St; tel: (978) 745-7665; open for lunch and dinner.* The restaurant side is formal, the bar more casual, but dark wood and white linens dominate both. Both rooms give stylish updates to classic dishes.

Grapevine Restaurant $$–$$$ *26 Congress St; tel: (978) 745-9335.* This stylish trattoria specialises in seafood and has a broad wine list.

The Salem Inn $$–$$$ *7 Summer St; tel: (800) 446-2995 or (978) 741-0680; www.saleminnma.com.* Lodgings are spread through three historic buildings. The big suites in the Peabody House are good for families; the Curwen House is for adults only.

Suggested tour

Total distance: 65 miles with detour.

Time: 2 hours' driving. Allow 1½ days. Those with limited time should focus on Salem and Newburyport.

Links: From Newburyport at the end of this route, join the New Hampshire and Southern Maine Coast Route (*see page 234*) or return via I-95 Rte 1 to Boston (*see page 40*).

Route: From Boston's Callahan Tunnel follow Rte 1A north 6 miles through the lively beach community of Revere Beach and on to Lynnway, taking the right fork in Swampscott for 6 miles on to Rte 129, which provides fleeting glimpses of an ever-rockier shore as the geology shifts from rivermouth to limestone cliffs en route to **MARBLEHEAD ❶**. Pleasant St at Washington Sq becomes Rte 114 west, a residential district until it enters **SALEM ❷** in 4 miles.

Cogswell's Grant
$$ *60 Spring St, Essex; tel: (978) 768-3632; www.historicnewengland.org. Open Jun–mid-Oct, Wed–Sun, tours on the hour, 1100–1600.* 18th-century farmhouse is filled with folk art assembled by some of the most knowledgeable collectors of the 20th century.

The coastline becomes more rugged between Salem and Cape Ann, a peninsula of solid granite jutting 15 miles out to sea. Follow Rte 1A north 2 miles through Beverly to the intersection with Rte 127 east, the scenic cliffside road to **GLOUCESTER ❸**. In 10 miles turn right on to Hesperus Ave for a 2-mile ocean drive, past craggy cliffs topped with millionaires' mansions. Hesperus Ave rejoins Route 127 just before entering Gloucester at Stage Fort Park. Rte 127 circles Cape Ann, going 4 miles through wooded countryside to **ROCKPORT ❹**.

Woodman's of Essex $ *Main St, Essex; tel: (978) 768-6057.* The family claims to have invented the fried clam circa 1915 at this outstanding 'in-the-rough' seafood restaurant.

Rte 133 in Essex is lined with antiques shops for more than a mile. Most dealers feature small 20th-century collectibles.

Crane Properties *290 Argilla Rd, Ipswich; tel: (978) 356-4351. Open late May–Oct. House tours ($$) Wed–Sat 1000–1300. Landscape Tours ($) Sat 1000.*

Route 127A is the alternative, slightly longer route that skirts the eastern coast of the peninsula for steady views of crashing waves. At Rockport, Rte 127 continues for 7 scenic anticlockwise miles through the summer villages of Lanesboro and Annisquam to return to Gloucester.

In Gloucester, veer right on to Rte 133. The landscape switches abruptly from granite cliffs to tidal marshes and barrier beaches for the rest of the route. Continue 4 miles to **Essex ❺**, a town dedicated to fried clams and antiques shops.

Detour: Three miles past Essex on the right is a turn on to Northgate Rd, which connects to Argilla Rd. Two miles off Rte 133 are the **Crane Properties ❻**, a turn-of-the-century, 2000-acre estate donated by Chicago industrialist Richard T Crane to the Trustees of Reservations. The Stuart-style mansion and formal plantings of Castle Hill serve as the backdrop to informal picnics and many weddings, but the 5 miles of sandy **Crane Beach ❼** are the chief summer draw. Surrounding marshes and dunes comprise a famous bird habitat.

Route 1A continues 1 mile into Ipswich village. The 11 miles to **NEWBURYPORT ❽** pass through farmland – much of it planted with flowers for cutting – and protected wetlands.

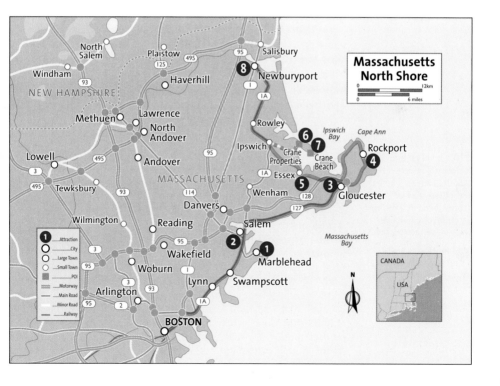

Southeastern Massachusetts

Ratings

History	●●●●●
Nature/ scenery	●●●●●
Arts and culture	●●●●○
Museums	●●●●○
Beaches	●●●○○
Children	●●○○○
Food and drink	●●○○○
Shopping	●●○○○

In the pantheon of American legend and lore, the Pilgrims are right up there with George Washington, Ben Franklin, Abe Lincoln, Mickey Mouse and baseball slugger Babe Ruth. A fervent group of religious dissidents, they crossed the Atlantic aboard the crowded *Mayflower*, eventually landing on the Massachusetts coast in December 1620, at what they nostalgically called Plymouth – England's first permanent New World settlement north of Virginia, which makes that town a prime destination for patriotic British visitors.

By meandering elsewhere on a swing past Cape Cod, you'll come upon grey-shingled coastal villages, plus a pair of working-class towns: New Bedford, awash in whaling history, and Fall River, with worn-out textile mills for possibly your first impression. Don't let those distract you from Battleship Cove, another source of star-spangled patriotism.

FALL RIVER

Fall River Chamber of Commerce *200 Pocasset St; tel: (508) 676-8226; www.fallriverchamber.com*

Heritage State Park *200 Davol St West; tel: (508) 675-5759. Free admission.*

Carousel *$ Tel: (508) 324-4300. Open late Jun–Aug daily 1100–1700; Sept–mid-Oct weekends only.*

This blue-collar city attained prominence as a thriving centre of cotton textile manufacturing from 1811 until the Great Depression of the 1930s. Now some of the huge mills have been converted to factory-outlet shopping warehouses. Fall River remains best known for the unsolved hatchet murder allegedly perpetrated by Lizzie Borden on her father Andrew Jackson Borden and her stepmother Abby in 1892.

Riverfront **Heritage State Park** is a multiple attraction, having textile-mill historical exhibits as well as providing visitor information. It's alongside a pavilion featuring a 1920s **Carousel**. Dwarfing all else is **Battleship Cove**, where the USS *Massachusetts* can be boarded for on-deck touring (as well as cafeteria-style luncheon meals in the ward room). Also at permanent anchor and open to the public are the USS

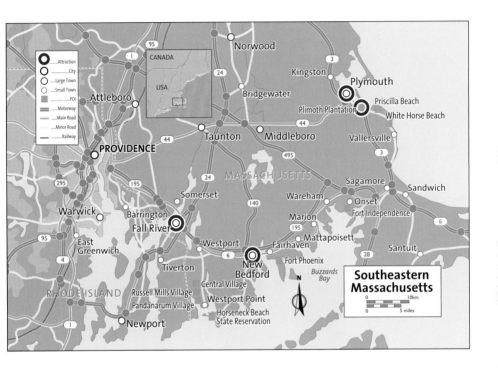

Battleship Cove $$
Take Exit 5 off I-195 or Exit 7 off Rte 24 south-bound; tel: (800) 533-3194 or (508) 678-1100; www.battleshipcove.com. Open daily 0900–1700.

Marine Museum $
70 Water St; tel: (508) 674-3533. Open Mon–Fri 0900–1700, Sat 1200–1700, Sun and holidays 1200–1600; weekends only in winter.

Fall River Historical Society $ 451 Rock St; tel: (508) 679-1071; www.lizzieborden.org. Open Tue–Fri 0900–1630; Jun–Sept Sat and Sun 1300–1700; closed Jan–Apr.

Joseph P. Kennedy destroyer and USS *Lionfish* submarine, plus the *Hiddensee*, a Russian missile corvette acquired by reunified Germany's Baltic fleet. Two PT torpedo boats (small attack boats used in World War II) stand high and dry in an adjacent shed.

For more nautical stuff, stroll from that armada to Fall River's **Marine Museum**, showcasing an array of *Titanic* memorabilia, including Mrs John Jacob Astor's life jacket, numerous documents and other artefacts and an intricately detailed 28-ft model of the doomed White Star liner, made for a 1953 Hollywood melodrama.

Uptown, in a 19th-century mill owner's mansion, the **Fall River Historical Society** concentrates on period furnishings, decorative arts and, inevitably, details of the notorious Borden case.

Accommodation and food in Fall River

Hampton Inn $ *53 Old Bedford Rd, Westport; tel: (800) 426-7866 or (508) 675-8500; www.hamptoninn.com.* Off the I-195 motorway on the east side of town, this 133-room hotel features an indoor pool and serves complimentary continental breakfast.

Waterstreet Café $ *36 Water St; tel: (508) 672-8748.* Pleasantly casual and conveniently situated on the fringe of the riverfront park, this value restaurant near Battleship Cove also has live music on weekends.

The Abbey Grill $$ *100 Rock St; tel: (508) 679-9108.* In a former church of 1865 in Fall River's Historic Highlands neighbourhood ('the Hill'), this is the dining room of the International Institute of Culinary Arts, so you can look forward to fine, creative cooking.

Regatta $$ *392 Davol St; tel: (508) 679-4115.* Right on the shoreline in the park, it has a huge bar, menu selections suiting everyone's taste and an umbrella-shaded deck for broadside views of Battleship Row's war vessels.

Considering Fall River's strong Portuguese, Azorean and Cape Verdean ethnicity, you're in luck if you'd like to sample some tasty Portuguese cooking at **Sagres $$** *177 Columbia St; tel: (508) 675-7108.*

Right
Many of the buildings in New
Bedford feature in Herman
Melville's novel *Moby Dick*

New Bedford

ⓘ Whaling National Historical Park *33 William St; tel: (508) 996-4095; www.nps.gov/nebe. Sponsors free walking tours.*

ⓜ New Bedford Whaling Museum *$ 18 Johnny Cake Hill; tel: (508) 997-0046; www.whalingmuseum.org. Open Mon–Sat 0900–1700, Sun 1300–1700; Jul and Aug 1100–1700.*

Seamen's Bethel *15 Johnny Cake Hill; tel: (508) 992-3295. Open mid-May–mid-Oct daily 1000–1700; rest of year Mon–Fri 1100–1300, Sat 1100–1600, Sun 1300–1600. Free admission.*

Rotch-Jones-Duff House & Garden Museum *$ 396 County St; tel: (508) 997-1401. Open Mon–Sat 1000–1600, Sun 1200–1600.*

Founded in 1652 by Baptists and Quakers from the Plymouth Colony, named after Britain's Duke of Bedford, and surpassing Nantucket as the world's leading whaling centre by 1830, New Bedford was home port to 329 whale-hunting ships at the height of its prosperity in 1857 – when whalebone was a desirable commodity, used for products including corset stays, umbrella handles and knitting needles; lamps fuelled by whale oil illuminated entire cities. *Moby Dick*, Herman Melville's allegorical masterpiece, immortalised the city and that heady era. The historical park brings the past to life, while the city still harbours one of the largest commercial fishing and scalloping fleets in the US.

The New Bedford Whaling Museum is reason enough to come this way. Devoted to local maritime history, its centrepiece is a walk-on, half-scale model of the *Lagoda*, a square-rigged whaling barque. Here, too, are a 98-ft mural depicting a round-the-world whaling voyage, a humpback whale's skeleton, galleries displaying scrimshaw (etchings on whalebone), ship models, figureheads, whaling implements, photographs, folk art and paintings. A 22-minute film captures the adventure of an actual whaling chase.

In *Moby Dick*, Melville set an evocative scene in the grey clapboard **Seamen's Bethel**, an 1832 chapel with a preacher's pulpit shaped like the bowsprit of a whaleboat. Marble cenotaphs memorialise crewmen lost at sea.

A 22-room Greek Revival mansion is the focal point of the **Rotch-Jones-Duff House & Garden Museum**. Built by a whaling merchant, it reflects the lifestyles of three privileged families who resided here between 1834 and 1981.

Accommodation and food in New Bedford

Orchard Street Manor $ *139 Orchard St; tel: (508) 984-3475; www.the-orchard-street-manor.com.* This lovely Georgian Revival home from 1845 features two spacious rooms and three suites as a welcome alternative to the area's chain hotels.

Freestone's City Grill $–$$ *41 William St; tel: (508) 993-7477.* The historic district's standout, in a rock-solid former 19th-century bank building with fireplace and mahogany woodwork; casual atmosphere for fish chowder, grilled seafood, chargrilled hamburgers and serious salads.

Davy's Locker $$ *1480 E Rodney French Blvd; tel: (508) 992-7359.* Overlooking Clark's Cove, primarily a seafood restaurant but also serving steak, chicken and ribs.

PLIMOTH PLANTATION

Plimoth Plantation $$$ *Rte 3A;* tel: (508) 746-1622; www.plimoth.org. Open late Mar–Nov daily 0900–1700.

A recreated 1627 village where interpreters attired in Pilgrim garb cook, harvest, tend farm animals, make candles and clapboards, play games and speak to visitors in authentic Elizabethan dialect. Just outside the stockade settlement, a Wampanoag campsite demonstrates Native American life at the time of the Pilgrims' arrival. Stay in Plymouth (just 3 miles away) if you are visiting Plimoth Plantation.

PLYMOUTH

Plymouth Visitors Information Center *130 Water St;* tel: (800) 872-1620 or (508) 747-7533; www.visit-plymouth.com

Pilgrim Hall Museum $ *75 Court St;* tel: (508) 746-1620. Open Feb–Dec daily 0930–1630.

Sites recalling Pilgrim endurance of circa 1620 are close together in this handsome old town. In Plymouth centre, **Pilgrim Hall Museum** houses pertinent portraits, furniture, maps, and humble clothing and personal effects. A remarkable number of artefact-filled historic dwellings can be visited – among them the 1749 **Spooner House**, owned by generations of Spooners for 200 years.

Down on harbourside Water St, a Grecian portico shelters **Plymouth Rock**, supposedly the stepping-stone where the newcomers clambered ashore after their 66 days at sea.

That suspicious boulder is outmatched by the *Mayflower II*, a faithful replica of the original three-masted barque. Sailing from

The Pilgrims

Early in the 17th century, a group of religious dissidents – many from the northern English village of Scrooby – rebelled under the strict rules and rituals imposed by the Church of England. Led by William Brewster and William Bradford, these Separatists were systematically hunted down and arrested for their defiant beliefs. A sizeable number of families sailed from England to Leyden in the Netherlands; once there, however, they became concerned about losing their English way of life. So some of them decided to emigrate to colonial America, where they believed they could have religious freedom while remaining English.

On 16 September, 1620, 102 passengers and a crew of 26 began the long and difficult journey across the frigid Atlantic. They sailed aboard the *Mayflower*, a small-capacity merchant vessel. It measured merely 104ft long, 25ft wide and, because of a late start, encountered the season's stormiest weather. The passengers spent much of their time below deck in cramped quarters while the ship bucked winds and downpours.

The Pilgrims had planned to sail for Virginia, but raging gales blew them north. They finally stepped ashore at what is now Provincetown on Cape Cod on 21 November, then at Plymouth on 16 December. Scurvy and the extremely harsh weather claimed the lives of about half the Pilgrims during the first gruelling winter on land.

With the help of Native American inhabitants, the new arrivals learned how to grow vegetables, and how to fish and hunt. Pilgrims and tribespeople joined together for a harvest festival in 1621, which Americans now celebrate on the fourth Thursday in November as Thanksgiving Day.

Above
Plimoth Plantation

Spooner House $
27 North St; tel: (508)
746-0012. Closed for
restoration.

Mayflower II $
State Pier off Water St;
tel: (508) 746-1622.
Open late Mar–Nov daily
0900–1700. Available:
combination **$$$** Plimoth
Plantation/ *Mayflower II*
admittance.

Plymouth, England, in 1954, it followed the original vessel's transatlantic course. On-board narrators provide vivid insights into the 17th-century Pilgrims' seagoing hardships while making their long journey to the New World.

The **Pilgrim Trail**, a 10-mile walking route that begins and ends at the Visitors Information Center, encompasses the major and many minor sites related to Plymouth history.

Accommodation and food in Plymouth

Two properties, each with a restaurant and swimming pool, are recommendable. Overlooking the waterfront is the **Governor Bradford on the Harbour $** *98 Water St; tel: (800) 332-1620 or (508) 746-6200.* The **John Carver Inn $–$$** *25 Summer St; tel: (800) 274-1620 or (508) 746-7100,* is downtown.

For seafood dining, choose from among three harbour-view eateries: **Wood's Seafood Market & Restaurant $** *15 Town Pier; tel: (508) 746-0261;* **East Bay Grille $$** *173 Water St; tel: (508) 746-9751;* and **Weathervane $$** *6 Town Wharf; tel: (508) 746-4195.*

Above
The *Mayflower II* replica in Plymouth

Suggested tour

Total distance: 97 miles.

Time: You'll need enough time for adequate, non-rushed sightseeing – especially in Fall River, New Bedford and Plymouth. So allow at least 2 full days.

Links: Driving west beyond Fall River, you can join the Providence/ Pawtucket Route (*see page 158*). From the Plymouth vicinity, you connect with the Cape Cod, Mass. Route (*see page 82*) or the Boston Route (*see page 40*). A summer-season ferry-boat service from New Bedford links that city with Martha's Vineyard (*see page 87*).

Route: Leaving Fall River, take the time for a scenic drive by forsaking the I-195 motorway at Exit 10. Head south 10 miles on Rte 88, leading to the high sand dunes of 2-mile-long **Horseneck Beach State Reservation** ❶. Tiny communities worth seeking out on the way within the Westport and South Dartmouth townships are **Pandanarum Village** ❷, **Russell Mills Village** ❸, **Central Village** ❹ and **Westport** ❺, all dating from US Colonial times. Then follow signs for a north-by-east loop via salt marshes and boat harbours.

At North Dartmouth, take Rte 6 to head 1 mile into **NEW BEDFORD** ❻; follow Kempton St to reach downtown's historic waterfront area. Back on Rte 6, cross the Acushnet River bridge to arrive in **Fairhaven** ❼, where Rte 6 coincides with Huttleston St, named after Standard Oil tycoon Henry Huttleston Rogers, a native son and civic benefactor. His generosity becomes evident in Centre St's 1894 **Town Hall** ❽, resembling a Flemish castle. Standing directly across the street is the equally flamboyant 1893 **Millicent Public Library** ❾, an Italian Renaissance showpiece inside and out. Continue west on Centre St to Old Fort Rd, where you'll reach **Fort Phoenix** ❿, bristling with six Revolutionary War cannons; here US militiamen repulsed British invaders on 7 September 1778. High ground affords panoramic views of Buzzards Bay and New Bedford's harbour.

East from Fairhaven, Rte 6 curves alongside jagged coastline. After 3 miles, you'll be in **Mattapoisett** ⓫, where most of New Bedford's

ⓘ Fairhaven Visitors Center *43 Center St, Fairhaven; tel: (508) 979-4085.*

Cape Cod Canal Region Chamber of Commerce *70 N Main St, Buzzards Bay; tel: (508) 759-6000.* Provides information about the Marion/Onset/Wareham area.

whaling ships were built between 1752 and 1878 – barques, brigs, sloops, schooners, launched at six shipyards. Herman Melville's 1841 sea duty on the *Acushnet* inspired the *Moby Dick* saga. Early 19th-century shingle-sided houses line Water St. Next comes **Marion ⑫**, the most affluent village on Buzzards Bay's western shore, with a sizeable millionaire population and, at Sippican Harbor, the 1872 Beverly Yacht Club, America's second-oldest after its counterpart in New York City.

Passing cranberry bogs, continue another 6 miles to Wareham. Consider a short detour to **Onset ⑬**, a placid Victorian hamlet overlooking Onset Bay and the public beach at **Fort Independence ⑭**. Departing Wareham, drive through Buzzards Bay village, then follow Rte 6 alongside the Cape Cod Canal in order to reach Rte 3. (This entails careful sign-reading, and you'll encounter two daredevil roundabouts at cross-bridge approaches to Cape Cod. Stay calm.) Shortly after turning on to Rte 3, take Exit 2 for scenic Rte 3A to head north past cranberry bogs while enjoying ocean views along Cape Cod Bay. At Manomet Point, **White Horse Beach ⑮** and the adjoining **Priscilla Beach ⑯** form a sandy crescent. They're 1 mile south of **PLIMOTH PLANTATION ⑰** which, in turn, is 3 miles south of **PLYMOUTH ⑱**.

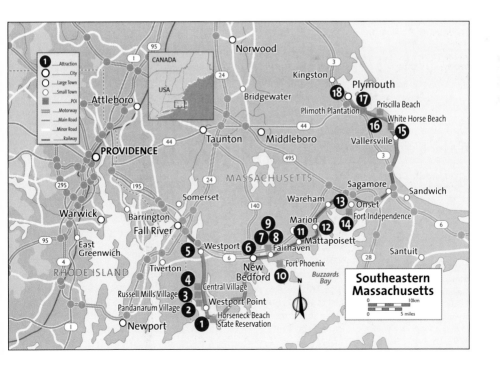

Cape Cod and its Islands

Ratings

Beaches	●●●●●
Nature/scenery	●●●●●
Children	●●●●○
Food and drink	●●●○○
Museums	●●●○○
Shopping	●●●○○
Arts and culture	●●○○○
History	●●○○○

On a map, Cape Cod resembles a strongman's flexed arm, with Falmouth on the triceps, Chatham at the elbow and Provincetown the clenched fist. Many New Englanders equate Cape Cod with summer, as it has been the holiday spot of choice for nearly a century. The finest recreational beaches in the Northeast attract literally millions of visitors to a region with a winter population of tens of thousands. Yet much of the Cape remains seemingly deserted, a landscape of windswept dunes and relentless surf, or of tranquil farmland dotted with windmills and saltbox houses. Depending on the town, Cape Cod can spell days of indolence in the sun or non-stop partying, dining and shopping.

CAPE COD BAY

ⓘ Sandwich Glass Museum $ *129 Main St; tel: (508) 888-0251; www.sandwichglassmuseum. org. Open Apr–Dec daily 0930–1700; Feb and Mar Wed–Sun 0930–1600.*

Thornton Burgess Museum $ *4 Water St, Sandwich; tel: (508) 888-4668; www. thorntonburgess.org. Open May–Oct Mon–Sat 1000–1600, Sun 1300–1600.*

The placid communities of Cape Cod Bay are strung along the old King's Highway, Rte 6A. They are preserves of 18th- and early 19th-century houses (many converted to B&Bs), village greens and antiques dealers. Closest to Boston, **Sandwich** features three museums. The **Sandwich Glass Museum** chronicles the local pressed glass industry that flourished 1828–88. The charming **Thornton Burgess Museum** features a collection of the author's children's books and original illustrations. **Heritage Museums and Gardens** has spectacular rhododendron gardens and several buildings exhibiting Indian artefacts, Colonial furniture and weapons, and vintage cars. Along with sea captains' homes, **Dennis** boasts the **Cape Cod Playhouse**, last of the summer stock venues. On the same grounds, the **Cape Cod Museum of Art** displays work by local artists. Almost at the

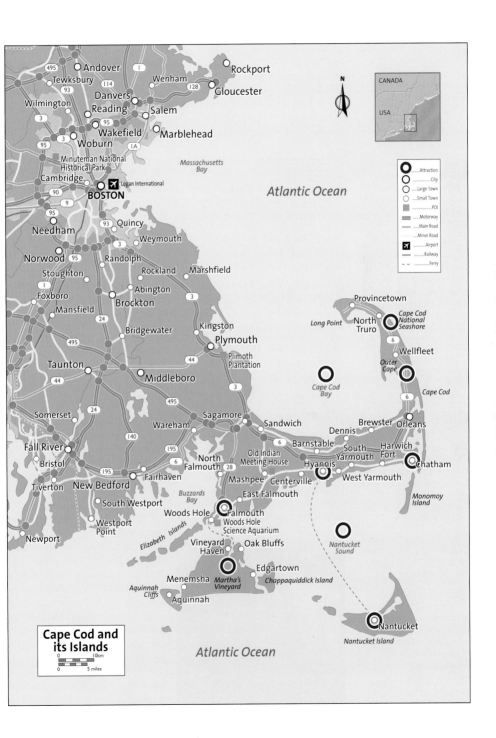

Cape Cod and its Islands

⊞ Heritage Museums and Gardens $$$ *Grove and Pine Sts, Sandwich; tel: (508) 888-3300; www. heritagemuseumsand gardens.org. Open Apr–Oct daily 1000–1700; Nov–Mar call for hours.*

Cape Cod Museum of Art $$ *Main St, Rte 6A, Dennis; tel: (508) 385-4477; www.ccmoa.org. Open late May–mid-Oct Mon–Sat 1000–1700, Sun 1200–1700; call for winter hours.*

Cape Cod Museum of Natural History $$ *Rte 6A, Brewster; tel: (508) 896-3867; www.ccmnh.org. Open Jun–Sept daily 0930–1600; call for off-season hours.*

⊙ Cape Cod Playhouse *Main St, Dennis; tel: (508) 385-3911.*

geographic centre of Cape Cod, **Brewster** capitalises on its sedate landscape. The activities at the **Cape Cod Museum of Natural History** target younger children, but the 82-acre site also contains three self-guided nature trails. The 2000 acres of **Nickerson State Park** are dotted with glacial kettle ponds and tracked with trails. Directly across Rte 6A from Nickerson is **Linnell Landing Beach**, with excellent wheelchair access.

Accommodation and food on Cape Cod Bay

Nickerson State Park *3488 Main St, Rte 6A; tel: (508) 896-3491, camping reservations (877) 422-6762; www.reserveamerica.com.* Nickerson's 420 tent and RV pitches ($) are the Cape's most popular.

Sandy Neck Motel $–$$ *669 Rt 6A, E Sandwich; tel: (800) 564-3992 or (508) 362-3992; www.sandyneck.com.* Superb older motel on landscaped grounds sits at road to Sandy Neck Beach.

Ocean Edge Club $$–$$$ *2907 Main St, Brewster; tel: (800) 343-6074 or (508) 896-9000; www.oceanedge.com.* Lodging choices include rooms in a massive stone hotel or self-catering condo units on this property with a private beach and the Cape's best golf course.

Chillingsworth $$$ *2449 Main St, Brewster; tel: (508) 896-3640; open for lunch and dinner.* This classic French restaurant is a top Cape dining destination.

CAPE COD NATIONAL SEASHORE

ⓘ Cape Cod National Seashore Salt Pond Visitor Center *Rte 6, Eastham; tel: (508) 255-3421; www.nps.gov/caco. Open daily 0900–1630; summer 0900–1700.*

Province Lands Visitor Center *Rte 6, Provincetown; tel: (508) 487-1256. Open May–Oct 0900–1700.*

◑ Explore the marsh near Nauset Light Beach by canoe or kayak, either of which can be rented from **Goose Hummock Shop $$$** *15 Rte 6A, Orleans; tel: (508) 255-0455; www.goose.com*

The National Seashore encompasses almost 45,000 acres of fragile dunes, fertile marshes, woodlands and deserts, cranberry bogs, cedar forest and long sandy beaches along a 40-mile stretch between **Chatham** and **Provincetown**. Ranger-led programmes explore these varied ecosystems. Little explanation is required to enjoy the beaches, which include **Coast Guard Beach**, with excellent surfing; **Nauset Light Beach**, with good surfing and surf-casting; **Head of the Meadow Beach**, with great views of Provincetown and Truro dunelands; **Race Point Beach**, with spectacular dunes and some of the Cape's finest swimming; and **Herring Cove Beach**, which has the calmest waters and faces west into the sunset. Lifeguards are posted late June–early September. Watch for heavy surf and rip tides.

CHATHAM

ⓘ Chatham Chamber of Commerce Info Booth *533 Main St; tel: (800) 715-5567 or (508) 945-5199; www.chathaminfo.com. Open May–Oct Mon–Sat 1000–1700, Sun 1200–1700.*

ⓜ Old Atwood House Museum $ *347 Stage Harbor Rd; tel: (508) 947-2493. Open Jun–Oct Tue–Sat 1300–1600.*

Monomoy National Wildlife Refuge Visitor Center *30 Wikis Way; tel: (508) 945–0594; www.fws.gov. Open late May–Oct 1000–1600; call for winter hours. Free admission.*

ⓝ Band Nights *Tel: (508) 945-5199.* Fri evening band concerts held in Kate Gould Park during July and August are best enjoyed while eating chocolate-covered cranberries from Chatham Candies on Main St.

Chatham is a close-knit community, where shell fishermen harvest some of the world's finest clams, oysters and mussels and where the whole town turns out for civic band concerts. Art galleries and boutiques dominate the village. The **Old Atwood House Museum** details local history and displays provocative murals by Alice Stallknect depicting Christ as a modern fisherman. Sheltered **Oyster Pond Beach**, just a block from Main St, is superb for small children. The long strand of **Chatham Light Beach** is reached from the lighthouse car park. **South Monomoy Island**, a barrier island bird sanctuary, is accessible by boat.

Accommodation and food in Chatham

Above right South Beach, Chatham

Marley's Restaurant $–$$ *Rte 28; tel: (508) 945-1700; open for dinner.* Casual spot to sample Chatham shellfish.

Impudent Oyster $$ *15 Chatham Bars Ave; tel: (508) 945-3545; open for lunch and dinner.* A good place for fresh fish and cold draught beer.

Chatham Wayside Inn $$–$$$ *512 Main St; tel: (800) 242-8426 or (508) 945-5550; www.waysideinn.com.* In the village centre, an 1860 inn with restored rooms lies at the heart of a recent expansion.

Old Harbor Inn $$–$$$ *22 Old Harbor Rd; tel: (800) 942-4434 or (508) 945-4434; www.chathamoldharborinn.com.* Elegant inn just steps from town features eight rooms, some with fireplaces.

FALMOUTH

ⓘ Falmouth Chamber of Commerce 20 Academy Ln; tel: (800) 526-8532 or (508) 548-8500; www.falmouthchamber.com. Open Mon–Fri 0900–1700; late May–mid-Oct Sat 1000–1600.

ⓜ Woods Hole Oceanographic Institution Exhibit Center $ 15 School St, Woods Hole; tel: (508) 289-2663; www.whoi.edu. Open May–Oct Mon–Sat 1000–1630; call for off-season hours.

Woods Hole Science Aquarium Albatross St, Woods Hole; tel: (508) 495-2267. Open Jun–Sept Tue–Sat 1100–1600; Oct–May Mon–Fri 1100–1600. Free admission. ID required for adults.

Handsome **Falmouth**, with its fine old village centre and green, is usually bypassed in the rush to get to **Woods Hole**, but has fine architecture, a striking yacht harbour and good swimming beaches.

The picturesque village of **Woods Hole** is an enclave of oceanographic research. The **Woods Hole Oceanographic Institution Exhibit Center** focuses on underwater research. The **Woods Hole Science Aquarium** eschews high tech in favour of educational exhibits of commercially important local fish.

Accommodation and food in Falmouth

Shoreway Acres $–$$$ *Shore St; tel: (800) 352-7100 or (508) 540-3000; www.shorewayacresinn.com.* Near town and beach, Shoreway has both motel rooms and inn-style rooms in former sea captains' houses.

Quarterdeck Restaurant $$ *164 Main St; tel: (508) 548-9900.* Traditional spot specialises in seafood classics such as crab cakes, scallops and steamed lobster.

Palmer House Inn $$–$$$ *81 Palmer Ave; tel: (800) 472-2632 or (508) 548-1230; www.palmerhouseinn.com.* Full-blown Victorian frills in the village centre. There is a separate suite in the grounds that is ideal for romantic getaways.

HYANNIS

ⓒ Hy-Line Harbor Cruises $$$ Ocean St Dock; tel: (800) 492-8082 makes a narrated hour-long tour past the Kennedy family compound.

All Cape highways converge in Hyannis, the sprawling commercial centre of the Cape haunted by memories of President Kennedy. The exhibits at the modest **John F Kennedy Hyannis Museum** include many of the most memorable photographs of the president and his family, taken at the nearby Kennedy compound.

**John F Kennedy
Hyannis Museum $**
397 Main St; tel: (508) 790-3077. Open late May–mid-Oct Mon–Sat 0900–1700, Sun 1200–1700; call for off-season hours.

Accommodation in Hyannis

Hyannis Travel Inn $–$$ *18 North St; tel: (800) 352-7190 or (508) 775-8200; www.hyannistravelinn.com.* Modern motel strategically located just off the bustle of Hyannis.

Right
Nobska lighthouse stands between Falmouth and Woods Hole

MARTHA'S VINEYARD

**Martha's Vineyard
Chamber of
Commerce** *Beach Rd, Vineyard Haven; tel: (508) 693-0085; www.mvy.com. Open Mon–Fri 0900–1700.*

**Martha's Vineyard
& Nantucket
Steamship Authority**
Tel: (508) 477-8600; www.islandferry.com. Provides the only year-round and only car crossings (reservation essential) to Martha's Vineyard. Operates all year between Woods Hole and Vineyard Haven and adds a summer service to Oak Bluffs.

Of the two large islands off Cape Cod, 100-square-mile Martha's Vineyard offers more for day-trippers who often don't get beyond the tourist shops and ice cream parlours of **Vineyard Haven**. **Oak Bluffs** is the home of Martha's Vineyard Camp Meeting Association, with more than 300 gingerbread cottages. The downtown carousel is one of America's oldest. The majestic homes of the whaling captains in **Edgartown**, with their signature white clapboards and black shutters, lend historic charm to the Vineyard town with the most amenities and best beach access. **Martha's Vineyard Preservation Society** offers a tour of two houses and the 1843 Old Whaling Church. Three-mile **Katama Beach** has good surfing and many shore birds. A ferry at the foot of Dock St makes a 2-minute crossing to **Chappaquiddick Island**, where the **Cape Pogue Wildlife Refuge** has 2 miles of stunning beach. **Menemsha** is the Vineyard's last working fishing village. The Aquinnah Wampanoag tribe owns the **Aquinnah Cliffs** at the southwestern end of the island. The brightly coloured cliffs, sacred to the tribe, capture 100 million years of geological history in layers of sand, gravel and clay.

Accommodation and food on Martha's Vineyard

Martha's Vineyard Preservation Trust *$ 99 Main St, Edgartown; tel: (508) 627-4400.* Tours of three historic properties offered May–mid-October; call for schedule.

Striped Bass and Bluefish Derby *Tel: (508) 693-0085.* Martha's Vineyard is known for sport fishing. This competition takes place mid-September–mid-October.

Martha's Vineyard Regional Transit Authority $ *Tel: (508) 693-9440; www.vineyardtransit.com.* Year-round bus service connects Edgartown, Oak Bluffs, Vineyard Haven and West Tisbury, with additional beach stops. **Martha's Bike Rentals $$$** *4 Lagoon Point Rd, Vineyard Haven, tel: (508) 693-6593* is next to the steamship docks. **Vineyard History & Ghost Tours $$** *Tel: (508) 627-8619.* Walking tours with knowledgeable local guide mid-May–mid-October.

Martha's Vineyard Family Campground $ *569 Edgartown Rd, Vineyard Haven; tel: (508) 693-3772; www.campmv.com.* Cabins augment tent and RV sites on shuttle bus line.

Larsen's Fish Market $–$$ *Menemsha Harbor; tel: (508) 645-2680; open daily 0900–1800.* Fish market cooks steamers, lobsters and mussels to order and always has a supply of chowder and crab cakes.

Nancy's $–$$ *Oak Bluffs Harbor; tel: (508) 693-0006; open for lunch and dinner.* Excellent fish and chips, lobster rolls and stuffed quahogs (round-shell clams) to eat at picnic tables overlooking the harbour.

Seafood Shanty $$ *31 Dock St, Edgartown; tel: (508) 627-8622; open for lunch and dinner.* Spacious room looks out on the harbour; specialises in local shellfish.

Clarion Martha's Vineyard $$–$$$ *227 Upper Main St, Edgartown; tel: (800) 922-3009 or (508) 627-5161; www.clarionmv.com.* Modest rooms with modern conveniences at (by local standards) modest prices.

Colonial Inn $$–$$$ *38 N Water St, Edgartown; tel: (508) 627-4711 or (800) 627-4701; www.colonialinnmvy.com.* One of Edgartown's larger properties, central to the shopping district and waterfront.

Mansion House Inn $$–$$$ *9 Main St, Vineyard Haven; tel: (800) 332-4112; www.mvmansionhouse.com.* Luxurious rooms and sybaritic spa combine with grand sea view. Elegant restaurant rounds out the package.

Wesley Hotel $$–$$$ *70 Lake Ave, Oak Bluffs; tel: (800) 638-9027 or (508) 693-6611; www.wesleyhotel.com.* Victorian resort hotel overlooking the harbour also has modern rooms in a new annexe.

Right
This horseshoe crab is for studying by naturalists, not for eating

NANTUCKET ISLAND

ⓘ Nantucket Island Chamber of Commerce *40 Main St; tel: (508) 228-1700; www.nantucketchamber.org. Open Mon–Fri 0900–1700.*

Ⓟ Nantucket Regional Transit Authority $ *Tel: (508) 228-7025; www.shuttlenantucket.com operates a bus service between villages and a seasonal beach shuttle.* At Steamship Wharf, **Nantucket Bike Shop** *tel: (508) 228-1999 rents bicycles and mopeds and* **Young's Bicycle Shop** *tel: (508) 228-1151 rents bicycles, cars and jeeps.* **Great Point Natural History Tours $$$** *tel: (508) 228-6799 traverse the beaches in four-wheel-drive vehicles June–September.*

Ⓜ Nantucket Whaling Museum *$$$ Broad and South Beach Sts; tel: (508) 228-5646; www.nha.org. Open late May–Oct daily 1000–1700; call for off-season hours.*

First Congregational Church *$ 62 Centre St; no tel. Tower open mid-Jun–mid-Oct Mon–Sat 1000–1600.*

Ⓐ Daffodil Festival *Tel: (508) 228-1700. Celebrates the bloom of more than three million daffodils in late April.*

Nantucket Film Festival *Tel: (508) 228-1700; www. nantucketfilmfestival.org. June event focuses on screenwriting.*

Some thirty miles out to sea, the island of Nantucket stands aloof from the Cape's hubbub. Quaker whalers made Nantucket's fortunes, and their Spartan mien still influences local style. The island is small enough to negotiate on a bicycle, yet dense enough with natural and historic sites to be endlessly beguiling.

The **Nantucket Whaling Museum**, kingpin site of the Nantucket Historical Society, illuminates the enterprise and adventure that made Nantucket rich. The landscape and layout of the island are best appreciated from the belfry lookout of the **First Congregational Church**. Tiny houses with roses climbing their walls and roofs dominate the former fishing village of **Sconset**, now an upmarket preserve on the east end of the island.

Accommodation and food on Nantucket Island

Camping is prohibited on Nantucket and caravans are not permitted on the island.

Straight Wharf Fish Store $ *Harbor Sq; tel: (508) 228-1095; open daily.* Outstanding takeaway items include lobster rolls, seafood gumbo and swordfish sandwiches.

Roberts House $–$$$ *11 India St; tel: (800) 872-6830 or (508) 228-0600; www.robertshouseinn.com.* Cosy rooms have Victorian whaling era decor as well as free wireless internet and cable TV. Quick walk to village centre.

Café at Le Languedoc $$ *24 Broad St; tel: (508) 228-2552; open for dinner and weekend lunch.* Cheery basement café is the bargain sibling of one of Nantucket's best French restaurants.

Jared Coffin House $$–$$$ *29 Broad St; tel: (800) 248-2405 or (508) 228-2400; www.jaredcoffinhouse.com.* This brick mansion is a social centre of island life; sixty rooms are spread among six buildings. Enjoy a complimentary glass of port in the library in the afternoon.

Ships Inn $$$ *13 Fair St; tel: (508) 228-0040 or (888) 872-4052; www.shipsinnnantucket.com.* There are 12 guest rooms (two with shared bath) in this 1831 whaling captain's home, as well as a gourmet restaurant ($$$) where the chef creates a new lobster dish each year.

The Wauwinet $$$ *120 Wauwinet Rd; tel: (800) 426-8718 or (508) 228-0145; www.wauwinet.com.* Posh resort next to Great Point Nature Preserve houses the island's leading gourmet restaurant.

NANTUCKET SOUND

Roadside development has run amok on Rte 28 between Hyannis and Chatham, but good bargain motels are to be found here, and striking sandy beaches usually lie less than a mile south of the highway.

Accommodation on Nantucket Sound

Grindell's Ocean View Park $ *61 Old Wharf Rd, Dennisport; tel: (508) 398-2671.* Park with 160 RV pitches and 11 cottages sits at edge of Nantucket Sound beach.

Town 'n Country Motor Lodge $–$$ *452 Main St, Rte 28, W Yarmouth; tel: (800) 992-2340 or (508) 771-0212; www.towncountry-capecod.com.* This complex about 5 miles from the beach has 150 rooms, 3 pools, sauna, whirlpool and barbecue area.

Pilgrims at Provincetown

Popular history forgets that the *Mayflower* Pilgrims didn't make their first landfall on Plymouth Rock, but on the sandy shores of Provincetown. After raiding the grain stores of the Nauset tribe in nearby Wellfleet, they sailed on to settle at Plymouth – but not before signing the Mayflower Compact, which would become the first building block of American self-governance. That first landing is commemorated by Provincetown's 255ft Pilgrim Monument, the tallest granite structure in the US.

OUTER CAPE

Art's Dune Tours $$$ *Standish and Commercial Sts, Provincetown; tel: (508) 487-1950 or (800) 894-1951; www.artsdunetours.com.* The best way to tour the environmentally sensitive dune habitat. Book early for the sunset tour.

Dolphin Fleet $$$ *Tel: (800) 826-9300; www.whalewatch.com.* Whale-watching boats staffed by naturalists April–October.

The most dynamic landscapes of the forearm of Cape Cod belong to the **Cape Cod National Seashore**, but the towns of Wellfleet and Provincetown pulse with human activity. **Provincetown** combines an art colony, a Portuguese fishing village and a gay and lesbian resort. **Provincetown Art Association and Museum** has an outstanding collection of work by some of America's leading artists – including Edward Hopper and Robert Motherwell – who chose to paint the conjunction of sea, land and sky on the outer Cape. Naturalist excursions include **guided dune tours** and **whale-watching cruises**. Wellfleet Bay Wildlife Sanctuary, with nearly every natural habitat found on Cape Cod, is a magnet for birdwatchers. Wellfleet Drive-In, one of the region's last outdoor cinemas, turns its car park to good use by day when it serves as the venue for a huge flea market. Walk around in Wellfleet's centre to browse art galleries and appreciate the ambience of a harbour village.

Provincetown Art Association and Museum $ *460 Commercial St; tel: (508) 487-1750; www.paam.org. Open Oct–May Thur–Sun 1200–1700; late May–Sept Mon–Thur 1100–2000, Fri 1100–2200, Sat and Sun 1100–1700.*

Wellfleet Flea Market *Rte 6A; tel: (508) 349-7176.* Cape Cod's largest flea market ($) is held *mid-Apr–Sept Sat and Sun; Jul and Aug Wed and Thur.*

Wellfleet Drive-In $$ *Rte 6A; tel: (508) 349-7176; www.wellfleetcinemas.com.* Screens first run double features late April–October.

Wellfleet Harbor Actors Theater *Town Pier (1 Kendrick Ave) and 2357 Rte 6, Wellfleet; tel: (508) 349-9428 or 866-282-9428; www.what.org.* Modern 200-seat Julie Harris Stage augments the original 90-seat Harbor Stage for a year-round resident company known for its provocative contemporary work, including new play development.

Accommodation and food on the Outer Cape

Squealing Pig $–$$ *335 Commercial St, Provincetown; tel: (508) 487-5804; open for lunch and dinner.* Bar food with panache includes lean burgers, curries and vegetarian sandwiches.

Wellfleet Motel & Lodge $–$$$ *Rte 6, S Wellfleet; tel: (800) 852-2900 or (508) 349-3535; www.wellfleetmotel.com.* Well maintained 65-room property is across the street from a wildlife sanctuary and close to Cape Cod Rail Trail.

Catch of the Day Seafood Market & Grill $$ *975 Rte 6, Wellfleet; tel: (508) 349-9090.* Savour famous Wellfleet oysters and littleneck clams or select fish from the case and have it grilled.

Surfside Hotel & Suites $$–$$$ *543 Commercial St, Provincetown; tel: (508) 487-1726 or (800) 421-1726; www.surfsideinn.cc.* Large motor inn, which boasts a private beach. Rooms have refrigerators and microwaves or full kitchens.

Right
Artists are everywhere in Provincetown

ⓘ **Cape Cod Chamber of Commerce and Visitor Bureau** *Jct Rtes 6 and 132, at exit 6 Hyannis;* tel: *(888) 33-CAPECOD or (508) 362-3225;* www.capecodchamber.org. *Open Mon–Fri 0830–1700, Sat 0900–1700; May–Aug Sun 1000–1400.* Offers information for the entire Cape.

② Two bottleneck bridges cross Cape Cod Canal: **Bourne Bridge** (Rte 28) on the west and **Sagamore Bridge** (Rte 6) on the east.

✪ Aficionados cite the semi-professional **Cape Cod Baseball League** *www.capecodbaseball.org* as the purest surviving example of the all-American game. Its schedule is posted in the *Cape Cod Times.* Free admission.

Above
Cape Cod National Seashore

Suggested tour

Total distance: 192 miles; ferry detours add 66 miles.

Duration: 8 hours' driving in Jul and Aug, 5 hours' rest of year. Allow 5–6 days. Those with limited time should follow Rte 6 and focus on Cape Cod National Seashore.

Links: Connects via Rte 3 or Rte 6 to Southeastern Massachusetts Route (*see page 74*).

Route: Begin at Bourne Bridge at the west end of Cape Cod Canal, heading south 4 miles on Rte 28. Veer right on to Rte 28A to follow shoreline road past beaches and quiet villages for 5 miles before returning to Rte 28, 3 miles north of **FALMOUTH ❶**. At Falmouth, follow Woods Hole Rd 4¹/2 miles to Woods Hole.

Detour: Take the ferry to **MARTHA'S VINEYARD ❷**.

Backtrack from Woods Hole to Falmouth and follow Rte 28 east for 10 miles. Turn left on Great Neck Rd N to **Mashpee ❸**, a village set aside in 1660 as a Wampanoag reservation. Turn left on Rte 130 to visit the poignant graveyard at the **Old Indian Meeting House ❹**. Follow Rte 130 south 2 miles to rejoin Rte 28, which passes through several wealthy villages in the 10 miles into **HYANNIS ❺**.

Detour: Take the ferry to **NANTUCKET ISLAND ❻**.

The 23 miles of Rte 28 east of Hyannis en route to **CHATHAM ❼** usually suffer the Cape's worst traffic. Periodic breaks for oceanfront scenery along **NANTUCKET SOUND ❽** can be made by turning south on any large street. At Chatham, Rte 28 doglegs north, following the Nauset Marsh 10 miles to Orleans, where Rte 6 is the only road extending the length of the **OUTER CAPE ❾**, passing all of the entry points to the **CAPE COD NATIONAL SEASHORE ❿** in a 34-mile stretch to **Provincetown ⓫**.

From Provincetown, backtrack 34 miles to the Orleans traffic roundabout and take Rte 6A for 5 miles to Brewster, another 6 miles to Dennis and another 18 miles to **Sandwich ⓬**, watching for art potters, art galleries and antiques dealers along the way. Just over a mile west of Sandwich, Rte 6A joins Rte 6 at Sagamore. A 5-mile drive west along the Cape Cod Canal returns to the starting point. Alternatively, Rte 3 from the flyover crosses the Sagamore Bridge and continues north to Plymouth.

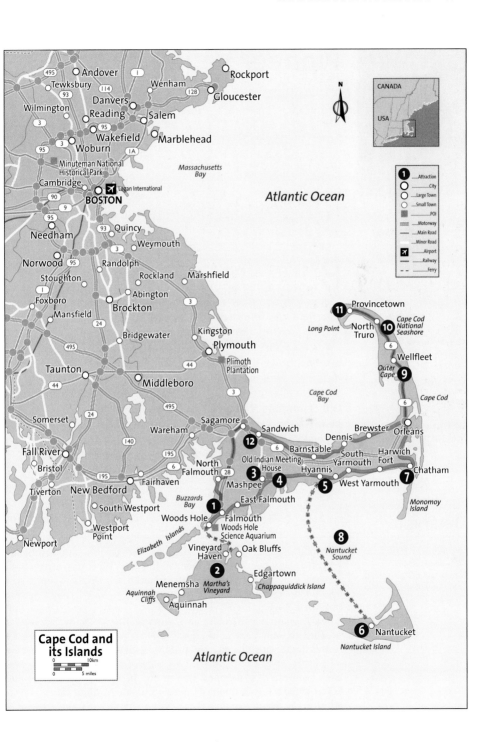

Cape Cod and its Islands

Pioneer Valley

Ratings

Arts and culture	●●●●○
History	●●●●○
Museums	●●●●○
Food and drink	●●●○○
Children	●●○○○
Nature/ scenery	●●○○○
Shopping	●●○○○
Beaches and watersports	●○○○○

By the time it reaches Massachusetts, the Connecticut River is wide and imposing, carving a flat floodplain hemmed by rolling hills on either side. Farms have flourished here since tiny Deerfield was founded as a colonial outpost in the early 1700s, and homes from that era still grace village greens.

For travellers, the highlights of the centre of Massachusetts are two quite different historical villages, of different eras, different styles and with different artefacts and interpretation. Serious collectors should visit Historic Deerfield which, unlike Old Sturbridge Village, is not a museum village showing how people lived. Deerfield focuses on the artefacts, and it has a fine collection. Families and those who are interested to learn how people lived in other times and places shouldn't miss Old Sturbridge Village. Most visitors try to see both.

DEERFIELD

 **Pioneer Valley Tourist Information Center** *Rte 5/10, South Deerfield; tel: (413) 665-7333.*

Deerfield's several museum houses are seen by tours, unfortunately scheduled so you cannot see them all in a day. When you arrive, head straight away for the Visitors Center opposite the Deerfield Inn to sign up. All tour groups are of limited numbers, so early arrivals get the day's best choices.

Ask first for the **Hinsdale and Anna Williams House**, home of a prosperous merchant in the early 1800s, and **Stebbins House**, an earlier home with fine examples of decorative arts. For an interesting look at the village in the mid-1700s, when revolutionary plotting was afoot, you can visit **Barnard Tavern** and its upstairs assembly room. Some of the finest examples of needlework are in **Allen House**: this is a bit of a hodge-podge, but well worth asking for; it is often the only

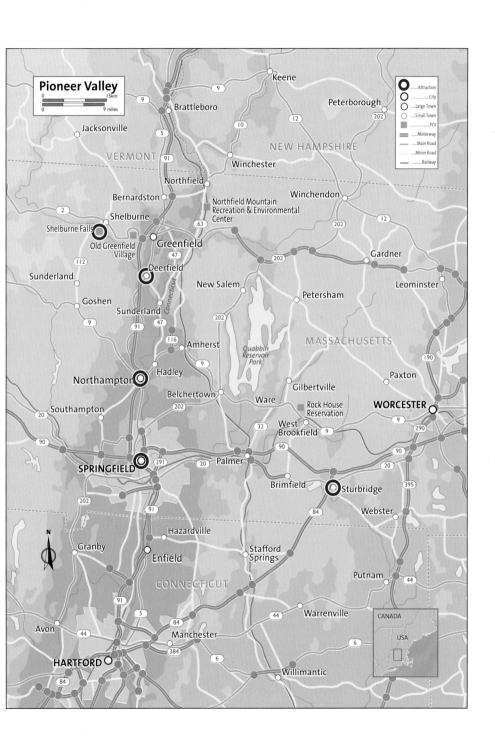

Historic Deerfield
$$ *Rte 5; tel: (413)
774-5581; www.historic-
deerfield.org. Open daily
0930–1630, tours
1000–1600.* All houses
shown only on guided
tours. Special advance
arrangements for private
tours (up to four people)
focusing on special
interests, such as
needlework.

Memorial Hall Museum
$ *Memorial St;
tel: (413) 774-3768;
www.memorialhall.mass.edu.
Open May–Oct daily
0930–1630.* Admission
free with Historic
Deerfield unlimited tour
ticket.

way to see the extraordinary **Textile Museum** with its collections of early costumes and bed coverings. These and the **Silver and Metalware Collection** are grouped into one tour.

However discouraging these arrangements may be, the two largest assemblages are open on a regular schedule without tours. Deerfield's 'don't miss' attraction is the local historical society's **Memorial Hall Museum**, which traces Deerfield's history from its most famous event, when in 1704 the entire town was destroyed in an Indian raid and its inhabitants taken prisoner to Canada. You can see at your own pace excellent examples of the famous Deerfield embroidery, quilts and everything from kitchen utensils to ladies' fans.

The entire village, including private homes, is a National Historic District, worth strolling through even if the buildings are closed. Few places offer such outstanding domestic architecture of late Colonial and Federal periods.

Accommodation and food in Deerfield

Deerfield Inn $$–$$$ *Old Deerfield; tel: (413) 774-5587 or (800) 926-3865; www.deerfieldinn.com; open daily for dinner 1800–2100.* A fine old inn, restored and furnished with antiques, with an outstanding dining room ($$–$$$), in which the menu features such specialities as venison and rack of lamb.

NORTHAMPTON

**Smith College Art
Museum** $ *Elm St;
tel: (413) 585-2760;
www.smith.edu/artmuseum.
Open Tue–Sat 1000–1600,
Sun 1200–1600, second Fri
of the month 1000–2000*
(free admission 1600–
2000).

Lyman Plant House
*College Lane, tel: (413) 585-
2740; www.smith.edu/garden.
Open daily 0830–1600.*
Free admission.

A college town with the usual attendant cultural and social life, Northampton is known for its restaurants and trendy shops. The **Smith College Art Museum**, one of the nation's most important college art collections, is strong in paintings by Connecticut Valley and American artists, plus French Impressionist paintings, Greek vases, Dutch landscapes and sculptures by Rodin.

Smith College's **Lyman Plant House** is a glasshouse world of growing things, with 3500 species indigenous to places from the Amazon to Zanzibar. Fourteen solaria sit amid gardens and an arboretum.

Accommodation and food in Northampton

The Knoll $ *230 North Main St; tel: (413) 584-8164; http:// theknollbedandbreakfast.com.* Intimate B&B in a 12-room Tudor-style mansion built in 1910 and close to the five colleges; Wi-Fi available.

Hotel Northampton $$ *36 King St; tel: (413) 584-3100 or (800) 547-3529; www.hotelnorthampton.com.* Well-kept downtown hotel with inn flavour; at **Wiggins Tavern** ($$) you can sample traditional New England dishes.

SHELBURNE FALLS

ⓘ Tourist Information Center *75 Bridge St; tel: (413) 625-2544.*

Ⓜ McCusker's Market *State St; tel: (413) 625-2548; http:// greenfieldsmarket.coop.* Deli counter with fresh salads and other picnic food.

Ⓡ From Shelburne Falls you can continue west on Rte 2, known as the **Mohawk Trail**. This scenic route climbs over the southern end of the Green Mountains, then drops dramatically into the Hoosic Valley before connecting to Rte 7, the main road through the Berkshires.

The river that divides Shelburne Falls in half also gives it two of its attractions. In the riverbed below the falls, at the foot of Deerfield St, are dozens of glacial potholes in the ledges, formed millions of years ago by the swirling and falling waters of melting glaciers. As large as 40ft in diameter, the potholes are the town's swimming 'beach' in the summer.

Above the falls is the unusual **Bridge of Flowers**, a colourful linear garden atop the arches of a redundant trolley bridge. To see the trolley car that once travelled it, drive up the hill to the **Shelburne Falls Trolley Museum** *(tel: (413) 625-9443 or 625-6707; www.sftm.org).*

Right
The potholes at Shelburne Falls

SPRINGFIELD

Greater Springfield CVB
1441 Main St; tel: (413) 787-1558 or (800) 723-1548; fax: (413) 781-4607; www.valleyvisitor.com

The Quadrangle Museums $ 21 Edwards St; tel: (413) 263-6800 or (800) 625-7738; www.springfieldmuseums.org. Open Tue–Sun 1000–1600.

Basketball Hall of Fame $$ 1000 West Columbus Ave; tel: (413) 781-6500 or (800) 446-6752; www.hoophall.com. Open Tue–Fri & Sun 1000–1600, Sat 1000–1700.

The Student Prince $–$$ 8 Fort St; tel: (413) 788-6628; www.studentprince.com. Open daily for lunch and dinner; a local tradition for hearty German/American fare.

Springfield is filled with chain hotels, concentrated around I-91 to the north of the city, and along Rte 5 adjacent to the Interstate Highway.

Right
Freeman Farm, Old Sturbridge Village

Remarkably for a small city, Springfield has an entire complex of museums known as **The Quadrangle** (or 'The Quad'). The buildings themselves are interesting, ranging from Italianate to art deco, and together they create one of New England's finest art ensembles. At the **George Walter Vincent Smith Art Museum** are Asian collections including Japanese armour, netsuke, carved jade, silk embroidery and cloisonné. The **Museum of Fine Arts**, opposite, represents American painters from John Singleton Copley to Winslow Homer and Georgia O'Keefe, as well as French Impressionists.

Springfield Science Museum (tel: (413) 263-6800) is perfectly designed for children, spotlighting the region's many palaeontological finds with a life-sized replica of *Tyrannosaurus rex* and a dinosaur footprint large enough to climb into. The fourth museum in 'The Quad' is the **Connecticut Valley Historical Museum**, with the work of itinerant painters and fine New England-made furniture shown in period rooms.

A virtual outdoor museum of Victorian architecture includes more than 400 elegant homes dating from 1890–1910 in the **McKnight District** east of the Quadrangle.

The **Basketball Hall of Fame** has films on the sport, memorabilia and high-tech displays, fun even for those who don't give a hoot about hoops.

STURBRIDGE

Old Sturbridge Village $$$ Tel: (508) 347-3362; www.osv.org. Open late May–mid-Oct daily 0930–1700; late Oct–mid-Apr Tue–Sun 0930–1600.

Old Sturbridge Village is New England's finest restoration, recreating an entire mid-19th-century village of homes, workshops, mills and barns brought from all over the region. Costumed interpreters farm, cook, weave and work just as people would have done in a small 1840s village. In a tidy circle facing the village green are a church, general store, tavern, bank, the **Tinsmith's Shop** and several houses, including the handsome **Salem Towne House**, the most formal, with painted murals, fine furnishings and an excellent period ornamental garden.

Reached by a walk through the woods, or by oxcart ride, is the **Freeman Farm**, with working gardens, barns, animals and fields, as well as a **Cooper's Shop**. Something interesting is always happening here, from cheese-making to the birth of a lamb. Nearby is the **Blacksmith Shop** and **Bixby House**, home of the village blacksmith.

Water-powered mills from the early 1800s grind grain, card wool, and saw boards, and you can see their great wheels at work. Throughout the village are demonstrations of home industries, perhaps dyeing wool with plant colours or pressing apples into cider. Several homes have gardens, but the showpiece is the large, well-designed **Herb Garden**, with period plant varieties. Special displays show other facets of 19th-century life, and the Museum Shop is filled with reproductions, books and crafts.

Accommodation and food in Sturbridge

Commonwealth Cottage $–$$ *11 Summit Ave; tel: (508) 347-7708; www.commonwealthcottage.com*. Hilltop cottage B&B with afternoon tea.

Comfort Inn & Suites $$ *215 Charlton Rd, Rte 20; tel: (508) 347-3306; fax: (508) 347-3514; www.sturbridgecomfortinn.com*. This centrally located chain hotel offers good value for money: Queen suites with two queen beds, sofabeds, coffee makers, microwaves and refrigerators. Pluses are the restaurant, pool, free car park and free wireless internet.

The Publick House $$ *Rte 131; tel: (508) 347-3313 or (800) PUBLICK; www.publickhouse.com; open 0730–2200*. Fine old inn with excellent traditional food.

Cedar Street Restaurant $$$ *12 Cedar St; tel: (508) 347-5800; www.cedarstreetrestaurant.com*. Dine on entrées of bouillabaisse, fresh salmon or mushroom risotto at this upmarket bistro, and finish off with a decadent dessert.

Brimfield Flea Market $ *Tel: (508) 764-4920*. Held one weekend each in May, July and September.

Emily Dickinson Museum: The Homestead and The Evergreens $ *280 Main St, Amherst; tel: (413) 542-8161; www. emilydickinsonmuseum.org. Open Mar–May and Sept–Dec Wed–Sun 1000–1700; Jun–Aug Wed–Sun 1100–1600. Closed Jan–Feb. Reservations strongly recommended.*

Hadley Farm Museum *147 Russell St (Rte 9), Hadley; tel: (413) 549-2863. Open mid-May–mid-Oct Wed–Sat 1100–1600, Sun 1000–1600. Free admission.*

Suggested tour

Total distance: 155 miles; 183 miles with detour.

Time: 4 hours' driving. Allow 2 days for the main route, 3 days with detours. Those with limited time should concentrate on Sturbridge or Deerfield.

Links: I-91 leads north to Brattleboro, joining the Upper Connecticut Valley Route (*see page 196*), and south to the Lower Connecticut Valley Route (*see page 130*). I-90 connects Springfield and Boston (*see page 40*).

Route: From I-91 north of **SPRINGFIELD** ❶ take I-91 and I-90 to Palmer (Exit 8), then follow Rte 32 to **Ware** ❷.

Chicopee, just north of Springfield, holds one of the USA's largest St Patrick's Day parades and celebrations each March.

Allen House Inn
$–$$ 599 Main St, Amherst; tel: (413) 253-5000; www.allenhouse.com. Victorian B&B near downtown Amherst.

Salem Cross Inn $$
260 W Main St (Rte 9), West Brookfield; tel: (508) 867-2345; www.salemcrossinn.com. Country restaurant serving traditional New England dishes.

Northfield Mountain Recreation and Environmental Center and *Quinnetukut II $$* 99 Millers Falls Rd (Rte 63), Northfield; tel: (413) 659-3714 or (800) 859-2960; www.northquabbinwoods.org

Old Greenfield Village $ Rte 2, Greenfield; tel: (413) 774-7138. Open mid-May–mid-Oct Sat and holidays 1000–1600, Sun 1200–1600.

Barton Cove Campground $ Rte 2, Gill; tel: (800) 859-2960, reservations (413) 863-9300. Tent pitches in a grove of tall pines on the riverbank.

To connect this suggested route to the Upper Connecticut Valley via a more scenic route than the I-91, follow Rte 5 as it winds northwards from Bernardston to Brattleboro, Vermont.

Detour: Instead of leaving the highway, continue on I-90 to **STURBRIDGE ❸**, then follow Rte 20 to Brimfield and Rte 19 north through Warren to West Brookfield, going northwest on Rte 9, past **Rock House Reservation ❹**, where trails lead to a huge overhanging rock uncovered by glaciers. The cave-like area beneath it was used by Native Americans as a winter hunting camp, and their implements have been found there. Trails lead to other exposed rocks and around a small pond. Continue to Ware, where you rejoin the main route.

From Ware, follow Rte 9 past the huge **Quabbin Reservoir Park ❺**, with scenic picnic sites overlooking the water, through **Amherst ❻**. This attractive college town was home to poet Emily Dickinson, whose house, **Emily Dickinson Museum ❼**, is open to tour. Continue on Rte 9 to Hadley, where you will pass the **Hadley Farm Museum ❽**, a three-storey 1782 barn packed full of old-time implements, vehicles and treasures of rural life in the past. Highlights are a Concord coach and a peddler's wagon, as well as a dugout canoe.

From Hadley, follow the winding Rte 47 north along the river to Sunderland, crossing the river to South Deerfield. From there, Rte 5 leads north to **DEERFIELD ❾**. Continue north on Rte 5 to Rte 2A, which leads east to Rte 2 and back over the river on the French King Bridge and to Rte 63. Follow this north to the **Northfield Mountain Recreation and Environmental Center ❿**. Here you can walk the nature trail to an abandoned stone quarry, climb to panoramic river views or take a tour (reservations *tel: (800) 859-2960*) to the top of the mountain to learn how water is pumped from the river to the mountaintop at off-peak times, then used to generate electricity for high-usage hours. The Visitor Center's animated displays tell the story, too, along with the history of the river valley.

Beside the river is a large picnic area and a dock where the open-air riverboat *Quinnetukut II* ⓫ meets passengers for a 12-mile cruise on this scenic part of the Connecticut River. The banks are densely wooded here, giving way to ledges, then to bird-filled grassy marshes downstream. Eagles are often spotted over the water.

Just beyond, Rte 63 becomes the main street of **Northfield** ⓬, lined with Colonial-era homes. At the northern end of town, side streets are filled with fine Victorian homes, one of which houses the AYH Hostel, a programme which had its American origins in Northfield, in 1934.

From Northfield, cross the Connecticut River on Rte 10 and follow Rte 5 south to Greenfield. From there, take Rte 2 west, the Mohawk Trail, past **Old Greenfield Village** ⓭, a museum of entire workshops and stores, housed in 14 buildings, including a general store, an original pharmacy, blacksmith's shop, tinshop, butcher, soda fountain, doctor's office, barber shop and more. No costumed guides or videos, just the real things, arranged just as they were.

Just off the Mohawk Trail, **SHELBURNE FALLS** ⓮ is at the intersection of Rte 112, which leads south to Rte 9, where a left turn (southeast) takes you into **NORTHAMPTON** ⓯. From there, I-91 leads back to Springfield.

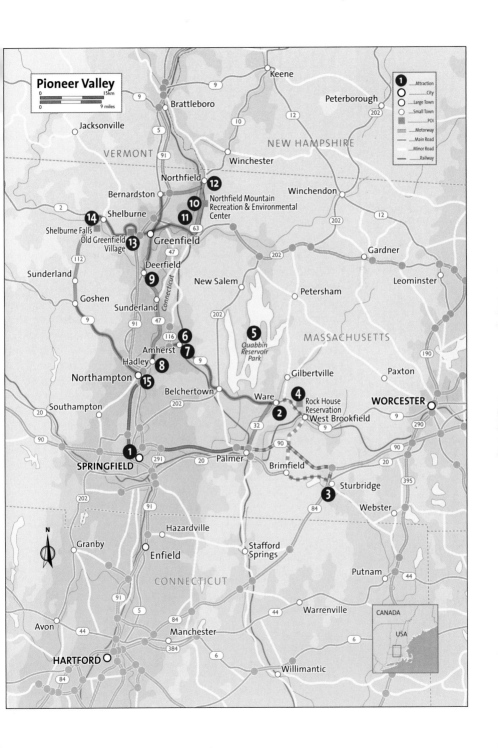

The Berkshires

Ratings

Arts and culture	●●●●●
Nature/ scenery	●●●●○
Food and drink	●●●○○
Shopping	●●●○○
History	●●○○○
Museums	●●○○○
Beaches	●○○○○
Children	●○○○○

The tame and rounded mounds of the Berkshire Hills in western Massachusetts are the best places in New England to spend summer days hiking up a mountain or perusing art galleries while enjoying orchestral and chamber music, modern dance or theatre by starlight. Wealthy rusticators from New York and Boston transformed the sleepy farms and hill towns of the region at the end of the 19th century by building lavish summer homes and turning the Berkshires into a chic scene for high society in the late summer and early autumn. Vestiges of this booming age of conspicuous consumption persist in private estates (many now refitted as museums or inns) and in the modern social flutter associated with the most prestigious of the performing arts groups, particularly the theatres and the Boston Symphony Orchestra.

GREAT BARRINGTON

Monument Mountain Rte 7 S, 3 miles south of Stockbridge; tel: (413) 298-3239; www.thetrustees.org

Aston Magna Festival $$ Several locations, Rte 7; tel: (413) 528-3595; www.astonmagna.org. Baroque and classical chamber music is performed on period instruments July–early August.

Great Barrington's counter-cultural ambience, so evident in its craft galleries and New-Age emporia, scarcely hints at a progressive past, when the town was the first in the world to enjoy electric streetlights and electric lights in its homes (local inventor William Stanley pioneered the use of alternating current for street lights, then sold the rights to the General Electric Company). In-town shops will excite the interest of antiques hunters, but the greater concentration of dealers is found in the houses and barns along Rte 7 south of the town.

Perhaps the most accessible mountain peak in the area is 1735ft **Monument Mountain**, where the summit gives a sweeping overview of hills and valleys. Two trails, each taking 45 minutes, diverge from the roadside trailhead. The ³/₄-mile Hickey Trail is steeper, while the 1¹/₄-mile Monument Trail is more gradual.

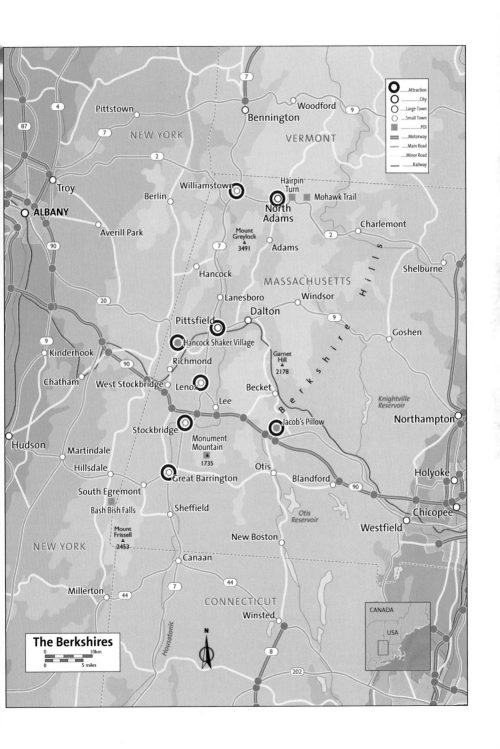

Attraction
City
Large Town
Small Town
POI
Motorway
Main Road
Minor Road
Railway

87
4
Pittstown
Woodford
9
Bennington
NEW YORK
VERMONT
2
Troy
Williamstown
Hairpin Turn
Berlin
North Adams
Mohawk Trail
ALBANY
Charlemont
Averill Park
Mount Greylock
3491
Adams
2
90
7
Shelburne
Hancock
MASSACHUSETTS
Lanesboro
Windsor
20
Pittsfield
Dalton
9
Goshen
9
Kinderhook
Hancock Shaker Village
Richmond
Garnet Hill
2178
Chatham
90
Lenox
West Stockbridge
Lee
Becket
Jacob's Pillow
Knightville Reservoir
Hudson
Martindale
Stockbridge
Monument Mountain
1735
Otis
Northampton
Hillsdale
Great Barrington
Blandford
Holyoke
South Egremont
90
Bash Bish Falls
Sheffield
Otis Reservoir
Chicopee
Mount Frissell
2453
New Boston
Westfield
NEW YORK
Canaan
Millerton
44
44
7
CONNECTICUT
Winsted
8
202

The Berkshires

0   10km
0   5 miles

CANADA

USA

Above
The spare simplicity of the Shaker lifestyle

Right
The Daniel Chester French Studio in Lenox

Accommodation and food in Great Barrington

Castle Street Café $$ *10 Castle St; tel: (413) 528-5244; open for dinner.* The menu of this stylish café features produce from the area's organic and speciality farmers.

Day's Inn $$–$$$ *372 Main St; tel: (413) 528-3150.* Moderately priced and well located for walking to the shopping and dining district.

HANCOCK SHAKER VILLAGE

🔴 **Hancock Shaker Village $$$** *Rtes 20 and 41; tel: (413) 443-0188; www.hancockshaker-village.org. Open Apr–Nov daily 1000–1600; call for off-season hours.*

🔵 **Country Inn at Jiminy Peak**
$$–$$$ Brodie Mountain Rd, Hancock; tel: (413) 738 5500 or (800) 882-8859; www.jiminypeak.com. Ski-style self-catering lodgings at the foot of ski mountain.

Among the most enduring Shaker settlements, the 'City of Peace' was inhabited between 1790 and 1959 by the celibate communal sect. Twenty buildings, most from the 19th century, illustrate their ways. For example, although Shaker brothers and sisters did not live together, they ranked as equals. Thus, the five-storey 1830 brick dwelling is built in two separate but identical sections. Pegs for hanging clothes, tools, chairs and brooms speak of the Shaker penchant for order and cleanliness. 'There is no dirt in heaven', an eldress once declared.

The striking 1826 **Round Stone Barn** was built to speed the care of 50 cattle, yet its practical design is also aesthetically appealing, almost as a prayer in stone. Hancock's architecture strongly influenced non-Shaker builders throughout New England, just as the spare and elegant Shaker furniture and baskets had a lasting impact on domestic design. Hancock has the largest collection of Shaker furniture and artefacts in an original site.

JACOB'S PILLOW

⬥ Jacob's Pillow Dance Festival $$
George Carter Rd off Rte 8, Becket; tel: (413) 243-9199; www.jacobspillow.org. Performances late June–late August Wednesday–Sunday.

At the end of a twisty mountain road from Becket stands America's summer Mecca of modern dance, Jacob's Pillow. For more than seven decades, Pillow programming has promoted ground-breaking choreography and the integration of folk dance, modern ballet and ethnic dance into the modern repertoire. Works in progress appear on a small stage in the woods. The Ted Shawn Theatre, with its back opening to the mountain nightscape, was the first stage built specifically for dance in the US.

LENOX

ℹ Lenox Chamber of Commerce
The Curtis at 5 Walker St; tel: (413) 637-3646; www.lenox.org. Open Jun–Aug daily 1000–1800; Sept–May Wed–Sat 1000–1600.

🏛 The Mount $$$
Plunkett St and Rte 7; tel: (413) 551-5111; www. edithwharton.org. Open May–Oct daily 1000–1700.

⬥ Hoadley Gallery *21 Church St; tel: (413) 637-2814. Displays a superb selection of ceramic art.*

Sienna Gallery *80 Main St; tel: (413) 637-8386. Open Jun–Aug daily 1100–1700. Elegant gallery offers contemporary jewellery from artists around the world.*

⬥ Shakespeare & Company $$$ *70 Kemble St; tel: (413) 637-1199; www.shakespeare.org. Performances year-round.*

Tanglewood *Rte 183, West St; tel: (888) 266-1200 or (617) 266-1492; www.bso.org. Concerts late June–early September.*

In the decades before income tax, Lenox flourished as a seasonal playground of the rich, many of whom built estates here (which they called 'cottages') between 1890 and 1910. The Berkshires social season, which revolves around music, theatre and dance, is still centred in Lenox. Although small, the town boasts more boutiques, restaurants and upmarket lodgings than any nearby community.

Several 'cottages' are open as museums, of which the most interesting is **The Mount**, completed in 1902 for the novelist Edith Wharton, who wrote extensively about architecture and design. She practised what she preached by designing and decorating this estate, basing the building on a Lincolnshire manor in England, then adding French and Italian accents. Her interior decoration eschewed the Victorian overstuffed vogue of her day in favour of more classical spareness.

Based on a 33-acre wooded compound, **Shakespeare & Company** performs in all seasons, but is best known for magical summer presentations of the Bard's works in the Founder's Theatre. Shorter, more contemporary plays are also presented.

Another summer estate turned to artistic purposes is **Tanglewood**, the summer home of the Boston Symphony Orchestra. In addition to the BSO, concerts feature chamber music, jazz and contemporary artists. The priciest tickets are for seats in 'the Shed', a roofed open auditorium built in 1938 that seats 5000. Less expensive 'lawn' tickets are more fun and concertgoers have raised the Tanglewood picnic to an artform of its own.

Above
Edith Wharton's splendid mansion, The Mount, in Lenox

🅗 **Frelinghuysen Morris House & Studio $$** *92 Hawthorne St; tel: (413) 637-0166; www.frelinghuysen.org. Open late Jun–early Sept Thur–Sun 1000–1500; Sept–mid-Oct Thur–Sat 1000–1600.* Bauhaus-style villa built and decorated by American abstract artists is a striking contrast to the Gilded Age sensibility of much of the Berkshires.

Accommodation and food in Lenox

Café Lucia $$–$$$ *80 Church St; tel: (413) 637-2640; open for dinner.* The tables on the covered wooden deck of this northern Italian trattoria are in great demand.

Church Street Café $$–$$$ *65 Church St; tel: (413) 637-2745; open for lunch and dinner.* A comfortable, casual spot to enjoy freshly prepared meals, including light pastas and bright salads.

The Village Inn $$–$$$ *16 Church St; tel: (413) 637-0020 or (800) 253-0917; www.villageinn-lenox.com.* There are 32 guest rooms in this 1771 inn in the heart of the downtown shopping and dining district.

The Yankee Inn $$–$$$ *461 Pittsfield Rd; tel: (413) 499-3700; www.yankeeinn.com.* Spacious rooms (a quarter of them with fireplaces) and indoor and outdoor pools make this 96-room complex a relaxing base for exploring the area.

NORTH ADAMS

Western Gateway Heritage State Park *Rte 8; tel: (413) 663-6312. Open daily 1000–1700. Free admission.*

Massachusetts Museum of Contemporary Art *$$$ 1040 Mass MoCA Way; tel: (413) 662-2111; www.massmoca.org. Open Jul–Sept daily 1000–1800; Oct–Jun Wed–Mon 1100–1700.*

Mount Greylock Reservation Headquarters *Rockwell Rd, Lanesboro; tel: (413) 499-4262; www.mass.gov/dcr/parks/mtGreylock. Open late May–early Sept 0900–2000; call for off-season hours.*

Porches $$$ *231 River St; tel: (413) 664-0400; www.porches.com.* Complex of workers' houses converted to hip, luxury hotel; complements contemporary art museum across the street.

Abandoned by industry, gritty North Adams has turned its strategic location and empty buildings into an incubator for education, computing and the arts. A smattering of bookstores, galleries and coffee bars hints at approaching prosperity.

Western Gateway Heritage State Park relates North Adams' role as a 19th-century boom town, thanks to the construction of the Hoosac Tunnel to link the Berkshires by train to Boston to the east and New York to the west. Under construction for more than a decade, the **Massachusetts Museum of Contemporary Art** began mounting exhibitions in 1999. Housed in a cavernous factory building, the museum specialises in art on a scale too immense for other institutions.

North Adams is also a gateway to the 12,500-acre **Mount Greylock State Reservation**. The 3491ft mountain is laced with more than 45 miles of marked trails. Some short loops near the summit can be traversed in an hour or less. Rare alpine flora is found on higher elevations and the reservation provides a nesting habitat for more than 100 bird species. The auto road and Bascom Lodge at the summit are open late May to October (parking $).

Hoosac Tunnel

Steep gradients kept trains out of the Berkshires until the 1870s, when the Boston & Albany Railroad decided to dig its 4³/₄-mile Hoosac Tunnel. At a staggering cost of $14 million, the tunnel was the longest bore in the world when it opened in 1875. Workers dug from both ends, meeting in a final dynamite blast. The engineering was so precise that the two sides lined up with an error of less than 1 inch in 25,000ft.

PITTSFIELD

Berkshire Visitors Bureau *3 Hoosac St, Adams; tel: (800) 237-5747 or (413) 743-4500; www.berkshires.org. Open Tue–Sat 1000–1600.* Provides information on the entire Berkshires region.

Barrington Stage Company *30 Union St; tel: (413) 236-8888; www.barringtonstageco.org.* Innovative regional company.

All major Berkshire roads converge at Pittsfield; moreover, a cultural renaissance has also made the city a regional centre for live theatre and music, and a hothouse for visual arts. The **Berkshire Museum** (*$$; 39 South St; tel: (413) 443-7171; www.berkshiremuseum.org*) augments a fine collection of 19th-century American and European art with imaginative contemporary exhibitions. The **Berkshire Athenaeum** (*Wendell Avenue; tel: (413) 499-9486; open daily except Sun*), contains the Herman Melville Memorial Room, with some of the author's books and his writing desk. Melville's home from 1850 to 1863 is **Arrowhead** (*$$; 780 Holmes Rd; tel: (413) 442-1793; open late May–mid-Oct Fri–Wed 1030–1600*). Few of the author's personal belongings remain, but the window of the study where he wrote *Moby Dick* overlooks the whale-like hump of Mount Greylock.

STOCKBRIDGE

Norman Rockwell Museum $$$ *Rte 183; tel: (413) 298-4100; www.nrm.org. Open May–Oct daily 1000–1700; Nov–Apr Mon–Fri 1000–1600, Sat and Sun 1000–1700.*

Chesterwood $$$ *Williamsville Rd; tel: (413) 298-3579; www.chesterwood.org. Open May–Oct daily 1000–1700.*

Naumkeag $$ *Prospect Hill Rd; tel: (413) 298-3239; www.thetrustees.org. Open late May–mid-Oct daily 1000–1700.*

Berkshire Theater Festival *Main St; tel: (413) 298-5576; www.berkshiretheatre.org.* One of the oldest summer theatres in the nation, BTF performs in a Gilded Age playhouse.

Main Street at Christmas *Tel: (413) 298-5200.* This holiday event recreates Norman Rockwell's well-known painting *Stockbridge Main Street at Christmas.*

Founded in 1734 as a Puritan mission to the Indians, Stockbridge today bears little trace of either. Like Lenox, it contains many vast 'cottages', but unlike its neighbour, it still feels like a rustic village endeavouring to live up to its Norman Rockwell image. The **Norman Rockwell Museum** chronicles the illustrator's prolific career, which held a small-town mirror up to American popular culture in the mid-20th century. Stockbridge was also the summer home of sculptor Daniel Chester French, best known for his *Seated Lincoln* in Washington DC's Lincoln Memorial. Tours of his estate, **Chesterwood**, feature both house and studio, filled with drawings, plaster casts and bronze models. **Naumkeag**, residence of Joseph Choate, ambassador to England 1899–1905, is an example of how the rich and famous summered in the Berkshires. Original furnishings and Chinese decorative arts fill the 26-room 1886 mansion. No visit to Stockbridge is complete without a stint in a rocking chair on the porch of the **Red Lion Inn**, the town's de facto social centre.

Accommodation and food in Stockbridge

Daily Bread $ *31 Main St; tel: (413) 298-0272; open for breakfast and lunch.* This excellent bakery produces several styles of bread as well as flaky scones and pastries. Soups and sandwiches available for lunch.

Red Lion Inn $$–$$$ *30 Main St; tel: (413) 298-5545; www.redlioninn.com.* One of the few American inns in continuous use since the 18th century, the Red Lion's rooms have an updated country style. The semi-formal dining room (**$$$**) where Norman Rockwell ate once a week serves updated traditional cuisine featuring local foodstuffs.

The Inn at Stockbridge $$$ *Rte 7; tel: (413) 298-3337 or (888) 466-7865; www.stockbridgeinn.com.* This 1906 country inn, a mile from town, has 15 guest rooms in the original house, a cottage and a barn were added in 2001.

WILLIAMSTOWN

🚩 Sterling and Francine Clark Art Institute $$
225 South St; tel: (413) 458-2303; www.clarkart.edu. Open Sept–Jun Tue–Sun 1000–1700; Jul and Aug daily 1000–1700. Admission charge June–October only.

Williams College Museum of Art *Main St;* tel: (413) 597-2429; www.wcma.org. Open Tue–Sat 1000–1700, Sun 1300–1700. Free admission.

🎭 Williamstown Theatre Festival
Adams Memorial Theater, 1000 Main St; tel: (413) 597-3400; www.wtfestival.org. June–August season includes classics, premieres, cabaret and free performances.

The artistry of **Williamstown Theatre Festival** is a good reason to visit this pleasant college town in the summer. The **Sterling and Francine Clark Art Institute** makes a stopover essential in any season. The Clarks inherited a large industrial fortune and amassed impressive collections of works by Pierre Auguste Renoir, Claude Monet, J M W Turner and Winslow Homer. Blessed with the presence of 'the Clark', the **Williams College Museum of Art** instead emphasises modern, contemporary and non-Western art. One American masterpiece is Edward Hopper's *Morning in a City*.

Accommodation and food in Williamstown

Northside Motel $–$$ *45 North St; tel: (413) 458-8107; www.northsidemotel.com.* This 30-room motel is conveniently located in the downtown district.

Field Farm Guest House $$–$$$ *554 Sloan Rd; tel: (413) 458-3135; http://guesthouseatfieldfarm.thetrustees.org.* This 1948 modern-design masterpiece offers a distinct change from the usual Victorian B&B. The grounds include 4 miles of hiking trails flanked by wild flowers and some rare ferns.

Mezze Bistro & Bar $$–$$$ *16 Water St; tel: (413) 458-0123.* Eclectic fusion cooking brings worldly sophistication to American food.

Suggested tour

Total distance: 87 miles; 110 miles with detours.

Time: 3–4 hours' driving. Allow 3 days.

Links: Connects via Rte 7 at Williamstown or Rte 100 at North Adams with Southern Green Mountains Route (*see page 168*), via Rte 2 at North Adams to northern end of Pioneer Valley Route (*see page 94*), via Massachusetts Turnpike at Lee to southern end of Pioneer Valley Route, or via Rte 7 south from Sheffield to Litchfield Hills Route (*see page 122*).

Route: The ideal route for touring the Berkshires begins by taking the scenic mountain road known as the **Mohawk Trail ❶**. through the aptly-named **Hairpin Turn ❷** on Rte 2 into **NORTH ADAMS ❸**.

Left
The Stockbridge home of the Berkshire Theater Festival

Egremont Inn
$$–$$$ *Old Sheffield Rd, South Egremont; tel: (800) 859-1780 or (413) 528-2111; www.egremontinn.com.* Classic circa-1820 country inn with original architecture and modern comforts.

Devonfield $$–$$$
85 Stockbridge Rd, Lee; tel: (800) 664-0880 or (413) 243-3298; www.devonfield.com. Federal-era mansion where Queen Wilhemina and Princess Beatrix (now queen) of the Netherlands spent a summer while taking refuge in Canada during World War II. Now a fine country inn.

Rouge Restaurant & Bistro $$ *3 Center St, West Stockbridge; tel: (413) 232-4111; www.rougerestaurant.com.* Chef cooks traditional menu of his native Provence as well as offering an array of small plates to accompany drinks.

Charles H Baldwin & Sons *1 West Center Road, West Stockbridge; tel: (413) 232-7785. Open Mon–Sat 0900–1700; call for Sun hours.* Family-owned business has been making vanilla and other flavour extracts, such as anise and almond, since 1888. Small shop is also stocked with a wide range of baking supplies.

Prime Outlets at Lee
Route 20 East, Lee; tel: (413) 243-8186; www.primeoutlets.com

Detour: One mile west of North Adams centre is Notch Rd, a 5-mile drive to the summit of Mount Greylock, which is open late May to October.

Rte 2 continues past meadows and gentle uplands west for 5 miles to **WILLIAMSTOWN** ❹, where it meets Rte 7 descending from Bennington, Vt. Rte 7 follows the broad north–south valley of the Housatonic River between the Hoosac and Taconic ranges of the Berkshires. In Lanesboro, 18 miles south, is a turn-off for Rockwell Rd, the 12-mile ascent of Mount Greylock. Rte 7 continues 6 miles south to **PITTSFIELD** ❺. In the centre of town, Rte 20 leads west for 5 miles to **HANCOCK SHAKER VILLAGE** ❻. Some of New England's most fertile farmland lies in the river plain south of Hancock along Rte 41. **West Stockbridge** ❼, something of an outpost for craftspeople, lies 8 miles south. Rte 41 returns to the Housatonic's banks at **GREAT BARRINGTON** ❽ in 18 miles. **South Egremont** ❾, a handsome village with several good antiques shops and a fine inn, lies 3 miles further south on Rte 41. South of Egremont, Rte 41 trails the eastern edge of a mountain range, hence the highway is known as Under Mountain Rd. In 4 miles, a left turn on to Berkshire School Rd leads 3$^{1}/_{2}$ miles into the centre of **Sheffield** ❿, distinguished by having the largest number of antiques dealers in the Berkshires. Most of them ply their trade along Rte 7, which leads north 7 miles back to Great Barrington, then another 6 miles north past **Monument Mountain** ⓫ to bucolic **LENOX** ⓬. Most travellers connect to the Massachusetts Turnpike from Lenox by driving 4 miles east on Rte 20 to **Lee** ⓭, which has a dusty, old-fashioned downtown and a huge cluster of factory outlet shopping on the edge of town.

Detour: Rte 8 joins Rte 20 in Lee to go east for 15 miles to George Carter Rd, which winds 3 miles north to **JACOB'S PILLOW** ⓮.

Also worth exploring

Bash Bish Falls

Fine riverside walking trails and dramatic, picturesque falls make Bash Bish worth the wooded drive through thickets of mountain laurel and along old fields where deer often graze. From South Egremont village, follow Rte 41 south half a mile. Turn right onto Mount Washington Rd, which doglegs left in 3 miles and continues 2 miles south into Mount Washington village. In 1$^{3}/_{4}$ miles, a right turn leads to Bash Bish Falls on a narrow, steep road alternating between pavement and dirt for 3 miles to a car park with a steep trail. In another half-mile (over the New York line) a second trailhead offers easier walking access to the falls along a woodland trail that follows the river upstream for a mile. The 80-ft waterfall divides around a huge basalt boulder. According to legend, an Indian maiden dived over the falls to escape lecherous white trappers and was never seen again.

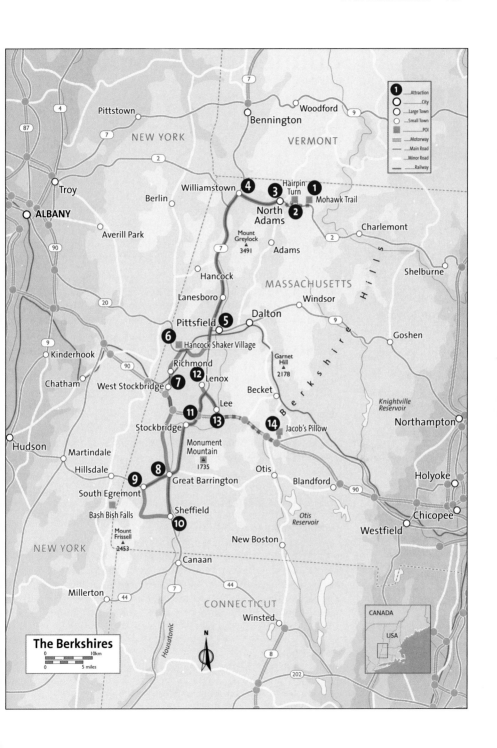

The Berkshires

0   10km
0   5 miles

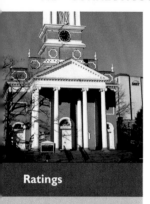

Connecticut's Midlands

Ratings

Arts and culture	●●●●●
History	●●●●●
Food and drink	●●●●○
Museums	●●●●○
Nature/ scenery	●●●●○
Children	●●●○○
Shopping	●●●○○
Beaches	●●○○○

Two of Connecticut's most noteworthy cities, just about equal in population, have distinctive, contrasting identities. State capital Hartford is the headquarters base for several nationally recognised insurance companies. Directly south from there – less than an hour's drive via an interstate motorway – New Haven takes particular pride in Yale, an elite university in the US's Ivy League. However, both places have more to offer than big business and higher education. Hartford has an outstanding art museum, plus the houses where authors Mark Twain and Harriet Beecher Stowe lived. In New Haven, treat yourself to such cultural perks as Yale's Center for British Art and its Peabody Museum of Natural History. Communities of varying size comprise a high-density sprawl between Hartford and New Haven. Some of those which merit a stopover are pointed out in this chapter.

Hartford sights

ⓘ **Greater Hartford Tourism** *31 Pratt St, Hartford; tel: (800) 446-7811 or (860) 244-8181; www.enjoyhartford.com*

② **Hartford**, 102 miles from Boston, rises amid a bridge-crossing tangle of highways and interstate motorways at the pivotal, busy junction of north–south I-91 and east–west I-84.

Bushnell Park and Carousel

Hartford's premier open space, amounting to 37 acres, lies in the heart of the city. At its centre, the **Corning Fountain** honours the region's original Native American inhabitants. On the greenery's east side is a tall brownstone **Soldiers & Sailors Memorial Arch** erected in 1886. The park's **Carousel** is a 1914 merry-go-round with 48 hand-carved horses, spinning to the tunes of a 1925 Wurlitzer band organ – in a pavilion emblazoned with folk art and more than 800 light bulbs.

Center Church

Dating from 1807, and modelled on London's St-Martin-in-the-Fields, the interior is embellished by stained-glass windows, including six by Louis Comfort Tiffany. Outside is the **Ancient Burying Ground**, where Hartford's 17th-century founders are interred.

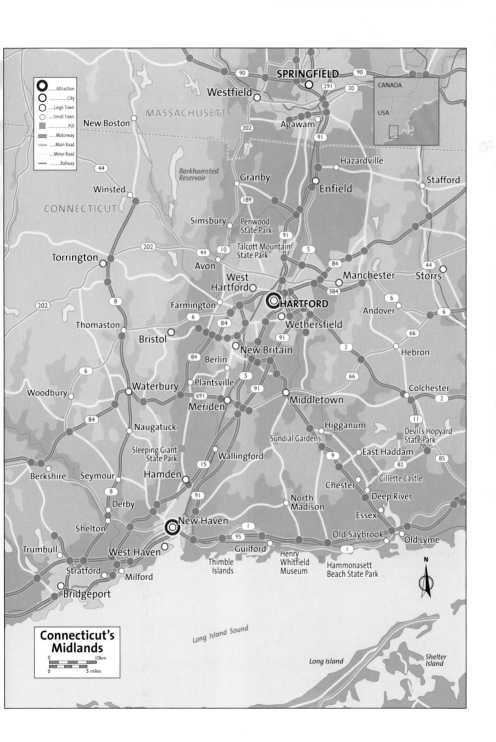

Connecticut's Midlands

🎠 Bushnell Park Carousel $ *Park at Jewell St; tel: (860) 585-5411. Phone for opening times at various times of year.*

Center Church *675 Main St; tel: (860) 249-5631. Open Wed and Fri 1100–1400.*

Connecticut State Capitol *210 Capitol Ave; tel: (860) 240-0222. Hourly guided tours daily. Free admission.*

Elizabeth Park Rose Gardens *Prospect Ave; tel: (860) 231-9443. Open dawn–dusk. Free admission.*

Harriet Beecher Stowe House $ *Farmington Ave at Forest St; tel: (860) 522-9258; www.harrietbeecherstowe.org. Open Tue–Sat 0930–1630, Sun 1200–1630. Also Jun–mid-Oct and Dec, Mon 0930–1630.*

Connecticut State Capitol

Hartford's hilltop showpiece, opened in 1879, bristles with Gothic spires and classical and Second Empire-style adornments, topped by a dome sheathed in gold leaf. Medallions and bas-reliefs are carved on the white marble façades. Interior features include bullet-riddled Civil War battle flags and a statue of Connecticut patriot Nathan Hale.

Elizabeth Park Rose Gardens

The nation's first municipal park devoted to roses (14,000 bushes, 900 varieties) also includes greenhouses, perennials, a rock garden and pathways on its 1000-acre expanse.

Harriet Beecher Stowe House

In what was Hartford's semi-rural Nook Farm enclave a century ago, the celebrated author of *Uncle Tom's Cabin* lived in this 'cottage' from 1873 to 1896. It includes her writing table, period furnishings and personal memorabilia.

Mark Twain House

Close to the Stowe abode, the turreted 'steamboat Gothic' Victorian manse – with multicoloured brickwork exterior and Tiffany-designed interiors – was the writer's home for 17 years beginning in 1874. Samuel Langhorne Clemens (aka Mark Twain) wrote seven of his best-known books here, including *Tom Sawyer*, *The Adventures of Huckleberry Finn*, *The Prince and the Pauper* and *A Connecticut Yankee in King Arthur's Court*.

Museum of Connecticut History

Displays include the colony's 1662 royal charter, Connecticut-made clocks and Colt firearms, governors' portraits and the desk upon which Abraham Lincoln signed the 1863 slave-freeing Emancipation Proclamation.

Mark Twain House

$ 351 Farmington Ave; tel: (860) 247-0998; www. marktwainhouse.org. Open Mon–Sat 0930–1730, Sun 1200–1730. Closed Jan–Mar Tue, 1 Jan, Easter Sun, 4 Jul, Thanksgiving and 24–25 Dec.

Museum of Connecticut History

231 Capitol Ave; tel: (860) 757-6693. Open Mon–Fri 0900–1600. Free admission.

Old State House

800 Main St; tel: (860) 522-6766. Open Mon–Fri 1000–1600, Sat 1100–1600. Free admission.

Travelers Tower Observatory

1 Tower Sq; tel: (860) 277-0111. Open Mon–Fri 1000–1500. Free admission.

Wadsworth Atheneum

$$ 600 Main St; tel: (860) 278-2670; www. wadsworthatheneum.org. Open Tue–Fri 1100–1700 (1st Thur each month 1100–2200); Sat and Sun 1000–1700.

Old State House

A 1796 brick-and-brownstone Federal-style classic, the Old State House was Boston architect Charles Bulfinch's first public building – and the nation's first state capitol, site of the drafting of colonial America's first written constitution, the Fundamental Orders (in 1639).

Travelers Tower Observatory

A vantage point for panoramic views of the city and surroundings from an altitude of 527ft at the top of the skyscraper headquarters of Hartford's pioneer insurance company.

Wadsworth Atheneum

America's oldest continuously functioning public art museum (founded in 1842) is especially strong on Hudson River School landscapes, Flemish/Dutch and Impressionist paintings and Early American furniture.

Accommodation and food in Hartford

Exodus to suburbia has sucked considerable life out of downtown. Nevertheless, a few bright spots do exist.

Pump House Grill $ *80 Elm St; tel: (860) 728-6730.* For meat eaters.

City Steam Brewery Café $$ *942 Main St; tel: (860) 525-1600.* Chatty and casual, with drinks and meals served on seven floors of this centrally located establishment.

Mayor Mike's $$ *283 Asylum St; tel: (860) 522-6463.* Old-time American tavern atmosphere; favoured hangout for local politicians. Recommended for its Italian specialities.

Goodwin Hotel $$–$$$ *1 Haynes St; tel: (800) 922-5006 or (860) 246-7500.* An 1881 Queen Anne-style beauty, built as a town house for billionaire J P Morgan. Fine cuisine downstairs in his namesake restaurant, **Pierpont's ($$)**.

Max Downtown $$$ *185 Asylum St; tel: (860) 522-2530,* is downtown's classiest eatery.

Suggested walk

Total distance: Walking a bit more than 1 mile, 2 miles at most, is all it takes to 'do' central Hartford thoroughly. The Harriet Beecher Stowe and Mark Twain Houses are approximately 1$^{1}/_{2}$ miles from downtown.

Time: Allow half a day, more for getting to the Stowe and Twain houses by foot, car or public transportation. The Wadsworth Atheneum deserves a minimum of 2 hours of your time.

Opposite
Mark Twain House

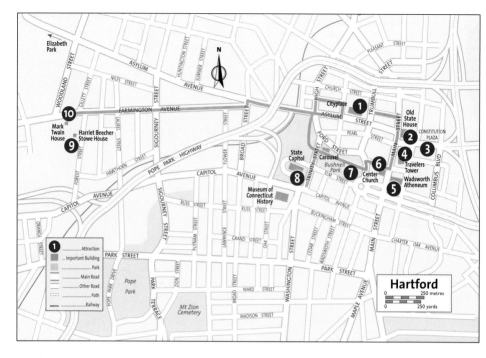

Starting at downtown's **Cityplace** skyscraper ❶, where Asylum and Trumbull Sts intersect, walk eastward via Pratt St to Main St. The **OLD STATE HOUSE** ❷ stands where Main St meets Asylum St. Behind the Old State House – between Market St and Columbus Blvd – **Constitution Plaza** ❸, overlooking the Connecticut River, is a 1960s urban-renewal complex encompassing office buildings and mall-type shops.

Continuing south on Main St brings you to the **TRAVELERS TOWER** ❹, then the **WADSWORTH ATHENEUM** ❺. From that castellated edifice, take Gold St past **CENTER CHURCH** ❻ to the eastern perimeter of **BUSHNELL PARK** ❼. Crossing Trinity St midway in the park, you're sure to see Connecticut's hilltop **STATE CAPITOL** ❽. After meandering in a northeasterly direction on park walkways, return to the Civic Center via High Street and turning right on to Allyn St.

To reach the **HARRIET BEECHER STOWE** ❾ and **MARK TWAIN HOUSES** ❿, go west on Asylum St, leading to Farmington Ave.

New Haven sights

Beinecke Rare Book & Manuscript Library
A sunken sculpture garden graces this Yale institution, with

ⓘ Greater New Haven Convention & Visitors Bureau; 169 Orange St; tel: (800) 322-STAY or (203) 777-8550; www.newhavencvb.org

Yale Visitor Information Center 149 Elm St; tel: (203) 432-2300.

❷ New Haven, 101 miles west of Providence, is reachable via two Interstate Highways: east–west I-95 and north–south I-91.

⓫ Beinecke Rare Book & Manuscript Library 121 Wall St; tel: (203) 432-2977. Open Mon–Thur 0830–2000, Fri 0830–1700, Sat 1000–1700. Free admission.

New Haven Green Bordered by Church, Elm, College & Chapel Sts; split by Temple St.

Peabody Museum of Natural History $ 170 Whitney Ave; tel: (203) 432-5050. Open Mon–Fri 1000–1700, Sat and Sun 1200–1700.

Yale Center for British Art 1080 Chapel St; tel: (203) 432-2800. Open Tue–Sat 1000–1700, Sun 1200–1700. Free admission.

Yale University Art Gallery 1111 Chapel St; tel: (203) 432-0600. Open Sept–Jul Tue–Sat 1000–1700, Sun 1300–1800. Free admission.

collections including an original Gutenberg Bible, Charles Dickens manuscripts and rare Audubon *Birds of America* prints.

New Haven Green

Textbook example of a New England town common, laid out in 1638, the site of three churches regarded as outstanding exemplars of Federal, Georgian and English Gothic design. On this 16-acre open space is the Philip Sherman Bennett Fountain (1907) and the Memorial to New Haven Soldiers of World War I (1928).

Peabody Museum of Natural History

Built in 1866 as part of Yale, this museum ranks among the world's best, with global 'finds' by generations of university archaeologists. In the Great Hall is a 67ft brontosaurus skeleton and an enormous mural entitled *The Age of Reptiles*.

Yale Center for British Art

The Yale Center houses the largest and broadest-ranging collection of British art to be found outside the UK: a bequest from philanthropist and Yale alumnus Paul Mellon, housed in the last building to be designed by big-name US architect Lewis Kahn.

Yale University Art Gallery

America's oldest academic art museum, founded in 1832, with paintings, sculptures, artefacts and decorative arts from ancient Egypt through the Italian Renaissance to the French and American Impressionist periods.

Accommodation and food in New Haven

New Haven is small but Yale is big, exerting a favourable influence on the lodging and dining scene.

Frank Pepe's Pizzeria Napoletana $ *157 Wooster St; tel: (203) 865-5762*, takes credit for baking the first US pizzas, in 1925.

Louis' Lunch $ *263 Crown St; tel: (203) 562-5507*, claims to be the birthplace (in 1895) of the original American hamburger sandwich.

The Colony Inn $$ *1157 Chapel St; tel: (800) 458-8810 or (203) 776-1234; www.colonyatyale.com*. A good, close-to-everything choice.

Omni New Haven $$ *155 Temple St; tel: (800) THE-OMNI or (203) 772-6664*. Convenient hotel near the green and the campus.

Scoozi Trattoria & Wine Bar $$ *1104 Chapel St; tel: (203) 776-8268*. A trendy pasta place.

Three Chimneys Inn $$ *1201 Chapel St; tel: (800) 443-1554 or (203) 789-1201; www.threechimneysinn.com*. Be pampered in a centrally located Victorian mansion reborn as a ten-room bed & breakfast.

Union League Café **$$** *1032 Chapel St; tel: (203) 562-4299.* Casual French bistro ambience.

Suggested walk

Total distance: Expect about 2 miles of walking if you concentrate on the compact downtown district and adjacent Yale University area. Add another 2 miles if you decide to extend your touring to the neighbourhood around Wooster Square.

Time: Despite those short in-town distances, treat yourself to a full day's sightseeing, thereby allowing time for sufficient looking around. But doing justice to any of Yale's compelling museums necessitates an extra 2–3 hours, at the very least, for each of them.

Route: Begin by walking west across the **NEW HAVEN GREEN** ❶, split by north–south Temple St. On the green, note its trio of early 19th-century churches: **United** ❷ (Federal), **Center** ❸ (Georgian), **Trinity** ❹ (Gothic Revival). Retrace your steps, and crossing Church St you'll see New Haven's 1862 clock-towered **City Hall** ❺, a polychrome limestone and sandstone High Victorian whopper. Go south down Church St to Chapel St; here at the scruffy edge of downtown, turn left; cross a bridge spanning railway tracks to reach elegant **Wooster Square** ❻ and its Christopher Columbus monument. Wooster St here on this east side of town defines New Haven's Italian–American neighbourhood.

Back downtown, walk west across the green; cross College St to reach the **Yale campus** ❼. Pass through Phelps Gate to reach the Old Campus quadrangle, where the university's oldest building, **Connecticut Hall** ❽, dates from 1750. The brick dormitory is where Nathan Hale, Noah Webster and US president-to-be William Howard Taft resided as undergraduates. Cross High St to a latter-day campus courtyard, dominated by 221ft **Harkness Tower** ❾.

Turn right on to York St to reach Broadway on the left, locale of the **Yale Co-op** ❿, a modernistic students' store designed by Finnish architect Eero Saarinen. Or, for a small variation, back on York St, head north to Grove St, thereby reaching **Grove Street Cemetery** ⓫, burial place of such Connecticut luminaries as lexicologist Noah Webster and inventors Eli Whitney, Charles Goodyear and Samuel F B Morse.

From York St, turn on to Wall St, then right on to High St to pass Yale's **Sterling Memorial Library** ⓬ and the **Cross Campus Library** ⓭. Former 'Yalie' Maya Lin, creator of Washington DC's Vietnam Veterans Memorial, designed the fountain sculpture on the latter building's plaza. Continuing south along High St gets you to Chapel St, where Yale's **UNIVERSITY ART GALLERY** ⓮, **CENTER**

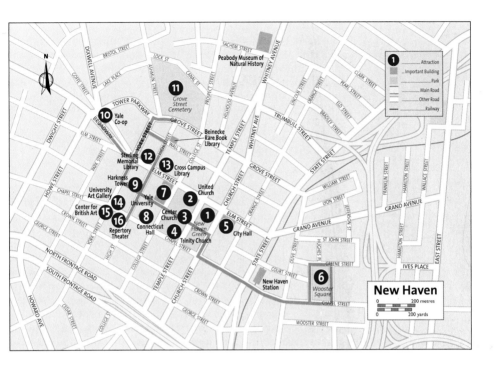

New Haven

0   200 metres

0   200 yards

Farmington Valley Visitors Association 33 E. Main St, Avon; tel: (800) 4-WELCOME or (860) 676-8878.

Farmington Valley Visitors Association PO Box 1015, Simsbury; tel: (800) 493-5266 or (860) 651-0822.

Webb-Deane-Stevens Museum $ 211 Main St; tel: (860) 529-0612. Open May–Oct Wed–Mon 1000–1600; Nov–Apr Sat and Sun 1000–1600.

Sleeping Giant State Park 200 Mount Carmel Ave (off Rte 10), Hamden; tel: (203) 789-7498. So-named because the crest resembles a gigantic head.

FOR BRITISH ART ⑮ and **Repertory Theater** ⑯ are prestigious landmarks.

Suggested driving tour

Total distance: 36–40 miles; 80–85 miles with detours.

Time: 1–1¹/₂ hours' driving. But allow half a day for an easy-going drive on the main route. If you have limited time, focus your sightseeing on downtown Hartford and New Haven, allowing at least half a day in each city centre. Allow a full day if you choose detours.

Links: Heading north from Hartford, connect on to the Pioneer Valley Route (*see page 94*) at Springfield, Mass. By driving 15 miles south from Hartford, via I-91 and Rte 9, to Middletown, you can link with the Lower Connecticut Valley Route (*see page 130*).

Route: Head south from central **HARTFORD** ❶ on the featureless I-91 motorway. After 3 miles, exit on to much more scenic Rte 99, which brings you to charming little **Wethersfield**, where Main and Broad Sts are lined with houses spanning the 17th, 18th and 19th centuries. Three of them comprise the **Webb-Deane-Stevens Museum** ❷,

**① Eli Whitney
Museum $** *915*
Whitney Ave, Hamden; tel:
(203) 777-1833. Open
Wed–Fri and Sun,
1000–1600, Sat
1000–1500.

Hill-Stead Museum $ *35*
Mountain Rd, Farmington;
tel: (860) 677-4787;
www.hillstead.org. Open
May–Oct Tue–Sun
1000–1700; Nov–Apr
Tue–Sun 1100–1600.

**International Skating
Center of Connecticut**
1375 Hopmeadow St,
Simsbury; tel: (860) 651-
5400. Open daily
0600–2400; phone ahead
for schedules. Public skating
times (rentals available):
Wed and Fri 0815–2215,
Sat 1300–1500,
1800–2000, 2115–2215,
Sun 1300–1500,
1800–2000.

**❶ Central
Connecticut
Tourism District**
1 Grove St (Suite 310), New
Britain; tel: (860) 225-3901.

**① New Britain
Museum of
American Art $**
56 Lexington St, New Britain;
tel: (860) 229-0257;
www.nbmaa.org. Open
Tue–Fri 1200–1700, Sat
1000–1700, Sun
1200–1700. Free admission
Sat 1000–1200.

**American Clock &
Watch Museum $** *100*
Maple St, Bristol; tel: (860)
583-6070. Open Apr–Nov
daily 1000–1700; Dec Fri
and Sat 1000–1700,
Sun 1300–1700.

showcasing the lifestyles of a wealthy merchant, diplomat and tradesman. From there, drive west on Rte 175, then 5 miles south via Rte 5 (the Berlin Turnpike) to Berlin. Switch on to westbound Rtes 71 and 364 through Southington and Plantsville to reach Rte 10 in the midst of mid-Connecticut tobacco-growing country. Take Rte 10 due south past **Sleeping Giant State Park ❸** to Hamden and its **Eli Whitney Museum ❹**, devoted to the Hamden-born inventor of the agriculturally revolutionary cotton gin. Then continue on into suburban sprawl outside **NEW HAVEN ❺**, overall a 23-mile drive. Follow signs leading into the downtown district.

Detour: From metro Hartford, drive 9 miles west on Rte 4 to Farmington, home of preppy Miss Porter's School (where the future Jackie Kennedy studied) and **Hill-Stead Museum ❻**, an industrialist's turn-of-the-century mansion designed by his architect daughter, showcasing their impressive collection of French and American Impressionist paintings (Degas, Manet, Monet, Cassatt, Whistler) along with antique furnishings, Chinese porcelains and Japanese woodblock prints, with a sunken garden on the 152-acre site. Via Rte 10, continue 7 miles through the lush, fertile (and affluent) Farmington River Valley to Avon. At the Rte 185 junction, turn east to indulge in some 'nature time' in **Penwood/Talcott Mountain State Parks ❼**, extensive side-by-side green spaces with hiking trails, picnic shelters, lakes and scenic viewpoints – especially from the Heublein Tower on the 1000ft summit of Talcott Mountain. Otherwise go another 5 miles on Rte 10 from Avon to Simsbury, giving you an opportunity to visit that town's **International Skating Center of Connecticut ❽**, home ice of US, World and Olympic ice-skating medallists – where you can watch Olympic figure-skaters' workouts and performances. Return southbound to Hartford on Rte 189.

Also worth exploring

Take the I-84 motorway (the Yankee Expressway) from Hartford to New Britain, an 11-mile drive, worthwhile because of that small city's **Museum of American Art**, housed in a 19th-century mansion. The collection contains over 5000 paintings, graphics and sculptures spanning national art history from 1740 to present times – including the pre-Revolutionary period, Impressionism, the Hudson River and Ash Can Schools, plus Thomas Hart Benton's 1930s *The Arts of Life in America* murals. Then head west an additional 7 miles on Rte 372 through Plainville to Bristol, where the **American Clock & Watch Museum** pays homage to timepieces made in Bristol and vicinity, filled with more than 3000 ticking, striking and chiming instruments, from stately grandfather and church-steeple clocks to the earliest Mickey Mouse watches, initially produced in nearby Waterbury.

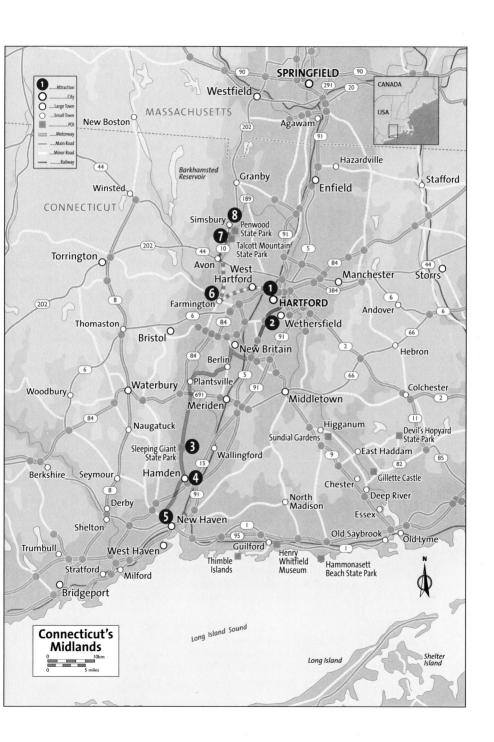

The Litchfield Hills

Ratings

Nature/scenery	●●●●●
Food and drink	●●●
History	●●●
Museums	●●●
Arts and culture	●
Beaches	●
Children	●
Shopping	●

It doesn't get better than this, at least not in inland New England. The state's northwestern corner offers travellers with a zest for wandering a mix of hilly topography, pastoral farmlands, wayward side roads, covered bridges, state parks and wooded nature sanctuaries, clear-water lakes and prototype Connecticut Yankee villages with white-steepled churches and grassy commons. Old-timers might grumble that their upstate region has become more than a little bit gentrified over recent years. True enough: increasing numbers of celebrities – often escapees from high-profile glamour cities – are pleased to count themselves as full- or part-time residents. Among them are actresses Meryl Streep and Mia Farrow, fashion guru Oscar de la Renta, novelist Philip Roth, TV newsman Tom Brokaw and elder statesman Henry Kissinger. But their affluence and visibility are understated, even hidden away in here-and-there enclosures of Litchfield-country valleys and hills.

KENT

ℹ For overall coverage: **Northwest Connecticut Convention & Visitors Bureau** PO Box 968, Litchfield, CT 06759-0968; tel: (860) 567-4506; fax: (800) 1663-1273; www.litchfieldhills.com Locally: **Kent Chamber of Commerce** PO Box 124; tel: (860) 927-1463.

ℹ **Kent Falls State Park** $ Rte 7; tel: (860) 927-3238. Open Apr–Dec daily 0800–dusk.

Iron-ore mines and blast furnaces in the bucolic Litchfield Hills? Indeed, pig-iron production was the region's economic engine for a century and a half beginning in 1750, and Kent was the centre of it all. Now that all evidence of industrial toil has faded into history, this tweedy, upmarket town has emerged as an arts community. You'll come across galleries and studios (crafts shops, too) on Station Sq and the inevitable Main St – plus an ice-cream parlour and a cluster of gift and clothing boutiques.

If that's too mercantile for you, head 5 miles north to **Kent Falls State Park**, where wooden stairs lead to the top of the cascade's 200ft plunge over white limestone. Also, Kent is merely 2 miles from **Macedonia Brook State Park**, where hikers reaching the summit of Cobble Mountain enjoy vistas of New York state's Catskill and Taconic ranges.

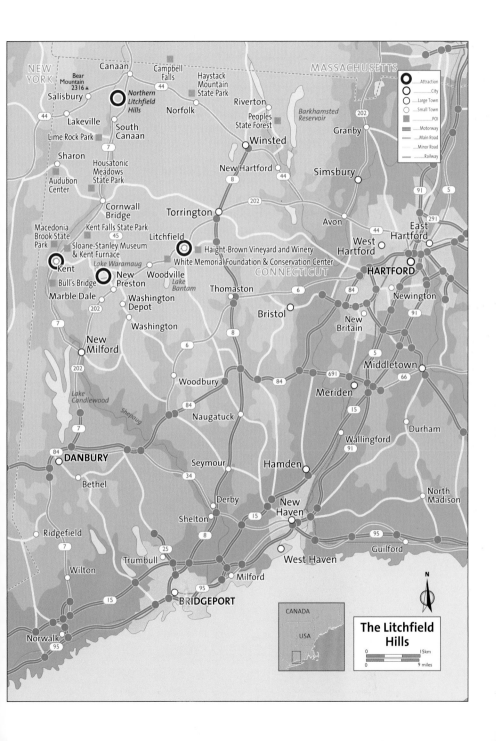

THE LITCHFIELD HILLS

NEW YORK

Canaan

Bear Mountain 2316 ▲

Salisbury

Campbell Falls

Northern Litchfield Hills

Haystack Mountain State Park

MASSACHUSETTS

Riverton

Barkhamsted Reservoir

Lakeville

Norfolk

Peoples State Forest

Granby

Lime Rock Park

South Canaan

Winsted

Sharon

Housatonic Meadows State Park

New Hartford

Simsbury

Audubon Center

Cornwall Bridge

Torrington

Avon

East Hartford

Macedonia Brook State Park

Kent Falls State Park

Litchfield

West Hartford

Sloane-Stanley Museum & Kent Furnace

Haight-Brown Vineyard and Winery

HARTFORD

Lake Waramaug

White Memorial Foundation & Conservation Center

CONNECTICUT

Kent

New Preston

Woodville

Bull's Bridge

Lake Bantam

Thomaston

Newington

Marble Dale

Washington Depot

Bristol

New Britain

Washington

New Milford

Woodbury

Middletown

Lake Candlewood

Shepaug

Meriden

Naugatuck

Durham

Wallingford

DANBURY

Seymour

Hamden

Bethel

Derby

New Haven

North Madison

Ridgefield

Shelton

West Haven

Guilford

Wilton

Trumbull

Milford

Norwalk

BRIDGEPORT

CANADA

USA

The Litchfield Hills

0 — 15km
0 — 9 miles

N

Attraction
City
Large Town
Small Town
POI
Motorway
Main Road
Minor Road
Railway

⊕ Macedonia Brook State Park
Macedonia Brook Rd (off Rte 341); tel: (860) 927-3238. Free admission.

Sloane-Stanley Museum & Kent Furnace $ *Rte 7; tel: (860) 927-3849. Open mid-May–late Oct Wed–Sun 1000–1600.*

Going 4 miles in the opposite direction gets you to **Bull's Bridge** (1842). Spanning the Housatonic River, it's one of only two Connecticut covered bridges still open to motor vehicles. View the river and its gorges from rocky ledges, ideal for an impromptu picnic spread. And if old-time ironworks perk your curiosity, tour the **Sloane-Stanley Museum & Kent Furnace**. The house and studio of 20th-century landscape painter Eric Sloane is on the site of a furnace that belched tool-making fire between 1826 and 1892.

Accommodation and food in Kent

Bull's Bridge Inn $ *333 Kent Rd; tel: (860) 927-1000.* Basic but satisfying meat-and-potatoes fare, plus a salad bar and fireplace.

Stroble's Bakery $ *14 N Main St; tel: (860) 927-4073.* For heavenly buttered baguettes and apricot tarts.

The Villager $ *28 N Main St; tel: (860) 927-1555.* A favourite for all-American burgers and milkshakes as well as heavy-duty breakfasts.

Constitution Oak Farm $$ *36 Beardsley Rd; tel: (860) 354-6495.* An ex-dairy farm where the house dates from the late 18th century.

Fife 'n Drum Restaurant & Inn $$ *53 N Main St; tel: (860) 927-3509; www.fifendrum.com.* Centre-of-town convenience; sizeable wine list in the barnwood restaurant.

Below
Bull's Bridge

LAKE WARAMAUG

Lake Waramaug State Park *Off Rte 45 from New Preston; tel: (860) 868-0220. Free admission.*

Hopkins Vineyard *Hopkins Rd, New Preston; tel: (860) 868-7954. Call ahead for different hours at various times of year; guided winery tours. Free admission.*

Institute for American Indian Studies *$ 38 Curtis Rd, Washington; tel: (860) 868-0518. Open Mon–Sat 1000–1700, Sun 1200–1700. Closed Jan–Mar Mon and Tue.*

The Silo *44 Upland Rd, New Milford; tel: (860) 355-0300; www.thesilo.com*

Its shores comprising one of the Litchfield Hills' many state parks, this 680-acre body of water is popular for swimming, boating and camping (88 sites in woods and open fields). Verdant hills surrounding the lake give it a Swiss-Austrian aura. As an extra treat, several idyllic villages are close by: notably New Preston, Woodville, Marble Dale, Washington/Washington Depot and New Milford. So is **Hopkins Vineyard** for the pleasure of wine tasting in an old red barn. For all manner of trendy cookware, drive to **The Silo** on New Milford's northerly outskirts, run by New York Pops conductor Skitch Henderson and his cookbook-collaborator wife.

Washington's **Institute for American Indian Studies** covers 10,000 years of Native American life, highlighted by a replica 17th-century Algonquian village, garden and rock shelter.

Accommodation and food in the Lake Waramaug vicinity

The Pantry $ *5 Titus Rd, Washington Depot; tel: (860) 868-0258.* Village-centre restaurant, deli, bakery and health-food store handy for picnic supplies.

Curtis House $$ *506 Main St, Woodbury; tel: (203) 263-2101.* Connecticut's oldest inn, circa 1754, contains 14 guest rooms in the main house (eight with private bath), plus four rooms (all with private bath) in the former carriage house. Furnished with antiques; cheerful pub and tavern.

Hopkins Inn $$ *22 Hopkins Rd, New Preston; tel: (860) 868-7295; www.thehopkinsinn.com.* A Federal-style country inn and Swiss-Austrian restaurant, across the road from the vineyard, overlooking the lake.

Le Bon Coin $$$ *Rte 202, New Preston; tel: (860) 868-7763.* Out here in the sticks, big-city standards for a French haute-cuisine dining experience.

Boulders Inn $$$ *East Shore Rd, New Preston; tel: (800) 552-6853 or (860) 868-0541; www.bouldersinn.com.* Classy, casual lodgings in an 1895 Victorian mansion; fine restaurant with lake and Pinnacle Mountain views.

Mayflower Inn $$$ *118 Woodbury Rd, Washington; tel: (860) 868-9466.* The crème de la crème of posh New England country inns, on a 28-acre site including woods, duck ponds and hillside gardens, plus a health spa and a stellar gourmet restaurant.

LITCHFIELD

Towns described as having 'quintessential New England' charm possess several requisite components: at least one pointy white church

ⓘ Northwest Connecticut Chamber of Commerce *333 Kennedy Dr, Torrington; tel: (860) 482-6586.*

ⓗ Litchfield Congregational Church *On the Green, East St/South St intersection. Open Mon–Fri 0900–1700, Sun services 1030, summer 0930.*

Tapping Reeve House $ *82 South St; tel: (860) 567-4501. Open mid-May–mid-Oct Tue–Sat 1100–1700, Sun 1300–1700.*

Historical Society Museum $ *7 South St; tel: (860) 567-4501. Open Apr–mid-Nov Tue–Sat 1100–1700, Sun 1300–1700.*

Haight-Brown Vineyard and Winery *29 Chestnut Hill Rd (off Rte 118); tel: (800) 577-9463 or (860) 567-4045. Open Mon–Sat 1030–1700, Sun 1200–1700. Hourly winery tours.*

White Memorial Foundation & Conservation Center *Rte 202; tel: (860) 567-0857. Open daily dawn–dusk.*

ⓞ Warner Theater $–$$ *68 Main St, Torrington; tel: (860) 489-7180.*

spire, a central common, a row or two of small local-colour shops, streets lined with old trees and impeccably cared-for Early American houses, and scenic surroundings. A courthouse, historical society and respectable library would clinch the title.

Litchfield qualifies on all counts. What's more, it's the birthplace of Revolutionary War hero Ethan Allen and Harriet Beecher Stowe, whose abolitionist (ie anti-slavery) bestseller, *Uncle Tom's Cabin*, came out in 1852. Her father, an equally outspoken abolitionist, was minister of the much-photographed **Congregational Church** from 1810 to 1826. Add to that pedigree the **Tapping Reeve House**, the nation's first independent law school, established in 1784, with an honour roll of graduates including Vice Presidents Aaron Burr and John C Calhoun along with 6 cabinet ministers, 26 senators, 3 Supreme Court justices and 16 state governors.

A browse through the Litchfield **Historical Society Museum** acquaints newcomers with the area's early years. For Chardonnay/Riesling/Merlot wine tasting, reaching **Haight-Brown Vineyard and Winery** entails a short drive into hill country east of town. Drive westward to Connecticut's biggest nature sanctuary: 4000-acre **White Memorial Foundation & Conservation Center**, pine-forested and boggy terrain bordering **Bantam Lake** and **Bantam River** for camping, swimming, birdwatching, bicycling and hiking (35-mile trail network). A 1¼-mile boardwalk encircling **Little Pond** puts you in close touch with a virginal wetland environment.

With just enough of a commercial core and the obvious past significance of its Naugatuck River millworks, nearby **Torrington** is more of a small city than a large town. Its standout landmark is the **Warner Theater**, exemplifying over-the-top art deco design, now a venue for stage shows and Nutmeg Ballet performances.

Accommodation and food in Litchfield and Torrington

Yankee Pedlar Inn $ *93 Main St, Torrington; tel: (860) 489-9226 or (866) 484-8247; www.pedlarinn.com.* A spruced-up 1891 oldie with 60 rooms and in-town convenience; pub-style downstairs restaurant.

Tollgate Hill Inn $$ *Rte 202 and Tollgate Rd, Litchfield; tel: (800) 445-3903 or (860) 567-1233.* Two 18th-century buildings amid a grove of white birch trees; hearty food in the original tavern.

West Side Grill $$ *West St, Litchfield; tel: (860) 567-3885.* Great for celebrity-watching and internationally inspired food, plus great home-made bread.

Stone House Café and Gallery $$$ *637 Bantam Rd, Litchfield; tel: (860) 567-3326.* As the name and address imply, a stone house overlooking the Bantam River and featuring an art gallery. Extra-good cuisine and wine list.

NORTHERN LITCHFIELD HILLS

Lime Rock Park $$
Rte 112, Lakeville;
tel: (800) 722-3577 or (860)
435-5000; www.limerock.com.
Open Apr–Nov.

Audubon Center *325*
Cornwall Bridge Road,
Sharon; tel: (860) 364-0520;
http://sharon.audubon.org.
Open Tue–Sat 0900–1700,
Sun 1300–1700. Closed
Mon and hols.

Battell Chapel *12 Village*
Green, Norfolk; tel: (860)
542-5721.

**Norfolk Chamber
Music Festival $$**
Tel: (860) 542-3000.
Jun–Aug.

Speckled with glacial lakes and ponds, the landscape a mix of rolling highlands and small farm fields, the Litchfield Hills' less populous upper half could be mistaken for the far reaches of New Hampshire or Vermont. Just about every town and village is near a state forest or park.

Amid the prevailing tranquillity, the eight-turn course at **Lime Rock Park** is a hotbed of pro/am car racing. **West Cornwall** shares noteworthiness with Kent for having the other of Connecticut's two covered bridges still accessible to vehicular traffic. Sharon's **Audubon Center** is a wildlife sanctuary with herb and wildflower gardens. High-altitude **Norfolk**, with a perfect village green, hosts a major **Chamber Music Festival**; the Congregational Church's **Battell Chapel** features art nouveau stained-glass windows crafted by Louis Comfort Tiffany.

Accommodation and food in the northern Litchfield Hills

Collins Diner $ *53 Main St, Canaan; tel: (860) 824-7040.* One of five classic US diners listed on the National Register of Historic Places.

Old Riverton Inn $–$$ *Rte 20, Riverton; tel: (800) 378-1796 or (860) 379-8678.* Countrified seclusion beside the Farmington River in an inn dating from 1796; cosy Colonial dining room.

Brookside Bistro $$ *Rte 128, West Cornwall; tel: (860) 672-6601.* French bistro fare, indoors or on the deck alongside Mill Brook.

Mountain View Inn $$ *67 Litchfield Rd, Norfolk; tel: (860) 542-6991.* An 1875 Victorian dowager in a well-nigh perfect New England village; Saturday–Sunday fireside dinners.

White Hart Inn $$ *Village Green, Salisbury; tel: (800) 832-0041 or (860) 435-0030; www.whitehartinn.com.* Landmark village-centre inn; seafood specialities in the restaurant.

Suggested tour

Total distance: 120 miles; 130–135 miles with detour.

Time: You're in hill country with curving roads, plus scenery and villages worthy of en-route stopovers, so allow a full day.

Link: Starting on the region's eastern flank connects you with the Connecticut Midlands Route (*see page 112*).

Route: Begin by heading west from metro Hartford on Rte 44; 3 miles beyond New Hartford, turn on to Rte 181, passing Pleasant Valley for an 8-mile drive through **Peoples State Forest** ❶ alongside the **Barkhamsted Reservoir** ❷ (a secondary road through the pine groves

ℹ Housatonic Valley Tourism District
30 Main St, Danbury; tel: (800) 841-4488 or (203) 743-0546.

Ridgefield Chamber of Commerce 9 Bailey Ave, Ridgefield; tel: (203) 438-5992.

⌂ Charles Ives Center for the Arts $$ Western Connecticut State University, Mill Plain Rd, Danbury; tel: (203) 837-9226. Jun–Sept.

🏛 Aldrich Museum of Contemporary Art $ 258 Main St, Ridgefield; tel: (203) 438-4519; www.aldrichart.org. Open Tue–Sun 1200–1700, Fri 1200–2000.

Weir Farm 735 Nod Hill Rd, Ridgefield/Wilton; tel: (203) 834-1896. Call for studio tours at designated times. Free admission.

gets you to Riverton, if desired). Reach Rte 20 for a southbound swing to Winsted, followed by a 16-mile, Rte 44 drive to Norfolk in the Berkshire foothills – temptingly close to **Haystack Mountain State Park ❸** and **Campbell Falls ❹** with its multiple cascades – and tiny Canaan.

Continue on Rte 44 towards Salisbury and Lakeville. If you're energetic, hike to the summit of 2361-ft **Bear Mountain ❺** for panoramic vistas of Connecticut, Massachusetts and New York.

Once past Falls Village and Lime Rock, swing over to Rte 7 to reach West Cornwall's historic **covered bridge ❻** after 4 miles. Continue a further 10 miles through **Housatonic Meadows State Park ❼** to Kent Falls State Park and another **covered bridge ❽**. The super-scenic West Cornwall–Kent segment features lofty cliffs flanking the Housatonic River, with maple and oak trees at the water's edge. Upon arrival in Cornwall Bridge, consider a 7-mile westbound sidetrack to Sharon, with its **Audubon Center ❾** and cluster of stone and brick Early American houses.

Detour: From Kent, take Rte 341, then Rte 45 for a 2-mile loop around LAKE WARAMAUG ❿. Veer south for some short distance meandering through **New Preston ⓫**, **Marble Dale ⓬**, **Washington Depot ⓭** and **Washington ⓮** – the latter an enchantingly quaint hilltop hamlet overlooking the **Shepaug River Valley ⓯**, a habitat for bald eagles.

Via Rte 202 going past **Lake Bantam ⓰**, reach Litchfield after 10 miles, or Torrington after 16 miles. From that mini-city, take Highway 8 for a quick northbound jaunt to Winsted, which gets you back on to east–west Rte 44.

Also worth exploring

Upstate Litchfield hill country's predominant river continues its southward course to form the **Housatonic Valley** in a more urbanised patch of Connecticut. But you'll discover plenty of open spaces, small communities and a distinct artistic heritage. Focus your touring on two close-together cities. Danbury is the birthplace of composer Charles Ives, hence the **Charles Ives Center for the Arts** on a college campus, an outdoor summer-concert venue where the stage perches on an island in a pond.

Smaller Ridgefield beckons with the world-class **Aldrich Museum of Contemporary Art**, complete with a sculpture garden. Also worth a visit is 50-acre **Weir Farm**, a National Historic Park where the painter J Alden Weir became one of the founders of American Impressionism.

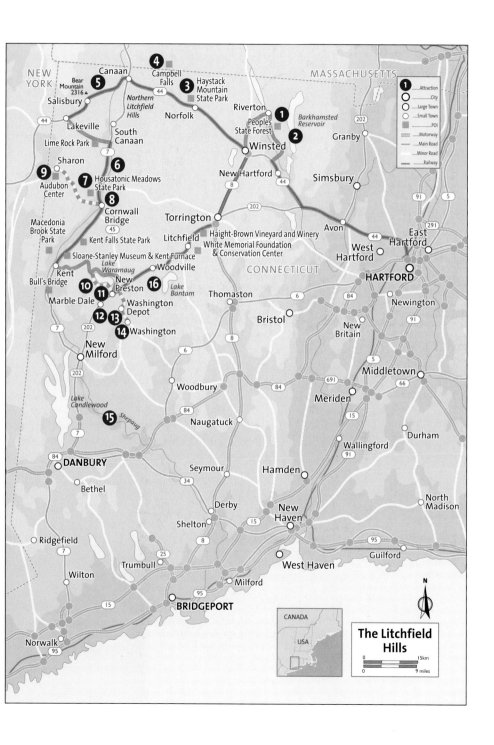

NEW YORK

MASSACHUSETTS

Bear Mountain 2316▲

Canaan

④ Campbell Falls

⑤ Salisbury

③ Haystack Mountain State Park

Northern Litchfield Hills

Riverton

① Barkhamsted Reservoir

② Granby

202

Lakeville

44

Norfolk

Peoples State Forest

Winsted

Lime Rock Park

South Canaan

7

Sharon

⑥

New Hartford

Simsbury

⑨ Audubon Center

⑦ Housatonic Meadows State Park

8

44

91

5

Macedonia Brook State Park

⑧ Cornwall Bridge

45

Torrington

202

Avon

East Hartford

291

Kent Falls State Park

Litchfield

Haight-Brown Vineyard and Winery

White Memorial Foundation & Conservation Center

West Hartford

HARTFORD

Sloane-Stanley Museum & Kent Furnace

Woodville

CONNECTICUT

Kent

Bull's Bridge

Lake Waramaug

New Preston

Lake Bantam

Thomaston

6

84

Newington

⑩ Marble Dale

⑪

⑯

Lake Bantam

New Britain

91

⑫ ⑬ Washington Depot

7 202

⑭ Washington

8

5

New Milford

6

Middletown

66

202

Woodbury

84

691

Meriden

Lake Candlewood

⑮ Shepaug

84

Naugatuck

15

Wallingford

91

Durham

7

DANBURY

Seymour

Hamden

North Madison

Bethel

34

Derby

New Haven

Ridgefield

Shelton

15

95

Guilford

7

8

Wilton

25

Trumbull

West Haven

Norwalk

Milford

95

15

BRIDGEPORT

95

N

CANADA

USA

The Litchfield Hills

0   15km
0   9 miles

① Attraction
○ City
○ Large Town
○ Small Town
■ POI
Motorway
Main Road
Minor Road
Railway

The Lower Connecticut Valley

Ratings

Arts and culture	●●●●●
Beaches	●●●●●
Nature/ scenery	●●●●○
Children	●●●○○
Food and drink	●●○○○
History	●●○○○
Museums	●●○○○
Shopping	●○○○○

After curving for 410 miles from the Quebec–New Hampshire border, Connecticut's namesake river spills into Long Island Sound. Shipbuilding, fishing and furniture-making were important regional occupations when America was a British colony and then a young republic.

But this part of the state never underwent heavy-industry development – evident in the estuary's pristine salt marshes, a tidal wetland protected to impressive extent by the US Nature Conservancy. Unlike other major northeastern US rivers, there's no commercial port city at the Connecticut's mouth. That's because the delta's shifting sand bars impede deep-draft shipping – another plus for the area's ecology. Enthralled by the reflective 'painters' light' and contrasting colours of river, sky, marshes, salt meadows and foliage, prominent American Impressionists (notably Childe Hassam, Willard Metcalf and William Chadwick) made Old Lyme famous as an art colony during the first two decades of the 20th century.

CHESTER

ⓘ Town Office Building *65 Main St, Chester; tel: (860) 526-0013; www.chesterct.com*

Like many New England towns, this one got rich as an 18th-century mercantile trading centre, switched to mundane industrial production during the following century (when workers turned out knitting needles by the umpteen thousands), subsequently declined and ultimately revived to the present-day extent of spruced-up riverside charm. Also as usual, local history includes a titbit of Yankee ingenuity: Chester's Samuel Silliman invented the inkwell here in 1857. For

Right
Autumn in the valley

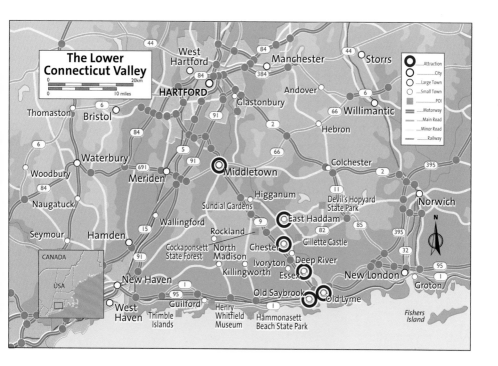

Chester–Hadlyme Ferry $ Tel: (860) 594-2550. Carrying eight to nine vehicles per crossing, Selden III service operates Apr–Nov Mon–Fri 0700–1845, Sat and Sun 1030–1700.

Connecticut River Artisans Cooperative 5 W Main St, tel: (860) 526-5575.

Nilsson Spring Street Studio 1 Spring St; tel: (860) 526-2077.

Cockaponsett State Forest Tel: (860) 345-8521. Via Rte 148 from Chester/Deep River; car park off Cedar Lake Rd. Free admission.

orientation, pick up a free pamphlet at the Town Office Building; it maps out self-guided walking tours ranging from 1³/₄ to 3¹/₂ miles through Chester's immediate surroundings. For a quirky way of getting here westbound by car, drive on to the **Chester–Hadlyme Ferry**, a cross-river service in continuous operation since 1769.

Chester has become an arty community – apparent in a cluster of galleries and craft shops, the most prominent being **Connecticut River Artisans Cooperative** and **Nilsson Spring Street Studio**.

Nature lovers should delve into **Cockaponsett State Forest**, the state's second-biggest at 15,652 acres. Alongside **Deep River**, Chester's neighbouring hamlet, 300-acre **Canfield-Meadow Woods Nature Preserve** features 13 trails wending through a wooded realm of ridges and valleys.

Accommodation and food in Chester

Mad Hatter Bakery & Café $ 16 Main St; tel: (860) 526-2156. A funky hangout for light lunch or early supper; delectable hearth-baked breads.

Fiddlers $$ 4 Water St; tel: (860) 526-3210. Specialises in fresh seafood.

🅗 Canfield-Meadow Woods Nature Preserve *Tel: (860) 526-6020. Off Rte 154 in Deep River. Free admission.*

◭ Chester Agricultural & Mechanical Society Fair *Rte 154; tel: (860) 526-5947 has been a folksy event in late August since 1877.*

Goodspeed-at-Chester/Norma Terris Theater *Tel: (860) 873-8668.* One of the town's recycled knitting-needle factories and a try-out venue for new musicals produced by **East Haddam**'s Goodspeed Opera House company, staged in summer and autumn.

Ancient Fife & Drum Muster and Parade Biggest in the US, rattles Deep River's Main St windows on the third Sat in July; *tel: (860) 526-5947.*

The Inn & Vineyard at Chester $$ *318 W. Main St; tel: (800) 949-7829 or (860) 526-9541.* A modernised 42-room country inn, colonial décor and 'Post and Beam' dining room.

Restaurant du Village $$$ *59 Main St; tel: (860) 526-5301.* Chester's haute-cuisine eatery, with French-Alsatian accentuation.

Right
Rural bridge near Chester

EAST HADDAM

◭ Goodspeed Opera House $$$ *Rte 82, East Haddam; tel: (860) 873-8668; www.goodspeed.org. Apr–Dec season, performances Wed–Sun. Definitely purchase tickets well in advance.*

A single eye-catching landmark is reason enough for a stopover here. It's a six-storey 'wedding-cake' built in 1876 by shipping/banking tycoon William H Goodspeed that's become the appropriately named **Goodspeed Opera House**, renowned for staging world premieres of such bound-for-Broadway musical successes as *Man of La Mancha* (1966) and *Annie* (1977). Another attraction is 2³/4 miles downriver, on the outskirts of Hadlyme: a state park on a promontory leading to **Gillette Castle**, a craggy fieldstone edifice with melodramatic

Gillette Castle State Park $
67 River Rd, East Haddam; tel: (860) 526-2336. Open end May–mid-Oct daily 1000–1700; mid-Oct–mid-Dec 1000–1600. Plan at least an hour for an absorbing tour.

Devil's Hopyard State Park *Rte 82 from East Haddam; tel: (860) 873-8566. Free admission.*

Rhineland inspiration, completed in 1919 for actor William Gillette, long-time portrayer of Sherlock Holmes. With river views from on high, the park is delightful for picnicking. So is **Devil's Hopyard State Park** and its 60ft Chapman's Falls, reached via a scenic 6-mile drive east from East Haddam. The park's hiking trails total 15 miles.

Accommodation and food in East Haddam

Wolf's Den Campground $ *Rte 82; tel: (860) 873-9681,* has 205 pitches, plus swimming and tennis facilities.

Bishopsgate Inn $$ *7 Norwich Rd; tel: (860) 873-1677.* This bed-and-breakfast alternative dates from the early 19th-century shipbuilding boom.

Gelston House $$ *8 Main St; tel: (860) 873-1411.* Predating the adjacent opera house by 23 years, this comparable gingerbread-Victorian pile is recommended for lodging and food.

ESSEX

Essex Steam Train & Riverboat Ride
$$ Board at 1 Railroad Ave near Exit 3 off Rte 9 at the west end of Essex; tel: (800) 377-3987 or (860) 767-0103; www.essexsteamtrain.com. Phone for seasonal schedules. The **North Cove Express** *dinner train runs May–December.*

Connecticut River Museum $ *67 Main St; tel: (860) 767-8269; www.ctrivermuseum.org. Open Tue–Sun 1000–1700.*

Ivoryton Playhouse *103 Main Street, Ivoryton; tel: (860) 767-7318; www.ivorytonplayhouse.org*

In 1995, the residents became more self-satisfied than ever. That's when their community topped one publication's list of 100 entries – in the 5000–15,000 population range – as the Best Small Town in America. Essex qualifies in many respects, appreciated by strolling the tree-shaded streets, poking into a modest number of cute shops, admiring the Georgian and Federal domestic architecture and exploring the riverfront with its North and South Coves, piers, boatyards, town dock and not-too-snobbish Essex Yacht Club.

Main St dead-ends at Steamboat Landing, site of the **Connecticut River Museum**, occupying an 1878 warehouse converted into a repository of riverine and maritime history. Displays include a model of colonial America's first custom-built warship, the *Oliver Cromwell*, launched in 1775 and a full-scale replica of the world's first seaworthy submarine, the Connecticut-built *Turtle* (1776).

Essex Station is the embarkation point for the **Essex Steam Train & Riverboat Ride**, beginning with a 90-minute rail trip aboard 1920s coaches. At Deep River Landing, passengers can optionally transfer on to the triple-deck *Becky Thatcher* for an hour-long cruise past **Chester** to **East Haddam** and back.

In neighbouring Ivoryton, the **Ivoryton Playhouse** (*103 Main St*), originally a factory recreation hall, is the summer-stock home of the River Rep Players, who present half a dozen productions, June–September. This is small-town straw-hat stuff with a big reputation. Over the decades, such stars as Katherine Hepburn, Marlon Brando, Tallulah Bankhead and Gloria Swanson have been on stage here.

Accommodation and food in Essex

Copper Beech Inn $$ *46 Main St, Ivoryton; tel: (888) 809-2056 or (860) 767-0330*, was constructed for one of the village's 19th-century ivory merchants and named after the copper beech tree standing to the front of it. A more intimate, secluded alternative to the 'Gris' (see below) for lodging and meals.

The Griswold Inn $$ *36 Main St, Essex; tel: (860) 767-1776; www. griswoldinn.com.* Essex wouldn't be Essex without the 'Gris', reputedly Connecticut's first three-storey structure. Along with guest rooms and suites, appealing features include Currier & Ives steamboat prints in the Covered Bridge dining room. More nautical illustrations embellish the timber-beamed tavern, a local watering hole with musical entertainment. An enormous 'Hunt Breakfast' is served every Sunday, 1100–1430.

MIDDLETOWN

General Mansfield House $ *151 Main St; tel: (860) 346-0746. Phone for times of Sun–Mon guided tours.*

America's Cup $$ *80 Harbor Dr; tel: (860) 347-9999. Lunch and dinner served in what used to be the riverside Middletown Yacht Club, built in 1915.*

Wesleyan Center for the Arts *283 Washington Terrace; tel: (860) 685-3355. Galleries open during school year Tue–Fri 1200–1400, Sat and Sun 1400–1700; summer Tue–Sat 1200–1600. For the Center's theatre and concert tickets, call the box office: (860) 685-2695.*

Make the Lower Valley's only bona fide city a pitstop for petrol, supplies, whatever you need. Students attending Wesleyan University exert a generally well-behaved influence, so there's no lack of budget stores and eateries, including three all-American diners right downtown. Wesleyan's **Center for the Arts** comprises three performance halls plus two avant-garde galleries: Davis Art Center (prints and photographs) and the Zilkha Gallery (contemporary paintings and sculpture). The circa-1810 **General Mansfield House** is big on US Civil War history and 18th- to 19th-century decorative arts. Crave fresh air and exercise? Hike up the **Mattabesett Blue Trail**, reaching rocky ledges for panoramas of Middletown and the river.

Right
The Florence Griswold Museum in Old Lyme

Right
Old Lyme's Congregational
Church

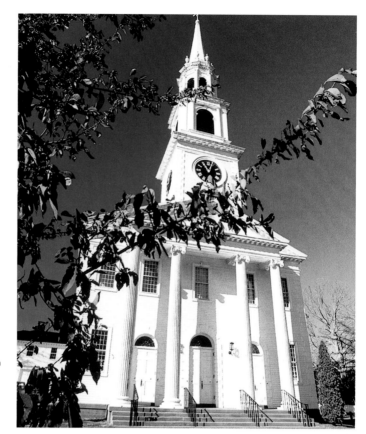

For train-travel
access to Old
Lyme/Old Saybrook and
vicinity, Old Saybrook is
one of the station stops on
Amtrak's southern New
England rail route –
midway between New
London and New Haven
station stops.

OLD LYME/OLD SAYBROOK

**Old Saybrook
Chamber of
Commerce** 655 Boston
Post Rd, Old Saybrook; tel:
(860) 388-3266.

James Pharmacy
2 Pennywise Lane, Old
Saybrook; tel: (860) 395-
1229.

**Florence Griswold
Museum** $ 96 Lyme
St, Old Lyme; tel: (860) 434-
5542; www. flogris.org. Open
Jun–Nov Tue–Sat 1000–
1700; Dec–May Wed–Sun
1300–1700.

Divided by the river but connected by the interstate motorway's
Baldwin Bridge, these are the closest towns to the Connecticut River's
delta. Hustle and bustle? A commercial centre? You'll find neither in
staid Old Lyme. Owners of its stately homes tend toward an anti-
development attitude, willing to drive to bland strip malls on the
outer fringe or to stores over in busier Old Saybrook. That said, Old
Lyme's reputation as an 'American Barbizon' is undeniable, thanks to
a sea captain's daughter who turned her inherited 1817 mansion into
a boarding house for American Impressionists – the result is today's
Florence Griswold Museum, bedecked with their paintings, as well as
self-portrait caricatures on the dining room mantel.

Map-read your way to Smith Neck Rd, off Rte 156, to reach Old
Lyme's **Bird Observation Platform**, vantage point for spotting
nesting ospreys in their Great Island habitat. Extending across a

Thimble Islands Cruise $ *Stony Creek dock; tel: (203) 481-3345; www.thimbleislands.com. Mid-May–mid-Oct. Phone ahead for weekday and weekend timetable.*

Sundial Gardens $ *Brault Hill Rd, Higganum; tel: (860) 345-4290; www.sundialgardens. com. Open Apr–mid-Oct Sat and Sun 1000–1700.*

causeway south from downtown Old Saybrook, Rte 154 loops around **Fenwick**, an enclave of exclusive summer houses, site of the lighthouse depicted on Connecticut licence plates. In town, don't bypass the genuinely old-time **James Pharmacy**, complete with an 1896 soda fountain. Yale University began its stellar existence as the Collegiate School, located in Old Saybrook from 1707 to 1716, when it moved to New Haven.

Accommodation and food in Old Lyme/Old Saybrook

Bee & Thistle Inn $$ *100 Lyme St, Old Lyme; tel: (800) 622-4946 or(860) 434-1667.* In the historic district.

Dock & Dine $$ *Saybrook Point, Old Saybrook; tel: (860) 388-4665.* A casual seafood restaurant where picture windows and an outdoor deck overlook the confluence of the Connecticut River and Long Island Sound.

The Old Lyme Inn $$ *85 Lyme St, Old Lyme; tel: (800) 434-5352 or (860) 434-2600.* Also in the historic district.

Saybrook Point Inn & Spa $$$ *2 Bridge St, Old Saybrook; tel: (800) 243-0212 or (860) 395-2000.* Modernistic design, fitness facilities, a grillroom restaurant and a gorgeous waterfront setting.

Suggested tour

Total distance: 68–70 miles; 98–100 miles with detour.

Time: 3 hours' leisurely driving. Figure on a full morning or afternoon at that pace; allow a full day or a bit more with detour.

Links: At **Old Lyme**, connect with the Connecticut's Southeastern Corner Route (*see page 138*). By driving east from Middletown, you can join the Connecticut's Midlands Route (*see page 112*). The detour to Stony Creek connects with the Connecticut's Midlands Route by way of Branford on New Haven's eastern outskirts.

Route: Heading west from **OLD LYME ❶**, cross the I-95/Baldwin Bridge to reach Rte 154 in **OLD SAYBROOK ❷** for a scenic riverside-marshland drive north to **ESSEX ❸** and **CHESTER ❹**. Cross the river aboard the Chester–Hadlyme Ferry if you'd like to visit **Gillette Castle ❺** on the east bank. Otherwise, continue on Rte 154 to Tylerville; cross the river's Swing Bridge (a 1913 iron-girder contraption, 'swingable' for passage of tall-masted boats) for arrival in East Haddam. If you wish, sidetrack via Rte 82 to **Devil's Hopyard State Park ❻** Otherwise, backtrack across the bridge; continue north on Rte 154 to Higganum, locale of 18th-century-style **Sundial Gardens ❼** with topiary and herb gardens. West of that village, connect on to Rte 9 for a swift drive into **MIDDLETOWN ❽**. Complete the loop by returning

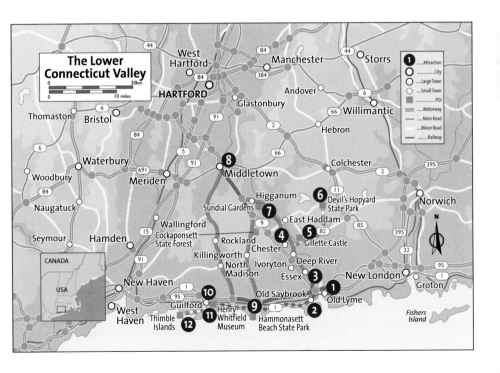

Hammonasett State Beach Park $
Rte 1, Madison; tel: (203) 453-2457. Open year-round 0800–dusk.

Henry Whitfield State Museum $
248 Old Whitfield St, Guilford; tel: (203) 453-2457; www.guilfordct.com. Open Feb–mid-Dec Wed–Sun 1000–1630. The house museum is well supplied with visitor information for Guilford and vicinity.

southbound to the coast. Two idyllic country byways, with miles of stone fences, are Rte 79 through Rockland to Madison and Rte 81 through Killingworth to Clinton.

Detour: Begin it at **Old Saybrook ❷**; drive close to shoreline and marshy wetlands via Rte 1 (the old Boston Post Rd) through Westbrook to above-mentioned Madison and Clinton. Midway between those pleasant towns, **Hammonasett Beach State Park ❾** features Connecticut's longest beachfront (2 miles), nature trails and 550 tent pitches.

Continue to very photogenic **Guilford ❿**, wrapped around an extra-large town green and locale of the **Henry Whitfield Museum ⓫**, eminent as New England's oldest stone house, built in 1639. Pink granite shipped to New York City from a quarry near here went into the construction of Grand Central Station and the pedestal of the Statue of Liberty.

From Guilford, steer on to Rte 146 for a super-scenic 10-mile jaunt with close-ups of coves and salt marshes, reaching tiny Stony Creek – port of call for cruises through the scattered, rocky, partially residential **Thimble Islands ⓬**, purported pirates' hideaways in past times.

Ratings

Children	●●●● ○
History	●●●● ○
Art and culture	●● ○○○
Beaches	●● ○○○
Food and drink	●● ○○○
Museums	●● ○○○
Nature/ scenery	●● ○○○
Entertainment	● ○○○○

Connecticut's Southeastern Corner

Connecticut's contrasts are especially apparent in the state's southeastern corner. Compare, for instance, the picturesque fishing-boat villages of Noank and Stonington Borough with citified New London and Norwich. In between, depending upon where you choose to travel, are spectacular stretches of indented coastline and some of the prettiest forested hills in all of New England – in the midst of which the world's largest casino complex attracts thousands of daredevil gamblers every day. The further reward of opting for a close-to-shore drive, with Long Island Sound in view, is Mystic Seaport, the nation's biggest, best and best-known maritime museum.

Because point-to-point distances are short throughout this region, you're never far from adjacent Rhode Island's southwesternmost edge of land, where the Watch Hill resort community and Misquamicut State Beach are summertime favourites.

FOXWOODS RESORT & CASINO

ⓘ Foxwoods information *39 Norwich-Westerly Road; tel: (800) FOXWOODS; www.foxwoods.com. Exit 92 off the I-95 motorway for a Rte 2 drive to the complex. From just about any direction in southern New England, roadside signs point the way. Free admission.*

For some miraculous reason, drowsy little Ledyard hasn't been swallowed up by its colossal neighbour dominating the Mashantucket Pequot Tribal Nation's 5000-acre chunk of territory: namely, **Foxwoods Resort & Casino**, whose turquoise and teal buildings rise Oz-like out of cornfields and cow pastures in hilly farm country. What began in 1986 as a bingo parlour is now a mighty complex comprising three vast gambling halls (buzzing and jingling around the clock) where get-rich-quick hopefuls play all conceivable games of chance. There is also a Vegas-type nightclub starring showbiz entertainers, Cinetropolis movie theatre, high-tech pastimes for the kids, loads of eateries and shops and three hotels of various sizes.

Along with all this the **Mashantucket Pequot Museum & Research Center** provides insights into the Pequot tribe's Native American culture and 10,000-year history.

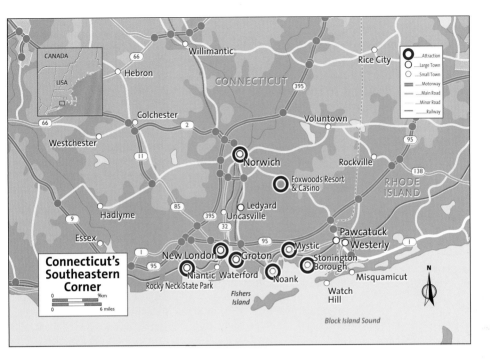

Connecticut's Southeastern Corner

Accommodation and food at Foxwoods

ⓗ Mashantucket Pequot Museum & Research Center $$
110 Pequot Trail; tel: (800) 411-9671; www.mashantucket.com. Open daily 1000–1600.

Foxwoods Resort Hotel $$ has copious amenities despite the high-wattage glitz, or there's the 800-room **Grand Pequot Tower $$–$$$**. For something more rustic: **Two Trees Inn $$**. Reserve well in advance in any season. Restaurants at the resort include: **Cedars Steak House $$** combining a grill room and seafood raw bar, **Al Dente $$** for Italian meals and **Han Garden $–$$** for its Chinese atmosphere. **Branches $$** is a fireside lounge in Two Trees Inn. *Tel: (800) FOXWOODS for reservations at all of the above.*

GROTON

ⓘ Eastern Regional Tourism District
32 Huntington St, PO Box 89, New London; tel: (800) TO EN-JOY or (860) 444-2206; www.mysticmore.com. Visitor enquiry services cover south-coast New London/Groton along with the state's entire eastern region.

Don't be put off by first impressions of Groton's outward junkiness. Westbound lorries and cars, after negotiating a tangle of motorway interchanges, rumble towards the Gold Star Memorial Bridge – an arched span high above the Thames River. With that milieu, drivers encounter consistently heavy traffic, billboards galore, a shopping 'plaza' and random motels.

But a short diversion, north alongside the river, is worthwhile for anyone interested in undersea strategy and technology. Explore the tight innards of the **USS *Nautilus***, the world's first nuclear-powered

USS Nautilus & Submarine Force Museum *Naval Submarine Base, 1 Crystal Lake Rd (off Rte 12); tel: (860) 694-3174 or (800) 343-0079. Open mid-Apr–mid-Oct Wed–Mon 0900–1700, Tue 1300–1700; mid-Oct–mid-Apr Wed–Mon 0900–1600.*

submarine (launched in 1954) and the first (in 1958) to cross beneath the North Pole's ice cap. That main attraction is augmented by the **Submarine Force Museum**, displaying scale models, periscopes, torpedoes, sonar equipment, signal flags, mini-subs and much else connected with what Navy veterans call the 'silent service'.

Fort Griswold Battlefield State Park (*Monument St and Pratt Ave; tel: (860) 449 6877; open daily*) harks back to earlier warfare, commemorating a bloody American defeat or a British victory (depending upon your allegiance) in 1781, when 800 Redcoats commanded by traitor General Benedict Arnold attacked the fort. Gun emplacements remain intact and the 17-acre site is a peaceful picnic spot. For coastal vistas from a height of 134ft, climb the spiral staircase inside the granite monument tower to the observatory platform.

MYSTIC

Mystic Chamber of Commerce *14 Holmes St, Mystic; tel: (860) 572-9578.*

Mystic Seaport $$$ *75 Germanville Ave (Rte 27); tel: (888) 9-SEAPORT or (860) 572-5315; www. mysticseaport.org. Open daily year-round. Call for times, variable depending upon time of year.*

Mystic Marinelife Aquarium $$ *55 Coogan Blvd (Exit 90 off I-95); tel: (860) 572-5955; www.mysticaquarium.org. Open daily 0900–1900 summer; 0900–1800 otherwise.*

Argia Schooner $$$ *73 Steamboat Wharf; tel: (860) 536-0416. Half-day cruises depart daily 1000 and 1400, sunset cruises 1800 (May–Oct only).*

Recreating a 19th-century New England seaport village and keeping it from becoming a trite theme park is no small accomplishment. **Mystic Seaport** succeeds (as Connecticut's foremost tourism attraction) because of its authenticity, craftspeople and interpreters, interactive demonstrations, informational facilities and – above all – fully rigged vessels that really went to sea in years gone by. Tied to the shipyard docks, they include the 1841 *Charles W. Morgan* (the last surviving wooden whaling ship), an 1882 square-rigger and a Gloucester fishing schooner. The 1907 *Sabino*, one of the last coal-fired steamers afloat, takes passengers on Mystic River excursions.

Another crowd-pleaser is **Mystic Marinelife Aquarium**, populated by more than 3500 aquatic creatures including sharks, stingrays, seals, sea lions, a penguin colony, Beluga whales and bottle-nose dolphins.

From Mystic's town centre, where the oddest (and traffic-delaying) landmark is a 1922 bascule drawbridge, the gaff-rigged schooner *Argia* goes cruising on Fishers Island Sound.

Accommodation and food in Mystic

S & P Oyster Co $ *1 Holmes St; tel: (860) 536-2674.* Dine overlooking the drawbridge and river.

Bravo Bravo $$ *20 E Main St; tel: (860) 536-3228.* Italian/Continental/American choices and a waterfront terrace.

Inn at Mystic $$ *3 Williams Ave, Mystic; tel: (800) 237-2415 or (860) 536-9604; www.innatmystic.com.* Lauren Bacall and Humphrey Bogart honeymooned here. On-site: the praiseworthy **Flood Tide Restaurant** $$.

Opposite
The harbour at Mystic

Downtown Mystic's sidewalks are taken over by a juried **Outdoor Arts & Crafts Festival** during the first weekend of August, 1000–dusk.

Seamen's Inne $$ *105 Germanville Ave; tel: (860) 572-5303.* Right next to Mystic Seaport, a seafood restaurant and pub.

The Steamboat Inn $$ *73 Steamboat Wharf, Mystic; tel: (860) 536-8300.* Stands alongside the drawbridge.

Whalers' Inn $$ *20 E Main St, Mystic; tel: (800) 243-2588 or (860) 536-1506; www.whalersinnmystic.com.* A grouping of four 19th-century buildings.

NEW LONDON

ⓘ Connecticut East Tourism District
See Groton, page 138.

ⓑ Ye Antientist Burial Ground
Between Hempsted and Huntington Sts downtown.

Perkins-Shaw Mansion
$ 11 Blinman St; tel: (860) 443-1209. Open May–Oct Wed–Fri 1300–1600, Sat 1000–1600.

Robert Mills US Custom House Museum 150 Bank St; tel: (860) 447-2501. Limited hours, so phone ahead. Free admission.

Monte Cristo Cottage
$ 325 Pequot Ave; tel: (860) 443-0051. Open late May–early Sept Tue–Sat 1000–1700, Sun 1300–1700.

Lyman Allyn Art Museum $ 625 Williams St; tel: (860) 443-2545. Open Tue–Sat 1000–1700, Sun 1300–1700. Free admission.

US Coast Guard Academy 15 Mohegan Ave (off Rte 32); tel: (860) 444-8270. Visitors' pavilion open May–Oct Mon–Fri 0900–1700, Sat and Sun 1000–1700. Museum open May–Oct Mon–Fri 0900–1630 (Thur 0900–2000), Sat 1000–1700, Sun 1200–1700. Free admission. When in port, the Eagle can be boarded Mon–Fri 1300–dusk, Sat and Sun dawn–dusk.

Nothing's fancy or overtly touristy here. Mid-size New London has deep-water harbour facilities near the mouth of the Thames River (pronounced like 'James' on this side of the Atlantic). That location made quite a few people wealthy during the whale-hunting era, which began locally in 1784 and peaked by the mid-19th century.

A free walking-tour map acquaints you with what's historically interesting about compact inner New London. It covers places with such evocative names as the **Captain's Walk** and **Whale Oil Row**, the latter lined with stately 1830s Greek Revival houses. Also on the route are: **Ye Antientist Burial Grounds**, with headstones dating from Puritan settlement in the mid-1600s, the 1756 **Perkins-Shaw Mansion**, Connecticut's Naval Office during the Revolutionary War, and the **Robert Mills US Custom House Museum**, America's oldest functioning custom house, built in 1833.

Nobel and Pulitzer Prize-winning playwright Eugene O'Neill spent his boyhood years in New London's **Monte Cristo Cottage**, named after his actor father's signature stage role and the setting of two O'Neill plays: *Long Day's Journey Into Night* and *Ah! Wilderness*.

The **Lyman Allyn Art Museum** is strong on colonial furniture, paintings, silver, china and glassware. If you're here with children, treat them to the museum's collection of dolls, doll's houses and antique toys.

The **US Coast Guard Academy**, upriver from downtown, is New London's link with its seagoing past. The academy's campus, on high ground overlooking the river, is pleasantly walkable. For orientation and background see a multimedia presentation in the visitors' pavilion and historical displays in Waesche Hall's Coast Guard Museum. The cadet's tall-masted training ship, the barque *Eagle*, captured from the Germans and brought here after World War II, is occasionally away on tour. If not, it's open to the public.

Accommodation and food in New London

Lorelei $ 158 State St; tel: (860) 442-3375. A fun place with tin ceilings and a convivial bar.

The Queen Anne Inn $ 265 Williams St; tel: (800) 347-8818 or (860) 447-2600. As the name implies, a Victorian 'painted lady' bed & breakfast.

Lighthouse Inn $–$$ 6 Guthrie Pl; tel: (800) 678-8946 or (860) 443-8411. Waterfront lodgings in a pink stucco 1902 mansion with the elegant **Mansion Restaurant** $$–$$$.

Bulkeley House $$ 111 Bank St; tel: (860) 444-7753. In an 18th-century tavern for Early American atmosphere.

NIANTIC

Rocky Neck State Park $ *Rte 156; tel: (860) 739-5471. Open daily 0800–dusk.*

Children's Museum of Southeastern Connecticut $ *409 Main St; tel: (860) 691-1111. Open Tue–Sat 0930–1630, Fri 0930–2000, Sun 1200–1600.*

Millstone Discovery & Science Center *278 Main St; tel: (800) 428-4234 or (860) 691-4670. Open in summer Mon–Tue 0900–1600, Wed–Fri 0900–1900, Sat and Sun 1200–1700; Sept–Jun Mon–Fri 1000–1600. Free admission.*

Driving southwest from New London brings you to a string of specks on the map – Jordan Village, Graniteville, Crescent Beach – where a general store, petrol pumps and perhaps a clam shack are the primary sources of income and social activity. Another such speck is Niantic, better known because of desirably plump Niantic Bay scallops. The village is 4 miles from **Rocky Neck State Park**, with a crescent-shaped beach, promontories, boardwalk, woodland hiking trails, picnic grounds and a stone pavilion constructed by WPA (Works Progress Administration) labourers during the 1930s Depression. Edged by salt marshes, Bride's Brook flows through the park.

If you're touring with youngsters, take them to the interactive **Children's Museum of Southeastern Connecticut**. Walk from there to Northeast Utilities' **Millstone Discovery & Science Center** to learn about the workings of a nuclear power station.

Accommodation and food in Niantic and vicinity

The Shack $–$$ *324 Flanders Rd (Rte 161); tel: (860) 739-8898.* Three miles inland from Niantic, in Flanders Village, part of another speck on the map – East Lyme. Down-home cooking, all-you-can-eat fish fry daily. Serves Niantic Bay scallops.

Inn at Harbor Hill Marina $$ *60 Grand St, Niantic; tel: (860) 739-0331.* Eight water-view rooms in an 1870s building; continental breakfast included.

NOANK

This coast-of-Maine lookalike, clustered on a rocky outcrop and complete with lobster traps stacked on weatherbeaten piers, merits a sidetrack while you're driving in either direction between Groton/New London and Mystic. At an easygoing pace, you can see all that's in the nationally registered historic district – mainly fine old houses, a general store, grocery store and a couple of art galleries – in less than an hour.

Accommodation and food in Noank

Abbott's Lobster in the Rough $$ *117 Pearl St; tel: (860) 536-7719.* A setting at the sea edge for New England shore dinners (clam chowder, boiled lobster, 'steamer' clams, corn on the cob).

The Palmer Inn $$ *25 Church St; tel: (860) 572-9000.* Epitomises a Yankee bed & breakfast, in this case built by a shipwright in 1907.

NORWICH

ⓘ Norwich Tourism Office *77 Main St; tel: (860) 886-4683; www.norwichct.org*

ⓝ Christopher Leffingwell House *$ 348 Washington St; tel: (860) 889-9440. Open mid-May–mid-Oct Tue–Sun 1300–1600.*

Slater Memorial Museum and Converse Art Gallery $ *108 Crescent St; tel: (860) 887-2506. Open Jun and Sept Tue–Fri 0900–1600, Sat and Sun 1300–1600; Jul and Aug Tue–Sun 1300–1600.*

Not flashy but historic, Norwich was founded in 1635 by three dozen English settlers who knew a favourable locale when they saw one. It's situated at the confluence of three rivers which form the Thames – an ideal location for water-powered mills. The tourism office provides three walking-tour maps for $5^1/_4$ miles of independent sightseeing. They cover three episodes of local history – Norwichtown is the Colonial-era district, with houses in every Early American style. Among the oldest is Norwichtown's circa-1675 **Christopher Leffingwell House**, built by an original settler, then used as a meeting place for Revolutionary War patriots.

On the campus of Norwich Academy, **Slater Memorial Museum** is an attention-getter because of its major, rather weird collection of plaster casts of Greek, Roman and Renaissance sculptures, among them *Winged Victory*, *Venus de Milo* and Michelangelo's *Pietà*.

Accommodation and food in Norwich

Americus on the Wharf $$ *1 American Wharf; tel: (860) 887-8555.* The wharf symbolises downtown Norwich's Thames riverside revitalisation; the restaurant's décor is appropriately nautical.

The Spa at Norwich Inn $$$ *607 W Thames St (Rte 32); tel: (800) 275-4772 or (860) 886-2401; www.thespaatnorwichinn.com.* Luxurious late 19th-century country inn with up-to-date resort amenities.

Below
Stonington Borough's shoreline

Right
Stonington Borough's Cannon Square commemorates Yankee victories over the British during the American Revolution

STONINGTON BOROUGH

Old Lighthouse Museum $ *7 Water St; tel: (860) 535-1440. Open May, Jun, Sept & Oct Tue–Sun 1000–1700; Jul and Aug daily 1000–1700.*

Although Stonington is just another 'gasoline alley' village on the Boston Post Rd, its Stonington Borough appendage vies with Noank as Connecticut's most charming shoreline community. Squeezed on to a narrow spit of land, the village is home port for Connecticut's only remaining commercial fishing fleet. Maritime miscellany crams the 1823 **Old Lighthouse Museum.**

Accommodation and food in Stonington

Noah's $$ *113 Water St, Stonington Borough; tel: (860) 535-3925.* Just what you'd expect in a fishing village. Fresh-caught seafood served in an ever-popular downtown hangout where locals rub shoulders with out-of-towners. Appealing choices of American and Portuguese specialities appear on daily lunch and dinner menus.

Randall's Ordinary $$ *Rte 2, North Stonington; tel: (860) 599-4540.* Rooms in a colonial homestead and a converted 1819 dairy barn; costumed waiters and waitresses serve hearth-cooked meals.

Mystic Pizza

Among the thousands of pizza parlours scattered throughout the US, **Mystic Pizza $** is arguably the best-known of them all. Credit that to 1988's MGM film of the same name, which featured cinema superstar Julia Roberts in her first big role. Cast and crew actually did their thing in nearby Stonington Borough, with a Water St antiques shop transformed into the film's version of a small New England seacoast town's pizzeria. You'll find Mystic's real-life, very popular version – in business since 1973 – at *56 W. Main St; tel: (860) 536-3700; www. mysticpizza.com*

Suggested tour

Total distance: 45–50 miles, 57–62 miles with detours.

Time: Maximum 2 hours' driving; add half a day for detours. Allow at least half a day for Mystic Seaport.

Links: Join the Newport/Narragansett Bay Route (*see page 148*) at Stonington or Westerly. Join the Lower Connecticut Valley Route (*see page 132*) at Niantic/Rocky Neck State Park.

Route: From **NEW LONDON** ❶, go north on Rte 32 through Uncasville to reach **NORWICH/NORWICHTOWN** ❷, a 12-mile drive. For a same-distance southbound return to **GROTON** ❸ on the opposite side of the Thames River, cross over to Rte 12.

If you are coming from the west, head east from Rocky Neck State Park to **NIANTIC** ❹, then follow rural Rte 156 to Waterford; from there via Rte 1 into **New London** for connection with I-95 across the Gold Star Memorial Bridge to reach **Groton**. Rte 12 gets you south into town or north to the US' Submarine Base. Beyond Groton, take Rte 1 to the Rte 215 junction in order to swoop down and through **NOANK** ❺, continuing past Beebe Cove to **MYSTIC** ❻. Resume driving on Rte 1. At Rte 1A in Stonington, signs sidetrack you a bit south to **STONINGTON BOROUGH** ❼. Rte 1 continues $4^1/_2$ miles to the Connecticut/Rhode Island state line at the Pawcatuck River.

Above
Mystic Seaport

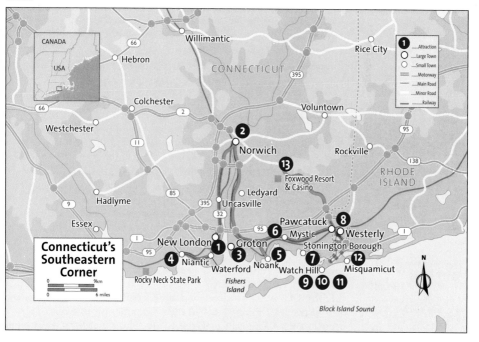 **Westerly-Pawcatuck Chamber of Commerce** / *Chamber Way, Westerly; tel: (800) 732-7636 or (401) 596-7761.*

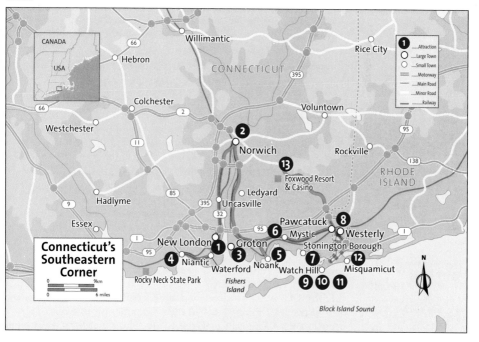 A stopover in **Westerly** is worthwhile, if only to stroll through Victorian **Wilcox Park**, *Granite St.*

Flying Horse Carousel *$ Bay St, Watch Hill. Open Mon–Fri 1300–2100, Sun and holidays 1100–2100.*

Misquamicut State Beach *$ Car entrance on Atlantic Ave, off Rte 1A (Shore Rd).*

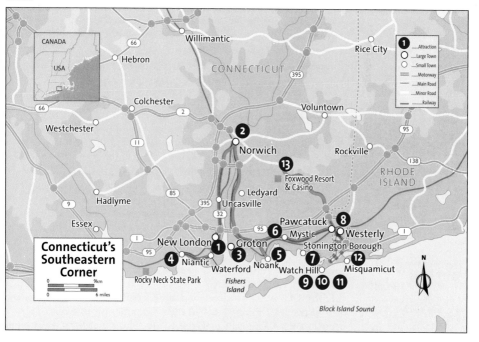 **Olympia Tea Room** *$ 74 Bay St, Watch Hill; tel: (401) 348-8211. For breakfast, lunch and dinner.*

Detour: Immediately upon arriving in Rhode Island, you're in Westerly ❽. Turn on to Rte 1A for a 5-mile drive past Avondale to the peninsular **Watch Hill ❾**, which began attracting urban holiday-makers, who turned it into a mini-Newport during the Gilded Age (late 19th century). It's still a popular warm-weather destination, thanks to breezy air, nearby beaches and plenty of lodgings in inexpensive-to-moderate price categories. Grown-ups and kids alike enjoy the 19th-century **Flying Horse Carousel ❿**, with each steed sculpted out of a single block of wood. Watch Hill's **Olympia Tea Room ⓫** has been in business non-stop since 1916. Splendid sand-and-dunes **Misquamicut State Beach ⓬** is 3 miles away.

Once you're at the Connecticut/Rhode Island state line, Rte 2 northbound takes you (12 miles) to **FOXWOODS ⓭**.

Also worth exploring

Uncasville, midway between New London and Norwich, would be unassuming were it not for adjacent **Mohegan Sun** (*tel: (888) 226-7711; www.mohegansun.com*), the second of Connecticut's gambling palaces – this one on Mohegan Tribal Nation land. If you haven't gone bankrupt at Foxwoods, try your luck at this less overwhelming place, with nightclub, 24-hour restaurants and shops in addition to the essential table games and slot machines.

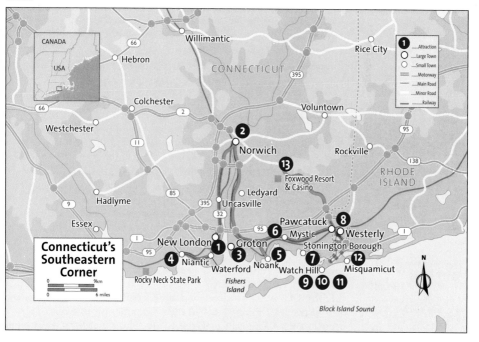

Newport

Ratings

Arts and Culture	●●●●●
Beaches	●●●●●
History	●●●●●
Museums	●●●●○
Children	●●○○○
Food and drink	●●○○○
Nature/ scenery	●●○○○
Shopping	●●○○○

For several primary reasons, Newport heads the list of Rhode Island's most popular visitor destinations. First of all: the palatial Gilded Age 'summer cottages' on and near Bellevue Ave. To those exemplars of conspicuous consumption, add intriguing aspects of US colonial and Revolutionary War history, complete with public buildings and clapboard houses dating from the era. Furthermore, this small peninsular city on Aquidneck Island still exudes the yachting aura of its America's Cup heyday. Make Newport your base for bridge-connected drives to Conanicut Island and – along Narragansett Bay's western shore – charming towns and terrific beaches. East Bay scenery and villages are compelling, too. As an extra bonus, Newport is a port of embarkation for car-ferry crossings to Block Island and Providence, ideal bicycling and nature-walking terrain.

Sights

National Museum of American Illustration $$ 492
Bellevue Ave; tel: (401) 851-8949;
www.americanillustration.org.
Open Jun–Aug Sat and Sun 1000–1600 or by reservation.

National Museum of American Illustration
The previously closed mansion of Vernon Court has been restored to original condition as the home of the new National Museum of American Illustration. The stunning collection of more than 2000 original paintings includes those created for magazine covers, book illustration and advertising by such artists as Norman Rockwell and N C Wyeth. It is the largest collection of Maxfield Parrish works anywhere, and includes a large number of his murals.

International Tennis Hall of Fame $ 194
Bellevue Ave; tel: (401) 849-3990; www.tennisfame.com.
Open daily 1000–1700.

International Tennis Hall of Fame
Originally Newport's shingle-sided casino (not a gambling joint, but a country club in its previous existence), from 1881 to 1914 it was the site of the US National Lawn Tennis Championships which became the US Open. The Hall of Fame is the sport's Valhalla; a museum

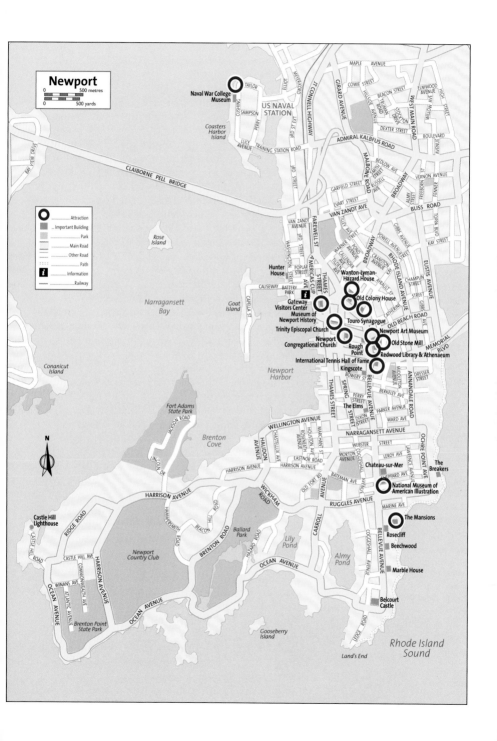

Newport

0 — 500 metres
0 — 500 yards

Naval War College Museum

US NAVAL STATION

Coasters Harbor Island

ADMIRAL KALBFUS ROAD

CLAIBORNE PELL BRIDGE

MAPLE AVENUE
COWIE STREET
GIRARD AVENUE
BEACON STREET
ELMWOOD AVENUE
WEST MAIN ROAD
HIGH STREET
HILLSIDE AVENUE
TRUMAN ST
DEXTER STREET
BOULEVARD

JT CONNELL HIGHWAY

GARFIELD STREET
BROADWAY
EVART STREET
VAN ZANDT AVE
VAN ZANDT AVENUE
BLISS ROAD
VERNON AVENUE

Rose Island

TAYLOR
JOTH
SAMPSON
LUCE AVENUE
TRAINING STATION ROAD
MALBONE ROAD

Attraction
Important Building
Park
Main Road
Other Road
Path
i Information
Railway

Narragansett Bay

Goat Island

Hunter House

Wanton-Lyman-Hazard House

Gateway Visitors Center
Museum of Newport History

Trinity Episcopal Church

Touro Synagogue

Old Colony House

Newport Art Museum

Old Stone Mill

Newport Congregational Church

Rough Point

Redwood Library & Athenaeum

International Tennis Hall of Fame

Kingscote

Newport Harbor

Conanicut Island

The Elms

N

Fort Adams State Park

JACKSON ROAD

Brenton Cove

WELLINGTON AVENUE
NARRAGANSETT AVENUE

HARRISON AVENUE

LINCOLN DR

HARRISON AVENUE
HARRISON AVENUE

WICKHAM ROAD

RUGGLES AVENUE

Chateau-sur-Mer

The Breakers

National Museum of American Illustration

Castle Hill Lighthouse

RIDGE ROAD
CASTLE HILL AVE
CASTLE HILL ROAD

Ballard Park

BRENTON ROAD

Newport Country Club

Lily Pond

OCEAN AVENUE

Almy Pond

The Mansions

Rosecliff

Beechwood

Marble House

WINANS AVE
COMMONWEALTH AVE
ATLANTIC AVENUE
HARRISON AVENUE

OCEAN AVENUE

Brenton Point State Park

Gooseberry Island

Land's End

Belcourt Castle

Rhode Island Sound

covers the history of tennis, and the original 13 courts are America's only competition grass courts available for public play.

The Mansions

Collectively, the city's paramount attraction consists of eight open-to-the-public 'summer cottages'. Six are maintained by the Newport Preservation Society:

The Breakers, *Ochre Point Ave*, emulating a 16th-century Italian palazzo, was built for railroad tycoon Cornelius Vanderbilt in 1895. **Chateau-sur-Mer**, *Bellevue Ave*, a shipping magnate's abode dating from 1852, exemplifies full-blown mid-Victorian architecture. A 1901 extravaganza resembling a French château, **The Elms**, *Bellevue Ave*, was the summer residence of a Pennsylvania coal-mining magnate. An 1839 Gothic Revival spread, **Kingscote**, *Bellevue Ave*, was built for the George Noble Jones family of Savannah, in Georgia. Inspired by the Grand and Petit Trianons at Versailles, William K Vanderbilt's 1892 **Marble House**, *Bellevue Ave*, cost a then-outrageous $9 million. Terracotta **Rosecliff**, *Bellevue Ave* (1902), with its 22 bedrooms, heart-shaped staircase and Newport's biggest private ballroom, was modelled on Versailles' Grand Trianon by Stanford White, the era's most sought-after architect.

Three additional mansions can be visited: **Beechwood** belonged to William Backhouse Astor and his wife, the grande dame of 1890s Newport society. Offers the liveliest tour, with costumed actors re-enacting the mansion's colourful life in the Gilded Age. Sixty-room **Belcourt Castle**, another little Vanderbilt getaway, sports the first-ever indirect lighting, installed by Thomas Edison in 1894. **Rough Point**, mansion of the legendary heiress Doris Duke, is one of the few with its original – and breathtaking – furnishings and art collections.

Museum of Newport History

Overviews of colourful local history and accomplishments can be found here through artefacts, displays, dioramas, paintings, photographs, decorative arts, cinema, interactive computers and videos. The 1762 Brick Market building, an attraction in its own right, was designed by Peter Harrison, architect of the Redwood Library.

Naval War College Museum

As the name implies, this museum covers global maritime warfare, with emphasis on US Navy exploits on Narragansett Bay. Collections include ship models and photographs of World War II sea battles. Also displayed is the first American torpedo, made in Newport in 1869.

Newport Art Museum

The main building is the main attraction: the former Grisold mansion of 1864, a stick-style Victorian house designed by celebrity architect Richard Morris Hunt. The art collection leans heavily towards 19th- and 20th-century Americana, including paintings by Winslow Homer and Fitz Hugh Lane.

Sidebar

ⓘ The Mansions $$
For days, times and individual or combination admittance prices at the six maintained by the **Preservation Society of Newport County**
tel: *(401) 847-1000*;
www.newportmansions.org.
Regarding the other two, call ahead for opening times and prices:
Beechwood *580 Bellevue Ave*; tel: *(401) 846-3772*;
www.astors-beechwood.com.
Belcourt Castle *657 Bellevue Ave*; tel: *(401) 846-0669*; *www.belcourtcastle. com*.

Rough Point *680 Belleview Ave*; tel: *(401) 849-7300*; *www. newportrestoration.org* (tours by reservation only, ask at Visitors Center).

Museum of Newport History $
Brick Market at 120 Thames St; tel: *(401) 841-8770*; *www. newporthistorical.org*. Open Mon and Wed–Sat 1000–1700, Sun 1300–1700.

Naval War College Museum *Coasters Island, 686 Cushing Rd (US Naval base)*; tel: *(401) 841-4052*. Open Mon–Fri 1000–1600; Jun–Sept Sat and Sun 1200–1600.

Newport Art Museum $ *76 Bellevue Ave*; tel: *(401) 848-8200*;
www.newportartmuseum.org. Phone ahead for seasonal hours.

🏛 Newport Congregational Church *Cnr Spring & Pelham Sts; tel: (401) 849-2238. Open to visitors summer Tue and Thur 1000–1200.*

Old Colony House *Washington Sq; tel: (401) 846-2980. Open summer Mon–Sat 1000–1600, Sun 1200–1600. Free admission.*

Old Stone Mill *Off Bellevue Ave between Mill & Pelham Sts.*

Redwood Library & Athenaeum *50 Bellevue Ave; tel: (401) 847-0292; www.redwoodlibrary.org. Open Mon–Sat 0930–1730. Free admission.*

Newport Congregational Church

Even if you're an atheist, look inside to admire the breathtaking interior, all of it – floor-to-ceiling, including opalescent windows – the masterwork of American art nouveau maestro John La Farge.

Old Colony House

A 'hallowed hall' of American patriotism, where General Washington and the French Comte de Rochambeau planned the civil-war-winning Battle of Yorktown – also where the legislature denounced its allegiance to King George III on 4 May 1776, making Rhode Island the first colony to declare independence. One of Rhode Island's two original Gilbert Stuart portraits of George Washington is here. The other hangs in the Rhode Island State House (*see page 161*).

Old Stone Mill

Flimsy legend has it that Norse Vikings erected this oddity – made of clamshell mortar and stones – long before Columbus crossed the Atlantic. Less carried-away theorists date what was probably a farmer's grain silo and windmill closer to 1660.

Redwood Library and Athenaeum

No, this oldest US library (1747) isn't constructed of redwood; it's named after its founder, Abraham Redwood. Peek inside the reading room to imagine frequent patrons Edith Wharton and Henry James scribbling on their manuscripts. The portrait gallery includes six by Gilbert Stuart, and a full-length statue of George Washington stands out the front. Turn toward the building's left side to see a portion of the chain formerly extended across the Hudson at West Point, New York, thwarting upriver passage of the enemy British warships.

Touro Synagogue
85 Touro St;
tel: (401) 847-4794;
www.tourosynagogue.org.
Open Sun–Fri 1000–1600.
Fri religious services 1800
winter, 1900 summer; Sat
services 0900.

Trinity Episcopal
Church *Queen Anne Sq;*
tel: (401) 846-0660. Open
Mon–Fri 1000–1300; Sun
services 0800, 1030.

Wanton-Lyman-Hazard
House $ *17 Broadway; tel:*
(401) 846-0813. Open
Thur–Sat 1000–1600, Sun
1300–1600 in summer.

Below
Spring Street antiques

Touro Synagogue
Dedicated in 1763 for stature as North America's first Jewish house of worship. Another of Peter Harrison's architectural commissions, this one is a Georgian-style beauty.

Trinity Episcopal Church
Patterned after those designed in Britain by Christopher Wren and in use since 1726. Queen Elizabeth II and the Archbishop of Canterbury attended services here during America's 1976 bicentennial. Look out for pew No 81, where George Washington sat, also No 66, where the Vanderbilts prayed.

Wanton-Lyman-Hazard House
Newport's oldest restored dwelling, dating from 1675, exemplifies American-style Jacobean architecture, with fine furnishings and an 18th-century herb garden. Site of the inflammatory Stamp Act Riot of 1765, a pivotal event leading to American independence.

Entertainment

Refer to listings in the *Newport Daily News (www.newportdailynews.com)* and the free *Newport This Week* tabloid.

Sundry nightspots along Thames St pack 'em in for jazz, rock, rhythm 'n blues, even karaoke sing-alongs. The town's cheeriest Irish pubs are **O'Brien's**, *501 Thames St; tel: (401) 849-6623*, and **Sabina Doyle's**, *359 Thames St; tel: (401) 849-4466*. **The Red Parrot**, *348 Thames St; tel: (401) 847-3800*, is an 'in' spot for cool jazz.

Annually during the third week in August, Newport's **Jazz Festival** is famously big, showcasing fusion and modern jazz at **Fort Adams State Park**; *tel: (401) 841-0707*. It's the same location and phone number for early August's **Folk Music Festival**.

Two boat piers have become buzzing retail bazaars: **Bannister's Wharf** and **Bowen's Wharf**. Nearby **Brick Market Place** encompasses gift and souvenir shops, galleries and clothing boutiques. You'll find more such establishments along Thames St, and a Bellevue Ave shopping mall is situated where 'Mansion Row' begins. **Spring St** exudes small-scale mercantile charm with shops devoted to such items as antiques, pottery, quilts and ship models. **The Coop**, *99 Spring St; tel: (401) 848-2442*, is a crafts cooperative. Antiques and fine-art dealers occupy an 1894 heavyweight, the **Armory**, *365 Lower Thames St; tel: (401) 848-2398*.

ⓘ Newport County Convention & Visitors Bureau *23 America's Cup Ave, Newport;* tel: (800) 976-5122 or (401) 849-8048; www.GoNewport.com

Same location for the **Gateway Visitors Center**, where facilities include direct-access accommodation bookings.

ⓘ South County Tourism Council *4808 Tower Hill Rd, Wakefield;* tel: (800) 548-4662 or (401) 789-4422; www.southcountyri.com

⊘ Newport is 75 miles from Boston, 25 miles from Providence. To reach the city, choose scenic routes on either side of Narragansett Bay; both entail toll-bridge crossings. In town, be prepared for crowded traffic conditions during summer high season.

Ⓟ Anticipating midsummer traffic jams, savvy drivers opt for the 24-hour car park alongside downtown's Gateway Visitors Center.

Ⓠ Downtown Newport is squeezed between Washington Sq on the north and Memorial Blvd on the south. From there, the longest and swankiest section of Bellevue Ave's 'Mansion Row' runs due south. Bellevue Ave, in turn, leads to a sensational Ocean Drive loop around the tip of Aquidneck Island. City-wide transport is provided by **Rhode Island Public Transit Authority** (RIPTA) buses; tel: (401) 781-9400.

Accommodation and food

Because Newport is a small city (population around 30,000) on a point of land, you can count on staying close to or right on some part of its waterfront. Lodgings run from slick hotels to bed & breakfasts tucked away on neighbourhood side streets. In addition to the free booking service at the Visitors Center, there's no charge for bookings by **Taylor-Made Reservations**; *tel: (800) 848-8848 or (401)848-0300; www.citybythesea.com*

Ocean Coffee Roasters $ *22 Washington Sq; tel: (401) 846-6060.*

Brick Alley Pub & Restaurant $–$$ *140 Thames St; tel: (401) 849-6334.* Eat heartily but cost-effectively.

The Black Pearl $$ *Bannister's Wharf; tel: (401) 846-5264.* Seafood.

Christie's $$ *Christie's Landing; tel: (401) 847-5400.* Harbourside ambience and seafood menus.

Elizabeth's Café $$ *404 Lower Thames St; tel: (401) 846-6862.* Antique-filled café known for its English adaptation of seafood bouillabaisse.

La Forge Casino Restaurant $$ *186 Bellevue Ave; tel: (401) 847-0418.* Dine in the pub or on the covered porch overlooking the Tennis Hall of Fame's Horseshow Piazza grass court.

Francis Malbone House $$ *392 Thames St; tel: (800) 846-0392 or (401) 846-0392; www.malbone.com.* Like living in a colonial house museum without the visitor ropes, but with all the comfy mod cons – feather pillows, king-sized beds and sumptuous breakfasts.

Adele Turner Inn $$–$$$ *93 Pelham St; tel: (800)-845-1811 or (401) 847-1811; fax: (401) 848-5850; www.adeleturnerinn.com.* A luxurious B&B – rooms are beautifully furnished. Afternoon teas or wine and food pairing events are sure to ruin your dinner.

Castle Hill Inn $$–$$$ *590 Ocean Dr; tel: (888) 466-1355 or (401) 849-3800; www.castlehillinn.com.* A real Newport mansion overlooking the sea. The estate is beautifully transformed into an inn with even more luxuries than the original owners enjoyed here – and an excellent restaurant.

The Cheeky Monkey $$–$$$ *14 Perry Mill Wharf; tel: (401) 845-9494; www.cheekymonkey.com.* Serves really creative and delicious foods and encourages guests to share so everyone gets a taste.

Mill Street Inn $$–$$$ *75 Mill St; tel: (800) 392-1316 or (401) 849-9500; www.millstreetinn.com.* A 19th-century mill building that has become an all-suite hotel.

Newport Harbor Hotel & Marina $$–$$$ *49 America's Cup Ave; tel: (800) 955-2558 or (401) 847-9000; www.newporthotel.com*

Newport firsts

Newport claims many US 'firsts', including the first post office; first public library; first synagogue; first golf tournament (1895); first polo match (1876); first tennis championships; first rollerskating rink; first street (Pelham) to be illuminated by gaslights; first use of indirect electric lighting (for Belcourt Castle, installed by Thomas Edison in 1894); first jail sentence for speeding in a car (issued in Newport by Judge Darius Baker in 1904). Newport also lays claim to being the US first luxury resort community.

Newport Bay Club & Hotel $$$ *337 Thames St; tel: (401) 849-8600; www.newportbayclub.com.* Overlooks the yacht harbour.

White Horse Tavern $$$ *Marlborough/Farewell Sts; tel: (401) 849-3600.* Splurge at Newport's priciest and New England's oldest restaurant (cooking since 1687). Beef Wellington and Châteaubriand are specialities, as is high-calorie triple chocolate silk pie.

Suggested tour

Total distance: 10–12 miles.

Time: Whole day for full enjoyment, mixed with walking and driving or partially by public transport.

Starting at the **Gateway Visitors Center** ❶ on America's Cup Ave, do a harbourfront walk, poking into the shopping and boat-dock wharves. At the America's Cup Ave/Lower Thames St junction, backtrack to stroll along shop- and restaurant-filled Thames St, bringing you to Queen Anne Sq and its landmark, **TRINITY EPISCOPAL CHURCH** ❷. Go back to Washington Sq, site of **OLD COLONY HOUSE** ❸ and (nearby on Broadway) **WANTON-LYMAN-HAZARD HOUSE** ❹. From the square, head up Touro St in Newport's

Right
Marble House, on Bellevue Avenue, built for William Vanderbilt in 1892

ⓘ **Hunter House $**
  54 Washington St;
  tel: (401) 847-1000; www.
  newportmansions.org. Open
  daily 1000–1700.

The America's Cup

Newport remains virtually synonymous with the America's Cup, the world's most prestigious yacht-racing trophy. Its history dates from 1851, when the *America* recorded the fastest time while sailing around the Isle of Wight, in England. Subsequently, the York Yacht Club put together a remarkable string of consecutive US victories, beating every America's Cup challenger between 1870 and 1980. Newport became internationally known by hosting the races from 1930 to 1983.
  Since then, the home-port honours have been dominated by such 'Down Under' locations as Perth and Auckland, but Newport continues to host dozens of regattas annually, plus each September's International Boat Show, with the harbour filled with sleek sailing craft during warm-weather seasons. Two-time America's Cup winner *Courageous* is Flagship of the memorabilia-filled **Museum of Yachting $** *Fort Adams State Park; tel: (401) 847-1018; www.moy.org. Open May–Oct daily 1000–1700.*

Historic Hill ❺ neighbourhood, thereby reaching **TOURO SYNAGOGUE ❻**, then onward towards a right turn at Bellevue Ave, reaching the **REDWOOD LIBRARY ❼**, **ART MUSEUM ❽** and, centred on a park, the **OLD STONE MILL ❾**. Meander amid side streets in this vicinity, graced with rows of Early American houses.

Bellevue Ave's swanky segment begins where that thoroughfare meets Memorial Blvd. First comes the **INTERNATIONAL TENNIS HALL OF FAME ❿**, then the fabled 'summer cottages'. At Webster St, deviate a block from Bellevue Ave to see Cornelius Vanderbilt's **THE BREAKERS ⓫** on Ochre Point Ave. Also consider an oceanside **detour**: the **Cliff Walk ⓬**, extending 3½ miles from **Easton's Beach ⓭** southward to **Land's End ⓮**.

Bellevue Ave ends at Ocean Ave, whereupon you'll undoubtedly require transportation for the very scenic 7-mile Ocean Ave–Ridge Rd–Harrison Ave loop around the tip of Aquidneck Island – via **Brenton Point State Park ⓯**, **Castle Hill Lighthouse ⓰** and **Fort Adams State Park ⓱**. Harrison Ave, Halidon Ave and Wellington Ave meet Lower Thames St, so you've arrived back in downtown Newport.

Additional walking tour: The Point

This compact, walkable neighbourhood rivals Historic Hill for its abundance of 18th- and early 19th-century domestic architecture. Begin at the **Gateway Visitors Center ❶**; turn right on to Long Wharf St, right again on to Washington St, where **Battery Park ⓲** overlooks the bay and 1748 **Hunter House ⓳** contains an important collection of Colonial pewter and authentic Chippendale, Queen Anne and Hepplewhite furniture. Walk as far as Van Zandt Ave; return through The Point by way of Second St.

Also worth exploring

East Bay
Choosing Rte 138, drive 11 miles north through commercialised Middletown, then Portsmouth (*see Providence/Pawtucket, page 166*); cross the Sakonnet River bridge linking Aquidneck Island with **Tiverton**, where **Weetamoo Woods** has nature-hiking trails. Tiverton's Lawton Rd ends at **Fort Barton**, a Revolutionary War redoubt, now a park with river and bay panoramics. Head south via Rte 77, passing miles of stone fences and Nannaquaket Pond to **Tiverton Four Corners**, then along Pachet Brook Reservoir to arrive at **Little Compton**, an unspoiled hamlet clustered around a village green, church and cemetery. From Tiverton to Little Compton is 11 miles. Three miles south beyond Little Compton, Rte 77 ends at Sakonnet Harbor. At Little Compton's **Sakonnet Vineyards**, wines have such jaunty names as 'Eye of the Storm', 'America's Cup Red' and 'Spinnaker White'; *162 West Main Rd (off Rte 77); tel: (401) 635-8486; www.sakonnetwine.com*

Block Island Tourism Council
Water St, Block Island; tel: (800) 383-2474 or (401) 466-5200; www.blockislandinfo.com

Interstate Navigation Company *PO Box 482, New London; tel: (401) 783-4613 (in RI) or (860) 442-7891 (in CT); www. blockislandferry.com*

West Bay

From Newport, cross the 2-mile Newport Bridge (toll) to **Conanicut Island**, 9 miles long, 1 mile wide. **Jamestown** is the sole community, with appealing restaurants on Narragansett Ave and a resort hotel: **The Bay Voyage $$–$$$** *150 Conanicus Ave, Jamestown; tel: (401) 423-2100*. A north–south loop around the island via East Shore Rd and North Shore Rd features the **Conanicut Sanctuary** wildlife habitat, the 1789 **Jamestown Windmill**, standing in pastureland, clifftop **Fort Wetherill State Park** and a beach at **Mackerel Cove**. The 1856 **Beaver Tail Lighthouse** flashes signals from the island's southern tip.

Drive west across the Jamestown Bridge to reach Rhode Island's mainland; detour 3 miles north on Rte 1A to **Wickford**, where elm-shaded Main St leads to a boat harbour and has parallel rows of 18th-century clapboard dwellings and the oldest Episcopal church (1707) north of Virginia. Then backtrack via Rte 1A to **Narragansett Pier**, with elegant summer homes along Ocean Rd and a mile-long beach favoured by surfers. From there, drive 2 miles west to lively little **Wakefield**, then 5 miles on Rte 1 to Matunuck Beach Rd, your access to **Matunuck**, home of the May–Oct **Theater by the Sea**, in a converted barn at *364 Card's Point Rd; tel: (401) 782-8587*, and **Trustom Pond National Wildlife Refuge**, where a sand barrier shelters Rhode Island's only undeveloped salt pond. Here on the state's marshy south coast, **Block Island Sound** washes 20-plus miles of sheltered beaches.

Block Island

This 11-square-mile offshore haven has a year-round population of 850 or so; stoplights, parking meters and house numbers don't exist, and 25 per cent of the island is environmentally protected by the US Nature Conservancy. Car ferries operated by **Interstate Navigation Company** reach this 'Bermuda of the North' from Newport during summertime and year-round from Point Judith, RI, 12 miles away (also from New London, CT). **Old Harbor**, the arrival point, is a quaint village with Victorian-period hotels and laid-back eateries facing Block Island Sound.

Touring beyond Old Harbor by car or bicycle, the road opens on to grassy moors, bayberry shrubs, blackberry patches, rose bushes, salt marshes and freshwater ponds. Springtime brings countless daffodils into full bloom. Migratory birds travelling the 'Atlantic Flyway' make stopovers en route to South America. Four hundred miles of three-century-old stone fences criss-cross the terrain; sublime **Crescent Beach**, near Old Harbor, is 4$^1/_2$ miles long. The south-coastal **Mohegan Bluffs** – resembling West Ireland's Cliffs of Moher – tower above rocky coves. From the viewpoint, a wooden stairway clambers down to a pocket beach, and on the headland is brick **Southeast Lighthouse**. Ask at the Tourism Council for a Nature Conservancy trail map, detailing five walking pathways, exceeding 20 miles overall.

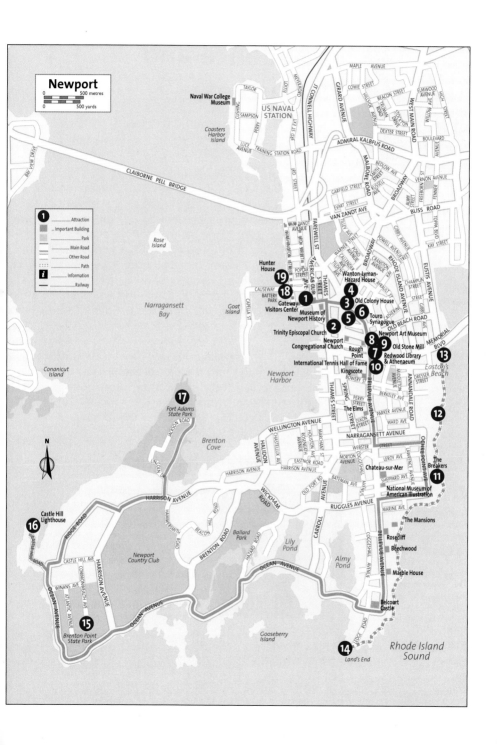

Newport

0	500 metres
0	500 yards

Naval War College Museum

US NAVAL STATION

Legend

- ① .... Attraction
- .... Important Building
- .... Park
- .... Main Road
- .... Other Road
- .... Path
- ℹ .... Information
- .... Railway

Coasters Harbor Island

CLAIBORNE PELL BRIDGE

Rose Island

Narragansett Bay

Goat Island

Conanicut Island

Hunter House ⑲

⑱ Gateway Visitors Center
① Museum of Newport History
Trinity Episcopal Church
②
Newport Congregational Church
Rough Point
International Tennis Hall of Fame
Kingscote
⑩

④
③ Old Colony House
⑥ Touro Synagogue
⑤
Wanton-Lyman-Hazard House
Newport Art Museum
⑧ ⑨ Old Stone Mill
⑦ Redwood Library & Athenaeum

⑬
Easton's Beach

Newport Harbor

The Elms

⑫

⑰
Fort Adams State Park

Brenton Cove

WELLINGTON AVENUE
HARRISON AVENUE

NARRAGANSETT AVENUE

Chateau-sur-Mer
National Museum of American Illustration
RUGGLES AVENUE

The Breakers ⑪

N

Castle Hill Lighthouse ⑯

Newport Country Club

Ballard Park

Lily Pond

Almy Pond

The Mansions
Rosecliff
Beechwood
Marble House

OCEAN AVENUE

Belcourt Castle

⑮
Brenton Point State Park

Gooseberry Island

Land's End ⑭

Rhode Island Sound

Providence and Pawtucket

Ratings

Architecture	●●●●●
Food and drink	●●●●●
Art	●●●○○
Museums	●●○○○
Shopping	●●○○○
Beaches	●○○○○
Children	●○○○○
Shopping	●○○○○

You won't find any such thing as a large city in America's smallest state. No matter, for Providence's abundant attractions and mini-metropolitan diversity are out of proportion to its modest size. Its stature is augmented by the prestige and energising influence of the excellent university and school of design. Furthermore, 'Little Rhody's' capital is a top-notch restaurant town, partly because the design school has a culinary curriculum and Johnson & Wales University educates future chefs.

Geographically, Providence qualifies as a waterfront city: the Seekonk River flows into the Providence River which, in turn, empties into breezy Narragansett Bay. But urban shorelines have mostly been industrialised for nearly 200 years – accounting for Pawtucket's inclusion in this chapter.

Getting there and getting around

ⓘ **Providence Warwick Convention & Visitors Bureau** (PWCVB) *1 W Exchange St, Providence; tel: (800) 233-1636 or (401) 456-0200; www.providencecvb.com.* The CVB's **Visitor Information Center** is located at 1 Sabin St (lower level of the Convention Center); *tel: (401) 751-1177.*

Right
Rhododendrons in a Providence front garden

Arriving and departing
Providence is 45 miles south of Boston via the I-95 motorway, so allow for about an hour's drive. You can also get here quickly from Boston via **Amtrak's Northeast Corridor rail service** (*tel: (800) 872-7245*). For air travel (from, for instance, Boston and Cape Cod), suburban Warwick's **T F Green Airport** is 8 miles from downtown Providence (*tel: (401) 737-8222*).

Getting around
After leaving the I-95, avoid misery by steering clear of inner downtown's tangle of narrow, one-way streets. Thanks to Providence's compact dimensions, it's easier to see the sights on foot and by using public transport. Kennedy Plaza near the Arcade is where **Rhode Island**

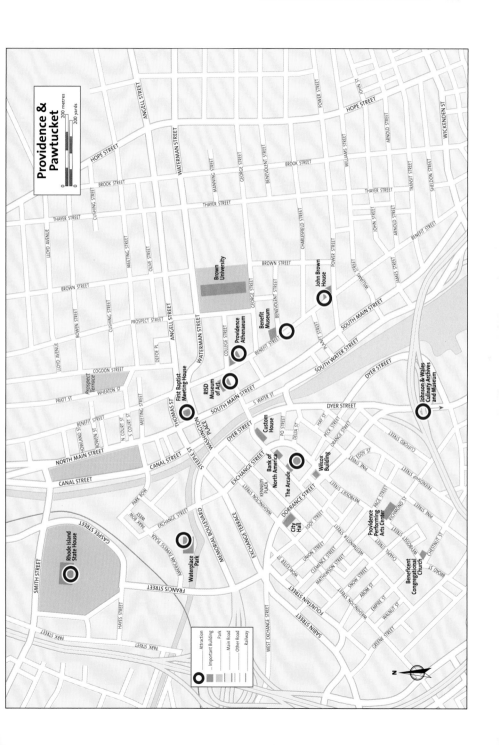

P For a long-term stay downtown, you're best advised to use downtown's Convention Center car park; entrances on West Exchange St. Other big-capacity car parks are on Eddy St downtown and alongside the Amtrak station on Gaspee St.

Public Transit Authority (RIPTA) buses fan out for service throughout the metro area, also to Newport *(tel: (401) 781-9400* for schedule and fare information). The third Thursday of each month year-round is Gallery Night, made convenient by the **ArTrolley**, free shuttle transport between galleries, museums, antiques shops and arts and performance events. *Service operates non-stop 1700–2100; tel: (401) 751-1177.*

Sights

The Arcade

Completed in 1828, this quaint little skylit enclosure qualifies as America's first indoor marketplace, the forerunner of thousands of look-alike shopping malls from coast to coast. A National Historic Landmark, the Greek Revival structure features massive Ionic columns, the original cast-iron railings and three tiers of speciality shops and inexpensive eateries.

Benefit St

East Side Providence's brick-paved 'Mile of History' – illuminated by antique gaslamps after nightfall – encompasses the US' most impressive

Benefit St On the East Side alongside College Hill. The street's most historic portion extends from Howland St south to James St.

First Baptist Meeting House 75 N Main St; tel: (401) 454-3418. Open Mon–Fri 0930–1530; guided tour following Sun 1100 worship service.

John Brown House $ 52 Power St; tel: (401) 273-7507. Tours Tue–Sat 1000–1700, Sun 1200–1600.

Johnson & Wales Culinary Archives & Museum $ 315 Harborside Blvd; tel: (401) 598-2805. Open Tue–Sun 1000–1700.

Providence Athenaeum 251 Benefit St; tel: (401) 421-6970. Open Mon–Thur 0900–1900, Fri and Sat 0900–1700, Sun 1300–1700. Free admission.

Rhode Island State House Enter at 82 Smith St; tel: (401) 222-2357. Free tours Mon–Fri 0830–1630.

concentration of clapboard Colonial bungalows and mansions, plus textbook examples of New England Federal and flamboyant Victorian styles, along with colonnaded terraces of houses from the Civil War period. Parallel and criss-crossing streets on higher ground – notably Prospect, Hope, Williams, Congdon, Charlesfield and Porter – exude comparable grace and charm. The fact that Benefit St was 'slum central' back in the 1950s makes it all the more remarkable today.

First Baptist Meeting House
Members of America's Baptist congregation regard this gem, topped by a 185ft steeple, as their 'Mother Church'. An outstanding example of Georgian architecture and design, the interior features a Waterford crystal chandelier dating from 1782.

John Brown House
The aggressive ship-owner merchants who made bundles of money during early America's China Trade spared no expense in building and furnishing lavish dwellings for themselves and their usually large families. Such is the three-storey pride of Power St, epitomising grand Georgian-style domestic architecture, fine craftsmanship and belongings befitting a refined late-18th-century lifestyle. The mansion is a veritable museum of porcelain, glassware, pewter, silver and paintings.

Johnson & Wales Culinary Archives & Museum
Known as the 'Smithsonian Institution of the food-service industry', this unique museum contains more than 300,000 items related to culinary arts and hospitality – including a gallery of chefs through the ages, cooking tools from as far back as the third millennium BC, 1000-year-old utensils, a bread ring from Pompeii(!), stoves from the past two centuries, silverware from famous hotels and restaurants, vintage menus, White House dinner invitations and much else connected with eating and drinking through the ages.

Providence Athenaeum
Benefit St's literary haven, a granite edifice built in 1828 to resemble a Greek Doric temple, is one of the country's oldest libraries and cultural centres. Creaky floorboards and cast-iron spiral stairs lead to shelves crammed with old and current books. Watch for announcements of exhibitions of volumes and folios from the Athenaeum's rare-book archives. As rumour had it, secluded in the recessed alcoves, Edgar Allan Poe and local socialite Sarah Helen Whitman conducted what was then regarded as a steamy courtship.

Rhode Island State House
Manhattan-based McKim, Mead and White – high society's pet architectural firm early last century – designed the gigantic state capitol, employing tons of white Georgia marble and a reported 15

Left
Providence Riverwalk and skyline

RISD Museum of Arts $ *224 Benefit St; tel: (401) 454-6500. Open Tue–Sun 1000–1700.*

Waterplace Park *North edge of downtown; midway between I-95 exit and Benefit St; downhill from Rhode Island State House, and a short walk from the Amtrak station. Free admission.*

million bricks. Visible from points near and far, this 1891–1904 hilltop whopper is crowned by one of the world's biggest self-supporting domes. Depending upon who's claiming what, the 250ft-high dome ranks second, third or fourth after that of St Peter's Basilica in the Vatican City. Displayed inside are regimental battle flags, cannons fired during Civil War combat and Rhode Island's original charter, on parchment and granted by King Charles II in 1663. Another attention-getter is Rhode Island-born Gilbert Stuart's portrait of George Washington. The head-and-shoulders engraving on US one-dollar bills comes from that full-length painting.

RISD Museum of Art

RISD: that's student shorthand for the Rhode Island School of Design. The museum's permanent collections total some 75,000 works of art, ranging from French Impressionist paintings by Cezanne and Manet to a 9ft Buddha; from a Kyoto temple to ancient Greek bronzes and Roman mosaics. There's also an unsurpassable assemblage of 18th-century American furniture and decorative art in the adjoining Pendleton House wing.

Waterplace Park

Four acres of ambitious urban redevelopment on what had been the city centre's decrepit backside, completed in 1994, this handsome open space features a stone-stepped amphitheatre overlooking a fountain-splashed pond, a Riverwalk and curved pedestrian bridges connecting the park with downtown's financial and theatre district. The amphitheatre has become a popular venue for open-air concerts and theatrical performances. A Venetian-type gondolier wearing a straw boater takes passengers on 45-minute rides, and on certain occasions a local artist lights up the summertime evening with a spectacle called Water Fire.

Entertainment

Providence packs a steady barrage of serious art and culture – both highbrow and mainstream, with much going on in the far-out realm of jazz, folk, blues, country and rock – into its relatively small size. To help you decide, consult the daily 'What's Happening' section of the *Providence Journal* (*www.projo.com*) and listings in two hip, alternative tabloids, the *Phoenix* and the *Nice Paper*.

A nationally acclaimed award-winner, the **Trinity Repertory Company** *201 Washington St; tel: (401) 351-4242*, produces classic and contemporary works. The extra-large stage at the **Providence Performing Arts Center** *220 Weybosset St; tel: (401) 421-2787*, accommodates roadshow versions of blockbuster Broadway musicals. **Veterans Memorial Auditorium** *1 Avenue of the Arts; tel: (401) 272-4862*, schedules ballet, opera and Rhode Island Philharmonic concerts.

Roger Williams

London-born Roger Williams arrived in Boston in 1631, became Anglican minister of the church in nearby Salem – and promptly fell foul of the no-nonsense Puritans who headed the Massachusetts Bay Colony. Not willing to tolerate his radically 'new and dangerous opinions' on religious freedom, they banished him to England in 1636. Instead, the renegade preacher ventured south. Finding a natural spring in what's now a downtown park, Williams drank the water, thankful for 'God's providence'. He purchased a tract of uninhabited land from the Narragansett Indians and established a plantation settlement dedicated to – of course – religious freedom. The smallest US state is still officially named the State of Rhode Island and Providence Plantation.

Groundwerx Dance Theater *95 Empire St; tel: (401) 454-4564*, concentrates on offbeat, cutting-edge choreography. **Brown University's Stuart Theater** *on campus, 77 Waterman St; tel: (401) 863-2838*, is a venue for visiting performers and student productions, as is **Rhode Island College's Roberts Auditorium** *600 Mount Pleasant Ave; tel: (401) 456-9765*. **AS220** *95 Mathewson St; tel: (401) 831-9327*, is an arts centre consisting of a café performance space and two studios showing works of present-day Rhode Island painters and sculptors.

During the second weekend in June, a **Festival of Historic Houses** (**$**) house and garden tour is sponsored by the **Providence Preservation Society** *21 Meeting St; tel: (401) 831-7440*.

Accommodation and food in Providence

The **PWCVB** *(tel: (800) 233-1636 or (401) 274-1636)* is a reliable source of updated lodging listings in all price ranges, but cannot make reservations on your behalf.

Providence has an impressively large number of very good restaurants where courageous young chefs habitually distance themselves from traditional New England cooking. Two dozen Italian–American trattorias and cafés draw visitors to the Federal Hill neighbourhood, bounded by Broadway and Atwells Ave.

Right
Rhode Island State House

Above
The oyster bar at Hemenway's in Providence

Blackstone Valley Tourism Council
175 Main St, Pawtucket; tel: (800) 454-2882 or (401) 724-2200; www.tourblackstone.com

Bristol County Chamber of Commerce *654 Metacom Ave, PO Box 250, Warren; tel: (888) 278-9948 or (401) 245-0750.*

Trinity Brewhouse $ *186 Fountain St; tel: (401) 453-2337.* Brew-pub serving inexpensive meals.

Union Station Brewery $ *36 Exchange Terrace; tel: (401) 274-2739.* Meals plus their house brand of beer and ale.

Café Nuovo $$ *1 Citizens Plaza; tel: (401) 421-2525.* Indoor and outdoor seating overlooking the Riverwalk. They serve Caribbean, Asian and US Southwest meals.

Federal Reserve $$ *66 Dorrance St; tel: (401) 737-3783.* A former bank lobby, complete with a turn-of-the-century vault, sets the tone for contemporary New England dining.

Hemenway's $$ *121 South Main St; tel: (401) 351-8570.* International seafood galore in the restaurant, plus an oyster bar.

Neath's New American Bistro $$ *262 S Water St; tel: (401) 751-3700.* Recommended for grilled steaks and spit-roasted chicken.

New Rivers $$ *7 Steeple St; tel: (401) 751-0350.* A classy bistro atmosphere for fusion cuisine with worldwide influences.

Old Court Bed & Breakfast $$ *144 Benefit St; tel: (401) 751-2002.* Advantageously situated on the 'Mile of History'. Originally the rectory for St John's Church.

Gilbert Stuart

Gilbert Stuart, whose depiction of George Washington appears on all US one-dollar bills, was born in 1775 in a humble grist mill in Saunderstown, a rural hamlet 30 miles south of Providence. Shipping off to London as a young man, he studied art under Sir Joshua Reynolds and Benjamin West. Back on his native soil, Stuart made his mark as the nation's most celebrated painter of well-known personages; the first six US presidents and each of their wives (except Thomas Jefferson's) posed for him. The prolific Rhode Islander produced at least 10 look-alike George Washington portraits. The full-length painting that hangs in the Rhode Island State House (see page 161) is one of two acknowledged 'dollar-bill Washingtons'. The other is a head-and-shoulders likeness on view in Boston's Museum of Fine Arts (see page 46). Yet another of Stuart's full-length GW portrayals can be seen in Connecticut – in Hartford's Old State House (see page 115).

For further insights, visit the **Gilbert Stuart Birthplace** $ *Between Rtes 1 and 1A, Saunderstown; tel: (401) 294-3001; www.gilbert-stuart.org. Open Apr–Oct Thur–Mon 1100–1600.*

Providence Biltmore $$ *11 Dorrance St; tel: (800) 843-6664 or (401) 421-0700; www.providencebiltmore.com.* Built in 1922, but completely renovated and offering spacious suites in a central location.

State House Inn $$ *11 West Park St; tel: (401) 351-6111.* Built circa 1889, this inn stands a few blocks from the state capitol building.

Al Forno $$$ *577 S Main St; tel: (401) 273-9760.* The city's best-known restaurant, acclaimed for its eclectic menu and excellent wood-grilled food.

Pot Au Feu $$$ *44 Custom House St; tel: (401) 273-8953.* Providence's haute cuisine French restaurant, with arguably the best wine list in town.

Westin Providence $$$ *1 West Exchange St; tel: (800) 228-3000 or (401) 598-8000; www.westinhotels.com.* In a central location downtown (which the locals call Downcity).

Suggested tour

Total distance: 4–5 miles (additional 8 miles for the zoo).

Time: Half day or full day. Since streets leading from downtown to College Hill are quite steep, you might prefer driving up that way or relying on public transport – and a car is needed to reach the zoo. So consider dividing your sightseeing into a downtown walking segment and a motoring segment for more distant touring. Major free-access points of interest are on the city-centre **Banner Trail**, marked by colour-coded flags for easy orientation.

Begin at Kennedy Plaza, Downcity's hub. On the plaza's Dorrance St side, view **City Hall** ❶, dating from 1874, a Second Empire-style showpiece of civic architecture. From there, walk north, crossing Exchange Terrace and Memorial Blvd to **Waterplace Park** ❷, then uphill further north via Francis and Hayes Sts to visit the **RHODE ISLAND STATE HOUSE** ❸. Return downhill, crossing Exchange St's bridge to reach Westminster St downtown; stroll through the **ARCADE** ❹. Several of the city's other landmark buildings face Weybosset St – including the **Providence Performing Arts Center** ❺ in a Beaux Arts movie palace from 1928, the 1857 **Custom House** ❻, the 1875 **Wilcox Building** ❼ with its cast-iron façade, the 1856 Italian palazzo-style **Bank of North America** ❽ and the early 19th-century **Beneficent Congregational Church** ❾. Parallel Westminster St also has notable examples of varied 19th-century motifs.

Cross one of the Riverwalk bridges to reach the East Side. **BENEFIT ST** ❿, with its rows of 200 historic houses and buildings, is two blocks from any bridge. First, though, head north; turn right on Meeting St, then left onto Congdon St to reach **Prospect Terrace** ⓫, site of a statue of Rhode Island's 'founding father' Roger Williams and an ideal

🄰 Roger Williams Park & Zoo $ *Rte 1000 Elmwood Ave, Exit 17; tel: (401) 785-9450 (park), (401) 785-3510 (zoo). Park open daily 0900–1900. Zoo open daily Nov–Mar 0900–1600; Apr–Oct 0900–1700.*

Slater Mill Historic Site $ *67 Roosevelt Ave; tel: (401) 725-8638. Phone ahead for opening days and times, depending upon the season.*

Blithewold Mansion & Gardens $ *101 Ferry Rd, Bristol; tel: (401) 253-2707. Grounds and arboretum open daily year-round, 1000–1700. Mansion open mid-Apr–late Sept Tue–Sun 1000–1600.*

Herreshoff Marine Museum $ *1 Burnside St, Bristol; tel: (401) 253-5000. Open May, Sept & Oct Mon–Fri 1300–1600, Sat and Sun 1100–1600; Jun–Aug daily 1000–1600.*

🄱 The East Bay Bike Path *extends 14½ miles between East Providence and Bristol.*

🄲 Colt State Park/Coggeshall Farm Museum *Off Poppasquash Rd, Bristol; tel: (401) 253-9062. Park open daily year-round. Farm Museum open summer 1000–1800, winter 1000–1600 (closed Jan). Free admission.*

Green Animals Topiary Gardens $ *Cory's Lane, off Rte 114, Portsmouth; tel: (401) 683-1267. Open May–Oct daily 1000–1700.*

perch for panoramic views of Downcity. Back on Benefit St, go uphill via either Waterman or George Sts to the campus of **Brown University ⑫**, an Ivy League academic stalwart founded in 1764. Thayer St is the liveliest College Hill thoroughfare for bookstores, clothing shops and student-budget eateries. Going nine blocks south on that street (or the same direction on Benefit St) gets you to hip and trendy **Wickenden St ⑬** in Providence's Fox Point neighbourhood (George M Cohan, old-time vaudeville's song-and-dance trouper, was born here). The street's determined funkiness is evident on telephone poles, festooned with goofy sculptural concoctions.

Roger Williams Park & Zoo, covering 435 acres on the southern edge of Providence, is far enough away from downtown to be considered a special-interest side trip. The park comprises waterways and formal gardens, greenhouses, boathouse, Planetarium and Museum of Natural History. The US' third-oldest zoo (1872) is widely regarded as the best in New England.

Northern Detour: From downtown Providence, drive 4 miles north on the I-95 motorway to Exit 27 for **Pawtucket**. At that city's Main St/Roosevelt St intersection, you'll come upon the riverside **Slater Mill Historic Site**, where in 1793 Yankee tinker Samuel Slater designed and built the US' first reliably operative textile-manufacturing machinery, thereby launching the American Industrial Revolution. The adjacent park is a pleasant picnic spot.

Southern detour: Leaving Providence via the I-95 motorway, head south to the I-95/I-195 intersection; turn right on to Rte 114 for a 6-mile East Bay drive to **Warren**, worth a stop if you'd like to browse through that town's numerous antiques shops. Continue 4 miles to photogenic **Bristol**, where an attraction overlooking Narragansett Bay is **Blithewold Mansion & Gardens**, former summer estate of a Pennsylvania coal baron, well known for its arboretum including a Japanese water garden, exotic bamboo stands and the biggest Redwood tree east of the Rockies. Elsewhere in town, the **Herreshoff Marine Museum** focuses on the boat works where eight America's Cup defenders were built (1893–1934) and includes the America's Cup Hall of Fame. Also in Bristol is **Colt State Park** (spacious picnic grounds) and its **Coggeshall Farm Museum**, a working farmstead relying solely on 18th-century agricultural methods, including seasonal sheep-shearing and maple sugaring.

Continuing southwards, drive 6 miles through bayside pastureland to **Portsmouth** via the Mount Hope Bridge (toll) if you'd like to tour **Green Animals Topiary Gardens**, a great place for children, with sculpted animals, birds and geometric forms made from English boxwood, as well as rose arbours, formal flower beds and a museum of Victorian toys.

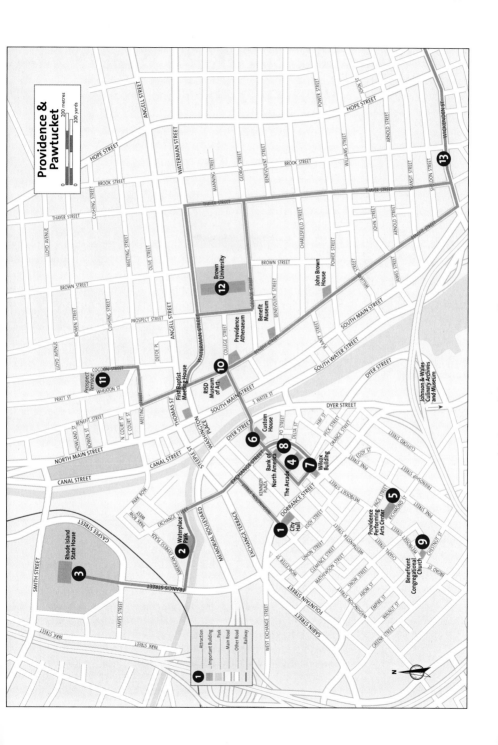

Providence &
Pawtucket

0 ___ 200 metres
0 ___ 200 yards

1 Attraction
Important Building
Park
Main Road
Other Road
Railway

N

Rhode Island
State House **3**

Waterplace
Park **2**

City Hall **1**

The Arcade
Bank of
North America **4**
8
7
Wilcox
Building

Custom
House **6**

Providence
Performing
Arts Center **5**

Beneficent
Congregational
Church **9**

RISD
Museum
of Art

First Baptist
Meeting House

11 Prospect
Terrace

10

Providence
Athenaeum

Benefit
Museum

Brown
University **12**

John Brown
House

13

Johnson & Wales
Culinary Archives
and Museum

Ratings

Arts and Culture	●●●○○
History	●●●○○
Museums	●●●○○
Nature/ scenery	●●●○○
Shopping	●●●○○
Food and drink	●●○○○
Beaches	●○○○○
Children	●○○○○

The Southern Green Mountains

Some of Vermont's most idyllic towns lie nestled in the rolling Green Mountains and the valleys that separate them from the Taconics in neighbouring New York state. From stylish Manchester to tiny Weston, isolated in its mountain vale, these towns blend scenery with history and the great outdoors.

Miles of hiking and walking trails criss-cross the mountains, and towering forests are reflected in lakes and streams, the latter often spanned by covered bridges. The region is small but filled with the elements that exemplify Vermont: green-clad mountains, skiing, white churches, country stores, summer theatres, craft studios and historic homes.

This is one of Vermont's most popular corners, especially in autumn, when maple trees paint the mountainsides red. Expect the heaviest traffic on Rte 9, especially in Wilmington, and around Manchester Center.

ARLINGTON

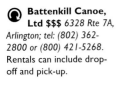

Battenkill Canoe, Ltd $$$ *6328 Rte 7A, Arlington; tel: (802) 362-2800 or (800) 421-5268.* Rentals can include drop-off and pick-up.

Nearly 200 notable buildings line the streets of the Historic District, for many years the summer home of the artist Norman Rockwell, who used its residents as models for his popular magazine covers. Some of these works are shown in the **Norman Rockwell Exhibition**, on Rte 7A (*tel: (802) 375-6423*).

Just north of town are the **Fisher-Scott Memorial Pines**, on Red Mountain Rd, $^1/_4$ mile from Rte 7a, a rare stand of huge first-growth trees that were here when the first colonists settled. Nearly all New England's 'King's Pines' were cut as masts for the Royal Navy or in later lumbering, making this hillside a rare sight. Leave your car to see the Battenkill Valley from the river itself, stopping at **Battenkill Canoe, Ltd** to rent a canoe. The narrow river offers easy paddling through farms and forests and under a covered bridge in West Arlington.

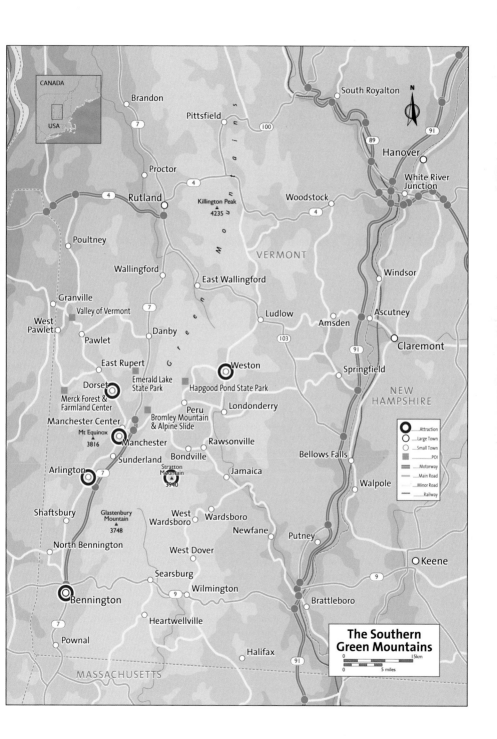

The Southern Green Mountains

BENNINGTON

ⓘ Bennington Chamber of Commerce *Rte 7A; tel: (802) 447-3311 or (800) 229-0252.*

ⓗ Bennington Battle Monument $ *Rte 9, Old Bennington; tel: (802) 447-0550; www. historicvermont.org/ bennington. Open mid-Apr–Oct daily 0900–1700.*

Bennington Museum $ *W Main St (Rte 9), Bennington; tel: (802) 447-1571; www. benningtonmuseum.com. Open daily 1000–1700.*

Park-McCullough House and Gardens $ *1 Park St (off Rte 67A), North Bennington; tel: (802) 442-5441; www. parkmccullough.org. Open mid-May–Oct daily, guided tours on the hour 1000–1500.*

The 306ft obelisk you see from nearly any point in town is the **Bennington Battle Monument** in Old Bennington. The battle it commemorates is considered the turning point of the Revolution, causing General Burgoyne to rethink and abandon his northward thrust to divide the colonies in half. A lift takes you to the top for views of three states.

Old Bennington is worth seeing, even for those to whom the monument is less than a shrine, since it is filled with finely restored colonial-era homes surrounding an 1806 church where Robert Frost is buried. You will hear this poet quoted throughout New England in such phrases as 'but I have promises to keep, and miles to go before I sleep'.

On Rte 9 on the way to the monument is **The Bennington Museum**, known for its collections of Early American glass, pottery, quilts and for the work of the primitive artist Grandma Moses. A poignant statue of President Lincoln stands in front.

Bennington Potters, in an old wooden factory building, is the outlet for seconds of high-priced Bennington Pottery, manufactured on site. Dinnerware, bakeware and accessories of first quality sell here at lower-than-gift-shop prices; seconds are a real bargain.

In nearby North Bennington is the Victorian **Park-McCullough House**, among America's earliest Second Empire homes. In the grounds are a carriage barn, striking flower gardens and a playhouse that is a miniature version of the mansion.

Accommodation and food in Bennington

Alldays and Onions $ *519 E Main St; tel: (802) 447-0043; www.alldaysandonions.com; open Mon–Sat for lunch and dinner, Sun brunch*

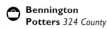 **Bennington Potters** *324 County St, Bennington; tel: (802) 447-7531 or (800) 205-8033; www.benningtonpotters.com. Open daily.*

0900–1300, Sat breakfast 0730–1030. Healthy wholegrains hold their sandwiches, but the pastries are positively sinful.

Blue Benn Diner $ *Rte 7; tel: (802) 442-5140.* An old-fashioned diner atmosphere, but with a modern twist to the menu.

Greenwood Lodge $ *Rte 9; tel: (802) 442-2547; www.campvermont. com/greenwood.* An American Youth Hostel high on a mountainside, close to hiking trails.

Four Chimneys Inn & Restaurant $$–$$$ *21 West Rd, Rte 9; tel: (802) 447-3500; fax: (802) 447-3692; www.fourchimneys.com.* In the heart of historic Old Bennington, this inn dates back to 1783, with spacious airy rooms, several with fireplace and patio. A full breakfast is included and the restaurant is known for fine dining.

DORSET

Dorset Summer Theatre Festival *104 Cheney Rd; tel: (802) 867-5777; www. dorsettheatrefestival.org. A professional company performing since 1929, late Jun–early Sept.*

The Dorset Historical Society Museum *Rte 30 at Kent Hill Rd; tel: (802) 867-0331. Open mid-Apr–mid-Oct Wed 1000–1200, Thur–Sat 1000–1400; mid-Oct–mid-Apr Wed–Fri 1000–1200, Sat 1000–1400. Call to confirm hours. Free admission.*

Emerald Lake State Park *Rte 7, East Dorset; tel: (802) 362-1655; www.vtstateparks.com. Open late May–mid-Oct. Free admission.*

In 1785, North America's first commercial marble quarries opened in Dorset, cutting over 15¹/₂ million cubic ft of stone in the next 150 years, including the marble for the Jefferson Memorial in Washington, DC.

Note the odd stones bordering the J K Adams workshop, south of the village. These are leftovers from cutting the columns for the New York Public Library. Shop here for chopping boards, salad bowls and other fine woodenware sold at factory prices.

Borrow the excellent **Dorset Walking Tour** recording from the **Historical Society Museum**, along with a book of photographs to help you spot each building. The museum displays local pottery, farm implements and old photographs of the quarries.

Stop to buy Vermont cheddar (but don't tell them Vermont didn't invent it!) from Peltier's Store (on Rte 30 in the centre of the village), which has been there for generations. Next door is the unique United Church, built entirely of marble, and decorated with beautiful stained-glass windows of local landscapes, by Tiffany Studios.

On the opposite side of the 'marble mountain', in East Dorset, **Emerald Lake State Park** surrounds a scenic lake with a swimming beach, picnic grounds and campsite with tent pitches and caravan park. A free booklet describes the half-mile nature trail; a steeper trail climbs 1¹/₂ miles to a natural bridge over a narrow gorge.

Accommodation and food in Dorset

Inn at West View Farm $–$$ *Rte 30; tel: (802) 867-5715 or (800) 769-4903; www.innatwestviewfarm.com.* A rambling, comfortable country inn – and an outstanding dining room, where the meals contain locally-grown ingredients.

Opposite
North Bennington's Park-McCullough House, built in the Second Empire style

The Marble West Inn $–$$ *Dorset West Rd; tel: (802) 867-4155 or (800) 453-7629; www.marblewestinn.com.* In a fine old home with antique features.

MANCHESTER

ℹ **Manchester & the Mountains Chamber of Commerce**
5046 Main St, Suite 1;
tel: (800) 362-4144;
www.manchestervermont.net

🏛 **Robert Todd Lincoln's Hildene $**
Rte 7A, Manchester Village;
tel: (802) 362-1788;
www.hildene.org. Open mid-May–mid-Oct for house tours; grounds open year round, cross-county skiing trails in winter.

Mount Equinox Skyline Drive $$ Rte 7A,
Manchester Center;
tel: (802) 362-1113;
www.equinoxmountain.com/skylinedrive. Open May–Oct.

American Museum of Fly Fishing $ Rte 7A,
Manchester Center; tel: (802) 362-3300; www.amff.com.
Open daily 1000–1600.

⛳ **Golf Club $$$** Rte 7a; tel: (802) 362-3223;
www.equinoxresort.com

⚒ **Ethan Allen Days**
Held at the meadows, Hildene, Manchester; tel: (802) 362-1788;
www.hildene.org/html/ethan_allen_days.html. Mid-June, with re-enactments of Revolutionary War skirmishes.

Southern Vermont Craft Fair $ Hildene Meadows, Manchester Village; tel: (802) 425-3399. Late July, with 250 craftsmen.

Don't confuse Manchester Village with Manchester Center. The former, to the south, is a genteel village with marble pavements and impeccable large homes surrounding the elegant pillared façade of The Equinox, Vermont's only vintage grand hotel. In the rarefied atmosphere of 'the village', wealthy New Yorkers once spent idyllic summers, and you'll still see their mansions here.

The best known is **Robert Todd Lincoln's Hildene**, built in 1902 by Abraham Lincoln's eldest son. Along with the family rooms, the servants' quarters and the surprisingly small kitchen are open to view. Carefully restored gardens overlook the valley, and are at their best in June and July.

Vermont State Craft Center is among the Equinox Shops, facing the hotel. Displayed and sold here are works by the state's top craftsmen in all media, from pottery and wood to weaving and fine art prints. Behind the craft centre, the **Golf Club** flows down the hillside, surrounded by mountain views. It's a championship course, beautifully designed.

Mount Equinox rises behind the hotel, and it can be yours without any exertion at all, via the 5-mile **Mount Equinox Skyline Drive**, a toll road to the top. Below, the **American Museum of Fly Fishing** covers the sport through history, with mementoes of fishing greats and examples of fine hand-crafted equipment.

Just north is Manchester Center, a succession of upmarket **factory outlet malls** selling off-price goods (some seconds, most simply last season's over-stocks). Most of the outlets sell designer and brand-name clothing and home decorations.

Accommodation and food in Manchester

The Inn at Ormsby Hill $$ *Rte 7A, 1842 Main St; (802) 362-1163 or (800) 670-2841; www.ormsbyhill.com.* Antique-furnished mansion built by Lincoln's law partner, now a classy inn with double whirlpool baths, fireplaces and a full-course breakfast served in a magnificent dining room.

The Equinox $$–$$$ *Rte 7A, Manchester Village; tel: (802) 362-4700 or (800) 362-4747; www.equinoxresort.com.* Golf course, spa and outdoor activities for guests; fine dining in the formal dining room or Scottish-themed restaurant.

STRATTON MOUNTAIN

ⓘ Stratton Mountain
Bondville; tel: (802) 277-2200 or (800) STRATTON; www.stratton.com

Ⓗ Sun Bowl Ranch $$
Stratton Mountain; tel: (802) 293-5837; www.sunbowlranch.com. Trail rides mid-Jun–mid-Oct 0900–1700.

Not just a ski area, Stratton Mountain presents a year-round sports and activities schedule, as well as a faux-Alpine village filled with shops, cafés and restaurants. The **Stratton Gondola** operates in good weather year-round to take visitors to the top of southern Vermont's tallest mountain. Golf, tennis, mountain biking and hiking are all within easy reach of this self-contained resort.

Sun Bowl Ranch offers trail rides on horseback, along with rides in their farm wagon drawn by two big Belgian draught horses. Sleighs replace the wagons on winter weekends.

WESTON

◓ The Vermont Country Store
657 Main St; tel: (802) 362-8460; www.vermontcountrystore.com. Open daily 0930–1730.

The remote location in a mountain valley doesn't keep visitors from finding this lovely little town that clusters around its village green and bandstand. The main draw is **The Vermont Country Store**, not a replica or a restoration, but a real original, complete with high button shoes, pot-bellied stove and rows of penny candy jars. But it's more than a museum, with carefully chosen natural fibre clothing, quality housewares, foods and necessities of gracious country living. The **Farrar-Mansur House** is a colonial tavern, which combines with an

Above left
Shopping at The Equinox

Right
The Vermont Country Store

Farrar-Mansur House and Mill Museum $ *On the Green, Weston; tel: (802) 824-8190. Open Jun–mid-Oct daily 1000–1600.*

Weston Playhouse $$ *On the Green; tel: (802) 824-5288; www.westonplayhouse.org. Presents Broadway musicals late June–early September, with pre-theatre dinner and cabaret afterwards.*

adjacent watermill to form the town's historical museum. Displays include antique furnishings, clothing, utensils and firearms.

Elsewhere in town are craft studios and shops selling quilts, braided rugs, pottery and needlework.

Accommodation and food in Weston

Colonial House Inn and Motel $ *287 Rte 100; tel: (802) 824-6286 or (800) 639-5033; www.cohoinn.com.* A homely B&B-cum-motel, with home-cooked meals and a bakery famed for its peach pie.

Village Sandwich Shop $ *Tel: (802) 824-5477; open daily.* Sandwiches, light meals and pastries.

The Inn at Weston $$ *636 Main St (Route 100); (802) 824-6789; www.innweston.com.* Two well-restored mid-1800s houses sit among gardens in the village centre, one of them furnished with antiques and handmade quilts. The excellent dining room (dishes such as quail stuffed with chestnuts, cranberries and cornbread will be on the menu) is open to the public, but advance booking is wise. Ask to tour the 670-square-foot orchid greenhouse to see the hundreds of different species and hybrids.

Ethan Allen and the Green Mountain Boys

Colonial Royal Governors of New Hampshire and New York each had a defensible claim, under their patents from the King, to what is now Vermont. New Hampshire granted over 100 towns to settlers who carved farms out of the forests.

When New York sheriffs began driving these farmers from their homes and giving their farms to New Yorkers, brothers Ira and Ethan Allen, a feisty pair of New Hampshire grant-holders, rallied a band of rowdy riflemen who sent the 'Yorkers' packing. The Allens had their eye on a separate province. These 'Green Mountain Boys' maintained a stand-off until the two sides temporarily joined forces during the American Revolution.

After the Green Mountain Boys captured Fort Ticonderoga, they were hailed as heroes of the Revolution. But this was just a skirmish in their larger battle, which they won with the formation of an independent Republic of Vermont and finally, in 1791, acceptance of Vermont as the 14th state.

Suggested tour

Total distance: 130 miles; 144 miles with detour.

Time: 3 hours' driving. Allow a day for the main route, with or without detour, more if you intend to stop at attractions. The route

Above
Autumn colour at Wardsboro, near Stratton Mountain

can be broken into two loops, each beginning in Manchester. Those with limited time should concentrate on Bennington or Manchester.

Links: To reach the Berkshires Route (*see page 102*), follow Rte 7 south from Bennington to Williamstown, Massachusetts.

To join the Upper Connecticut Valley Route (*see page 196*), take Rte 9 from Bennington over the Green Mountains and scenic Hogback Mountain to Brattleboro. This is a winding, but good road that literally goes over the tops of two mountain ranges; the best views are from Hogback. To the Lake Champlain and Northern Green Mountains Route (*see page 178*), follow Rte 7 or the more scenic Rte 30 north from Manchester to Middlebury.

Route: From downtown **BENNINGTON** ❶ follow Rte 7A to Rte 67A into North Bennington to the Park-McCullough House. Rte 67 connects to Rte 7A, which travels north to **ARLINGTON** ❷ and **MANCHESTER** ❸. From Manchester Center, follow Rte 30 to **DORSET** ❹ continuing through East Rupert to Pawlet.

🅘 **Vermont Marble Museum $** *52 Main St, Proctor (7 miles N of Rutland); tel: (800) 427-1396 or (802) 459-2300; www.vermont-marble.com. Open mid-May–Oct daily 0900–1730.* Learn about how the state's prime building and carving stone was used to create some of the USA's most famous landmarks, such as Washington's Jefferson Memorial. Stunning presentation covers the science, technology and art of building with marble.

Detour: At East Rupert, turn left (west) onto Rte 315, which leads to the **Merck Forest** ❺ and **Farmland Center** ❻ (*tel: (802) 394-7836; www.merckforest.com*). This working organic farm has miles of walking trails, including a labelled nature trail, along with farm animals, a maple sugar house and frequent special family programmes on farming and the environment. Take Rte 153 north to **West Pawlet** ❼. Almost the whole town was built in the 1890s to house stone-workers for the newly-opened quarries. These gabled American Queen Anne homes have decorated porches and trims. Each has a slate roof, and you'll see why, when you pass right through the slate quarry at the north end of the village. When Rte 153 meets Rte 30, turn right (south). The **Valley of Vermont** ❽, through which you've been driving, is enclosed by the Taconics on the west and the Green Mountains on the east. Here the valley widens into fertile farmlands;

ⓐ Mach's Market
Pawlet; tel: (802) 325-3405. Open Mon–Sat 0700–1830, Sun 0800–1230.

Marion Waldo McChesney Potter *746 Lilly Hill Rd, Pawlet; tel: (802) 325-3238; www.marionwaldomcchesney.com*

ⓝ Bromley Mountain
$$ Manchester Center; tel: (802) 824-5522; http://summer-bromley.com

ⓒ The Silas Griffith Inn *$$ Main St, Danby; tel: (802) 293-5567 or (888) 569-4660; www.silasgriffith.com.* Beautifully restored architectural details – such as an oval 'pocket' doorway and embossed tin ceilings – fill the Victorian mansion. In the garden gazebo is a hot-tub.

ⓡ Adams Farm *$ 15 Higley Hill, Wilmington; tel: (802) 464-3762; www.adamsfamilyfarm.com.* Visit the farm if you have children to see the baby animals and learn how a Vermont farm works. Pony and hay rides can be arranged there.

ⓟ Parking in Wilmington is available, off Rte 100, just south of the Rte 9 crossing.

Welsh Slate

The slate quarries in this part of Vermont and neighbouring New York State drew many skilled slate workers from the valleys of Wales. To this day the area is heavily populated with those of Welsh ancestry.

the several large farms with barns and silos dotting the landscape are still a vital part of Vermont's rural heritage.

Rte 30 intersects Rte 133 in the centre of Pawlet, where the **pottery studio ⑨** of Marion Waldo McChesney is in the ground floor of the brick house opposite **Mach's Market ⑩**. The store itself is worth a visit to see the cabinet in the back, whose glass top looks straight down into the chasm cut by the benign-looking **Flower Brook ⑪**.

From Pawlet take Rte 133 until you reach a right fork signposted 'Danby'. Follow this unnumbered road through Danby Four Corners, and over the hill.

You literally drop into **Danby ⑫**, once home of the author Pearl Buck, who wrote *The Good Earth*. She worked tirelessly to keep the little town alive as the marble industry declined and is largely responsible for saving its 19th-century buildings.

Go south on Rte 7, past **Emerald Lake State Park ⑬** to **MANCHESTER CENTER ⑭** where you take Rte 11 towards Peru. **Bromley Mountain ⑮**, 6 miles east of **MANCHESTER CENTER**, was one of the earliest ski resorts, built in the 1930s. A family-friendly area, it has trails for all skills and minimal ski lift queues. You can get your thrills on the mountain even in the summer, by riding the two-third-mile **Alpine Slide ⑯**, the longest alpine ride in the country.

In Peru, follow signs to **Hapgood Pond State Park ⑰** *(tel: (802) 362-2307)*, where you will find a swimming beach, tent pitches and walking trails. From here you will enjoy a real Vermont experience: travelling on an unpaved road to **WESTON ⑱**. If you shun gravel roads, return to Rte 11 and go north to Weston on Rte 100.

Leave Weston on Rte 100 south to Rawsonville, then take Rte 30 west to Bondville, and the entrance road to **STRATTON MOUNTAIN ⑲**. Returning to Manchester Center on Rte 30, you can reach your starting point in Bennington via fast, limited-access Rte 7.

Also worth exploring

Instead of returning to Manchester on Rte 30, continue down the winding, scenic Rte 100, 'The Skier's Highway', to **Wardsboro**, **West Dover** and **Wilmington**. At West Dover you will pass **Mount Snow Ski Area** (*www.mountsnow.com*), with its attendant businesses and lodgings. In Wilmington, at the crossroads of Rte 100 and Rte 9, are dozens of gift shops catering to tourists, in addition to some of the worst weekend traffic you are likely to see in the state. Rte 9 west takes you back to Bennington, through the **Green Mountain National Forest**.

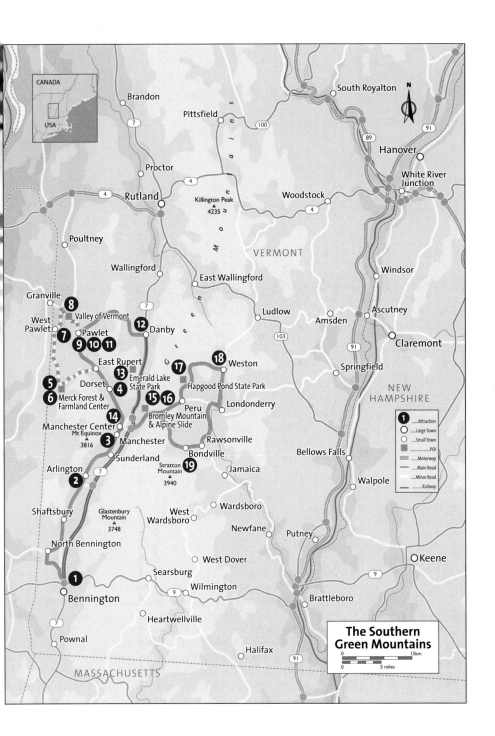

Lake Champlain to the Northern Green Mountains

Ratings

Nature and scenery	●●●●○
Art and culture	●●●○○
Food and drink	●●●○○
Shopping	●●●○○
Beaches and watersports	●●○○○
History	●●○○○
Museums	●●○○○
Children	●○○○○

Caught between the Green Mountains and the broadest part of huge Lake Champlain, Burlington rises from its marina to the University of Vermont's stately hilltop buildings. In between is downtown, centred on lively Church St, with shops, entertainment and abundant restaurants. From sailing on the lake to skiing in the mountains, Burlington has it.

Nearby Shelburne Village is an assemblage of historic buildings (even a steamboat that once plied the lake) filled with collections of Early Americana.

Expect steep, narrow, winding roads if you travel over the passes at Smugglers Notch or Appalachian Gap, but otherwise only gentle hills as you explore these routes.

BURLINGTON

ⓘ Lake Champlain Regional Chamber of Commerce 60 Main St; tel: (802) 863-3489; www.vermont.org

ⓐ Whistling Man Schooner Co $$ Pier, Burlington; tel: (802) 598-6504; www. whistlingman.com

The lake is a part of downtown Burlington, bordered by a greensward of parks and a cycling/footpath leading to beaches, marinas and playgrounds. **Church St Marketplace** is alive with activity, especially in good weather, when the pedestrian-only street is filled with pavement cafés, vendors, music and people. At any time of year shops, restaurants and entertainments keep things busy, and a free shuttle connects the area to the college and waterfront.

Departing from the waterfront are sailing tours of Lake Champlain on board the schooner **Whistling Man**. For an inexpensive alternative 'cruise' you can ride the ferry (except in winter) from Burlington to Port Kent, New York, on the opposite side of the lake. Another ferry runs from Charlotte, south of Shelburne. For a more conventional

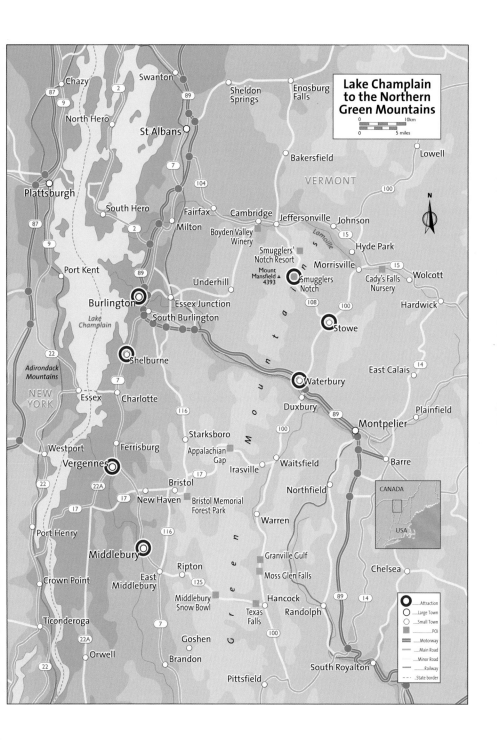

Lake Champlain to the Northern Green Mountains

0   10km
0   5 miles

Chazy
87
9
North Hero
Swanton
2
89
Sheldon Springs
Enosburg Falls
St Albans
7
104
Bakersfield
VERMONT
100
Lowell
Plattsburgh
87
9
South Hero
2
Milton
Fairfax
Cambridge
Jeffersonville
Johnson
15
Hyde Park
Port Kent
89
Underhill
Boyden Valley Winery
Smugglers' Notch Resort
Mount Mansfield 4393
Lamoille
Morrisville
Cady's Falls Nursery
15
Wolcott
Burlington
Essex Junction
Smugglers' Notch
108
100
Hardwick
Lake Champlain
South Burlington
Stowe
22
Shelburne
Waterbury
East Calais
14
Adirondack Mountains
7
Essex
Charlotte
116
Duxbury
Plainfield
NEW YORK
89
Montpelier
Westport
Ferrisburg
Starksboro
100
Barre
Vergennes
Appalachian Gap
17
Irasville
Waitsfield
CANADA
22
Bristol
22A
New Haven
17
Bristol Memorial Forest Park
Northfield
USA
Port Henry
116
Warren
Middlebury
Ripton
Granville Gulf
Moss Glen Falls
Chelsea
Crown Point
East Middlebury
125
Middlebury Snow Bowl
Texas Falls
Hancock
89
14
Ticonderoga
7
Goshen
Randolph
100
22A
Orwell
Brandon
South Royalton
22
Pittsfield

Mountains

Green

N

Attraction
Large Town
Small Town
POI
Motorway
Main Road
Minor Road
Railway
State border

Spirit of Ethan Allen III $ *Spirit Landing, Burlington Boathouse, College St; tel: (802) 862-8300; www.soea.com*

ECHO at the Leahy Center for Lake Champlain $ *Beside Boathouse, 1 College St; tel: (802) 864-1848; www.echovermont.org. Open daily 1000–1700.*

Ethan Allen Homestead $ *Signposted from North Ave and Rte 127; tel: (802) 865-4556; www. ethanallenhomestead.org. Open mid-May–mid-Oct Thur–Sat 1000–1600, Sun 1300–1600.*

Right
The Ethan Allen Homestead

excursion, board the *Spirit of Ethan Allen III* for a narrated dinner or sunset cruise. Children will have fun learning about the lake and the creatures that live there through interactive exhibits in **ECHO at the Leahy Center**.

Two centuries away from busy downtown is the **Ethan Allen Homestead**, where visitors learn about this cheeky Vermonter and his exploits during the Revolution. Along with the farmhouse, you can tour interpretative trails in the Wetlands Nature Center, identifying the abundant bird and plant life with a self-guiding brochure.

Accommodation and food in Burlington

Penny Cluse Café $–$$ *169 Cherry St; tel: (802) 651-8834; www.pennycluse.com.* Locals will likely suggest this downtown favourite for breakfast, for its heaped plates of fried potatoes, omelettes, biscuits (like a scone) and gravy, and stacks of pancakes. It's open for lunch, too, until 1500.

Trattoria Delia $–$$ *152 St Paul St (City Hall Park); tel: (802) 864-5253; www.trattoriadelia.com.* Unforgettable Mediterranean dining.

Butler's $$ *70 Essex Way, Essex Junction; tel: (802) 764-1413.* Many cuisines blend creatively at the hands of New England Culinary Institute students.

The Essex $$ *70 Essex Way, Essex Junction; tel: (802) 878-1100; www.vtculinaryresort.com.* Stylish hotel and full service spa run by New England Culinary Institute.

Historic Inns of Burlington $$–$$$ *www.historicinnsofburlington.com:* **Lang House** *360 Main St; tel: (877) 919-9799; www.langhouse.com.* **Willard Street Inn** *349 South Willard St; tel: (800) 577-8712; www.willardstreetinn.com.* Walk to everything in downtown Burlington from either of these charming turn-of-the-century inns. Luxurious accommodations, memorable breakfasts.

MIDDLEBURY

ℹ Chamber of Commerce 2 Court St; tel: (802) 388-7951; www.midvermont.com

🏛 The Sheldon Museum $ 1 Park St; tel: (802) 388-2117; www.henrysheldonmuseum.org. Open Jun–Oct Tue–Sat 1000–1700, Sun 1300–1700; rest of year Tue, Wed & Fri 1300–1700, Thur 1300–2000.

UVM Morgan Horse Farm $ 2½ miles from downtown Middlebury, at 74 Battell Drive (Rte 23), Weybridge; tel: (802) 388-2011; www.uvm.edu/morgan

🐎 Middlebury Snow Bowl Rte 125, Ripton; tel: (802) 388-4356. Ski lift $$$.

⛰ Summer Festival on the Green Tel: (802) 462-3555; www.festivalonthegreen.com. A mid-July week of performing arts.

College campus and town flow together seamlessly, each with its share of historic architecture. Marble is so plentiful in Vermont that you'll see entire buildings made of it, such as **The Sheldon Museum**, an 1829 merchant's home and the oldest community museum in the United States. Ten rooms show furniture, art and daily life of early Vermont. To see (and buy) fine contemporary craftwork, visit the **Vermont State Craft Center** (www.froghollow.org).

University of Vermont Morgan Horse Farm offers films on this remarkable breed and a chance to meet some horses in person during the tour.

Middlebury Snow Bowl is a unique, uncrowded place to ski, without the glitz, queues or high prices of many of its Vermont neighbours. Trails for Nordic skiers begin near the **Robert Frost Wayside Trail**, which leads to the cabin where the poet wrote for 22 summers.

Accommodation and food near Middlebury

Judith's Garden B&B $ 423 Goshen-Ripton Rd, Goshen; tel: (802) 247-4707. Guests get personal attention in a remote location amid gardens overlooking the Adirondack Mountains.

Chipman Inn $–$$ Rte 125, Ripton; tel: (802) 388-2390 or (800) 890-2390; www.chipmaninn.com. Payment for rooms in this historic home includes hearty breakfasts.

Blueberry Hill Inn $$–$$$ 32 Forest Rd, Goshen; tel: (800) 448–0707 or (802) 247-6735; www.blueberryhillinn.com. Berries and flowers fill the beautiful gardens; breakfast and dinner are included in the price of the rooms at this idyllic hideaway surrounded by Green Mountain National Forest.

SHELBURNE

🏛 Shelburne Museum $$ Rte 7; tel: (802) 985-3346; www.shelburnemuseum.org. Open late May–mid-Oct daily 1000–1700

Shelburne Farms $ Harbor Rd; tel: (802) 985-8686; www.shelburnefarms.org. Open daily mid-May–mid-Oct 0900–1730, mid-Oct–mid-May 1000–1700.

Ten miles south of Burlington, Shelburne is best known for the **Shelburne Museum**. Early New England quilts, painted tin and woodenware, roundabout horses, furniture, horse-drawn sleighs, carriages and entire buildings, even a covered bridge, lighthouse and the steamship SS *Ticonderoga* are among the 80,000 artefacts.

Baronial estates are not common in New England, which makes the grand barns and turreted farmyard at **Shelburne Farms** even more unexpected. On this 1400-acre working 'gentleman's farm' are gardens, historic barns, a children's farmyard where you can try milking a cow, and a dairy where cheese is made.

SMUGGLERS NOTCH

Smugglers' Notch Resort $–$$ *Rte 108, Smugglers Notch; tel: (802) 644-8851 or (800) 451-8752; www.smuggs.com.* Hotel or condos with kitchens, fireplaces and whirlpool tubs.

Boyden Valley Winery $ *Rtes 15 and 104; tel: (802) 644-8151; www.boydenvalley.com. Tours year-round Tue–Sun.*

Smugglers Notch Area Winter Carnival *Smugglers Notch; tel: (802) 644-8851;* early Feb. Nordic races, snow sculptures, food, snowshoe hikes and social events.

The road over Smugglers Notch is like no other in New England, so narrow that caravans are not allowed over it; they would be unable to manoeuvre the sharp turns between giant boulders that line its sides. Park between the stones and climb a short distance for sweeping views of Vermont, New York and Canada. Snow ploughs can't navigate the road, so it closes for the winter. On the other side from Stowe is **Smugglers' Notch Resort** (note that, for some reason, the resort name has an apostrophe whereas the area's doesn't). Smugglers' Notch is a self-contained resort with year-round sports facilities, including horse riding, kayaking, tennis, swimming and climbing. The skiing is superb. It is perfect for families, with many year-round programmes for children.

To the northwest is **Boyden Valley Winery**, set on a dairy farm, where they combine their own grapes, local berries and apples with maple syrup to make wines and cordials, along with hard cider.

STOWE

Apart from skiing, Stowe is also popular year-round for its shopping and restaurants. Crafts and handiwork dominate in the upmarket shops along Stowe's Main St, where the pace is relaxed and friendly.

Rent bicycles at **Mountain Sports** (*580 Mountain Rd; tel: (802) 253-7919*) to bike the paved 5¼-mile **Stowe Recreation Path** along the river, leading past lodging, dining, gardens and mountain vistas. Walkers, skaters and runners all enjoy the path.

In May–October Sundays 1100–1500, it leads past the **Stowe Farmers Market**, on Mountain Rd (*tel: (800) 24-STOWE*). Shop here

Above
Stowe, Vermont

Stowe Area Association *Main St;*
tel: (877) GO STOWE;
www.gostowe.com

Meadow Concerts
$$ *Trapp Family Lodge; tel: (877) GO STOWE; www.gostowe.com, www.vtmozart.org.* Late June–August; Vermont Mozart Festival late July.

Stoweflake Mountain Resort & Spa $$–$$$ *1746 Mountain Rd; tel: (802) 253-7355 or (800) 253-2232; in the UK: (0500) 892 522; www.stoweflake.com*

Topnotch Resort and Spa $$$ *4000 Mountain Rd; tel: (800) 451-8686; www.topnotchresort.com*

Vermont Ski Museum *1 South Main St; tel: (802) 253-9911; www.vermontskimuseum.org*

for locally produced picnic ingredients: freshly baked breads and goats' cheese, country sausage and fruits.

On Rte 108, near the ski area, is the short trail to **Bingham Falls**, one of the state's most beautiful. Above the falls look for potholes carved by swirling waters. For your own safety, and to protect fragile banks from further erosion, descend well away from the gorge's sides to view the falls from below.

A **Gondola Skyride $$** (*tel: (802) 253-3000; http://summer-stowe.com*) travels to the top of Mount Mansfield, Vermont's highest, for sweeping views and access to hiking trails, or you can drive to the summit on the 4¹/₂-mile Auto Road **$$**.

The **Trapp Family Lodge** (*www.trappfamily.com*), overlooking rolling meadows and mountains, is as much a part of Stowe as skiing itself. The hills are alive with the sound of music, all summer long, when the von Trapps host **Meadow Concerts** and the **Vermont Mozart Festival**. Bring a picnic and watch the sunset to music.

Take a look at the history of the sport that made Stowe a household word among skiers, at the **Vermont Ski Museum**, located in the 1818 town hall in the centre of the village. The building is on the National Register of Historic Places.

And if you're feeling stiff from a day's skiing, hiking or biking on the Recreation Path, Stowe has two high-quality spas, each of which has spa-and-stay packages or welcomes guests to day spa facilities. On the mountain is **Topnotch Resort and Spa**, and closer to the village is **Stoweflake Mountain Resort & Spa**. Both are also full-service resorts.

The Underground Railroad

From the first days of its statehood, Vermont prohibited slavery in its constitution. Abolitionist sentiment ran strong before the Civil War, and the state was a major conduit in the Underground Railroad. Several of the secret routes that carried escaped slaves to freedom in Canada followed Vermont rivers and mountain roads, over which slaves were transported, hidden under hay loads or in barrels labelled as everything from pork to molasses. Despite Federal law, which required courts to return slaves to their owners, many Vermont judges refused.

Accommodation and food in Stowe

Gracie's $ *1652 Mountain Rd; tel: (802) 253-8741; www.gracies.com.* Big burgers, sandwiches, generous dinners until 2400 daily.

The Gables $–$$ *1457 Mountain Rd; tel: (802) 253-7730 or (800) GABLES-1; www.gablesinn.com.* Warm and unpretentious family-owned inn with fireplaces, whirlpool tubs and mega-breakfasts. Restaurant $–$$ open to the public.

Green Mountain Inn $–$$ *Main St; tel: (802) 253-7301 or (800) 253-7302; www.greenmountaininn.com.* Canopy beds, whirlpool baths, terry robes, electric fireplaces, afternoon cider and fresh-baked cookies in the lobby.

Ten Acres Lodge $–$$ *14 Barrows Rd; tel: (802) 253-7638 or (800) 327-7357; fax: (802) 253 6589; www.tenacreslodge.com.* All mod-cons, but in a warm, inviting vintage Vermont farmhouse, with more rooms in a modern building just up the hill.

Right
Stowe landscape, looking towards Mount Mansfield

VERGENNES

🅘 Lake Champlain Maritime Museum
$$ *Basin Harbor Rd; tel: (802) 475-2022; www.lcmm.org. Open late May–mid-Oct daily 1000–1700.*

Rokeby Homestead $
Rte 7, Ferrisburg; tel: (802) 877-3406; www.rokeby.org. Open mid-May–mid-Oct Thur–Sun; tours 1100, 1230 & 1400.

Almost halfway between Burlington and Middlebury, Vergennes is one of the oldest towns in Vermont, and the smallest. Barely more than a mile square, it packs in a **Historic District** of 80 noteworthy buildings. In the basin below **Otter Creek Falls** the ships that prevailed at the Battle of Plattsburgh in 1814 were constructed.

This and other historical detail is provided at the **Lake Champlain Maritime Museum**, spread along the shore and into its waters. Interactive programmes for the public, which include boat-building workshops, are outstanding and are designed for all ages. Many of the boats there were recovered from the lake's floor. Blacksmiths and ship builders demonstrate, and exhibits tell tales of, the many shipwrecks and naval action during the War of 1812 with Britain. Sailing boats, rowing boats, canoes and kayaks are available for rent.

Rokeby Homestead is one of the few places in Vermont (or anywhere) with a well-documented history as a station in the Underground Railroad (*see page 183*). Written records of this clandestine network's activities were rarely kept, for fear of discovery and prosecution. Writer Rowland Robinson did keep records, and his home is now a museum chronicling this and other events in two centuries of a remarkable family's history.

Accommodation and food in Vergennes

Emerson Guest House $ *82 Main St; tel: (802) 877-3293; www. emersonhouse.com.* Comfortable Victorian home in downtown setting.

Roland's Place $–$$ *Rte 7 South, New Haven; tel: (802) 453-6309; www.rolands1796house.com.* Simply put, it's tops, with a French chef who values fresh local produce and farmed game. Open all year, serving dinner Thur–Sat and Sun brunch. A few charming rooms are also available for overnight guests.

Strong House Inn $$ *94 West Main St; tel: (802) 877-3337; www.stronghouseinn.com.* Beautifully restored Federal mansion overlooking the Adirondack.

WATERBURY

Ben and Jerry's Ice Cream Factory $
Rte 100; tel: (802) 846-1500. Open daily.

Cold Hollow Cider Mill $ *Rte 100, Waterbury Center; tel: (802) 244-8771; www.coldhollow.com. Open daily year-round 0800–1800 (until 1900 in summer).*

Green Mountain Coffee Roasters
Off Main St; tel: (888) 879-4627; www. greenmountaincoffee.com. Open Mon–Fri 0630–1700, Sat 0800–1300.

Free Thursday Concerts *Rusty Parker Memorial Park; tel: (802) 244-7352; summer only 1830.*

Most people come to Waterbury looking for the home of Vermont's favourite ice cream, at **Ben and Jerry's Ice Cream Factory**. If you haven't tried it, here's your chance not only to sample the stuff everyone raves about, but to see how it is made. Tours include samples.

At **Cold Hollow Cider Mill** you can watch the cider being pressed year-round, with free samples. Various apple products, including apple butter and cider jelly, as well as maple and other speciality foods, are sold, along with Vermont crafts, in the shop and bakery.

Waterbury has some fine Victorian buildings and a **Historical Society Museum** in the library building. It's a typical mix of local treasures, with a good collection of Berlin work, beading and handmade lace. Also downtown, **Green Mountain Coffee Roasters**, Vermont's coffee-of-choice, has a factory outlet store.

Accommodation and food in Waterbury

Grunberg Haus $–$$ *Rte 100, Duxbury; tel: (802) 244-7726 or (800) 800-7760; www.grunberghaus.com.* Rooms in an inviting Alpine chalet or cosy hillside cottages, all including sumptuous breakfast.

The Old Stagecoach Inn $–$$ *18 Main St (Rte 2); tel: (802) 244-5056 or (800) 262-2206; www.oldstagecoach.com.* Historic coaching stop with well-furnished rooms, genial hosts and fresh home-baked croissants. Wi-Fi is available.

Stowe Cabins $–$$ *Rte 100; tel: (802) 244-8533; www.stowecabins.com.* Modern, self-catering cabins, in pinewoods.

Michael's on the Hill $$–$$$ *Rte 100, Waterbury Center; tel: (802) 244-7476; www.michaelsonthehill.com.* Vermont-grown ingredients are on the inspired menus of the Swiss-born chef/owner. Plan dinner for sunset, since almost every table has a view.

Also worth exploring

The **Champlain Islands**, north of Burlington, stretch all the way to the Canadian Border. North of Colchester, take Rte 2 toward South Hero near **Sandbar State Park**. The landscape across the bridge is low, gentle farmland. Rte 2 passes **Grand Isle State Park** and **Knight Point State Park**, both with lakeshore beaches, and **Hyde Log Cabin**. Rte 129 leads to **St Anne's Shrine**, at the site of the first European settlement in Vermont, on **Isle La Motte**.

◖ **The Round Barn Farm** $$ *1661 East Warren Rd, Waitsfield;* tel: (802) 496-2276; fax: (802) 496-8832; *www.theroundbarn.com.* With an original round barn as its centrepiece, the inn offers stunning rooms and warm hospitality.

Shaker Barns

Round barns, now quite rare, were an invention of the Shakers. This religious group, whose members lived in farming communities, is credited with a number of inventions that made farming easier and more productive.

Suggested tour

Total distance: 140 miles; 158 miles with detours.

Time: 4 hours' driving. Allow 2 days for the main route, 2½ days with detours. Those with limited time should concentrate on Shelburne, Burlington, Smugglers Notch and Stowe.

Links: Follow Rte 7 south to Danby and the Southern Green Mountains Route (*see page 168*), or I-89 from Waterbury to Barre to join the Northeast Kingdom Route (*see page 188*).

Route: From **MIDDLEBURY** ❶ follow Rte 7 to **VERGENNES** ❷ and Ferrisburg ❸ with a detour at **Charlotte** ❹ to ride the ferry to Essex, New York and back.

Rte 7 continues through **SHELBURNE** ❺ to **BURLINGTON** ❻, with views east towards the **Green Mountains** ❼ and west over the lake to the **Adirondacks** ❽. From Burlington, follow Rte 15 through Essex Junction to Cambridge and to **Boyden Valley Winery** ❾. Follow Rte 15 alongside the **Lamoille River** ❿ to Jeffersonville ⓫. From here you can float through the scenic valley in a canoe, exploring the river environment during a Wetlands and Wildlife Tour with Green River Canoe. Guided tours include instruction for beginners. In Jeffersonville, Rte 108 leaves on its steep, winding route south over **SMUGGLERS NOTCH** ⓬ to **STOWE** ⓭.

Detour: In winter, or to avoid the notch in bad weather, continue on Rte 15 through **Johnson** ⓮ and **Hyde Park** ⓯ turning south on Rte 100 in Morrisville. Before the turn are acres of themed gardens at **Cady's Falls Nursery** ⓰. Rte 100 leads to Stowe.

Continue on Rte 100 to **WATERBURY** ⓱ and **Waitsfield** ⓲, home of a rare round barn at Round Barn Farm. In Irasville, Rte 17 heads over **Appalachian Gap** ⓳, 2300ft high at its dramatic summit on the spine of the Green Mountains. As you enter **Bristol** ⓴, notice the Lord's Prayer carved on a boulder beside the road.

Bristol is an attractive small town where, near the intersection of Rte 116 with Rte 17, you'll find **Bristol Memorial Forest Park** ㉑ with picnic sites overlooking a gorge and waterfalls. From Bristol, follow Rte 116 South to Rte 125 in East Middlebury, which leads back to the starting point in Middlebury.

Detour: Instead of climbing Appalachian Gap, continue on Rte 100 from Irasville through the wild cleft of **Granville Gulf** ㉒, past **Moss Glen Falls** ㉓, to Hancock. Follow Rte 125 past **Texas Falls** ㉔ and over the Green Mountains at Middlebury Gap, passing **Middlebury Snow Bowl** ㉕.

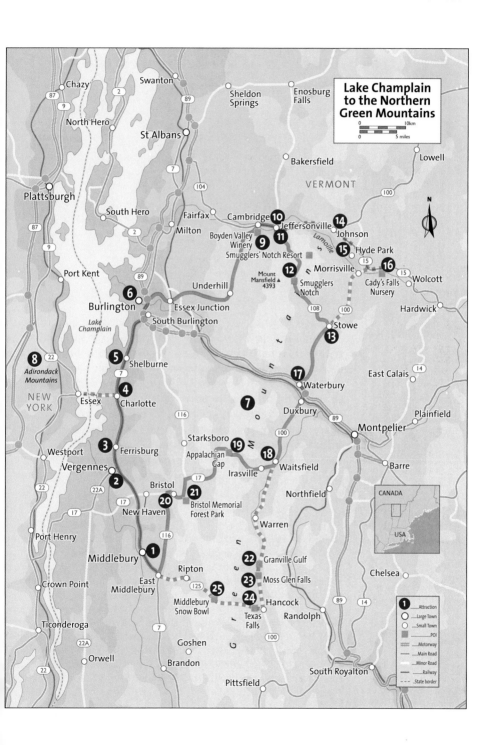

The Northeast Kingdom

Ratings

Nature/scenery	●●●●○
Arts and culture	●●○○○
Beaches/watersports	●●○○○
Children	●●○○○
Museums	●●○○○
Food and drink	●○○○○
History	●○○○○
Shopping	●○○○○

This remote corner of Vermont is rarely visited by tourists, so remains quiet and uncrowded. Covered bridges cross streams that have cut long narrow valleys through the hills, and in some areas the moose outnumber the people.

St Johnsbury is home to an entire hilltop of fine Victorian churches, homes and public buildings, which include a charmingly old-fashioned natural history museum. The subject is appropriate, since nature has blessed this region so abundantly, from the rich fine-grade granite of its bedrock to the wildlife that roams its woods and flies through its clean, clear air.

BARRE

Barre Opera House $ *City Hall; tel: (802) 476-8188; www.barreoperahouse.org.* A restored Victorian opera house with theatre, opera and classical concerts.

Rock of Ages $ *Websterville; tel: (802) 476-3119; www.rockofages.com. Open May–Oct Mon–Sat 0900–1700, Sun 1200–1700 (autumn Sun 0900–1730).*

Granite built Barre, literally and figuratively, and you can tour the world's largest granite quarry, the 450-ft deep **Rock of Ages**. Even the giant hills of tailings that surround its approach don't prepare visitors for the size of this man-made hole. Ride the shuttle to a working quarry; stone-cutting demonstrations complete the tour.

Barre's fine grade of granite is ideal for carving into monuments, and especially in the **Downtown Historic District** you will see public statuary, architectural ornamentation and even business signs made of granite. But nowhere will you see a finer collection than at **Hope Cemetery**, on Merchant St (Rte 14). Here the most skilled Italian stone carvers created monuments to their loved ones – and themselves. These range from lifelike figures and art deco designs to granite representations of everything from an aeroplane to a football.

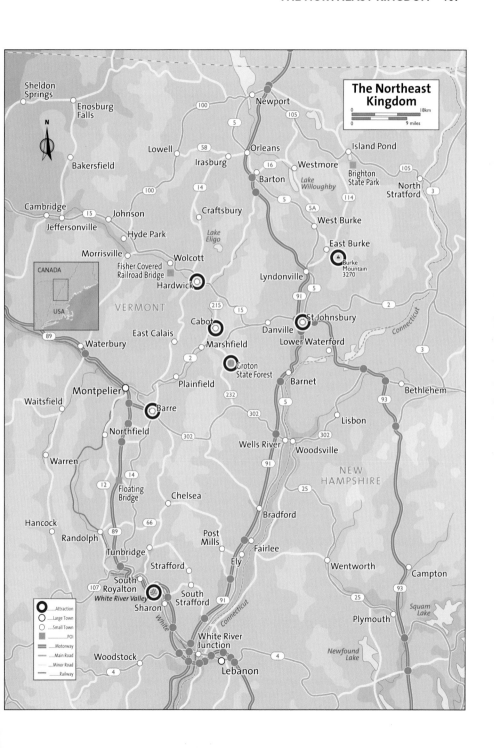

The Northeast
Kingdom

BURKE MOUNTAIN

Burke Mountain Ski Area *Mountain Rd, East Burke; tel: (802) 626-3305, (802) 626-7300 or (888) 287-5388; ski conditions (866) 496-1699; www.skiburke.com*

The Snack Shack $ *Rte 14; tel: (802) 479-5508.* Hamburgers, grilled hot dogs, sausage and hand-cut chips.

Northeast Kingdom Sled Dog Races *Eden Mountain Lodge, 1390 Square Road, Eden Mills; tel: (802) 635-9070; www.edendogsledding.com*

Bailey's & Burke Country Store (*Rte 114, East Burke; tel: (802) 626-9250; www.baileysandburke.com*) is a combination local general store and gift shop for tourists. Look here for Vermont crafts, picnic food and the mosquito repellent you'll need if you are hiking. A few café tables at the front offer a place to sit and enjoy their handmade sandwiches.

Overlooking town, **Burke Mountain** is a family ski area with a novice trail from the top of the mountain. It becomes **Burke Mountain Auto Road** when the snow melts, so you can enjoy the view any time of year. Cross-country ski trails traverse 50 miles of forest and meadows. Volkswalks are sponsored by the Kingdom Kickers, the area's very active Volkssporting group, which also sponsors an **Oktoberfest** at Burke Mountain.

Wildflower Inn spreads across a ridge with views over the mountains framed by perennial gardens. A barnful of baby animals, sleds for the sledding hill, a lighted skating rink, and sleigh- and hayrides are features of this small family-run resort/B&B. The outstanding dining room is open to the public.

The entire ridge was part of an 8000-acre farm. Drive further along Darling Hill Rd to see the mansion and several huge barns.

Accommodation and food around Burke Mountain

Above
Residents at the family-friendly Wildflower Inn

River Garden Café $–$$ *East Burke; tel: (802) 626-3514; www.rivergardencafe.com; open Tue–Sun year-round for lunch and dinner.* Has an eclectic menu.

Wildflower Inn $–$$ *Darling Hill Rd, Lyndonville; tel: (802) 626-8310 or (800) 627-8310; www.wildflowerinn.com.* One of the rare inns where children are not only welcome but positively doted upon. Kids' activities are available, but don't intrude; especially welcome are evening programmes that allow parents to enjoy fine dining while the kids watch movies. Dining room ($$) reservations advisable.

CABOT/HARDWICK

Perennial Pleasures *Brick House Rd, East Hardwick; tel: (802) 472-5104; www.perennialpleasures.net. Open late May–Sept Tue–Sun 1000–1700.*

Cabot Creamery *$ Main St (Rte 215), Cabot; tel: (800) 837-4261 or (888) 792-2268; www.cabotcheese.coop. Open Jun–Oct daily 0900–1700, shorter winter hours.*

Perennial Pleasures is the loving work of a professional restorer of almost-lost gardens. Painstaking research and searches for historically accurate plants led to the opening of a nursery to help others in similar quests.

The modern **Cabot Creamery** makes Vermont cheddar and other cheeses. After watching the process through glass windows on a tour, you can sample all their cheeses in the shop (you can also sample and buy without the tour).

Lamoille Valley Railroad, which once served the quarries of Hardwick, passes through **Fisher Covered Railroad Bridge** over the Lamoille River, the last covered railroad bridge still in use in the United States. There are picnic tables on the riverbank near the bridge.

Food in Cabot/Hardwick

Brick House *Perennial Pleasures, 2 Brick House Rd, East Hardwick; tel: (802) 472-5104; www.perennialpleasures.net.* Serves a lovely afternoon tea, by reservation.

GROTON STATE FOREST

Groton State Forest Headquarters *Marshfield, Rte 232; tel: (802) 584-3820. Excellent booklets are available on the natural and human history of the area.*

Geological and natural sights and plenty of trees fill the 25,000 acres of Groton State Forest. Three campsites (one with caravan facilities), a swimming beach and miles of hiking trails are spread along the 14-mile stretch of Rte 232 north of Groton. A good place to get an overview of the park's natural history is at the **Nature Center**, a museum with displays of local plants and animals. Diagrams illustrate the region's geology, from its origins at the bottom of a sea

Right
Groton State Forest

to scouring by glaciers. A **Nature Trail** begins here, described in a booklet available at the museum.

Hawks often circle above **Owls Head**, a 10-minute walk from the upper parking area, or a stiff climb from the bottom. This granite knob was scraped clean by glaciers, exposing stripes of different-coloured rock formed during earlier volcanic action.

St Johnsbury

ℹ️ **Northeast Kingdom Chamber of Commerce** *30 Western Ave; tel: (802) 748-3678 or (800) 639-6379; www.nekchamber.com*

🅟 **Fairbanks Museum and Planetarium $** *Main St; tel: (802) 748-2372; www.fairbanksmuseum.org. Open Mon–Sat 0900–1700, Sun 1300–1700. Planetarium shows Sat and Sun 1330, daily Jul and Aug. Closed Mon Nov–Mar.*

St Johnsbury Athenaeum and Art Gallery $ *Main St; tel: (802) 748-8291; www.stjathenaeum.org. Open daily, varying hours.*

Maple Grove Maple Museum and Factory $ *167 Portland St; tel: (802) 748-5141; www.maplegrove.com/museum.asp. Open mid-May–late Dec Mon–Fri 0800–1600.*

Main St, uphill from the business district (everything here is up- or downhill), is an avenue of fine **Victorian buildings** clustered around the Romanesque-style red sandstone **Fairbanks Museum** and the perpendicular gothic **Congregational Church**. This outstanding ensemble is described in a walking-tour brochure available at the museum.

Inside the **Fairbanks Museum and Planetarium**, collections centre on natural history, ethnology and history, plus just plain 'curiosities', once the private collections of the town's benefactor. The interior is also of architectural note, with an oak barrel-vaulted ceiling and arcade of cherrywood display cases along the upper gallery. Don't miss the bizarre Victorian 'bug art' portrait of George Washington.

Just down the street is the **St Johnsbury Athenaeum and Art Gallery**, with Albert Bierstadt's monumental painting *The Domes of Yosemite* on display. The street clock in front of the Athenaeum is from the old Grand Central Station in New York.

Maple Grove Maple Museum and Factory is the world's oldest and largest maple candy factory, begun in the kitchen of a family farm in 1915. The museum shows old methods of gathering sap and making syrup, and a tour takes visitors through the candy-making process – with samples, of course.

Accommodation and food in St Johnsbury

Echo Ledge Farm Inn $ *Rte 2, East St; tel: (802) 748-4750; www.echoledgefarminn.com.* An old farmhouse with homely atmosphere and warm hospitality.

Rabbit Hill Inn $$–$$$ *48 Lower Waterford Rd, PO Box 55, Lower Waterford; tel: (802) 748-5168 or (800) 76 BUNNY (762-8669); www.rabbithillinn.com.* Gracious owners have thought of every comfort, from abundant reading lights to packets of information on local attractions designed for guests' special interests. In the summer, packages offer outdoor activities, including kayaking. The dining room is unquestionably one of Vermont's best, using fresh locally grown ingredients.

WHITE RIVER VALLEY

Porter Music Box Museum $
*Rte 66, Randolph; tel:
(802) 728-9694 or
(800) 635-1938;
www.portermusicbox.com.
Open May–Oct 0800–1700.*

**Tunbridge World's
Fair $** *Rte 110;
tel: (802) 889-5555;
www.tunbridgefair.com.* Mid-
Sept; traffic clogs the single
road to this tiny town's
famous agricultural fair.

Four almost parallel branches of the White River flow southwards to join the main river, each with a scenic road beside it. On Rte 110, in 8 miles between South Royalton and Chelsea, are six **covered bridges**, five of them within easy sight of the road.

The 1883 Mill Covered Bridge and an 1820 brick sawmill form the centrepiece of **Tunbridge Village Historic District**, a well-preserved agricultural settlement of about a hundred pre-1890 buildings.

Randolph Center Historic District, on the Second Branch, has a number of outstanding buildings arranged on a 19th-century plan.

In Randolph, which sits on Third Branch, **Porter Music Box Company**, the world's only manufacturer of large-disc music boxes, has a museum and gift shop, with a collection of historic music boxes and a unique reproducing piano.

Brookfield Floating Bridge spans a 320ft pond, and is suspended on the surface of the water by nearly 400 wooden barrels. As you cross (the bridge is still in daily use, except in winter), the roadway undulates and water creeps between the floorboards.

Suggested tour

**Brighton State
Park** *Rte 5, Island
Pond; tel: (802) 723-4360
or 888-409-7579;
www.vtstateparks.com.* Open
late May–mid-Oct.
Free admission.

**Justin Smith Morrill
Homestead $** *Strafford;
tel: (802) 765-4484;
www.morrillhomestead.org.
Open Jun–mid-Oct Sat and
Sun 1100–1700.*

Total distance: 233 miles; 272 miles with detours.

Time: 6 hours' driving. Allow 2 days for the main route, with or without detours. Those with limited time should concentrate on Barre or St Johnsbury and the White River Valley.

Links: I-89 connects Barre with Waterbury and Burlington on the Lake Champlain Route (*see page 178*) and with White River Junction on the Upper Connecticut Valley Route (*see page 196*).

Route: From downtown **BARRE** ❶ follow Rte 14 north to Rte 2. Follow Rte 2 north to Marshfield, then Rte 215 through **CABOT** ❷ to Rte 15, which leads to **HARDWICK** ❸. From there, follow Rte 14 north, leaving it just past **Lake Eligo** ❹ to take the scenic road through **Craftsbury** ❺.

In Irasburg, take Rte 58 to Orleans, then head south on Rte 5 to Barton. Follow Rte 16 to Westmore and the loch-like **Lake Willoughby** ❻, following Rte 5A along its cliff-lined shore to West Burke, where a short unnumbered road is signposted to **East Burke** ❼.

Detour: Rte 5A heads north from **Westmore** to an intersection with Rte 105, which leads to the outpost town of **Island Pond** ❽. A two-storey brick and granite **Railroad Station** ❾, now a local museum, hints at the town's history as an important rail junction (13 different lines once converged here). Behind it rises a neighbourhood of **Victorian houses** ❿ and the Gothic Revival Christ Church.

◑ The WilloughVale Inn $–$$ *Rte 5A, Westmore; tel: (802) 594-9102; www.willoughvale.com.* Overlooking Lake Willoughby from inn rooms or lakefront cottages, dine in the Taproom or dining room.

Lakefront Motel $ *Cross St, Island Pond; tel: (802) 723-6507; www.thelakefrontinn.com.* Just as it says, right on the lake.

The Inn at Montpelier $$ *147 Main St, Montpelier; tel: (802) 223-2727; www.innatmontpelier.com.* In two restored early-1800s homes, a block from the centre of town.

⑪ Jennifer's Restaurant $ *Cross St, Island Pond; tel: (802) 723-4172.* Three meals daily with generous portions.

P&H Truck Stop $ *Rte 302, Wells River; tel: (802) 429-2141.* Reliable and informal, with terrific pies.

La Brioche Bakery and Café $ *89 Main St, Montpelier; tel: (802) 229-0443.* Modern café with excellent pastries and sandwiches.

Main Street Grill and Bar $–$$ *118 Main St, Montpelier; tel: (802) 223-3188; www.necidining.com.* Food cooked by student chefs from the New England Culinary Institute.

To explore the lake on your own, **hire a canoe ⑪** at the Lakefront Motel, which also has a sailing boat and a fishing boat for hire.

On the opposite side of the lake, **Brighton State Park ⑫** has hiking trails, tent pitches, lean-to shelters, a beach and nature programmes, but few frills, making it a favourite of those who love the quiet Boreal forest and the cry of loons on the lake. Native animals seen there include deer, moose, black bears, bobcats, racoons and squirrels. Island Pond offer some of the best birdwatching in the state.

From Island Pond, follow Rte 114 back to **East Burke ⑦**. Rte 114 leads south into **Lyndonville ⑬**, where it joins Rte 5 to **ST JOHNSBURY**. Rte 5 continues down the **Connecticut River Valley ⑭**, through several historic river towns, to Wells River.

Detour: From St Johnsbury, follow Rte 2 west through Danville to Rte 232, which leads through the centre of **GROTON STATE FOREST ⑮**. This road ends at Rte 302, by which you can return to Wells River.

Continuing down Rte 5, when you reach Ely, take Rte 244 west along the shores of Lake Fairlee to Rte 113 in Post Mills. Follow this south to Thetford Center, keeping a sharp look-out for an unnumbered road across a covered bridge, signposted to South Strafford. When you reach Rte 132, turn west (right) into South Strafford.

Two miles north in **Strafford**, the **Justin Smith Morrill Homestead ⑯** is a 17-room Gothic Revival mansion, unchanged and complete with original furnishings, gardens and outbuildings. It is worth visiting just to see the hand-painted window in the library ceiling.

Rte 132 leads to Sharon, where you turn right on to Rte 14, heading west along the **WHITE RIVER VALLEY ⑰**. In 5 miles, Rte 110 heads north to Tunbridge, along the White River's First Branch. Past the village take the well-signposted route to East Randolph.

Rte 66 leads to Randolph, where you meet Rte 12. Follow it north through the Brookfield Gulf to Rte 65, which leads into Brookfield, crossing over the unusual **Floating Bridge ⑱**. From Brookfield, Rte 14 returns to the starting point in Barre.

Also worth exploring

Montpelier is America's smallest state capital. Next to the Capitol Building is the **Vermont Historical Society Museum** *(tel: (802) 828-2291; www.vermonthistory.org)*. Home of New England Culinary Institute, Montpelier is known for its **abundant restaurants. Morse Farm Sugar House and Museum** *(tel: (800) 242-2740; www.morsefarm.com)* shows the maple production process.

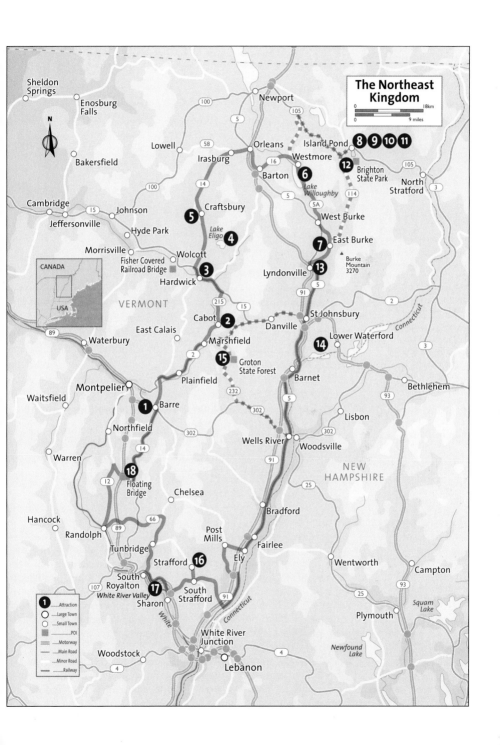

The Northeast Kingdom

Sheldon Springs
Enosburg Falls
Lowell
Bakersfield
Irasburg
Newport
Orleans
Island Pond
Westmore
Barton
Lake Willoughby
North Stratford
Cambridge
Johnson
Jeffersonville
Hyde Park
Craftsbury
Lake Eligo
West Burke
East Burke
Morrisville
Wolcott
Fisher Covered Railroad Bridge
Hardwick
Burke Mountain 3270
VERMONT
CANADA
USA
Cabot
Danville
St Johnsbury
Lyndonville
East Calais
Waterbury
Marshfield
Lower Waterford
Connecticut
Montpelier
Plainfield
Groton State Forest
Barnet
Bethlehem
Waitsfield
Barre
Lisbon
Northfield
Wells River
Woodsville
Warren
NEW HAMPSHIRE
Hancock
Randolph
Floating Bridge
Chelsea
Bradford
Tunbridge
Post Mills
Fairlee
Wentworth
Campton
Strafford
Ely
South Royalton
White River Valley
South Strafford
Squam Lake
Sharon
White
Connecticut
Plymouth
Woodstock
White River Junction
Newfound Lake
Lebanon

1 ....Attraction
○ ....Large Town
□ ....Small Town
■ ....POI
═══ ....Motorway
─── ....Main Road
─── ....Minor Road
····· ....Railway

The Upper Connecticut Valley

Ratings

Arts and culture	●●●●○
Nature/ scenery	●●●●○
Food and drink	●●●○○
History	●●●○○
Museums	●●●○○
Shopping	●●●○○
Beaches/ watersports	●○○○○
Children	●○○○○

The Connecticut River divides not just two states, but the ancient rocks of two continents. The eastern, New Hampshire side of the river is a bit of Africa left from the collision of continental plates, which accounts for the different landscapes and geology.

Interstate Highway 91 follows the valley, providing fine views across the winding river to New Hampshire. Nearby some of Vermont's most picture-perfect villages lie between the hills – Grafton, Chester and Newfane.

Roads here may wind through the countryside, but they are relatively level, with no mountains to climb in the beautiful Valley of the Connecticut River.

BRATTLEBORO

ⓘ Brattleboro Chamber of Commerce *On the Common, Putney Rd or 180 Main St; tel: (802) 254-4565 or (877) 254-4565; www.brattleborochamber.org*

Brattleboro Farmers Market *Rte 9 W May–Oct Sat 0900–1400; Main St May–Oct Wed 1000–1400 (craft fair first Sat in Dec).*

This small riverbank community has the relaxed air of people who have migrated back to the land. The New Age is alive and well here, and Main St shops reflect local interest in ethnic clothing, handicrafts, music, books and natural foods. One entire shop is filled with fabrics from all over the world. You'll also find five second-hand book shops, two breweries and one of New England's best sporting goods, camping and sportswear stores at **Sam's** *(tel: (802) 254-2933; www.samsoutfitters.com)*.

Nowhere is the 'Brattleboro Spirit' better experienced than at the **Brattleboro Farmers Market**. Small homestead farmers join craftsmen and makers of preserves, fresh-baked breads, maple syrup and organic honey. Many people go just to enjoy lunch at the international food

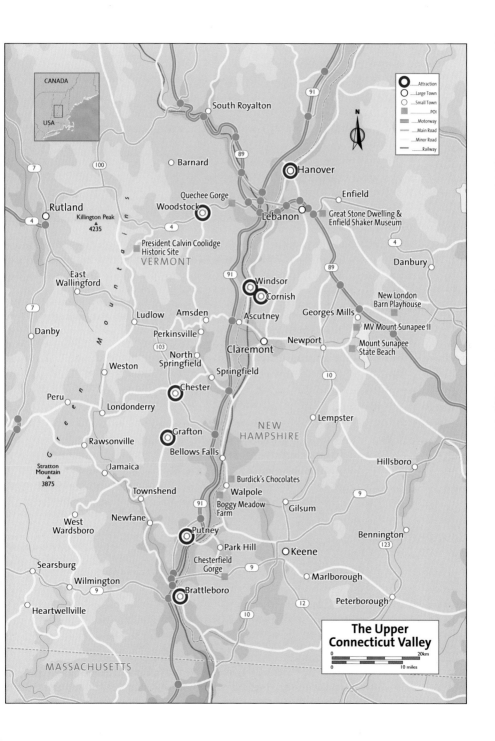

CANADA

USA

South Royalton

Barnard

Rutland

Killington Peak
4235

Woodstock

Quechee Gorge

Hanover

Enfield

Lebanon

Great Stone Dwelling &
Enfield Shaker Museum

President Calvin Coolidge
Historic Site

VERMONT

Danbury

East
Wallingford

Windsor

Cornish

Ludlow

Amsden

Ascutney

Georges Mills

New London
Barn Playhouse

Danby

Perkinsville

Newport

MV Mount Sunapee II

Weston

North
Springfield

Claremont

Mount Sunapee
State Beach

Springfield

Peru

Chester

Lempster

Londonderry

NEW
HAMPSHIRE

Grafton

Rawsonville

Hillsboro

Bellows Falls

Stratton
Mountain
3875

Jamaica

Burdick's Chocolates

Townshend

Walpole

West
Wardsboro

Newfane

Boggy Meadow
Farm

Gilsum

Putney

Bennington

Searsburg

Park Hill

Keene

Chesterfield
Gorge

Wilmington

Marlborough

Heartwellville

Brattleboro

Peterborough

MASSACHUSETTS

Attraction
Large Town
Small Town
POI
Motorway
Main Road
Minor Road
Railway

The Upper
Connecticut Valley

0   20km
0   10 miles

Brattleboro Museum and Art Center $ *10 Vernon St; tel: (802) 257-0124; www.brattleboromuseum.org. Open Thur–Mon 1100–1700.*

Vermont Canoe Touring Center $$$ *451 Putney Rd; tel: (802) 257-5008. Open May–Oct.* Kayak and canoe rentals.

stands and live music on the shaded lawn. Art and music are happening everywhere, with a busy schedule of concerts by local musicians and **Gallery Walks** on the first Friday evening of each month, when 15 art galleries serve up refreshments and host live music.

Estey organs were manufactured in Brattleboro and you can see examples, as well as changing exhibitions of art and antiquities, at the **Brattleboro Museum and Art Center**.

The *Belle of Brattleboro* (*tel: (802) 254-1263*), a canopied excursion boat, takes passengers on sunset, dinner and moonlight cruises from its dock where the West River flows into the Connecticut. Nearby, **Vermont Canoe Touring Center** rents kayaks and canoes. Blue herons, egrets, beavers and even eagles are seen along the low banks of the West River.

Accommodation and food in Brattleboro

Brattleboro Food Co-Op $ *2 Main St; tel: (802) 257-0236; open Mon–Sat 0800–2100, Sun 0900–2100.* Dining area where you can enjoy excellent à la carte deli meals, adjoining a certified organic grocery store where they sell rare cheeses from small Vermont farms. Often hosts special food events.

40 Putney Rd Bed & Breakfast $$ *Rte 5; tel: (802) 254-6268 or (800) 941-2413; www.fortyputneyroad.com.* An antique-filled French-style château near downtown.

Above
Brattleboro with the Connecticut River in the foreground

T J Buckley's $$ *132 Elliot St; tel: (802) 257-4922.* Tiny, eclectic and impeccable.

CHESTER

Well-kept Victorian buildings in the **Chester Village Historic District** surround the Green, described in a Walking Tour brochure from the TIC kiosk. Spanning the century from 1820 to 1920, they show how

Chester Area Chamber of Commerce *On the Green; tel: (802) 875-2939.*

The Green Mountain Flyer $$ *Tel: (802) 463-3069; www.rails-vt.com. Operates late Jun–early Sept Tue–Sun; Sept–mid-Oct Sat and Sun. Reservations advisable.*

Chester Art Guild *On the Green; tel: (802) 875-3767. Open Jun–Oct Tue–Sun 1400–1700.*

architecture evolved in streets lined with distinguished houses and perhaps Vermont's finest **Federal-style church**, topped by a five-layer spire reminiscent of the Boston architect Charles Bulfinch. The brick Academy is now the **Chester Art Guild**, displaying changing exhibits of the works of local artists.

Chester has three separate villages, the second surrounding the imposing Town Hall and the **Victorian Railway Station**. The **Green Mountain Flyer**, a sightseeing train, travels between Chester and Bellows Falls, with fully restored wooden coaches from 1913 and 1891. The train passes two covered bridges, and pauses suspended above the void of Brockaway Gorge.

The third, **Stone Village**, is built of granite quarried from the hill above. You will not see a finer ensemble of stone buildings than the school, church and nearly 30 houses facing each other across Rte 103.

Accommodation and food in Chester

Rose Arbour B&B and Tea Room $ *55 School St; tel: (802) 875-4767; www.rosearbour.com; open Tue–Sat 1000–1700, Sun 1200–1700.* Serves teas and ploughman's lunches; gift shop and attractive B&B rooms.

GRAFTON

Information Center *Next to the Old Tavern; tel: (802) 843-2255. Open May–Mar daily 1000–1800.*

Grafton Village Cheese Company *Townshend Rd; tel: (802) 843-2210 or (800) 472-3866; www.graftonvillagecheese.com. Open daily 1000–1700.*

Grafton Historical Society Museum $ *Main St; tel: (802) 843-1010; www.graftonhistory.org. Open Jun–mid-Sept Fri–Mon 1000–1600, mid-Sept–mid-Oct daily 1000–1600.*

The Old Tavern at Grafton $$ *Main St; tel: (802) 843-2231 or (800) 843-1801; http://old-tavern.com*

Many Vermonters claim that Grafton is not a town at all, but a carefully created museum. They may be right. The whole town is owned by the Windham Foundation, whose purpose is to keep it exactly as it is. That makes Grafton a pleasant place to visit, with its air of a 19th-century farming village – albeit a tidier and more 'kept up' version than the original.

Grafton Village Cheese Company makes cheddar: you can watch the process and sample the results. **Grafton Historical Society Museum** creates new exhibitions yearly, illustrating local life in past centuries. **Grafton Museum of Natural History** (*$ 186 Townshend Rd; tel: (802) 843-2111; www.nature-museum.org. Open Sat 1000–1600, Sun 1300–1600*) explains the surrounding natural world with live and interactive exhibits that allow visitors to watch bees make honey or learn why some minerals glow in the dark. At the **Grafton Blacksmith Shop** (*School St. Open Jun–mid-Oct Wed–Sun 1000–1500; demonstrations 1100–1200, 1300–1400*) you can see the tools of this ancient trade and watch a blacksmith at work. Walking trails (which metamorphose into cross-country ski trails) lead past an exhibition on sheep-raising and to the never-crowded **Grafton Swimming Pond**.

Upmarket galleries and shops emphasise the handmade and the antique; the Grafton Village Store (*tel: (802) 843-2348*) is a grocery and deli, but with fine wines, quilts and hand-knitted Guernseys (sweaters). **Plummer's Sugar House** (*tel: (802) 843-2207*), outside the 'pale' is a real farm, tapping trees and making maple syrup February–March; syrup and stencilled sap buckets are sold year-round.

HANOVER

🏛 **Hood Museum of Art** *Wheelock St; tel: (603) 646-2808; http://hoodmuseum.dartmouth.edu. Open Tue–Sat 1000–1700, Wed until 2100, Sun 1200–1700. Free admission.*

🅲 **The Hanover Inn** *$$–$$$ 2 South Main St; tel: (603) 643-4300; www.hanoverinn.com.* Beautiful rooms opposite the college.

🍴 **Molly's Restaurant** *$–$$ 43 South Main St; tel: (603) 643-2570; www.mollysrestaurant.com.* Lunch and dinner in a casual, upbeat atmosphere.

⬥ **Dartmouth Winter Carnival** *Dartmouth College; tel: (603) 646-3399; www.dartmouth.edu. Mid-Feb.* Featuring snow sculptures and sports events.

From its beginnings as a school to educate Native Americans, Dartmouth College has been at the centre of life in Hanover, providing the town's intellectual and cultural focus. The college's **Hood Museum of Art** has extensive collections ranging from 9th-century BC Assyrian reliefs to the entire suite of Picasso's Vollard etchings.

Less known are the treasures in Dartmouth's **Baker Memorial Library**, with fresco murals by the Mexican artist Jose Clemente Orozco (described in a free brochure). The **Baker-Berry Library** also displays selections from its vast collections of rare books and art in changing exhibits throughout the building. For a current list and locations, visit *http://library.dartmouth.edu* or enquire at the circulation desk.

The library faces a wide green, decorated in midwinter by the giant snow sculpture of **Dartmouth Winter Carnival**. Opposite is the **Hopkins Center for the Performing Arts** (*tel: (603) 646-2422; http://hop.dartmouth.edu*), with a diverse year-round concert, ballet, opera, jazz and theatre schedule.

PUTNEY

⬥ **Yellow Barn Music School and Festival** *$–$$ tel: (802) 387-6637; www.yellowbarn.org. Open late Jun–early Aug Tue–Sun afternoons and evenings.* Chamber music showcasing both known and rising artists.

Above
Dartmouth Winter Carnival

Wandering around Putney, you can be transported back into its world of the 1960s, when it was a haven for back-to-the-land homesteaders. The communes have gone, but Putney is still an enclave for artists and craft studios.

In the centre of the village is **Putney Clayschool**, a working pottery that is a riot of whimsical sculptures and practical dinnerware. **Green Mountain Spinnery** on Depot Rd (*tel: (802) 387-4528*), the smallest in the United States, produces knitting wool and patterns, and sells clothing knitted by local craftspeople. The **Putney Woodshed** offers handcrafted boxes, kaleidoscopes, toys, miniatures and more. Stop at the **Putney Co-op** (*I-91/Rte 5 interchange; www.putneycoop.com*) for picnic

Putney Clayschool *Kimball Hill; tel: (802) 387-4395. Open Wed–Mon 1000–1700.*

Putney Woodshed *Tel: (802) 387-4481.*

Basketville *8 Bellows Falls Rd (Rte 5); tel: (802) 387-5509; www.basketville.com. Open daily 1000–1730.*

supplies, local food specialities or to find out what's going on in the area. The bulletin board is on the porch. Or watch the town go by from the front porch of **Putney Hearth Bakery and Coffee House**, across the street.

The rambling world of **Basketville** has more baskets on display than you would ever have dreamed possible, from picnic hampers to beds for the dog. Before you think you are buying an authentic New England souvenir, however, be aware that Basketville makes no secret of the fact that their products are manufactured in China.

Accommodation and food in Putney

Putney Hearth Bakery and Coffee House $ *Putney Tavern; tel: (802) 387-2100; open Mon–Sat 0700–1700, Sun 0800–1500.* Adjoining this bakery, where you can also buy sandwiches, is a bookstore with a good selection of works by Vermont authors.

The Putney Inn $–$$ *Depot Rd (at Exit 4 of I-91); tel: (802) 387-2708; www.putneyinn.com.* Well-maintained old inn with adjacent motel rooms and well-known dining room.

WINDSOR AND CORNISH

American Precision Museum $ *196 Main St; tel: (802) 674-5781; www.americanprecision.org. Open late May–Oct daily 1000–1700.*

Old Constitution House $ *16 North Main St; tel: (802) 672-3773; www.historicvermont.org/ constitution. Open late May–mid-Oct Sat and Sun 1100–1700.*

Saint-Gaudens National Historic Site $ *Rte 12A, Cornish; tel: (603) 675-2175; www.nps.gov/saga. Open Jun–Oct daily 0900–1630.*

Windsor Station Pub $$ *27 Depot St; tel: (802) 674-2052; www.windsorstation.com. Open Tue–Sun 1730–2100.*

These twin towns are joined by the **longest historic covered bridge** in the United States, built in 1886. **Windsor Village Historic District** is lined by brick buildings from the 1800s, when the town led in founding the precision tool industry. The first interchangeable machine parts were designed and built here, as were the famed Enfield Rifles that won the Crimean War. This chapter in the Industrial Revolution is told at the **American Precision Museum**.

Old Constitution House, the tavern where Vermont was born, is a historical museum and the 1840 Windsor House contains the **Vermont State Craft Center**, featuring Vermont-made work; ask for the self-guided Architectural Tour brochure.

You can watch molten glass become useful and ornamental tableware at **Simon Pearce Glass** (*www.simonpearce.com*), housed in an industrial-looking building complex north of Windsor.

A century ago, Cornish was a summer colony of artists and writers, including the noted sculptor, Augustus Saint-Gaudens. His home is preserved as **Saint-Gaudens National Historic Site**, and many of his works are shown in the studio and throughout the lovely gardens.

The Connecticut River flows wide and calm between Windsor and Cornish, and the best way to enjoy it is by canoe. **North Star Canoe Livery** (*$$$; tel: (603) 542-6929; www.kayak-canoe.com*), south of the bridge, rents them and provides a shuttle service, as well as raft trips and guided river explorations.

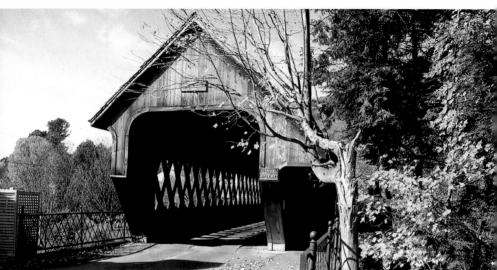

WOODSTOCK

 Woodstock Chamber of Commerce *18 Central St; tel: (802) 457-3555; www.woodstockvt.com*

Woodstock Historical Society *$ 26 Elm St; tel: (802) 457-1822; http://woodstockhistorical.org. Open most Sun 1000–1400.*

Billings Farm and Museum *$ 5302 River Rd; tel: (802) 457-2355; www.billingsfarm.org. Open May–Oct daily 1000–1700; Dec weekends, Christmas week 1000–1600; Sleigh ride weekends 1000–1500.*

The money that has always infused Woodstock is apparent from the well-kept homes and gardens and the stylish shops that line its streets. Around its **Village Green** are several historic buildings, and a covered bridge crosses a river only a block away.

Woodstock is the only town in America with five bells made by the patriot Paul Revere. The oldest is on the porch of the Congregational Church; another is at the Woodstock Inn and others are in churches and the Masonic Temple.

The Historical Society's **Dana House Museum**, a Federal-style 1807 merchant's home, recalls local history with collections of furniture, art, toys, costumes, textiles, kitchenware and farm equipment.

Still an active farm, **Billings Farm and Museum** mingles working barns and shops with exhibit areas and the home of the farm's manager. In the creamery downstairs is all the equipment used to make butter and cheese; special events highlight farm seasons.

In December the town is aglow with holiday decorations, and a **Wassail Parade** *(tel: (802) 457-1509)* the second weekend in December features horse-drawn carriages and wagons. This is horse country, and you can join an escorted trail ride, or a surrey, wagon or sleigh ride at **Kedron Valley Stables** in South Woodstock (**$$$**; *tel: (802) 457-1480; www.kedron.com*).

Accommodation and food in Woodstock

The Applebutter Inn $$ *Happy Valley Rd, off Rte 4, west of Woodstock; tel: (802) 457-4158 or (800) 486-1734; www.applebutterinn.com.* New England charm at its best, with nicely decorated rooms and

Above
Woodstock's covered bridge

Warning: Woodstock police impose fines on motorists who even slightly exceed the low speed limit.

Burdick's Chocolates $
Main St, Walpole;
tel: (603) 756-3701;
www.burdickchocolate.com.
Open Mon–Fri 0900–1800,
Sat and Sun 0900–1700.

Juniper Hill Inn
$–$$ 153 Pembroke
Rd, Windsor; tel: (802) 674-
5273 or (800) 359-2541;
www.juniperhillinn.com.
A gracious 1901 mansion overlooking the valley. Dinner (**$$**) by reservation in the candle-lit dining room.

Inn at Weathersfield
$$–$$$ 1342 Rte 106,
Perkinsville;
tel: (802) 263-9217;
www.weathersfieldinn.com.
Between Woodstock and Springfield, this is the epitome of a Vermont country inn, with no two rooms alike, each furnished with antiques. The chef creates memorable meals from the bounty of local farms.

sumptuous breakfasts. Ask the owners for suggestions to find the area's most beautiful country roads.

The Fan House $$ *Route 12, Barnard; tel: (802) 234-6704; www.thefanhouse.com.* Just north of Woodstock, Barnard is a good base for exploring the area, and the well-travelled owner of this charming B&B is just the person to advise you. Ask about the wildlife walks, with a guide from the local Audubon Society.

Suggested tour

Total distance: 172 miles; 231 miles with detours.

Time: 4½ hours' driving. Allow 2 days for the main route, with or without detours. Those with limited time should concentrate on Hanover, Woodstock and Chester.

Links: From Brattleboro, I-91 leads south to Northfield, Massachusetts and the Pioneer Valley Route (*see page 94*); Rte 9 goes west to Bennington and the Southern Green Mountain Route (*see page 168*).

Route: Leave **BRATTLEBORO** ❶ on Rte 5 north, running a gauntlet of shopping plazas to Rte 9, on which you will cross the river into New Hampshire. Stop at **Chesterfield Gorge** ❷ to walk the wooded half-mile path into the chasm carved into solid rock, or picnic under the pines. Return on Rte 9 to Rte 63 and follow it north through historic Park Hill, a settlement of exceptionally fine homes dating from the 1700s with one of New Hampshire's earliest (and best) meeting houses, built in 1762. The road winds through rich valley farms before reaching Rte 12.

At the intersection is Stuart & John's, a maple sugar house that's open year round (*tel: (603) 399-4486; www.stuartandjohnssugarhouse.com*).

Turn north on Rte 12 to find **Boggy Meadow Farm** ❸, where they make and sell (on the honour system) artisanal cheeses (*tel: (603) 756-3300; www.boggymeadowfarm.com*), and **Alyson's Orchard**. The hillside here is covered in apple trees, and there are beautiful views of the Connecticut River. More than 40 varieties of apple, many of them heritage varieties, grow here and are made into cider and wines (*tel: (800) 856-0549 or (603) 756-9800; www.alysonsorchard.com*).

Continue to **Walpole** ❹, making the short sidetrack into the hillside village to see its classic green surrounded by 18th- and 19th-century houses. Stop for a pick-me-up at **Burdick's Chocolates** ❺, where, along with the fine chocolates made here, they serve hot chocolate, tea or espresso with sinfully good pastries, as well as lunch and dinner.

Cross the river again into Vermont, heading north a short way to I-91. Follow it north, enjoying sweeping river views and exit at Ascutney

MV *Mount Sunapee II* $$ *Sunapee Harbor (off Rte 11); tel: (603) 763-4030; www.sunapeecruises.com. Cruising mid-May–mid-Jun Sat and Sun 1400; mid-Jun–Aug daily 1400; Sept–mid-Oct Sat and Sun 1400.*

Enfield Shaker Museum $ *Rte 4A, Enfield; tel: (603) 632-4346; www.shakermuseum.org. Open year-round Mon–Sat 1000–1700, Sun 1200–1700; last tour 1600.*

Calvin Coolidge Historic Site $ *Plymouth Notch; tel: (802) 228-5050. Open late May–mid Oct daily.*

Quechee Recreation Area $ *Rte 4; tel: (802) 295-2990. Tent pitches, picnic grounds and walking trails.*

Echo Lake Inn $–$$ *Rte 100, Tyson; tel: (802) 228-8602 or (800) 356-6844; www.echolakeinn.com. Attractive rooms and excellent dining.*

(Exit 8) and continue north on Rte 5 to **WINDSOR ⑥**. Cross the covered bridge to **CORNISH ⑦** and follow Rte 12A north to Lebanon.

Detour: From Lebanon, take Rte 4A along Mascoma Lake, where you can't miss the six-storey granite **Great Stone Dwelling** dating from 1841, the largest structure ever built by the Shakers. This religious sect built an entire village here, now **Enfield Shaker Museum ⑧**, with authentically restored gardens. Frequent events interpret the Shaker way of life and the shop sells baskets and Shaker crafts. The Stone Dwelling has been meticulously restored, with authentic Shaker furnishings and original built-in cabinetry. Continue on Rte 4A, turning right on Rte 11 and right again on to Rte 114 through the college town of New London. **New London Barn Playhouse ⑨** *(tel: (603) 526-4631 or (800) 633-2276)* has been operating since 1934, presenting summer performances of lively Broadway musicals in the renovated barn. Rte 114 rejoins Rte 11 to skirt Lake Sunapee, leading to the town of Sunapee Harbor, where the excursion boat **MV *Mount Sunapee II* ⑩** is docked. During the 1½-hour trip the Captain's narration is laced with local lore. Rte 103B leads to **Mount Sunapee State Beach ⑪**. Follow Rte 103 to Newport, then Rte 10, which joins with I-89 to return to Lebanon.

From Lebanon, take Rte 10 to **HANOVER ⑫**, crossing the river into Norwich, Vermont. Follow Rte 5 south to White River Junction and Rte 14 west to Rte 4, which crosses the 162-ft-deep **Quechee Gorge ⑬**. In Quechee, shops overlook a covered bridge, and the modern Quechee Gorge Village *(tel: (802) 295-1550)* has an Antique Center with over 450 dealers, and an Arts & Crafts Center representing 220 artisans.

Continue to **WOODSTOCK ⑭**, then follow Rte 106 to North Springfield, and Rte 10 to Rte 103, which leads south into **CHESTER ⑮**. Rte 35 takes you to **GRAFTON ⑯** and on to Townshend, with its attractive village green and meeting house.

Rte 30 heads south to **Newfane ⑰**, one of New England's 'postcard' towns, with fine buildings and the Sunday Newfane Flea Market. South of Newfane, cross the covered bridge over the West River on an unnumbered road through Dummerston Center to Rte 5. Two miles north on Rte 5 is **PUTNEY ⑱**. I-91 brings you back into **Brattleboro ①**.

Also worth exploring

West of Woodstock, Rte 4 follows the Ottauquechee River through Bridgewater to Rte 100A, which leads through Plymouth Notch and **President Calvin Coolidge Historic Site**. His family farm, where he took the oath of office, is a museum complex showing Vermont rural life. Rte 4A joins Rte 100, which leads to Ludlow, where Rte 103 leads back to the main route in Chester.

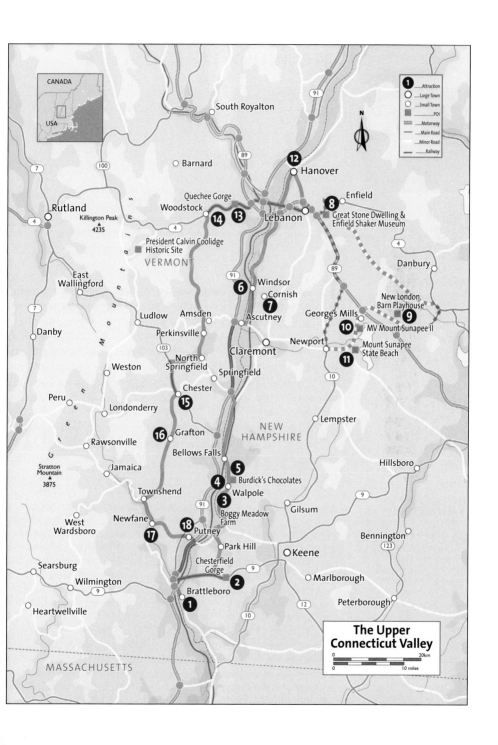

The Upper Connecticut Valley

The New Hampshire Lakes

Ratings

Beaches and watersports	●●●●○
Children	●●●●○
Shopping	●●●●○
Nature/ scenery	●●●○○
Food and drink	●●○○○
Museums	●●○○○
Arts and culture	●○○○○
History	●○○○○

The blue of Lake Winnipesaukee splashes unevenly across the centre of New Hampshire's map, making it the state's most popular region for sailing and watersports. The shores are dotted with resorts and camps, along with the diversions that such a concentration of holidaymakers inevitably brings. Recreation complexes, shops, craft and antique centres and big resorts congregate on Winnipesaukee's western shore, creating weekend traffic snarls. The eastern shore and nearby Squam Lake are quieter.

Surrounding the lakes are the mountains, one of them providing the state's best-known view: Mount Chocorua reflected in the lake at its feet.

CHOCORUA

ⓘ Greater Ossipee Chamber of Commerce *Rtes 16 and 25W, West Ossipee; tel: (603) 539-6201 or (866) 683-6295; www.ossipeevalley.org*

ⓗ White Lake State Park $ *Rte 16, Tamworth; tel: (603) 323-7350. Open late May–mid-Oct.*

Mount Chocorua (pronounced 'sho-KOR-oo-ah') is New Hampshire's signature mountain, shown on calendars and postcards in one of two poses: framed in white birch trees from a hilltop or rising from the deep blue foreground of Chocorua Lake. You can see both from Rte 16: the hilltop is just north of Chocorua Village, which lies clustered around its old stone dam. Below the hill is the lake, with benches along its scenic shore.

White Lake State Park is an idyllic campsite and picnic grove under tall pine trees, beside a clear lake with a sandy beach and another fine view of Mount Chocorua.

Practise casting with catch-and-release at **Sumner Brook Fish Farm** in nearby Ossipee or keep your trout, paying by the inch. Children enjoy watching the baby fish in growing pools.

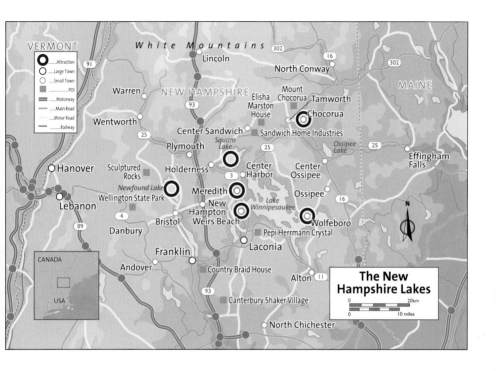

The New Hampshire Lakes

Sumner Brook Fish Farm $ *Rte 16, Ossipee; tel: (603) 539-7232. Open May and Sept Sat and Sun; Jun–Aug daily.*

Accommodation and food in Chocorua

Grammy Gordon's Bakery $ *29 Tamworth Rd; tel: (603) 323-2005.* Stop for fresh-made scones, biscuits and pastries, or browse the menu of ready-to-eat meals to take away (handy for those who are self-catering or having a picnic dinner).

The Yankee Smokehouse $ *Rtes 16 and 25, West Ossipee; tel: (603) 539-7427; open May–mid-November, mid-December–March daily.* Succulent pork, chicken and beef are barbecued over wood fires.

The Tamworth Inn $$ *Main St, Tamworth; tel: (603) 323-7721 or (800) 642-7352.* An 1833 inn, opposite Barnstormers Summer Theater.

MEREDITH

Information Center
Tel: (877) 279-6121; www.meredithcc.org. Open May–Oct daily.

The lively town borders a dock-lined lakefront with hotels, shops and eateries. At its centre, **Mills Falls Marketplace** *(tel: (603) 279-7006)* is a multistorey complex of 18 shops, selling everything from local books to ice cream and fashionwear.

Annalee Doll Museum *44*
Reservoir Rd; tel: (603) 279-3333; www.annalee.com. Open Jun–Oct daily 0900–1700. Free admission.

Annalee Doll Museum shows 35 years' worth of those flexible felt dolls prized by collectors. Posed and outfitted for favourite sports, including fishing and golf, or dressed for the holidays, each doll has a happy expression on its hand-painted face. The New Hampshire Craftsmen's League has a shop overlooking the lake.

Winnipesaukee Scenic Railroad $$ (*tel: (603) 745-2135; www.hoborr.com; open May–Oct*) runs passenger cars along the shore between the stations in Meredith and Weirs Beach for one- and two-hour scenic rides. An ice cream parlour car is popular or you can reserve a box lunch or turkey dinner.

Accommodation and food in Meredith

The Inn at Bay Point $$–$$$ *312 Daniel Webster Highway; tel: (603) 279-7006 or (800) 622-6455; www.millfalls.com*. Modern rooms all have views of Lake Winnipesaukee.

NEWFOUND LAKE

Wellington State Park $ *Rte 3A, Bristol; tel: (603) 744-2197. Open mid-May to Columbus Day daily.*

Polar Caves $$ *Rte 25, Plymouth; tel: (603) 536-1888 or (800)273-1886; www.polarcaves.com. Open mid-May–mid-Oct daily 0900–1700.*

Inn on Newfound Lake $$ *Rte 3A, Bridgewater; tel: (603) 744-9111; www.newfoundlake.com.* Nicely updated, this fine old lakeside inn has an excellent dining room. Sunday brunch is a speciality.

Right
Groton's sculptured rocks

A lovely lake close to I-93, but largely untrammelled, Newfound's shores are lined by trees and bird-filled marshlands instead of cottages. At its northern end is the protected area of **Paradise Point Nature Center** (*tel: (603) 744-3516*), where you can walk the trails helped by a descriptive pamphlet from the small museum, in which interactive exhibitions examine loons and other local wildlife.

Sculptured Rocks, farther along North Shore Rd in Groton, show how great the force of running water can be when it's given enough time. The tumbling river has worn giant potholes, some 10ft in diameter, in the solid granite over which it flows. Picnic tables overlook the gorge.

At **Wellington State Park**, on the lake's southern rim, a half-mile beach of fine white sand is ringed by tall pine trees. Never crowded, it is a good choice for swimming.

Polar Caves are not the true caves that form in limestone, but glacially constructed chambers and passages, through which children love to squirm. Deep in these cool rocky recesses you may find ice in the summer. Visit the Maple Sugar Museum and Mineral Display.

Accommodation and food in Newfound Lake

The Italian Farmhouse $–$$ *Rte 3 South, Plymouth; tel: (603) 536-4536; open Mon–Sat 1700–2100, Sun 1100–1400 and 1700–2030.* Rustic Italian menu and rural setting.

Glynn House Inn $$–$$$ *59 Highland St, Ashland; tel: (603) 968-3775; www.glynnhouse.com.* Queen Anne Victorian inn with four-poster beds, French wallpaper and fireplaces.

SQUAM LAKE

Squam Lake Association *Rte 3, Holderness; tel: (603) 968-7336; www.squamlakes.org*

Explore Squam Lake Cruises at Squam Lakes Natural Science Center $ *23 Science Center Rd, Holderness; tel: (603) 968-7194; www.nhnature.org. Departures Jun–Sept daily 1100, 1300 & 1500.*

Riverside Cycles *Rte 3, Ashland; tel: (603) 968-9676.* Bicycle rentals.

Squam Lakes Natural Science Center $–$$ *Rtes 3 and 113, Holderness; tel: (603) 968-7194; www.nhnature.org. Open May–Oct daily 0930–1630.*

A beautiful lake with little visible development to disturb its nesting loons or mar its quiet wooded shores, Squam is where *On Golden Pond*, starring Katherine Hepburn and Henry Fonda, was filmed. A map of bike and hiking trails is free from local shops.

At the **Squam Lakes Natural Science Center**, a wildlife sanctuary for rescued animals, you can meet a black bear, bobcat, river otter and a bald eagle as you walk the exhibit trail, or examine frogs up close from a boardwalk. A mile-long loop trail climbs Mount Fayal for views of Squam Lake. **Nature Cruises** explore the habitat of resident loons with a trained naturalist (*June Sat and Sun 1300; late June–mid-October daily 1100, 1300 & 1500*). Follow the trails to the end to enter Kirkwood Gardens (*tel: (603) 968-7194*) or drive to the beautiful free garden, on Rte 3.

Accommodation and food in Squam Lake

Little Holland Court $–$$, *Rte 3, Ashland; tel: (603) 968-4434.* Self-catering cottages set on Little Squam Lake, in addition offering boat rentals.

The Inn On Golden Pond $$ *Rte 3, Holderness; tel: (603) 968-7269; www.innongoldenpond.com.* Beautiful B&B accommodation in an 1879 lakeside farmhouse.

Squam Lake Inn $$ *Shepard Hill Rd, Holderness; tel: (603) 968-4417 or (800) 839-6205; www.squamlakeinn.com.* A Victorian-era home with nicely decorated and refreshingly unfrilly guestrooms, all with private baths, internet and air conditioning.

WEIRS BEACH

MV Sophie C $
Lakeside Ave, Weirs Beach; tel: (603) 366-5531; late May–mid-Oct daily, day and evening cruises.

MS Mount Washington Cruises $$ *Lakeside Ave, Weirs Beach; tel: (603) 366-BOAT; www.cruisenh.com. Departs Weirs Beach late May–mid-Oct daily 1230, weekends 1000 and 1230.*

MV *Sophie C* explores Winnipesaukee, sailing among its 365 islands and into secluded coves, all in a day's work for a genuine working mailboat. Day or sunset cruises last 2–3 hours. To tour on a larger boat, choose the venerable **MS *Mount Washington***, departing Weirs Beach for Wolfeboro, Center Harbor and Alton Bay. Evening cruises include dinner and dancing to live music.

If you like getting wet, **Weirs Beach Water Slide and Surf Coaster USA** (*www.weirsbeach.net*) have several water-soaked activities, including a wave tank, water slides, rafting and a spray ground for small fry. **FunSpot** (*www.funspotnh.com*) brings miniature golf, bowling, kiddy rides and a game arcade together. The short boardwalk at Weirs beach is backed by a row of brightly painted Victorian-style cottages.

WOLFEBORO AND EASTERN SHORE

Wolfeboro Area Chamber of Commerce *32 Central Ave; tel: (800) 516-5324(603) or 569-2200; www.wolfeboroonline.com*

Wright Museum $
77 Center St; tel: (603) 569-1212; www.wrightmuseum.org. Open May–Oct Mon–Sat 1000–1600, Sun 1200–1600.

Libby Museum $ *Main St (Rte 109), Wolfeboro; tel: (603) 569-1035; www.wolfeboronh.us. Open Jun–Sept Tue–Sun 1000–1600.*

Wentworth State Park $ *Rte 109; tel: (603) 569-3699. Open May and Jun Sat and Sun; Jul and Aug daily.*

Still in progress, showing life on the homefront and in the field during World War II, the **Wright Museum** has themed exhibits and an entire building of military hardware, including tanks and half-tracks. Stop to watch the video on women Air Corps pilots. The **Libby Museum** focuses on the area's natural history with exhibitions on native birds and animals and a collection of local Indian artefacts.

Board the ***Winnipesaukee Belle***, a replica turn-of-the-century lake paddleboat, at the **Wolfeboro Inn** (*tel: (603) 569-3016; www.wolfeboroinn.com*), or rent a boat at **Wetwolfe** (*Bay St; tel: (866) 413-3103*), to explore the lake on your own. You will pass a loon refuge, old boatyards and several of Winnipesaukee's many islands. **Wentworth State Park** has a small beach on Lake Wentworth, separated from Lake Winnipesaukee by a narrow strip of land at Wolfeboro.

Drive uphill to **Castle in the Clouds $** (*tel: (603) 476-2352*), the stone mansion of a former summer estate, for house tours, lake views, a tram ride to the source of a spring and a gift shop.

Accommodation and food in Wolfeboro and Eastern Shore

Tuc'Me Inn B&B $ *118 North Main St, Wolfeboro; tel: (603) 569-5702; www.tucmeinn.com.* Comfortable, unpretentious, and located downtown.

Dockside Grille $–$$ *11 Dockside St; tel: (603) 569-1910.* Seafood platters, burgers and sandwiches are served year round.

The Woodshed $$ *128 Lee Rd (off Rte 109), Moultonborough; tel: (603) 476-2311; open Tue–Sun for dinner.* Prime rib and more, served in an old farmhouse and rustic barn.

Above
Castle in the Clouds

Summer Retreat

On the shores of Lake Wentworth once stood the USA's first summer holiday cottage. Royal Governor Benning Wentworth built his 100ft by 40ft cottage here in 1768, travelling to it by coach from his mansion in Portsmouth.

The Shakers

Originally known as 'Shaking Quakers', Shakers came to the United States in 1774 from Manchester, England, led by the illiterate textile worker Anne Lee. Mother Anne's tiny group flourished despite early persecution, and by the 1840s had more than 6000 members living in farm-centred communities in New England, New York and the midwest. They led a celibate communal life stressing simplicity, work ethic and fine craftsmanship. Among the first to package and sell garden seeds, they also led in packaging medicinal and culinary herbs. Their practical inventions included home improvements such as the flat broom and the clothespeg. Shaker craftsmen were known for the strength and beauty of their furniture, and their styles have profoundly influenced American design ever since.

Ⓕ Pepi Herrmann Crystal *Off Lily Pond Rd near the airport, Gilford; tel: (603) 528-1020 or (800) HANDCUT. Open year-round, tours Tue–Sat 1000 and 1400.*

Elisha Marston House *4 Maple St, Center Sandwich; tel: (603) 284-6269. Open Jun–Sept Tue–Sat 1100–1700.*

Ⓒ Lakehurst Cottages *$ Rte 11-D, Alton Bay; tel: (603) 875-2492; www.lakehurstcottages.com. May and Jun nightly, Jul–Sept weekly only. Well-kept lakefront cottages.*

Ⓢ Sandwich Home Industries *32 Main St (Rte 109), Center Sandwich; tel: (603) 284-6831; www.nhcrafts.org. Open mid-May–mid-Oct Mon–Sat 1000–1700, Sun 1200–1700.*

Country Braid House *246 Main St (Rte 3), Tilton; tel: (603) 286-4511; www.countrybraidhouse.com. Open Mon–Sat 0900–1600.*

Suggested tour

Total distance: 120 miles; 183 miles with detours.

Time: 3 hours' driving. Allow 2 days for the main route, 3 days with detours or boat rides. Those with limited time should concentrate on Squam Lake, Wolfeboro and a boat tour.

Links: I-93 connects this route to the White Mountains (*see page 214*) and to Lowell, Massachusetts, on the West of Boston Route (*see page 54*).

Route: From Exit 23 of I-93 at New Hampton, follow Rte 104 east to **MEREDITH ❶**. Go south on Rte 3 to **WEIRS BEACH ❷** follow the lake shore on Rte 11B to Gilford. Here **Pepi Herrmann Crystal❸** creates hand-cut glassware, which you can watch being made during a studio tour.

Continue along the shore on Rte 11 to Alton Bay.

Follow signs to Rte 28A, hugging the opposite shore and leading to Rte 28, which climbs rolling hills and drops into **WOLFEBORO ❹**.

Rte 109 follows the shore to Moultonborough, from which you follow Rte 25 to West Ossipee. Turn north on Rte 16, past White Lake to **CHOCORUA ❺**.

After seeing **Mount Chocorua ❻**, just north on Rte 16, return to the village and head via Tamworth to Rte 25. Go west on 25, through Moultonborough, to Center Harbor, where Rte 25B climbs over the hill to Rte 3. Follow Rte 3 north along the quiet shore of **SQUAM LAKE ❼** to Holderness.

Detour: In Chocorua, follow winding Rte 113A past the tall pines and trails of Hemenway State Forest to the remote village of Wonalancet, and on to **Center Sandwich ❽**. One of the state's prettiest villages, it is home to several craftsmen whose studios you can visit.

Sandwich Home Industries ❾ displays and sells a wide selection of fine New Hampshire handicrafts, from hand-woven clothing and woodenware to stuffed toys and pottery. Sandwich Historical Society's **Elisha Marston House ❿** preserves the life and times of a village shoemaker in the 1850s. Rte 113 continues along the scenic northern shore of Squam Lake, rejoining the main route in Holderness.

Rte 3 leads to Ashland, crossing I-93 and heading north into Plymouth. Follow Rte 25 to Rumney Depot, then an unnumbered road south (left) signposted to Groton, where signs lead to **Sculptured Rocks ⓫**. Continue to Hebron, on **NEWFOUND LAKE ⓬**, and along its western shore, bearing left along the lake to Rte 3A in Bristol. Rte 104 leads to New Hampton.

Detour: Instead of returning to New Hampton, stay on Rte 3A to Franklin, following Rte 3 into Tilton. Shop for hand-braided rugs or learn how they are made in a studio tour of **Country Braid House ⓭**. Complete kits teach this traditional craft.

Tanger Factory Outlet Center
Off I-93 at exit 20, Tilton; tel: (603) 286-7880 or (888)-SHOP333. Open Mon–Sat 1000–2100, Sun 1000–1800.

Canterbury Shaker Village $$ *Exit 18 off I-95, Canterbury; tel: (603) 783-9511; www.shakers.org. Open May–Oct daily 1000–1700; Apr, Nov & Dec Fri–Sun 1000–1700.*

The Shaker Table $$–$$$ *Canterbury Shaker Village; tel: (603) 783-4238; www.theshakertable.com. Open daily for lunch 1130–1400, dinner 1700–2100. Reservations recommended for dinner.*

Tanger Factory Outlet Center is a huge outlet complex featuring overstocks and seconds of big labels like Reebok, Levi, Izod and more than 50 others, at low, tax-free prices (New Hampshire has no sales tax).

Rte 132 diverges from I-93 to Canterbury Center (at Exit 18), where you follow brown signs east (left) to **Canterbury Shaker Village ⓮**, a perfectly preserved set of 24 housing, farm and workshop buildings, now a museum perpetuating the art and ideals of the community. Tours not only show the buildings, but explain Shaker philosophy and daily life. The restaurant recreates authentic Shaker meals and the Summer Kitchen sells snacks.

Follow the road past the Shaker Village to Belmont, where a left turn on to Rte 140 brings you to I-93 at exit 20, two exits south of your starting-point in New Hampton.

Also worth exploring

From Chocorua, Rte 113 leads east to Madison, where you can see the gigantic **Madison Boulder**, perhaps the world's largest glacial erratic. Tiny **Crystal Lake** reflects picture-perfect **Eaton**, and Rte 153 leads along (and over) the Maine border, passing more lakes on its way to the beautiful **Wakefield Historic District**. Rte 109 leads back to Wolfeboro.

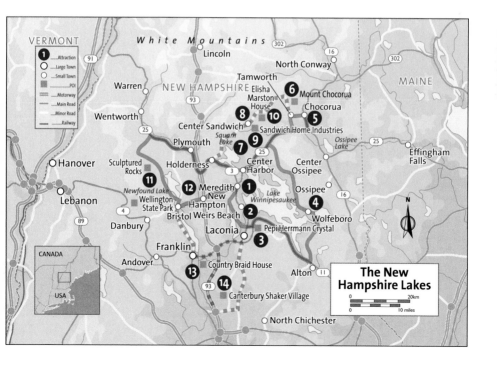

The White Mountains

Ratings

Nature/scenery	●●●●●
Children	●●●●○
Shopping	●●●●○
Food and drink	●●●○○
History	●●●○○
Museums	●●●○○
Arts and culture	●●○○○
Beaches/watersports	●○○○○

The White Mountains crown New England with its highest elevations. Almost since their first exploration, they have been a playground for hikers, climbers, skiers, fishermen and those who simply appreciate looking at the views and breathing the fresh, cool mountain air.

Views are everywhere, and some of the best spread before you as you drive: row upon row of mountains, tiny villages clustered around a white church and a covered bridge, crystal rivers rushing over rocky beds, even waterfalls dropping beside the road.

Expect some steep winding roads, and heavy traffic on summer weekends, especially around the shopping mecca of North Conway. Travelling in the evening or at night, be wary of moose, which have no fear of cars. In a head-on confrontation, the moose will win, so drive more slowly and scan the roadsides.

BRETTON WOODS

Mount Washington Cog Railway $$$ *Off Rte 302, Bretton Woods; tel: (603) 846-5406 or (800) 922-8825; www.thecog.com. Operates Sat and Sun in May, daily Jun–late Oct. Reservations suggested.*

The **Mount Washington Hotel** is far more than a place to stay; more even than a resort. It is a last reminder of an opulent era, gleaming in meticulous restoration. Its owners are keen to share it, offering free daily tours, and showing the conference table where the Bretton Woods Monetary Agreement was signed after World War II to set a world monetary standard. Frequent tours also visit the historic print shop and the Stickney Chapel, with Tiffany-signed windows.

The **Mount Washington Cog Railway**, first of its kind in the world, has puffed and steamed its way up the steep mountainside to the summit since the 1860s. The three-hour return trip allows time to explore New England's highest peak. On a clear day the views from the summit of **Mount Washington** seem endless. You can depend on wind; in April 1934, the highest wind gust ever recorded blew past the

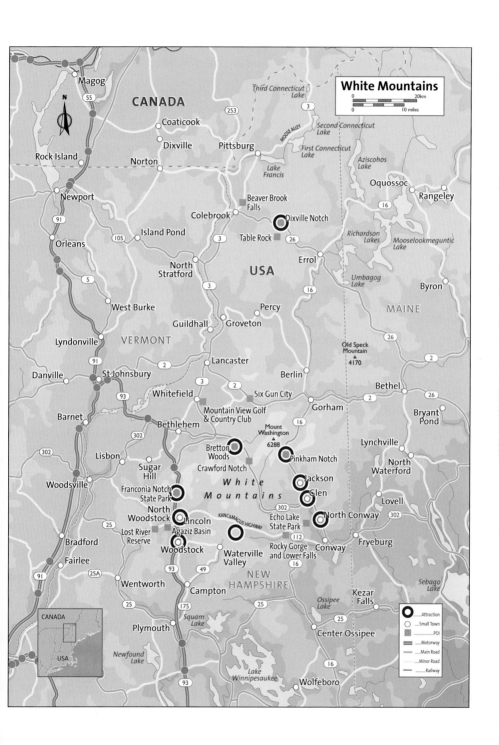

White Mountains

0   20km
0   10 miles

CANADA

Magog
Coaticook
Dixville
Pittsburg
Rock Island
Norton
Newport
Colebrook
Beaver Brook Falls
Dixville Notch
Island Pond
Table Rock
Orleans
North Stratford
Errol
West Burke
Percy
Guildhall
Groveton
Lyndonville
VERMONT
Danville
St Johnsbury
Lancaster
Berlin
Whitefield
Six Gun City
Barnet
Mountain View Golf & Country Club
Bethlehem
Gorham
Lisbon
Mount Washington 6288
Bretton Woods
Pinkham Notch
Sugar Hill
Crawford Notch
Woodsville
Franconia Notch State Park
White Mountains
Jackson
North Woodstock
Glen
KANCAMAGUS HIGHWAY
Echo Lake State Park
North Conway
Lincoln
Lost River Reserve
Agaziz Basin
Bradford
Woodstock
Rocky Gorge and Lower Falls
Conway
Fryeburg
Fairlee
Waterville Valley
Wentworth
Campton
NEW HAMPSHIRE
Kezar Falls
Plymouth
Squam Lake
Newfound Lake
Lake Winnipesaukee
Wolfeboro
Center Ossipee

Third Connecticut Lake
Second Connecticut Lake
First Connecticut Lake
Lake Francis
Aziscohos Lake
Oquossoc
Rangeley
Richardson Lakes
Mooselookmeguntic Lake
Byron
USA
Umbagog Lake
MAINE
Old Speck Mountain 4170
Bethel
Bryant Pond
Lynchville
North Waterford
Lovell
Sebago Lake
Ossipee Lake

N

CANADA
USA

⬤ ....Attraction
◯ ....Small Town
▪ ....POI
▬ ....Motorway
▬ ....Main Road
▬ ....Minor Road
▬ ....Railway

White Mountain National Forest

Charges **$$** per vehicle for a one-week pass (*tel: (603) 528-8721*).

Mount Washington Observatory (*www.mountwashington.org*) at 231 miles per hour. You can learn about the observatory and about the alpine habitat in a small museum at the top.

To ascend under your own steam, wait for good weather, begin early, and take layers of warm clothing. Perhaps the most scenic way, the **Ammonoosuc Ravine Trail**, begins at the Cog Railway's base station, passing a waterfall and breaking through the tree line to skirt Lake of the Clouds before the final climb to the summit. Expect to have plenty of company at the top.

A shorter, far easier climb with a view all its own, **Mount Willard** sits at the head of **Crawford Notch**. Its well-surfaced trail was a bridle-path for guests at the Mount Washington and other grand hotels that once lined the valley. The summit overlooks the grand sweep of the notch, with its steep walls.

Accommodation and food in Bretton Woods

Below
The Mount Washington Hotel, Bretton Woods

AMC Highland Center at Crawford Notch $–$$ *Rte 302, Bretton Woods; tel: (603) 278-4453; www.outdoors.org.* The best deal in the White Mountains may be the excellent dinners served nightly at the

Appalachian Mountain Club centre. Fresh-baked breads, hearty soups and choices of entrees that always include a vegetarian dish. Attractive rooms and free nature programmes make this an excellent choice for families.

The Mount Washington Hotel $$–$$$ *Rte 302; tel: (603) 278-1000 or (800) 314-1752; www.mtwashington.com.* Dinners are included in the rates.

DIXVILLE NOTCH

The Balsams Grand Resort Hotel $$–$$$ *Tel: (800) 255-0800 in NH, (800) 255-0600 elsewhere; www.thebalsams.com.* The only 'American Plan' hotel remaining, with all meals (and what meals they are!) and activities included in the room rate. The outstanding dining room ($$) is open to the public by reservation.

Dixville Notch is a wild, narrow cut though often jagged rocks, through which climbs a winding road. Around it is wilderness; wild animals, including moose, are common sights. So common, in fact, that at the eastern end of the notch a special platform has been built along Rte 26, overlooking a boggy area where moose munch in the evening.

Few resorts anywhere have so spectacular a setting as **The Balsams**, under the crest of Dixville Notch. This classic turn-of-the-century grand hotel nestles under steep walls, with mountain views from every window, its own lake, golf course and ski area. Visitors are welcome to stroll in the gardens and stop at the Spring House; guests have a full menu of activities taking advantage of the natural setting, with nature walks, fishing trips and climbs to the viewpoint at **Table Rock**, where the hotel looks like a toy far below.

FRANCONIA NOTCH STATE PARK

The Flume $$ *Tel: (603) 745-8391; www.nhstateparks.com/waterfalls.html. Open mid-May–late Oct daily 0900–1700.*

Old Man of the Mountain Museum *Tel: (603) 823-8800. Open Jun–mid-Oct daily 1000–1730. Free admission.*

Aerial Tramway $$ *Tel: (603) 823-8800; www.cannonmt.com. Open mid-May–Oct daily, and during winter ski season.*

Interstate Highway 93 briefly becomes the Franconia Notch Parkway – narrower, but still a dual carriageway. The first exit leads to **The Flume**, a natural chasm with vertical walls. A boardwalk runs through it close to river level.

The Basin is a 20ft natural pothole at the base of a small waterfall, where melting glaciers wore away the granite with their swirling force. A short walk beyond are the sloping ledges of **Kinsman Falls**, a lovely series of cascades.

High above Profile Lake once stood New Hampshire's symbol, the 40ft group of granite ledges forming the **Old Man of the Mountain**. At the base of the Aerial Tramway, the **Old Man of the Mountain Museum** explains the geology of the profile and efforts for its preservation, and shows collections of souvenirs picturing the 'Old Man' (*see box page 218*).

The **Aerial Tramway** begins here, carrying passengers to the 4200ft summit of Cannon Mountain. Views extend to Canada on clear days, and trails circle the summit. In the winter the tramway carries skiers.

One morning in May 2003 New Hampshire was stunned to discover that the ledges forming the Old Man of the Mountain had slid into the fog that filled the Franconia Notch the previous night, and The Old Man was no more. But you'll still see his likeness on everything from car license plates to road signs.

Accommodation and food in Franconia Notch

Lafayette Campground $ *Rte 3; tel: (603) 823-9513.* Well-spaced tent pitches and a campers' store.

Polly's Pancake Parlor $ *Rte 117, Sugar Hill; tel: (603) 823-5575; www.pollyspancakeparlor.com; open Mon–Fri 0700–1500, Sat and Sun 1700–1900.* Serves freshly made pancakes with real maple syrup.

Hilltop Inn $–$$ *Main St, Sugar Hill; tel: (603) 823-5695; www.hilltopinn.com.* B&B with well-decorated, very comfortable rooms and a lively atmosphere.

JACKSON/GLEN

Wentworth Resort Golf Club
$$$ *Rte 16B, Jackson; tel: (603) 383-9641; www.wentworthgolf.com.* Built in the 1890s when golfing was the latest rage, the club has the two oldest holes in the state, and you can still play them. Holes 12 and 13 are the original holes 1 and 2.

Storyland $$$ (all inclusive) *Rte 16, Glen; tel: (603) 383-4186; www.storylandnh.com. Open early Jun–Aug daily; Sept–mid-Oct Sat and Sun.*

The small village of **Jackson**, accessed through a red covered bridge, has always been a centre for summer resorts, a tradition carried on at the venerable **Wentworth Hotel**, whose beautifully restored Victorian buildings form the town's centrepiece. Behind the hotel stretches the green expanse of **Wentworth Resort Golf Club**, where golfers have enjoyed the greens and the mountain views since 1895. **Jackson Falls** cascades over a series of stair-stepped ledges beside Carter Notch Rd, providing natural picnic sites along the way.

Storyland is straight out of a fairy-tale book, where kids can ride in teacups or play house inside a giant pumpkin as favourite nursery rhymes and tales spring to life. Older children will prefer the rides in a separate section of the park that is designed for them.

Right
Wentworth Resort, Jackson

Attitash Bear Peak
$$ *Rte 302, Bartlett;*
tel: (603) 374-2368;
www.attitash.com. Open
mid-Jun–mid-Sept daily
(mid-Sept–mid-Oct Sat and
Sun only) 1000–1800.

Attitash Bear Peak is a multi-activity resort park with a ski area, an Alpine slide, water slides, mountain bike trails, horse riding and a chairlift to the top for 360-degree views.

Accommodation and food in Jackson/Glen

Carter Notch Inn $–$$ *Carter Notch Rd, Jackson; tel: (603) 383-9630 or (800) 794-9434.* Well-decorated rooms with character; great breakfasts.

Wentworth Resort Hotel $$–$$$ *Rte 16A, Jackson; tel: (603) 383-9700 or (800) 637-0013; www.thewentworth.com.* Fine old resort with year-round sports and an outstanding dining room.

KANCAMAGUS HIGHWAY (AND LINCOLN/WOODSTOCK)

White Mountain
Attractions
Association *Rte 112 at Exit 32 off I-93, North Woodstock; tel: (603) 745-8720 or (800) 346-3687; www.visitwhitemountains.com*

Loon Mountain
Park *Rte 112, Lincoln; tel: (603) 745-6281; www.loonmtn.com.*
Archery Range $ *ext 5569. Open late Jun–Aug daily 0900–1900.*
Equestrian Center $$$ *ext 5450. Open late May–mid-Oct daily.*

Clark's Trading Post $$
Rte 3, Lincoln; tel: (603) 745-8913; www.clarkstradingpost.com. Open late May–Jun and Sept–mid-Oct Sat and Sun; Jul and Aug daily 1000–1800.

Whale's Tale Water
Park $$$ *Rte 3, Lincoln; tel: (603) 745-8810; www. whalestalewaterpark.net. Open mid-Jun–Sept daily 1000–1800.*

The **Kancamagus Highway** stretches 35 miles from Conway in the east to Lincoln in the west. The steep and winding, but good road has a number of laybys, which you should take advantage of, since many fine vistas cannot be seen from the road itself. At the Conway end are **Rocky Gorge and Lower Falls**, on the Swift River, popular for swimming and picnics. Shortly after a covered bridge is the trail to **Sabbaday Falls**, where the stream flows through a gorge with 40ft of falls. Wooden railings make it possible to look straight down at the waterfall and potholes.

At the western end of the highway, **Loon Mountain Park** is best known for skiing, but its Equestrian Center offers trail rides for every skill level and the Archery Range has lessons and equipment. Mountain-biking trails lead to waterfalls, and a shuttle is provided if you want to take the cycle path through Franconia Notch. The gondola tramway that whisks skiers to the summit in the winter continues in the summer, giving access to views, a nature trail and a tumble of glacial boulders that form caves and passageways.

Clark's Trading Post is a wholesome, spotless theme park whose main theme is fun. Children love the steam train ride through the woods, parents appreciate the Victorian Main St, and the performing bears often prove popular. **Whale's Tale Water Park** is a good place to take kids on a hot summer day, with speed slides, a wave pool and two huge water slides.

Accommodation and food around Kancamagus Highway

Mountain Club on Loon $–$$ *Rte 112, Lincoln; tel: (603) 745-3441 or (800) 229-STAY; www.mtnclub.com.* Modern hotel with balconies and pools.

Woodstock Station & Brewery $–$$ *80 Main St, North Woodstock; tel: (603) 745-3951; www.woodstockinnnh.com.* Serves three meals a day.

Right
Conway Scenic Railroad

NORTH CONWAY

ⓘ Mount Washington Valley Chamber of Commerce *Rte 16;* *tel: (603) 356-5701 or (800) 367-3364;* *www.mtwashingtonvalley.org*

Ⓡ Conway Scenic Railroad $$ *Main St;* *tel: (603) 356-5251;* *www.conwayscenic.com. Operates mid-Apr–mid-May and Nov–mid-Dec Sat and Sun; mid-May–late Oct daily, Notch train late Jun–Aug Tue–Sun; Sept–mid-Oct daily.*

North Conway has one of the largest concentrations of outlet shops in the entire northeast, grouped into malls that line Rte 16. Settler's Green and Tanger Outlet Center are the foremost, but many other independent outlets lie all the way from Conway to North Conway. Seconds and overstocks are often drastically reduced, but not everything is a bargain. New Hampshire has no sales tax.

There's more to North Conway than factory outlets and the traffic congestion they create. Across the wide valley, Cathedral Ledge rises from **Echo Lake State Park** (*tel: (603) 356-2672; www.nhstateparks.org*). Rock climbers scale the cliffs in good weather, and a road leads to the top for views of the valley. The lake has a fine – although often crowded – swimming beach and picnic area.

Conway Scenic Railroad travels along the wide valley floor amid mountain views, or climbs through the narrow defile of Crawford Notch. At the Victorian North Conway Station, where trips begin, is a museum with vintage trains.

Accommodation and food in North Conway

Fox Ridge $–$$ *Rte 16; tel: (603) 356-3151 or (800) 343-1804.* Well-decorated motel with balconies and sports facilities.

The Ledges $–$$ *White Mountain Hotel, West Side Rd; tel: (603) 356-7100; www.whitemountainhotel.com.* Three varied meals daily.

Green Granite Inn $$ *Rte 16; tel: (603) 356-6901 or (800) 468-3666; www.greengranite.com.* Family-friendly modern hotel with pools, sauna.

The 1785 Inn $$–$$$ *Rte 16 N; tel: (603) 356-9025 or (800) 421-1785; www.the1785inn.com.* Pure old time New England inn, with inviting guest rooms and a giant fireplace in the dining room. The menu blends traditional and contemporary.

PINKHAM NOTCH

ⓘ Pinkham Notch Visitors Center *Rte 16; tel: (603) 466-2727. For an event schedule, write to AMC, PO Box 298, Gorham, 03581.*

ⓜ Mount Washington Auto Road $$$ *Rte 16; tel: (603) 466-3988; www.mt-washington.com. Open mid-May–late Oct daily 0730–1800 (shorter hours spring and autumn).*

Everything in Pinkham Notch is along Rte 16, which climbs from the village of Jackson. Although Pinkham is not the most dramatic of New Hampshire's mountain passes, known as notches, it offers fine views of Mount Washington, which forms its western slopes.

Your first stop should be at **Glen Ellis Falls**, a short walk from the road. Here a mountain stream rushes over cascades before dropping 65ft through a granite cleft. Native stone safety walls blend with the natural setting.

The **Pinkham Notch Visitors Center** is the headquarters of the Appalachian Mountain Club, and can supply a good selection of books, maps and other information about trails, wildlife and nature in the region, as well as a giant relief map of Mount Washington. It organises year-round programmes and classes, including nature hikes, mountaineering, botany, photography and travelogues. Some programmes are free, but classes require advance registration; some include lodging.

At the head of Pinkham Notch is the entrance to the **Mount Washington Auto Road**, 8 miles of 12 per cent climb with breathtaking views at every turn. Drive it or ride in a minibus with a guide pointing out historic sites and unusual geological formations along the way. If you drive, stop at the **Alpine Gardens**, where wild plants common to much higher elevations flourish on a windy heath; the flowers are at their best in June.

Opposite the Auto Road at the **Glen House Carriage Barns**, all that's left of one of the grand hotels, see vehicles that have carried passengers up the mountain: the first coach, wagons, a Pierce Arrow and others.

Great Glen Trails ($–$$$ *tel: (603) 466-2333; www.greatglentrails.com*) is an outdoor sports and trail centre for cross-country skiing, snowshoeing, ice skating, bicycling, guided nature walks, archery, concerts, barbecues and kite-flying. Rental bikes, skis, snowshoes and ice skates are available.

Accommodation and food in Pinkham Notch

Appalachian Mountain Club $ *Rte 16, Gorham; tel: (603) 466-2727; www.amc-nh.org.* Rustic lodging and three daily meals.

Mount Washington B&B $$ *Rte 2, Gorham; tel: (877) 466-2399 or (603) 466-2669; www.mtwashingtonbb.com*. This hospitable inn amid the celebrated Shelburne Birches, north of Pinkham Notch, has views of Mount Washington from its porch.

The grand hotels

In the 19th century, wealthy society families, fleeing the sweltering cities to seek cool mountain air, made the White Mountains their watering-hole-of-choice. Grand hotels adorned the most scenic settings, featuring opulent ballrooms, full orchestras, grand salons, wide porches for promenading in the evening, and gala activities to amuse the wives and offspring of the rich.

They had their portraits painted, rode the cog railway to the top of Mount Washington and rode horseback to the lookout on the summit of Mount Willard. Attending them was an army of nannies, personal maids and attendants who kept their ball gowns pressed and their collars starched.

This Golden Age died with World War I, and the hotels fell one by one until only a handful remain today. Three – The Balsams, The Mount Washington and The Wentworth – have been restored to their original grandeur to carry on the Golden Age traditions.

Suggested tour

The Valley Inn $–$$ *Waterville Valley; tel: (603) 236-8336 or (800) GO-VALLEY; www.valleyinn.com*. Hotel with the warmth of an inn; good dining room.

Black Bear Lodge $$ *Waterville Valley; tel: (603) 236-8383 or (800) 349-2327; www.black-bear-lodge.com*. Self-catering family suites, with pool.

Total distance: 143 miles; 413 miles with detours.

Time: 4 hours' driving, 9 with detours. Allow 2–3 days for the main route, 4 days with detours. Those with limited time should concentrate on Franconia Notch and Bretton Woods.

Links: I-93 leads north to St Johnsbury, Vermont and the Northeast Kingdom Route (*see page 188*), or south to New Hampton and the Lakes Route (*see page 206*). Maine's North Woods Route (*see page 228*) can be reached via Rte 2 east from Gorham.

Route: Begin at Plymouth, at I-93 Exit 25, and travel north on Rte 175 through Campton, which has three covered bridges.

Detour: From Campton, follow Rte 49 until it ends in a cul-de-sac in **Waterville Valley ①** (*tel: (603) 236-8311 or (800) 349-2327; www.waterville.com*), a mountain-surrounded resort, with golf, tennis, bicycling, hiking, swimming, a skateboard park, year-round ice skating rink, mountain biking and winter sports that centre around the ski area. Most activities are free for resort guests, but also open to the public. If unpaved roads don't scare you, return to Rte 175 on wooded Tripoli (pronounced 'triple-eye') Rd, or backtrack on Rte 49 to Campton.

Continue north on Rte 175, joining Rte 3 through Woodstock and into **NORTH WOODSTOCK ②**. **LINCOLN ③** lies a mile east on Rte 112. **Agaziz Basin ④** is a gorge with a waterfall, right beside Rte 112 just west of North Woodstock. A bridge over the falls makes viewing safe.

Making the Most of the Mountains

The White Mountains Attractions Association offers an easy and affordable way to experience some of the most popular places in the mountains. For about half the price of the normal entrance fees, visitors may purchase a single pass that admits 2 adults to each of 17 area attractions. These passes are also transferable, making them convenient for larger families travelling at different times, or several weekend trips. It is a good idea to buy it early in the season as the number of passes sold is limited. Order from **White Mountains Attractions**, *PO Box 10, VPB, North Woodstock, NH 03262; tel: (800) 346-3687; www.visitwhitemountains.com*

Use the White Mountains Visitors pass at: Attitash & Fields of Attitash (*page 219*); Cannon Mountain Aerial Tramway (*page 217*); Clark's Trading Post (*page 219*); Conway Scenic Railroad (*page 220*); Flume Gorge (*page 217*); Hobo Railroad, *tel: (603) 745-2135*; Loon Mountain (*page 219*); Lost River Gorge (*page 225*); Mount Washington Auto Road (*page 221*); Mount Washington Cog Railway (*page 214*); Polar Caves Park (*page 208*); Santa's Village, *tel: (603) 586-4445*; Six Gun City (*page 225*); Storyland (*page 218*); Whale's Tale Water Park (*page 219*); Wildcat Mountain Gondola, *tel: (800) 255-6439*.

Below
Clark's Trading Post in Lincoln

① Lost River $$
(garden free)
Rte 112, Kinsman Notch;
tel: (603) 745-8031;
www.findlostriver.com.
*Open mid-May–late Oct
daily 0900–1700, Jul and
Aug daily 0900–1800.*

**The Grand Victorian
Cottage $** *Berkley St,
Bethlehem; tel: (603) 869-
5755.* Elegant summer
mansion, furnished with
antiques.

⑩ Rosa Flamingo's $
Main St, Bethlehem;
tel: (603) 869-3111.
Favourite dishes; upbeat
setting.

**① The Spalding Inn
$$** *Mountain View Rd,
Whitefield; tel: (603) 837-
2572 or (800) 368-8439.*
Gracious inn with
excellent dinners daily.
Croquet on a proper lawn.

The Glen $$ *Rte 3,
Pittsburgh; tel: (603) 538-
6500 or (800) 445-GLEN;
www.theglen.org.* A classic
wilderness lodge and
surrounding log cabins on
a lake.

① Libby's Bistro $$
111 Main St, Gorham;
tel: (603) 466-5330;
www.libbysbistro.com. Just
north of Pinkham Notch,
Gorham might not seem a
likely location for a fine
dining restaurant worthy
of Boston or Providence,
but it's here – and without
the city prices.

Lost River ⑤ disappears under a tumble of glacial boulders, reappearing occasionally to plummet in waterfalls on its way down the steep ravine. You can explore all the rock caves and wriggle through tunnels or bypass them on boardwalks and stairs. The 'lemon squeezer' is one tight passage that the claustrophobic should avoid. At the top is a garden of woodland wild flowers, many rare.

Route 3 melds with I-93 through **FRANCONIA NOTCH ⑥**, beyond which Rte 18 leads into the valley village of Franconia, with the lovely **Sugar Hill ⑦** just above it on Rte 117. Views from **Sunset Hill Rd ⑧** are among the best in the mountains. Rte 142 leads from Franconia over a steep hill to **Bethlehem ⑨**. Nine antiques shops tempt travellers along Bethlehem's short Main St, Rte 302, which you follow to Twin Mountain.

Detour: From Bethlehem, take Rte 116 to Whitefield, rejoining Rte 3 to Lancaster. In Whitefield is one of the most scenic golf courses in the state, **Mountain View Golf and Country Club ⑩**, opposite the Mountain View Grand Hotel (*www.mountainviewgrand.com*).

Route 3 leads through Lancaster and Groveton to Colebrook, following the Connecticut River, which marks the border between New Hampshire and Vermont. Route 3 continues through Pittsburg to the Canadian border, past Lake Francis and the Connecticut Lakes, along a stretch known locally as **Moose Alley ⑪**, for the number of moose seen by its roadside. After exploring this road, backtrack to Pittsburg and take Rte 145 south (crossing a covered bridge) along a scenic ridge. Just before reaching Colebrook, you will pass **Beaver Brook Falls ⑫** on your left, a picnic park at its base.

From Colebrook, Rte 26 leads east over **DIXVILLE NOTCH ⑬**, passing The Balsams just before reaching its craggy height. The road follows Clear Stream to Errol, where Rte 16 leads south along the scenic Androscoggin River to Berlin. Climb steep Mount Forist St to see the gold-domed Russian Church before continuing on to Rte 2 at Gorham. Follow Rte 2 west to Rte 115A, with fine views of the Presidential Range to the south. In the early summer the fields near Jefferson are blue with lupins.

Six Gun City ⑭ provides kids lots of rootin'-tootin' fun with cowboy and Old West themed rides and a water park (*www.sixguncity.com*).

Rte 115A joins Rte 115 south to Rte 3, which ends the detour by rejoining the main route with a left turn on to Rte 302 in Twin Mountain. This road leads east to **BRETTON WOODS ⑮** and through the beautiful **Crawford Notch ⑯** to **GLEN ⑰**.

Detour: From Glen, Rte 16 leads north to **JACKSON ⑱**, accessed by a short loop on Rte 16B, and on through **PINKHAM NOTCH ⑲**. Backtrack for a whole new set of views as you head south through the notch, rejoining Rte 302 in Glen.

🌙 **Libby House B&B**
$ 55 Main St, Gorham;
tel: (603) 466-2271.
Victorian inside and out.

Notchland Inn $$–$$$
(including breakfast and
dinner) Rte 302 Bartlett,
Harts Location; tel: (603)
374-6131. Elegant rooms
and five-course dinners
with hiking trails from the
door.

Cranmore Inn $$ 80
Kearsarge St, North Conway;
tel: (800) 526-5502 or
(603) 356-5502;
www.cranmoreinn.com.
North Conway's oldest
continuously operating inn
has been welcoming guests
for 145 years, and serves a
full breakfast menu.

Below
Mount Washington Cog Railway

Rte 16 blends with Rte 302 south through **NORTH CONWAY ⑳**,
where they separate south of town and Rte 16 continues to Conway.
South of Conway's centre, take Rte 112 west (to the right), known as
the **KANCAMAGUS HIGHWAY ㉑**. This scenic road crosses the spine
of the mountain, passing Loon Mountain, and returns to Rte 3 and I-
93 in Lincoln/North Woodstock. Follow I-93 back to Plymouth.

Also worth exploring

From Sugar Hill, north of Franconia Notch, follow signs to Easton, a
town high in the mountains, where you can follow Rte 116 through
the wild and lonely Kinsman Notch. Rte 116 continues over
mountainous terrain until it reaches the stately old town of North
Haverhill, overlooking the Connecticut River. A short distance south
on Rte 10 is elegant Orford, with its Bulfinch-designed homes along
the common. Route 25A returns east over the mountains to
Wentworth, which is west of Plymouth on Rte 25.

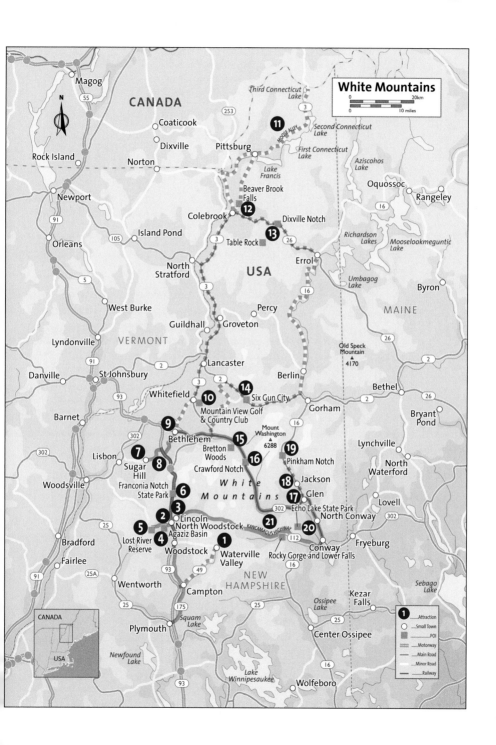

Maine's North Woods

Ratings

Nature/scenery	●●●●●
Food and drink	●●○○○
Arts and culture	●○○○○
Beaches	●○○○○
Children	●○○○○
History	●○○○○
Museums	●○○○○
Shopping	●○○○○

New England has many outdoor recreation areas, but only Maine's north woods have remained a true wilderness. For the most part, towns in this part of New England are outposts – places to sleep, eat and get supplies – and indoor attractions are few. The untamed landscape alternates between forested mountainsides, rolling spruce bogs and broad lakes and rivers. Moose and deer are so plentiful as to constitute a driving hazard. Travel in the north woods tends to be slow, often on poorly maintained roads or by canoe rather than car. But for the hiker, canoeist, fly-fisher or wildlife photographer, no other part of New England can match Maine's north woods.

ALLAGASH WILDERNESS WATERWAY

Allagash Canoe Trips Greenville
$$$ Tel: (207) 237-3077; www.allagashcanoetrips.com. A knowledgeable and reliable operator running wilderness expeditions on the Allagash. The Moosehead Lake Region Chamber of Commerce (see page 231) can supply a list of other outfitters.

Allagash Wilderness Waterway 106 Hogan Rd, Bangor; tel: (207) 941-4014.

Strictly controlled as wilderness (no permanent habitation, no development), this 92-mile ribbon of lakes, ponds, rivers and streams pierces the deep woods of northern Maine from just west of **Baxter State Park** to within a few miles of the northern border with Canada. The only way to travel the length of the wilderness is as the Abenaki tribe did: by canoe. The trip generally takes 7–10 days. Rapids are few, but some large lakes pose wind hazards and canoeing is best undertaken with a group.

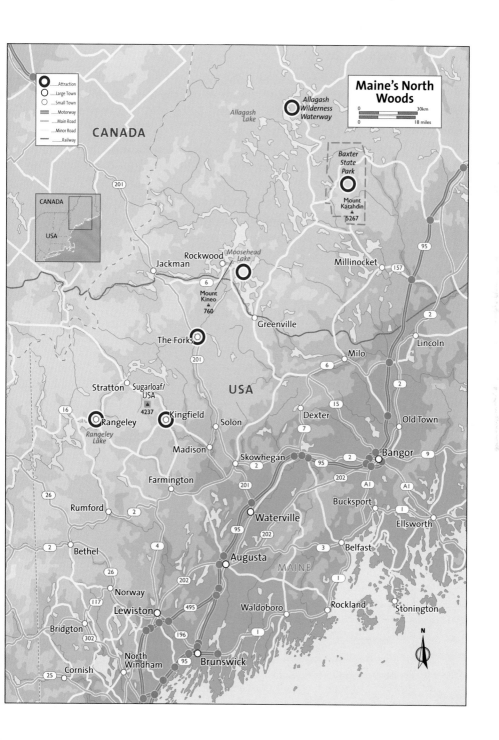

BAXTER STATE PARK

Entry is through Togue Pond Gate off Millinocket Rd, an extension of Golden Rd downstream from Ripogenus Dam.

ℹ️ **Baxter State Park Headquarters** 64 Balsam Dr, Millinocket; tel: (207) 723-5140; www.baxterstateparkauthority.com

🌙 **Campgrounds $** Ten facilities offer a range of accommodation including lean-tos, cabins, bunkhouses and tent pitches. Advance registration required, 4 months in advance. Contact reservations clerk at Baxter State Park Headquarters address (see above).

Professional rafting operators include **Magic Falls Rafting** tel: (800) 207-7238; www.magicfalls.com, **Moxie Outdoor Adventures** tel: (800) 866-6943 or (207) 663-2231; www.moxierafting.com, **Northern Outdoors** tel: (800) 765-7238 or (207) 663-4466; www.northernoutdoors.com, and **Professional River Runners** tel: (800) 325-3911 or (207) 663-2229; www.proriverrunners.com

This 201,018-acre wilderness park is named after a former governor who used his own money to purchase the land because short-sighted legislators would not create a state park. If Allagash is for canoeists, Baxter is for hikers, with 175 miles of trails for all abilities. The park contains 46 mountain peaks and ridges, including 18 higher than 3000ft. The chief attraction is **Mount Katahdin**, the second-tallest mountain in New England and the first place the sun rises on the US. The summit is 5267ft and the slopes support rare alpine plants surviving from the last ice age.

THE FORKS

The Dead River comes in from the west and the Kennebec from the east to create 'The Forks', a fast spill of white water famous for exhilarating rafting and kayaking ($$$). The season begins with spring run-off trips on both rivers and continues on the dam-controlled Kennebec until October. River rafting doesn't get any better than running the Kennebec Gorge, a 12-mile stretch of class II and III rapids with tall cliffs on either side.

Page 230
Allagash Wilderness Waterway

Above
Maine Woods sunrise

KINGFIELD

Sugarloaf/USA
$$–$$$ *Carrabassett Valley; tel: (800) 843-5623 or (207) 237-2000; www.sugarloaf.com.* Accommodation from chalets to motel rooms.

The resort of **Sugarloaf/USA** powers the economy along the Carrabassett River valley, including the farming community of Kingfield. At 4237ft, Sugarloaf Mountain provides dynamic skiing, the longest season in New England and a vertical drop second only to Killington, Vt. Summer activities include hiking, mountain biking, and golf on a Robert Trent Jones course.

MOOSEHEAD LAKE

Moosehead Lake Region Chamber of Commerce
Rtes 6 and 15, Greenville; tel: (207) 695-2702; www.mooseheadlake.org. Open Mon–Sat 1000–1600.

Moose Mainea
tel: (207) 695-2702. Moosehead Lake may have the largest moose population in Maine and celebrates this distinction with a month-long festival in May and June.

Moose on the loose

The moose (*Alces alces*) is the world's largest member of the deer family, with the bulls weighing up to 1400lb and cows reaching 900lb. The population has grown rapidly in recent years and moose are expanding from the northern wilds into urbanised areas. They are usually shy and gentle except during the October rutting season. Moose can be seen along northern roadsides in the spring, licking up the salt residue from winter de-icing efforts. They are also frequently spotted while feeding knee-deep in bogs and other swampy areas.

At 40 miles long and 20 miles wide at its extremities, Moosehead Lake is an inland sea trapped in the last ice age. The 350-mile shoreline is densely forested, and the lake itself is a legendary fishing ground. It's well named, since the shores (and often the waters) are full of moose. Two towns are gateways to the lake. **Greenville**, on the southeastern tip, began as a timber town and developed in the mid-19th century as a destination for adventurous (and wealthy) 'sports'. Until the current road system was built in the 1930s, steamboats were the chief transportation. The sole survivor, the 1914 SS *Katahdin* now makes scenic cruises late June to early October ($$$ *tel: (207) 695-2716*). Greenville is a primary base for wilderness outfitters and fishing guides and boasts the largest float plane fleet in New England. Hunting for moose (with cameras) ranks as the chief tourism activity, with options for various fitness levels, including motor trips, canoe trips and even 'bellyboats' (camouflaged flotation devices). The Chamber of Commerce updates its map of moose sightings daily. The other access to Moosehead is **Rockwood**, on the western shore at the narrowest and most dramatic point of the lake, with the best hunting and fly-fishing. Among the popular outings from Rockwood are trips across the water to 760ft **Mount Kineo**, a near-island peninsula that has been a popular hiking destination since the days of Henry David Thoreau.

Accommodation and food around Moosehead Lake

Greenville Inn $$–$$$ *Norris St, PO Box 1194, Greenville; tel: (888) 695-6000 or (207) 695-2206; email: gvlinn@moosehead.net; www.greenvilleinn.com.* Rooms in the historic country inn often share baths. The seasonal dining room ($$$) is an oasis of gourmet eating in an area rarely known for gastronomic finesse.

Lodge at Moosehead $$$ *Lily Bay Rd, PO Box 1167, Greenville; tel: (207) 695-4400 or (800) 825-6977; www.lodgeatmooseheadlake.com.* All rooms have whirlpool baths and fireplaces; rooms in the main lodge have hand-carved beds. This luxurious outpost on the lake also boasts stunning sunset views.

RANGELEY LAKES

ⓘ Rangeley Lakes Chamber of Commerce
Public Landing, Rangeley; tel: (207) 864-5364 or (800) 685-2537; www. rangeleymaine.com. Open Mon–Sat 0900–1700; reduced hours in winter.

ⓐ Dockside Sports Center $$$ *Town Cove, Rangeley; tel: (207) 864-2424. Rents canoes and powerboats in the summer and snowmobiles in the winter.*

Rangeley Region Sport Shop *2529 Main St, Rangeley; tel: (207) 864-5615. Sells fishing gear, canoes and camping gear and can recommend fishing guides.*

**ⓒ Rangeley Inn $–$$** *Main St, PO Box 160, Rangeley; tel (800) 666-3687 or (207) 864-3341; www.rangeleyinn.com. The main inn dates from 1877 and is the most atmospheric, but some rooms in the newer motel have wood stove fireplaces. The dining room ($–$$) serves good traditional New England food.*

The Rangeley Lakes are legendary for **fly-fishing** for land-locked salmon and native brook trout in a dramatic landscape where tall mountains surround deep glacial lakes. The chain of lakes includes Rangeley, Mooselookmeguntic (the largest at 2 miles wide and 11 miles long) and about ten others in an area of about 450 square miles. The town of Rangeley serves as the base for all outdoor activities in the region. Many fishermen camp at the 691-acre **Rangeley Lake State Park** (*www. state.me.us*), central to more than 40 trout and salmon ponds and lakes.

Suggested tour

Total distance: 509 miles.

Time: 14 hours' driving. Allow 4 days minimum.

Route: Few areas so exemplify the punchline of an old Maine joke, 'You can't get there from here.' Vast tracts of forest and rugged mountains divide road systems, which follow the north–south lines etched by the retreat of glacial ice. While the **RANGELEY LAKES ❶** and **KINGFIELD ❷** are best approached from the west via Rte 16 from the White Mountains (*see page 214*), the most direct route to **BAXTER STATE PARK ❸**, the **ALLAGASH ❹** and **MOOSEHEAD LAKE ❺** begins in **Millinocket ❻**, a timber-company town southeast of Baxter. From Portland, follow I-95 north 193 miles to exit 56, and turn west on Rtes 157 and 11 for 10 miles. Once you leave Millinocket you will be driving on roads that are, for the most part, unpaved. Watch for park signs west of town, turn right on to Golden Rd and continue 18 miles to the **BAXTER STATE PARK's ❸** Perimeter Rd at Togue Pond Gate. Golden Rd continues west through a timber-company gate (road-use fee $$$) for 24 miles to Ripogenus Dam and the Telos Rd turnoff. Although the beginning of the **ALLAGASH WILDERNESS WATERWAY ❼** is only 22 miles north on Telos Rd, the road is often deeply rutted and the drive can take up to two hours. Backtrack to Golden Rd and continue west. The road turns left and becomes more rutted as it becomes Greenville Rd, leading 35 slow miles through spruce bogs. The slowness of the road is an asset, as moose abound here, feeding in the roadside ponds and bogs. When the sealed road begins, Greenville is close. After the backwoods, it will seem like a metropolis. Greenville functions as the chief point of access to **MOOSEHEAD LAKE ❺**, with Rockwood, another 20 miles northwest on Rtes 6 and 15, serving as the other. To take the scenic route back to I-95, continue west for 31 miles to **Jackman ❽**, another wilderness outfitting town and turn south on Rte 201 to descend 26 miles to **THE FORKS ❾**. Views of the Kennebec River are extraordinary for the next 32 miles south to Solon, where Rte 201 turns inland, crosses through Skowhegan in 15 miles and then follows the Kennebec River for another 14 miles to exit 36 of I-95, 78 miles north of Portland.

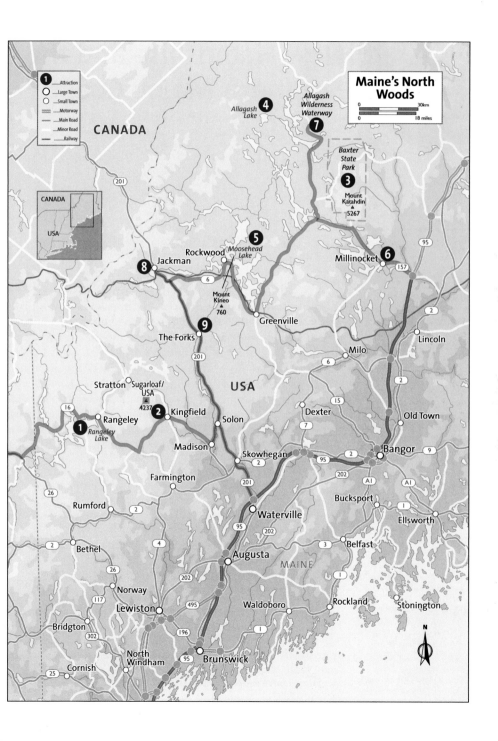

Maine's North Woods

0		30km
0		18 miles

Legend
- ① ....Attraction
- ○ ....Large Town
- ○ ....Small Town
- ....Motorway
- ....Main Road
- ....Minor Road
- ....Railway

CANADA

USA

New Hampshire and the Southern Maine Coast

Ratings

Beaches	●●●●○
Nature/scenery	●●●●○
Children	●●●○○
History	●●●○○
Museums	●●●○○
Shopping	●●●○○
Arts and culture	●●○○○
Food and drink	●●○○○

Old seafaring towns, raucous beach communities and upmarket summer resorts are interwoven along this stretch of coastal New Hampshire and southern Maine. Sudden spits of rock interrupt long sandy strands and the roadways skirt the ocean's edge along a coastal plain where bird-filled marshlands creep down to the sea. The beaches and associated attractions make this an excellent holiday area for families with children. Portsmouth, the Yorks and the Kennebunks also offer many historical attractions and Ogunquit has a lively art scene. Traffic is heavy and slow during July and August, so travellers should maintain patience and a sense of humour.

HAMPTON BEACH

ℙ Although metered parking is available on **Ocean Blvd**, all spaces are claimed early in July and August. There are numerous pay lots on streets leading toward the beach.

ⓘ **Village District** 22 C St; tel: (603) 926-8717; www.hamptonbeach.org. Open mid-Jun–Labor Day (first Mon in Sept) daily 0930–2030; Apr–mid-Jun and early Sept–Oct Sat and Sun only.

The mile-long strand of Hampton Beach offers superb swimming, with soft sand, rolling waves and water on the warm side of brutal. Very popular with Quebecers on holiday (it is the closest ocean beach to Montreal), Hampton is jammed with tanned bodies during July and August, yet tranquil and scenic in May and September.

Hampton Beach State RV Park $ (*Rte 1A; tel: (603) 926-8990*) is a prime recreational vehicle park south of the main beach with only 28 spots. It's open April–mid-October, but begins accepting reservations in January (*tel: (877) 647-2757*).

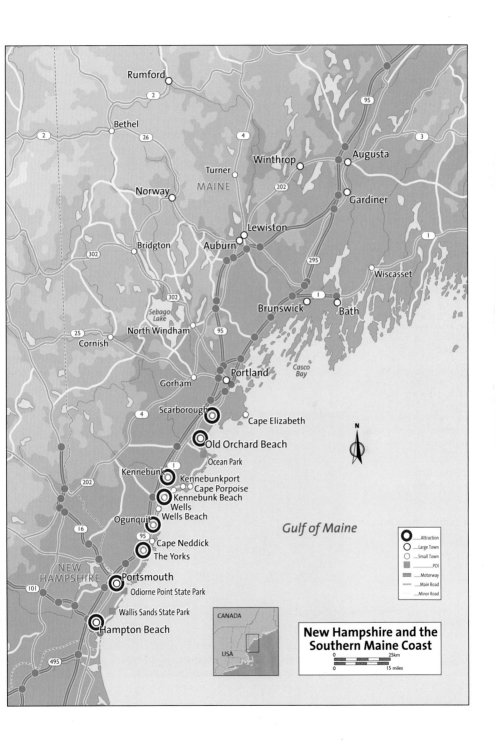

New Hampshire and the Southern Maine Coast

KENNEBUNK VILLAGES

ⓘ Kennebunk Chamber of Commerce *17 Western Ave; tel: (207) 967-0857 or (800) 982-4421; www. visitthekennebunks.com. Open Mon–Fri 0900–1700 (also 1000–1500 on weekends late May–mid-Oct).*

Ⓚ Kennebunk lies directly on Rte 1, while the other villages are strung along the waterfront on Rte 9. **Intown Trolley** **$$** *tel: (207) 967-3686. Tour relates Kennebunkport history as it travels past beaches, Blowing Cave, Spouting Rock and Bush estate. Late May–mid-Oct; re-boarding allowed all day.*

Ⓑ Brick Store Museum $ *Rtes 1 & 35; tel: (207) 985-4802. Open Tue–Fri 1000–1630, Sat 1000–1300. Ask about availability of architectural walking tours of historic district.*

Seashore Trolley Museum $$ *195 Log Cabin Road; tel: (207) 967-2800; www. trolleymuseum.org. Open late May–mid-Oct daily 1000–1700; early May and late Oct Sat and Sun 1000–1700.*

Page 234
Picknicking in Hampton Beach

Right
'Wedding-cake house', Kennebunk

Former president George Bush exemplifies the wealthy, politically conservative class that summers in the villages of Kennebunk (Kennebunk, Kennebunkport, Kennebunk Beach and Cape Porpoise). The town of Kennebunk grew wealthy from 19th-century shipbuilding, resulting in the trophy Colonial, Federal, Greek Revival and Victorian homes of the **Kennebunk National Historic District** (Main and Summer Sts and part of Rte 1). The **Brick Store Museum** occupies an 1825 store and three adjacent buildings in the district. Its exhibitions focus on local maritime history and on fine and decorative arts.

Kennebunkport is the liveliest of the villages; its heart is **Dock Square**, the former shipping centre now given to boutiques, restaurants and art galleries. The **Seashore Trolley Museum** features 50 refurbished trolley cars from around the world. Although the least prettified part of the Kennebunks, the working harbour of **Cape Porpoise**, marked at its entrance by Goat Island lighthouse, is perhaps the most scenic, with lobster fishermen and yachtsmen sharing the same anchorages.

Accommodation and food in the Kennebunks

Port Lobster $ *Ocean Ave, Kennebunkport; tel: (207) 967-5411; open daily 0800–1800.* Seafood market also sells superb takeaway lobster rolls.

Fontenay Terrace Motel $–$$ *128 Ocean Ave, Kennebunkport; tel: (207) 967-3556; www.fontenaymotel.com*. This small motel on a tidal inlet is a good spot to enjoy the natural beauty of the harbour.

Grissini Italian Bistro $$ *27 Western Ave, Kennebunk; tel: (207) 967-2211; open for dinner*. Northern Italian trattoria standards plus large pasta selection.

Historic Inns of Kennebunkport (*www.kportinns.com*) is a consortium of seven excellent B&Bs in historic homes with a strong emphasis on luxury and romance. One of the more relaxed members is **The Maine Stay $$–$$$** *34 Maine St, Kennebunkport; tel: (800) 950-2117 or (207) 967-2117*.

White Barn Inn $$–$$$ *37 Beach Ave, Kennebunkport; tel: (207) 967-2321; www.whitebarninn.com*. Luxurious retreat also has Maine's best white-linen gourmet dining (**$$$**).

OGUNQUIT

ⓘ Ogunquit Chamber of Commerce *36 Main St (PO Box 2289), Ogunquit; tel: (207) 646-2939; www.ogunquit.org. Open summer Mon–Thur and Sun 0900–1700, Fri 0900–2000, Sat 0900–1800; reduced hours rest of year.*

Ⓠ Ogunquit Trolley $ *Tel: (207) 646-1411.* Circles from town to beach to Perkins Cove. *Operates mid-May–mid-Oct.*

Ⓜ Ogunquit Museum of American Art *543 Shore Rd; tel: (207) 646-4909; www.ogunquitmuseum.org. Open Jul–mid-Oct Mon–Sat 1030–1700, Sun 1400–1700.*

Ⓞ Ogunquit Playhouse $$$ *Rte 1 S; tel: (207) 646-5511; www.ogunquitplayhouse.org.* Presents three musicals and two plays by touring companies mid-June–August.

Maine's most gay- and lesbian-friendly resort, Ogunquit has **superb sand beaches** (entrances at Beach St and 2 miles north of town via 'the footbridge'). Clusters of art galleries and boutiques are found both in the town centre and in **Perkins Cove**, a former fishing harbour that's now part art colony, part tourist emporium. **Marginal Way**, a 1¼-mile footpath on cliffs above the ocean, connects the cove with the beaches. Thickets of beach roses line the route and many benches are available to enjoy the view. Ogunquit's art colony began around 1900 but came into its own in the decades between the world wars. That heyday is well represented at the **Ogunquit Museum of American Art** which overlooks Perkins Cove, worth visiting for the Marsden Hartley paintings alone.

Accommodation and food in Ogunquit

Village Food Market $ *Ogunquit Sq; tel: (207) 646-2122; open daily 0630–1900*. Full-service grocer's deli counter, also makes excellent takeaway sandwiches.

Norseman Resort $–$$$ *135 Beach St; tel: (800) 822-7024 or (207) 646-7024; www.ogunquitbeach.com*. Sprawling motel at beach car park provides great beach access but limited peace and quiet.

Riverside Motel $–$$$ *50 Riverside Ln; tel: (207) 646-2741; www.riversidemotel.com*. Excellent motel complex connects to Perkins Cove over pedestrian drawbridge.

Beachmere Inn $$–$$$ *62 Beachmere Pl; tel: (800) 336-3983 or (207) 646-2021; www.beachmereinn.com*. Modernised Victorian inn and classic motel with grand views and gate on to Marginal Way. All rooms have cooking facilities.

Arrows $$$ *Berwick Rd; tel: (207) 361-1100; open May–late November for dinner.* Stunning gardens surround country restaurant dedicated to gourmet excess.

OLD ORCHARD BEACH

ℹ Old Orchard Beach Chamber of Commerce *First St; tel: (800) 365-9386 or (207) 934-2500; www. oldorchardbeachmaine.com. Open Jun–Aug daily 0830–1630; Sept–May Mon–Fri 0830–1630.*

Seven miles of sandy swimming beaches made Old Orchard one of New England's first summer resorts. A family destination, Old Orchard's giddy scene cranks up when school ends and halts abruptly on the first weekend in September. The 1898 **Ocean Pier** at the centre of town has a concentration of game arcades, souvenir stands and food vendors. Nearby amusement arcades feature old-fashioned games of 'skill' along with modern electronics. **Palace Playland** features mechanical rides, roller coaster and Ferris wheel. The least crowded beaches are north of the town centre along Rte 9.

Accommodation and food in Old Orchard Beach

Grand Ave is lined with dozens of modest motels, all steps from the beach. Eating here is more a continuous than a periodic activity, as stalls selling pizza, hot dogs and ice cream far outnumber actual restaurants.

The Edgewater $–$$$ *57 W Grand Ave; tel: (800) 203-2034 or (207) 934-2221; www.theedgewatermotorinn.com.* Lovingly maintained classic two-level motel situated right on the shore.

Atlantic Birches Inn $$ *20 Portland Ave; tel: (888) 934-5295 or (207) 934-5295; www.atlanticbirches.com.* Ten rooms in two buildings in a quiet location away from the beach.

Joseph's $$ *55 W Grand Ave; tel: (207) 934-5044; open for breakfast and dinner.* When cotton candy and clam rolls no longer suffice, Joseph's serves traditional American meals.

PORTSMOUTH

ℹ Strawbery Banke Museum $$$ *Marcy St; tel: (603) 433-1100; www.strawberybanke.org. Open May–Oct daily 1000–1700; Nov–Dec call for hours.*

Portsmouth's fervour for historic preservation saved its Colonial and Federal architecture, launching this small city's revival as a destination. Crafts shops, boutiques and restaurants fill the 18th-century chandleries and warehouses of the **Old Harbor** (Bow and Ceres Sts). The 10-acre **Strawbery Banke Museum** preserves 300 years of Portsmouth domestic life in 30 buildings. Walking to the six historic mansions scattered around the city on the **Portsmouth**

ⓘ Greater Portsmouth Chamber of Commerce *500 Market St, Portsmouth; tel: (603) 436-1118; www.portsmouthchamber.org.* Information kiosk in Market Sq provides Harbor Trail map. *Open late May–Oct daily.*

Harbor Trail gives a better sense of the intersection of history and modern life. Among them, they chronicle Portsmouth's merchant and privateer class from 1716 to 1807.

Accommodation and food in Portsmouth

Café Mediterraneo $–$$ *119 Congress St; tel: (603) 427-5563; open for lunch and dinner.* Pizza, calzones and contemporary Italian seafood.

Black Trumpet Bistro $$ *29 Ceres St; tel: (603) 431-0887; open for dinner.* New American bistro shows panache and innovation.

Inn at Strawbery Banke $$ *314 Court St; tel: (800) 428-3933 or (603) 436-7242; www.innatstrawberybanke.com.* Large 19th-century inn with striking wraparound porch near Strawbery Banke Museum.

Ale House Inn $$–$$$ *121 Bow St; tel: (603) 431-7760; www.alehouseinn.com.* Updated, modern rooms in a former brewery building near the harbour that also houses a professional theatre company.

Oar House $$–$$$ *55 Ceres St; tel: (603) 436-4025; open for lunch and dinner.* Old-style seafood restaurant with outdoor deck overlooking the harbour.

The Sise Inn $$–$$$ *40 Court St; tel: (877) 747-3466 or (603) 433-1200; www.siseinn.com.* Rich butternut woodwork sets elegant tone in Queen Anne-style mansion and carriage house with 34 rooms.

Below
Portsmouth Athenaeum

SCARBOROUGH

 Scarborough Marsh Nature Center *Pine Point Rd; tel: (207) 883-5100 or (207) 781-2330; www.maineaudubon.org. Open Jun–early Sept daily 0930–1730; May and late Sept Sat and Sun 0930–1730. Walking tours $$, canoe tours and rentals $$.*

Scarborough possesses a rough beauty rarely equalled along the New England coast. More than 3000 acres of tidal and freshwater marsh, salt creeks and uplands are protected in the **Scarborough Marsh Nature Center**, where a boardwalk nature trail is dotted with observation hides from where you can observe shy waterfowl. The exclusive summer community of **Prout's Neck** occupies a striking rocky knob where the artist Winslow Homer painted many of his best seascapes around the turn of the last century.

Accommodation and food in Scarborough

Bayley's Camping Resort $ *Rte 9; tel: (207) 883-6043.* Large wooded pitches; shuttle bus to beaches.

Black Point Inn Resort $$$ *Prout's Neck; tel: (800) 258-0003 or (207) 883-2500; www.blackpointinn.com.* This historic beachfront resort consists of the main inn plus several cottages; the amenities include hiking trails, a beach club and a golf course.

WELLS

 Wells Auto Museum $ *Rte 1; tel: (207) 646-9064. Open mid-Jun–early Sept daily 1000–1700.*

Wells National Estuarine Research Reserve $ *342 Laudholm Farm Rd; tel: (207) 646-1555; www.wellsreserve.org. Trails open daily 0700–dusk; visitor centre open late May–mid-Oct Mon–Sat 1000–1600, Sun 1200–1600. Call for off-season hours.*

Lighthouse Depot *Rte 1N; tel: (207) 646-0608.* This may not be in a real lighthouse but the selection of lighthouse-themed gifts and souvenirs is mind-boggling.

While adjacent Ogunquit caters for adult couples, Wells embraces families. The 7-mile-long strand of **Wells Beach** fronts on shallow waters and the town of souvenir shops has a naïve appeal. An attraction for all ages is the **Wells Auto Museum**, which displays a collection of nickelodeons and other Americana along with more than 80 antique and classic cars. Less than 2 miles from the hubbub of the beach and highway strip are a couple of striking wetland reserves. The **Wells National Estuarine Research Reserve** at Laudholm Farm preserves 1600 acres of field, forest, wetlands and beaches criss-crossed by 7 miles of nature trails.

The **Rachel Carson National Wildlife Refuge** (*www.fws.gov/ northeast/rachelcarson*) protects 4800 acres of wetland habitat critical to several migratory bird species. A mile-long interpretative nature trail begins at the headquarters car park, allowing you to explore on foot.

Accommodation and food in Wells

Pinederosa Camping Area $ *128 N Village Rd; tel: (207) 646-2492.* Mix of wooded and open field sites only 2 miles from Wells Beach.

Maine Diner $–$$ *Rte 1; tel: (207) 646-4441; open for breakfast, lunch and dinner.* Traditional diner makes good use of its vegetable garden out the back.

THE YORKS

ℹ Chamber of Commerce
1 Stonewall Ln;
tel: (207) 363-4422;
www.gatewaytomaine.org.
Open Mon–Sat 0900–1700,
Sun 1000–1600.

🏛 Old York Historical Society
$$ Jefferds Tavern Visitor Center on Lindsay Rd; tel: (207) 363-4974; www.oldyork.org. Open mid-Jun–mid-Oct Mon–Sat 1000–1700. Each building can also be toured for a small individual charge.

York is very proud to have been the first permanent English settlement in the region. The **Old York Historical Society** preserves nine 17th- and 18th-century buildings as a museum, with more than 30 galleries and period rooms. The most interesting and least visited of the bunch is the **Elizabeth Perkins House**. Its 20th-century owners had an idiosyncratic vision of Colonial life and strongly influenced New England's Colonial Revival movement.

Three other villages lie within York's boundaries. **York Harbor** and **Cape Neddick**, both lovely to stroll around, boast rich summer homes and yacht slips. Just off the tip of Cape Neddick is the much photographed **Nubble Light**. Brassy **York Beach** is the very public junction of two superb swimming beaches.

Accommodation and food in the Yorks

Camp Eaton $ *Rte 1A, York Harbor; tel: (207) 363-3424.* RV hook-ups and wooded tent pitches near Long Sands Beach.

Goldenrod Restaurant $–$$ *Railroad Rd and Ocean Ave, York Beach: tel: (207) 363-2621; open for breakfast, lunch and dinner.* Meals are simple 'home cooking' but the main appeal is an old-fashioned soda fountain and the salt water taffy (toffee) made on the premises.

York Harbor Inn $$–$$$ *Rte 1A, York Harbor; tel: (800) 343-3869 or (207) 363-5119; www.yorkharborinn.com.* A 19th-century inn with 54 rooms overlooking the harbour near Nubble Light. Formal dining room with grand ocean view serves traditional New England cuisine (**$$$**). The Ship's Cellar pub is more casual in menu and attire (**$$**).

Suggested tour

🍴 Stonewall Kitchen Company Store and Cafe $ *Stonewall Ln; tel: (207) 351-2712 (store), (207) 351-2719 (cafe); www.stonewallkitchen.com. Store open Mon–Sat 0800–1900, Sun 0900–1800; cafe open Mon–Sat 0800–1600, Sun 0900–1100, extended hours Jul and Aug. Factory outlet for local line of gourmet products has bargain-price café.*

Total distance: 110 miles with detours.

Time: 4–5 hours of often slow driving. Allow 2–3 days.

Links: The southern end of this route connects to the Massachusetts North Shore Route (*see page 64*), while the northern end runs into Portland (*see page 244*).

Route: From the New Hampshire Turnpike, take Exit 2 to **HAMPTON BEACH ❶**. At Ocean Ave turn north on to Rte 1A, which follows the ocean through Rye Beach, with fine swimming at **Wallis Sands State Park ❷** and gentle hiking and birdwatching at **Odiorne Point State Park ❸**, where a children's science museum highlights marine ecology.

🏖 Wallis Sands State Park $ *Rte 1A, Rye. Open late May–Oct daily. Beach accessible all year.*

Odiorne Point State Park $ *Rte 1A, Rye. Park open May–Oct daily.*

Seacoast Science Center $ *570 Ocean Blvd; tel: (603) 436-8043; www. seacoastsciencecenter.org. Open Apr–Oct daily 1000–1700; Nov–Mar Sat–Mon 1000–1700.*

🛍 Kittery Outlet Malls *Tel: (888) 548-8379; www. thekitteryoutlets.com*

Kittery Trading Post *Rte 1, Kittery; tel: (207) 439-2700 has been equipping travellers for camping, backpacking, fishing and other outdoor activities since 1938.*

🍴 Warren's Lobster House $–$$ *11 Water St; tel: (207) 439-1630. Simple seafood, lobster, chicken and steak in waterside location popular with families.*

🛍 Arundel Antiques *Rte 1, Arundel; tel: (207) 985-7965, about 3 miles north of Kennebunk, is one of the best multi-dealer group antiques shops along the Maine coast. Open daily 1000–1700; extended weekend summer hours.*

Route 1A rejoins Rte 1 as it enters **PORTSMOUTH ④** past about 2 miles of handsome Greek Revival houses, continuing into the Old Harbour district, and over the Piscataqua River on Memorial Bridge into Kittery and a traffic roundabout. Just north of the roundabout, 120 factory outlet stores in a mile-long thicket along Rte 1 constitute one of the largest concentrations of shops in the US.

Shopping-induced congestion suddenly eases as Rte 1 continues 5 miles to Rte 1A, which threads along the shoreline through the **YORKS ⑤** for another 5 miles before rejoining Rte 1 for the leafy 3-mile drive into **OGUNQUIT ⑥**. Route 1 continues another 4 miles north past strip malls to the Mile Rd turnoff to **WELLS BEACH ⑦**, then another 3 miles to the junction of Rte 9. Three miles north of the junction on Rte 1 is **KENNEBUNK ⑧**; Rte 9 goes 4 miles northeast into **Kennebunkport ⑨** (the two villages are joined by Rte 9A).

Route 1 is more direct, but the shoreline scenic route follows Rte 9 north for 16 miles into the towns of Biddeford and Saco, then down the north side of the Saco River to its mouth and north along the shore to **Ocean Park ⑩**, a summer cottage community with camp meeting origins, and then through **OLD ORCHARD BEACH ⑪**. At the Pier, Rte 9 becomes E Grand Ave and continues north 8 miles past uncrowded swimming and surfing beaches before turning inland at Pine Point to pass the Scarborough Marshes. Route 9 joins Rte 1 to continue north to **SCARBOROUGH ⑫** for 4 miles to Rte 207, Black Point Rd, which leads to Prout's Neck. Alternately, Rte 1 continues into Portland.

Also worth exploring

Isle of Shoals

These nine small, privately owned islands continue to spark the imagination of New Englanders, and legends persist of pirates' gold and rum-runners' fortunes buried in their mere 200 acres. One island was the site of the infamous (and unsolved) 1873 murders on which Anita Shreve's novel, *The Weight of Water*, is based. **Star Island** has a variety of self-guided nature walks. Poet Celia Thaxter planted flowers on **Appledore Island**, where she wrote her classic *An Island Garden*, illustrated by painter Childe Hassam. The 1894 book provided the plans that were used to restore the gardens in 1977. Tours are offered on Thursday afternoons mid-June–August by arrangement with **Shoals Marine Laboratory** $$$ *Cornell University, Ithaca NY 14853; tel: (607) 430-5220; www.sml.cornell.edu/sml_reservation.php.* Transportation is by **Portsmouth Harbor Cruises** *(www.portsmouthharbor.com).* **Island Cruises** $$$ *Rye Harbor State Marina, Rye; tel: (603) 964-6446; www.uncleoscar.com* does cruises of the group with 3-hour walkabouts on Star Island June–September.

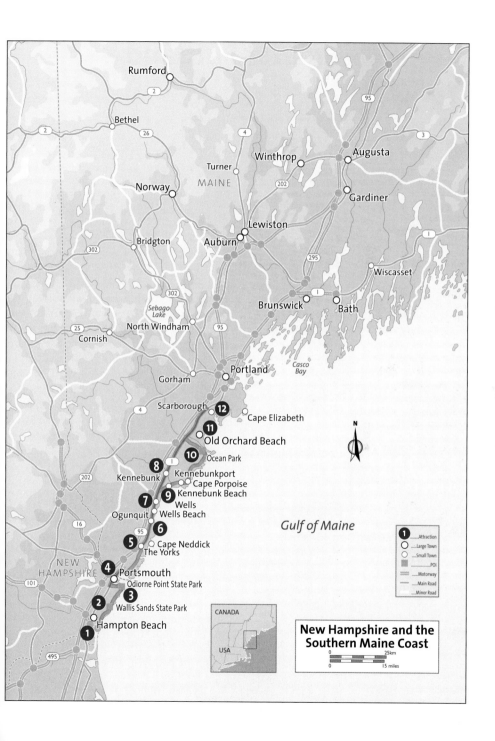

New Hampshire and the
Southern Maine Coast

Greater Portland

Ratings

Food and drink ●●●●○

Arts and culture ●●●○○

Shopping ●●●○○

Beaches ●●○○○

Children ●●○○○

History ●●○○○

Museums ●●○○○

Nature/ scenery ●●○○○

A s the cultural and business centre of New England's north coast, the small city of Portland has more shopping, dining, arts and entertainment than communities three times its population of just under 65,000. Situated on a peninsula in the focal point of sheltered Casco Bay, it is central to superb beaches to the south and Maine's woodlands only a few miles inland. Portland is often treated as a convenient departure point for winter skiing in Maine's rugged mountains or summer sightseeing through coastal villages, but the city itself is lively and engaging. Far-sighted city planning salvaged the architectural shell of Portland's 19th-century heyday as a shipping and shipbuilding centre, and an influx of young professionals to the software and banking industries has created a bustling cultural and entertainment scene.

Sights

ⓘ Convention and Visitors Bureau of Greater Portland *Visitor Center, 14 Ocean Gateway Pier; tel: (207) 772-5800; www.visitportland.com. Open Mon–Fri 0830–1700, Sat 0930–1600.*

ⓟ Public parking meters (2-hour maximum) are cheap. Off-street car parks charge slightly more, but most shops give validation stamps good for one hour of free parking at municipal lots and garages.

Arts District

In recent years Portland's commercial district along Congress St, between Mercy Hospital and the handsome Beaux-arts City Hall, has been spruced up and promoted to its own citizens as the 'Arts District'. Two museums give credence to the claim. The **Children's Museum of Maine** intentionally appeals to the under-14 set with many general science exhibits common to such institutions as well as some decidedly local exhibits, such as a lobster boat. The top-floor camera obscura that surveys Portland's skyline is an optical delight for all ages. The **Portland Museum of Art** occupies a strikingly modern building designed by the I M Pei firm and erected in 1983 – a welcome relief from the expanse of Victorian red brick around it. The museum has an outstanding collection of paintings and graphic art by late

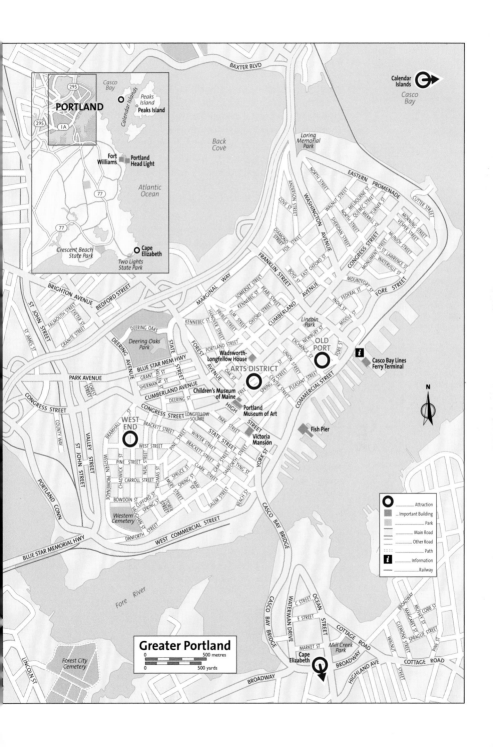

Greater Portland

0 — 500 metres
0 — 500 yards

Children's Museum of Maine $$
142 Free St; tel: (207)
828-1234; www.
childrensmuseumofme.org.
Open Mon–Sat 1000–1700,
Sun 1200–1700; Oct–Apr
closed Mon.

Portland Museum of Art $$ 7 Congress Sq;
tel: (207) 775-6148;
www.portlandmuseum.org.
Open late May–mid-Oct
daily 1000–1700 (Fri until
2100); late Oct–May
closed Mon.

Wadsworth-Longfellow House $$ 485–489
Congress St; tel: (207) 772-
1807; www.mainehistory.org.
Open May–Oct Mon–Sat
1000–1700, Sun
1200–1700.

Casco Bay Ferry $$–$$$
Commercial and Franklin Sts;
tel: (207) 774-7871; www.
cascobaylines.com. Offers
year-round ferry service
and a variety of summer
sightseeing tours.

Portland Discovery $$–$$$ Long Wharf; tel:
(207) 774-0808. Offers
cruises to Portland Head
Light and has a variety of
sightseeing and seal-
watching cruises.

Greater Portland Transit District $
Tel: (207) 774-0351;
www.gpmetrobus.com.
Although many attractions
are clustered near each
other, using the city bus
system cuts walking time,
especially on Portland's
steep hills.

19th- and early 20th-century artists who worked in Maine, including Andrew and N C Wyeth, Edward Hopper and Rockwell Kent. Its Winslow Homer oil paintings and watercolours, many of which were painted at nearby Prout's Neck, rank among the artist's finest.

Portland has a claim in the literary arts as well. Poet and translator Henry Wadsworth Longfellow was born in Portland and grew up in the **Wadsworth-Longfellow House**, a brick home now in the centre of town but far on the outskirts when Longfellow's grandfather, General Peleg Wadsworth, built it in 1786. Far more restrained than the mansions that Portlanders would build a century later, it reveals Longfellow's modest upbringing.

Calendar Islands

The Casco Bay archipelago across the mouth of Portland harbour is known as the Calendar Islands because legend has it that there are 365 of them (the actual number is closer to 200, and many of those are little more than ledges exposed at low tide). Similar exaggerations exist about the history of the islands, often involving unscrupulous characters who lured ships onto the rocks in storms to salvage them when the weather cleared. The larger islands are now pleasant residential neighbourhoods. **Peaks Island**, just offshore, has a fine waterfront park and beach ideal for a picnic. It enjoys a frequent ferry service on the **Casco Bay Lines** commuter boats. Cliff, Chebeague, Long, Little Diamond and Great Diamond islands are also accessible by ferry, but with limited service.

Cape Elizabeth

Although less than 2 miles south of downtown Portland, Cape Elizabeth boasts a radically different geography. Ancient geological forces pushed the seabed to the surface here, creating a buffer-zone of rocky promontories between sandy barrier beaches to the south and Casco Bay to the north. The contrast of landforms has haunted

Whales of New England

The most frequently spotted New England whales are the 5ft harbour porpoises, which sometimes even visit Boston's busy harbour. The offshore whales are larger, more striking baleen whales that feed on shrimp-like krill and plankton in the shallows from Cape Cod into the Gulf of Maine. Pilot whales, black and about 20ft long, are common in large pods spring and autumn. The streamlined minke whale, blue-grey on top and about 25ft long, is common in all but the coldest months. The 70ft finback also feeds off the New England coast in large numbers from March to November. The showman of the whales, the 40ft humpback whale, is famous for its great leaps, or 'breaches'. Although infrequently seen by commercial whale watches, almost the entire 300-individual population of the endangered northern right whale also swims in New England waters.

Fort Williams Park
1000 Shore Rd. Free
admission to grounds.
Lighthouse museum $
*tel: (207) 799-2661. Open
late May–mid-Oct daily
1000–1600; Apr, May, Nov
& Dec Sat and Sun
1000–1600.*

Free *Go* (a Thursday
supplement to the
Portland Press Herald)
provides complete listings
of theatre, concerts, club
performances, art galleries,
dance, film and performing
arts.

Portland Pirates
*Cumberland County Civic Ctr,
Spring St; tel: (207) 828-
4665;
www.portlandpirates.com.*
This minor-league hockey
team plays October–April.

Portland Sea Dogs $$
*Hadlock Field, Park Ave;
tel: (800) 936-3647 or
(207) 879-9500;
www.portlandseadogs.com.*
Minor league baseball team
plays April–September.

**Portland Stage
Company** *25 Forest Ave;
tel: (207) 774-0465;
www.portlandstage.com.* The
largest professional theatre
company in northern New
England produces
contemporary and classic
dramas and musicals
October–May.

**Portland Symphony
Orchestra** *20 Myrtle St;
tel: (207) 773-6128;
www.portlandsymphony.com;
box office tel: (207) 842-
0800; www.porttix.com.*
Performs classical, pops
and chamber concerts in
Merrill Auditorium.

Right
Portland Head Lighthouse

painters since the early 19th century. **Crescent Beach State Park** off Rte 77 offers excellent swimming on a south-facing beach that trails from sand at the east end to stones in the west. Less than half a mile away is **Two Lights State Park**, where a steep and rocky shoreline overlooks the Atlantic Ocean. The park is named after the two 19th-century lighthouses that still signal this southern opening of Casco Bay. Painter Edward Hopper so admired their stark desolation that he painted them from several viewpoints in 1927 and 1929. In general, Maine lighthouses warn sailors of rocks and ledges (as opposed to merely shallow water) and are therefore sited on prominent elevations that offer spectacular views. That is certainly true 3 miles north at **Fort Williams**, constructed in 1791 to defend Portland harbour from anticipated British attacks. Now a city park much favoured by kite fliers, the fortifications have crumbled but **Portland Head Light**

Victoria Mansion
$$$ *109 Danforth St;*
tel: (207) 772-4841;
www.victoriamansion.org.
Open May–Oct Mon–Sat
1000–1600, Sun
1300–1700; late Nov and
Dec Tue–Sun 1100–1700.

Cross Jewelers *570*
Congress St; tel: (207)
773-3107. Open Mon–Sat
0930–1700. Has an
excellent selection of
jewellery featuring the pink
and green tourmalines
mined in Maine.

Maine Potters Market
376 Fore St; tel: (207) 774-
1633. Open daily
1000–2100, reduced winter
hours. Provides one-stop
shopping for work by
many of Maine's best
ceramic artists.

remains intact. One of the most photographed lighthouses in Maine, Portland Head offers striking views down into swirling currents around ledges and islets. There is a small lighthouse museum inside the base.

Old Port

Many travellers spend their entire time in Portland in the Old Port district bounded by Commercial, Franklin, Congress and Union Sts. Portland's port and mercantile exchange area was completely rebuilt in red brick after the Great Fire of 1866, making it a later and more robust architecture than that found on most New England waterfronts. After World War II, most of Portland's sea traffic shifted to the deeper waters of South Portland and the waterfront fell into decay. Revived in the 1970s, the Old Port Exchange, as it is sometimes called, has boomed as a shopping, drinking and dining district, complete with cobblestone streets, pedestrian-only ways and artfully enhanced quaintness at every turn. Microbreweries and pubs have flourished and much of Portland's casual nightlife is found in the Old Port.

The wharves still constitute a working port, with sightseeing vessels berthed next to scallop draggers, lobster boats and offshore purse seiners. In fact, a substantial portion of Maine's catch is offloaded at Portland Fish Pier, where there's a **public fish auction** several afternoons each week.

West End

As in many port towns, the wealthy merchants built their homes on the highest point of land. As a result, Portland's West End managed to escape the flames of the 1866 conflagration, and it has survived the economic vicissitudes of much of the 20th century. Now the showpiece homes of one of the best-preserved Victorian residential districts in the US sparkle with fresh paint. The West End's neighbourhood park is the **Western Promenade**, a landscaped public walkway along the edge of a west-facing cliff some 175ft above sea level, an altitude sufficient for the White Mountains of New Hampshire to be visible in the distance on a clear day. The houses are the real marvels, and none is more marvellous than **Victoria Mansion**, an 1858 Italianate villa of inordinate flamboyance for a city where extravagance is always suspect. The original owner engaged an operatic set designer to create the interiors.

Accommodation and food in Portland

Many moderate chain motels line Rtes 1 and 9 south of Portland in Scarborough and South Portland.

Gilbert's Chowder House $ *92 Commercial St; tel: (207) 871-5636; open for lunch and dinner.* This casual spot near the docks is a good bet for chowder and baked fish.

Above
Old Port, Portland

Gritty McDuff's $ *396 Fore St; tel: (207) 772-2739; open for lunch and dinner.* Portland's first brew-pub serves English-inspired pub food.

Wassamki Springs $ *56 Saco St, Westbrook; tel: (207) 839-4276.* Convenient for Portland, this campsite for tents, trailers and recreational vehicles (RVs) is sited on a private 30-acre lake.

Two Lights Lobster Shack $$ *Two Lights Rd, Cape Elizabeth; tel: (207) 799-1677; open for lunch and dinner.* Oceanside picnic tables have a great ocean view.

Eastland Park Hotel $$–$$$ *157 High St, Portland; tel: (888) 671-8008 or (207) 775-5411; www.eastlandparkhotel.com.* Landmark hotel in Arts District at Congress Sq has 204 rooms on 12 levels.

Pomegranate Inn $$–$$$ *49 Neal St, Portland; tel: (800) 356-0408 or (207) 772-1006; www.pomegranateinn.com.* This 1884 Italianate home and carriage house near the Western Promenade has eight guest rooms.

Fore Street $$$ *288 Fore St; tel: (207) 775-2717; open for dinner.* Locals favour this restaurant for its roasted and wood-grilled entrées.

Inn by the Sea $$$ *40 Bowery Beach, Cape Elizabeth; tel: (800) 888-4287 or (207) 799-3134; www.innbythesea.com.* Striking resort-style complex of 57 guest rooms, suites and cottages on Crescent Beach, a short drive from downtown Portland.

Portland Regency Hotel & Spa $$$ *20 Milk St; tel: (207) 774-4200 or (800) 727-3436; www.theregency.com.* Boutique 93-room hotel with extensive spa services occupies historic Armory building in heart of Old Port.

Street & Company $$$ *33 Wharf St; tel: (207) 775-0887; open for dinner.* This restaurant is known for its innovative fish preparations.

Suggested walk

Total distance: 3½ miles.

Time: All day. Portland is a safe and compact city where walking is usually easier than driving. This walking tour concentrates on attractions in the Old Port, Arts District and West End.

Route: Begin at the corner of Commercial and Franklin Sts at the Ocean Gateway Information Centre, where architecture buffs may wish to purchase inexpensive brochures for four historic walking tours. Down Commercial St is **Fish Pier ❶**, site of the weekday fish auction. Walk three blocks along Commercial St past the working wharves to High St, turn right and walk two blocks to Danforth St, making a half-block detour to **Victoria Mansion ❷**. Continue four blocks up High St to Congress Sq to the **Portland Museum of Art ❸**. The **Children's Museum of Maine ❹** is practically next door on Free St, one block above the Civic Center Auditorium, the city's chief venue for concerts and expositions.

Beyond the Museum of Art, turn left on Congress St, passing through the last part of 'Portland's Downtown District' (as the merchants call the Arts District) with several interesting shops and the galleries associated with the Portland School of Art. Congress St meets State St at **Longfellow Sq ❺**, which honours Portland's most famous native son, Henry Wadsworth Longfellow.

Pine St leads off Congress Sq to the left, entering the **WEST END ❻** district of historic homes dating mostly from between 1865 and 1900, Portland's economic high point. Walking the streets perpendicular to Pine (Neal, Vaughan and Chadwick) for their modest four-block length is a pleasant way to tour the neighbourhood. At the end of this

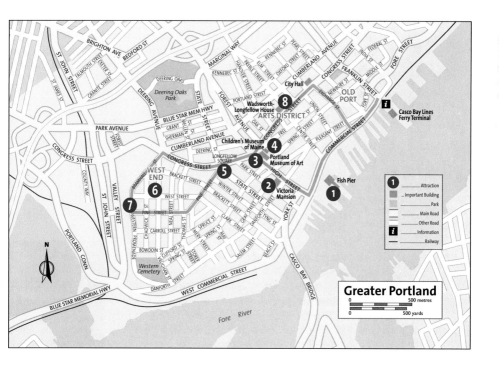 **Harraseeket Inn**
$$–$$$ *162 Main St;*
tel: (800) 342-6423 or
(207) 865-9377;
www.harraseeketinn.com.
Elegant country inn with
modern expansions; also
boasts exceptional
gourmet dining (**$$$**).

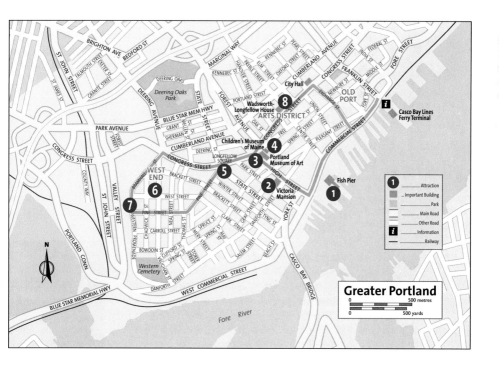 **Harraseeket Lunch
& Lobster $$** *On the
docks; tel: (207) 865-4888.
Open for lunch and dinner.*
A good place for dockside
dining away from the
outlet shopping.

cross-hatch lies **Western Promenade ❼**, where stately mansions on
one side contrast with long scenic vistas on the other.

Follow Western Promenade to its conclusion. Turn right on Bramhall
St and right on Congress St to return to the centre of town.
Approximately 1 mile down Congress St on the left is the **Wadsworth-
Longfellow House ❽**. Continue three blocks down Congress St and
turn right on to Exchange St, which enters the 'Old Port Exchange',
the former centre of shipping offices and warehouses. Portland's main
boutique and restaurant district begins two blocks downhill towards
the harbour. The warren of small streets and pedestrian walkways
eventually leads to Commercial St and the waterfront.

Also worth exploring

Freeport was once a sleepy town 18 miles north of Portland on either
I-95 or Rte 1. Now it is one of the busiest sites in northern New England,
thanks to the presence of more than 170 **outlet and retail stores**, within
walking distance in historic village buildings with a true small-town feel.
The legendary outdoors outfitter, **L L Bean**, opened here in 1905, long
before the outlets and continues to hold its own with every imaginable
item for a walk in the park or an expedition into the back woods.

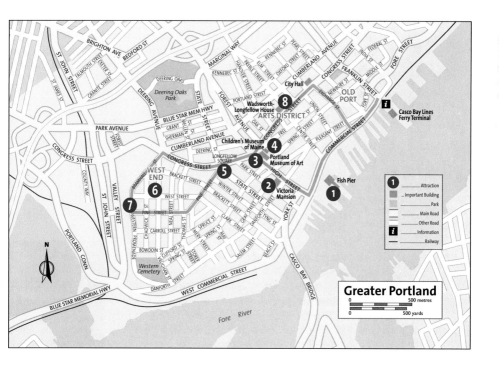

Midcoast Maine

Ratings

Nature/ scenery	●●●●●
Arts and culture	●●○○○
Beaches	●●○○○
Food and drink	●●○○○
History	●●○○○
Shopping	●●○○○
Children	●○○○○
Museums	●○○○○

Between Casco Bay and Penobscot Bay, the Maine coast fragments into hundreds of miles of long, narrow peninsulas that dangle off the mainland like a hank of crooked parsnips. With a stony and barren beauty, each peninsula harbours tiny villages where lobstering, clam-digging and scallop-dragging remain a dominant way of life. Route 1 joins the larger towns and villages at the mouths of rivers that once flowed with huge timber booms, and most travellers stay on this route towards Acadia National Park further north. But the midcoast is most rewarding to those who like to wander, to follow a twisting road down to the tip of a granite peninsula for the sheer exhilaration of watching the waves crash angrily on long grey ledges. Attractions, per se, are sparse. The look and feel of the place is everything.

BATH

 Maine Maritime Museum $$
243 Washington St;
tel: (207) 443-1316; www.
mainemaritimemuseum.org.
Open daily 0930–1700.

In an area of fishermen and sailors, Bath is a sprawling industrial town of riveters and steel workers. It began as a port for shipping mast timbers for the King's Navy, and at one point more than 200 Bath shipyards built nearly half of America's wooden ships. The **Maine Maritime Museum** deals in depth with this history. Its late 19th-century shipyard buildings trace the process of creating a wooden ship from preliminary designs to launch, and several historic boats can be toured at anchor. Now Bath makes destroyers for the US Navy. Excursion boat tours offered by the museum travel upriver to **Bath Iron Works**, where it's not unusual to see several large naval warships in for renovation.

Right
Bath

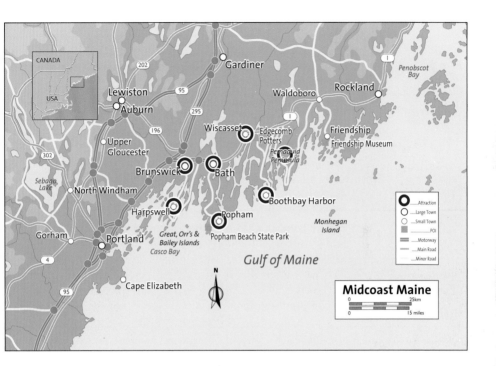

BOOTHBAY HARBOR

 **Boothbay Harbor Region Chamber of Commerce**
192 Townsend Ave;
tel: (207) 633-2353;
www.boothbayharbor.com.
Open Mon–Fri 0800–1700;
late May–mid-Oct also
Sat 1000–1700,
Sun 1100–1600.

Balmy Days Cruises $$–$$$ Pier 8; tel: (207) 633-2284; www.balmydayscruises.com. Offers harbour tours and fishing trips aboard a motor launch or 1½-hour sails on a 31ft sloop.

The self-styled yachting capital of **Boothbay Harbor** has been a summer resort community since 1870, and its popularity has earned it the best access highway of any town at the end of a midcoast peninsula. Souvenir shops and boutiques sit cheek-by-jowl in the harbourfront town, but some of the most scenic areas require drives (or bicycle rides) southwest to Southport Island, ringed with lighthouses, or east to Linekin Neck, where the single road overlooks favourite basking ledges of harbour and grey seals.

Boothbay Harbor's protected waters are a fine yachting anchorage, and fishing-boat captains at the docks offer deep-sea fishing excursions when the tuna are running. The waters surrounding Boothbay Peninsula are best appreciated from a boat, and Boothbay Harbor has no shortage of sightseeing cruises, ranging from half-day sails aboard the 64ft schooner *Appledore* (*Fisherman's Wharf; tel: (207) 633-6598*) to naturalist trips aboard the boats of **Cap'n Fish's Whale Watch and Scenic Nature Cruises** (*Pier 1; tel: (207) 633-3244*).

Accommodation and food in Boothbay Harbor

Ebb Tide $–$$ *43 Commercial St; tel: (207) 633-5692; open for breakfast, lunch and dinner.* This diner serves breakfast all day and also offers good chowder and home-made pies.

1830 Admiral's Quarters Inn Bed & Breakfast $$–$$$ *71 Commercial St; tel: (207) 633-2474 or (800) 644-1878; www.admiralsquartersinn.com.* The seven guest rooms in a renovated sea captain's home have fireplaces and views over the harbour.

Linekin Bay Resort $$$ *92 Wall Point Rd, East Boothbay; tel: (866) 847-2103 or (207) 633-2494; www.linekinbayresort.com.* This coastal resort has five lodges and thirty-five cabins. Rates include use of sailing boats and three meals a day.

Spruce Point Inn $$$ *Grandview Ave; tel: (800) 553-0289 or (207) 633-4152; www.sprucepointinn.com.* There is a broad variety of lodging choices in this turn-of-the-century inn with tennis courts, spa and pools. With a fabulous ocean view and an elegant New American menu, the dining room (**$$–$$$**) ranks among Maine's best.

BRUNSWICK

ℹ️ Southern Midcoast Maine Chamber of Commerce *2 Main St, Topsham; tel: (877) 725-8797 or (207) 725-8797; www.midcoastmaine.com. Open Mon–Fri 0830–1700.*

🏛️ Bowdoin College Museum of Art *Walker Art Bldg, Main St; tel: (207) 725-3275; www.bowdoin.edu/art-museum. Open Tue–Sat 1000–1700, Sun 1300–1700. Free admission.*

Peary-MacMillan Arctic Museum *Hubbard Hall, Main St; tel: (207) 725-3416; www.bowdoin.edu/arctic-museum. Open Tue– Sat 1000–1700, Sun 1400–1700. Free admission.*

🍴 Miss Brunswick Diner $ *101 Pleasant St; tel: (207) 721-1134.* Diner with Tex-Mex specialities.

This handsome town of sea captains' mansions is dominated by the park-like campus of Bowdoin College, Maine's first college of genteel education and alma mater of Nathaniel Hawthorne, Henry Wadsworth Longfellow and Arctic explorers Robert Peary and Donald MacMillan. The **Bowdoin College Museum of Art** is noted for Winslow Homer, Andrew Wyeth and late 19th- and early 20th-century American paintings. The **Peary-MacMillan Arctic Museum** pays tribute to the adventurers with a variety of artefacts, including the instruments with which Peary made the controversial 1909 observations to claim he had reached the North Pole.

HARPSWELL

Harpswell Inn $–$$
108 Lookout Point Rd;
tel: (207) 833-5509;
www.harpswellinn.com. This
1761 inn offers relative
sophistication in a
decidedly unsophisticated
region.

Lying due south from Brunswick on Rte 123, the town of Harpswell gathers seven villages and forty-five islands under a single place name. Except for the odd painter or poet, most residents earn their living from trapping lobsters and catching fish with hand lines from small boats. **Harpswell Neck** is a narrow granite peninsula where Rte 123 connects the four largest villages. A bridge from North Harpswell joins the peninsula to the scenic island villages of **Great, Orr's and Bailey Islands**.

Food in Harpswell

Cook's Lobster House $$ *Garrison Cove Rd; tel: (207) 833-6641* and **Estes Lobster House $$** *Rte 123; tel: (207) 833-6340; both open for lunch and dinner.* Large seafood houses supplied by local fishermen. Cook's has the better view.

PEMAQUID PENINSULA

Pemaquid Fishermen's Museum $ *Pemaquid Pt Lighthouse; no tel. Open late May–early Sept 1000–1700.*

The Pemaquid Peninsula is perhaps the most scenic and low-key of all the well-travelled parts of Maine's midcoast. **Damariscotta**, at the head of the peninsula, is bypassed by Rte 1, leaving intact a charming village renowned for 2000 years for its exquisite oysters – the Abenaki tribe left behind 20 centuries of shell middens. Some of the shells were as large as plates.

A dozen miles south at **Pemaquid Point**, interlaced streaks of granite and black lava produce some of the coast's most dramatic shoreline. Surmounting the promontory is Pemaquid Point Light, so quintessential an image that it frequently adorns tourism literature. The base of the 1827 lighthouse holds the **Pemaquid Fishermen's Museum**.

Accommodation and food on Pemaquid Peninsula

Sea Gull Shop $–$$ *Pemaquid Pt; tel: (207) 677-2374; open for breakfast, lunch and dinner.* This combination restaurant and souvenir shop makes good casual use of local provender in blueberry French toast, crisp fried clams and meaty crab rolls.

Shaw's Fish and Lobster Wharf Restaurant $$ *New Harbor; tel: (207) 677-2200; open for lunch and dinner.* A fish-lover's nirvana, Shaw's is the best among hundreds of Maine's 'in the rough' seafood restaurants serving local lobster, crab and finfish at picnic tables next to the boats that caught dinner.

Left
Pemaquid Peninsula's uplifted shales

Newcastle Inn $$–$$$ *60 River Rd, Newcastle; tel: (800) 832-8669 or (207) 563-5685; www.newcastleinn.com.* Federal-style inn on the Damariscotta River has 14 guest rooms, some with fireplaces. The guests-only pub is a quiet retreat.

POPHAM

 Fort Popham State Historic Site *Rte 209; tel: (207) 389-1335. Open late May–Sept 0900–dusk. Free admission.*

Popham Beach State Park $ *Rte 209; tel: (207) 389-1335. Open mid-Apr–Oct 0900–dusk.*

Popham was the site of the first English colony in New England (1606) as well as the spot where colonists built the first ocean-going vessel (1607) so they could rush home after the first brutal Maine winter. Nearby **Fort Popham** was erected during the Civil War to protect the Union shipyards in Bath from Confederate warships. The fortress's circular staircases rise to towers with sweeping views, including the white beaches of nearby **Popham Beach State Park**, one of the few places in Maine with soft sandy beaches and large waves for surfing.

WISCASSET

 Nickels-Sortwell House $ *Main and Federal Sts; tel: (207) 882-7169; www. historicnewengland.org. Tours given Jun–mid-Oct Fri–Sun 1100–1600.*

Musical Wonder House $$$ *18 High St; tel: (207) 882-7163. Open late May–Oct Mon–Sat 1000–1700, Sun 1200–1700.*

Known among regular drivers of Maine coastal roads as 'the prettiest little bottleneck on Rte 1', Wiscasset is a veritable architectural museum of late 18th- and early 19th-century architecture and its downtown is lined with antiques shops, cafés and art potters. The **Nickels-Sortwell House** reflects the fortunes of Wiscasset's sea-trade days, which came to a crashing halt with the Embargo Act of 1807, the year the house was built. Tours include the impressive period gardens. The **Musical Wonder House** is less historic but endlessly entertaining, with player pianos and music boxes from around the world.

Accommodation and food in Wiscasset

Red's Eats $ *Foot of Main and Water Sts; no tel; open for lunch and dinner.* Classic tiny food stand serves outstanding lobster and crab rolls.

Sea Basket $–$$ *Rte 1; tel: (207) 882-6581; open for lunch and dinner.* Unpretentious diner known for its lobster stew.

Sheepscot Harbour Village & Resort $$–$$$ *306 Eddy Rd, Edgecomb; tel: (207) 882-6343 or (800) 437-5503; www.midcoastresort.com.* Technically in Edgecomb, across the Sheepscot River, this combination of motel rooms, cottages and self-catering units was remodelled in 2007 and has striking views of Wiscasset Harbour.

Above
Cooking up a classic lobster
'bake' of steamed lobster and
corn in wet seaweed

Lobsters

Once so plentiful that they could be picked up off the beaches, the Maine lobster (*Homarus americanus*) was considered food fit only for prisons, poorhouses, orphanages and servants. Not until the 1940s did lobster begin to evolve as a 'gourmet' seafood in New England. The crustacean now fetches a high price because almost all of Maine's 55-million-pound annual catch (more than three-quarters the US haul) is harvested by small-boat fishermen tending heavy wooden or wire traps.

Lobsters are at their sweetest in June, before shedding their shells in early July. Most New England lobsters are relative youngsters, weighing 1¼–1¾lb, a size of maximum flavour. Traditionally, lobster is boiled or steamed and served with corn on the cob, boiled potatoes and copious quantities of drawn butter.

Suggested tour

Friendship Museum $ Rte 220; no telephone. Open Jul–early Sept Mon–Sat 1300–1600, Sun 1400–1600.

Moody's Diner $–$$ Rte 1, Waldoboro; tel: (207) 832-7468. Open for breakfast, lunch and dinner. Every trucker stops at Moody's for good road food at reasonable prices.

Edgecomb Potters Rte 27, Edgecomb, tel: (207) 882-9493 create high-fired porcelain with rich glazes and display high-quality work by other Maine artists working in craft media. Open summer Mon–Sat 0830–1800, Sun 0930–1800; call for off-season hours.

Total distance: 117 miles; 196 miles with detours.

Time: 4–5 hours' driving. Allow 2–3 days.

Links: Connects via Rte 1 to Portland (see page 244) at southern end, via Rte 1 to Penobscot Bay Route (see page 260) at northern end.

Route: The route barely begins before there are a couple of good reasons to depart from it. Begin at Pleasant St (Rte 1) in **BRUNSWICK** ❶, 6 miles north of Freeport (I-95, exit 22). Main St intersects in 1 mile, with Bowdoin College and fine Federal homes south of Rte 1.

Detour: Main St turns into Rte 123, Harpswell Rd, for a drive 13 miles through the rural fishing villages on the **HARPSWELL** ❷ peninsula. To reach **Orr's and Bailey Islands** ❸, backtrack 7 miles to the Ewin Narrows Rd bridge, explore the islands on Rte 24S, then return 15 miles north to Rte 1 via Rte 24.

Route 1 continues 5 miles into the centre of the active shipbuilding town of **BATH** ❹.

Detour: Rte 209 leads south from Bath for 15 scenic miles to **POPHAM** ❺ to visit the site of the first English colony in New England, or to swim or surf the high waves at **Popham Beach State Park** ❻, one of the few sandy beaches on the midcoast.

Back on Rte 1, cross the drawbridge from Bath to Woolrich and continue 10 miles to **WISCASSET** ❼. Two miles north, turn right on Rte 27. Two miles south on Rte 27 is the excellent art pottery, **Edgecomb Potters** ❽. **BOOTHBAY HARBOR** ❾ lies another 9 miles south on Rte 27. To see the peninsula's more rural side, return north 4 miles on Rte 27 and turn right on to River Rd, continuing north along the scenic banks of the Damariscotta River to join Rte 1B in Newcastle. Cross the old bridge in the village of Damariscotta, and turn right to drive south on the **PEMAQUID PENINSULA** ❿ for 3 miles on Bristol Rd (Rtes 129 and 130). At the fork, veer left on Rte 130 and continue 13½ miles to Pemaquid Point. Double back via Rte 130 for 3½ miles, then turn right on to Rte 32. This road passes through a string of small fishing villages separated by meadows and woodlands along the Muscongus Bay as it winds along the coast for 20 miles to rejoin Rte 1 in **Waldoboro** ⓫, another erstwhile shipbuilding centre now known for its antiques dealers, landmark diner and strict enforcement of the speed limit. At the bottom of the hill in Waldoboro, Rte 220 heads south for 10 miles into the village of **Friendship** ⓬, a fishing community noted for its boatbuilding since the 1750s. The Friendship sloop, an unusually responsive vessel created for the difficult conditions of Maine's peninsular waters, originated here and a 'homecoming' race of the sloops is held each July. The 1851 one-room

Monhegan Boat Lines \$\$\$ *Port Clyde landing; tel: (207) 372-8848.* Operates ferry service to Monhegan Island. Reservations recommended.

The Dip Net \$–\$\$ *Main St, Port Clyde; tel: (207) 372-6307.* Serves seafood on a deck overlooking the harbour.

schoolhouse holds the quirky **Friendship Museum** ⓭, with extensive boat construction and local history exhibits. Route 220 circles back northward and rejoins Rte 1 at South Warren, 1 mile west of Thomaston and the beginning of Penobscot Bay.

Also worth exploring

The Maine coast is dotted with literally thousands of islands, but few have the allure of **Monhegan Island**, which was a 15th- and 16th-century base for Basque fishermen, a 17th-century French–English battleground, an 18th-century pirate's lair, and has been one of New England's most successful fishing communities for the last 250 years. Beginning around 1905, it also became a seasonal retreat for many of America's most distinguished artists. Monhegan closes its commercial fishing in the summer and people with easels and brushes take over. Many species of birds alight here and whales favour Monhegan's coastal waters. Only 12 miles offshore, Monhegan can be reached by passenger boat year-round from Port Clyde, and in the summer from Boothbay Harbor and New Harbor.

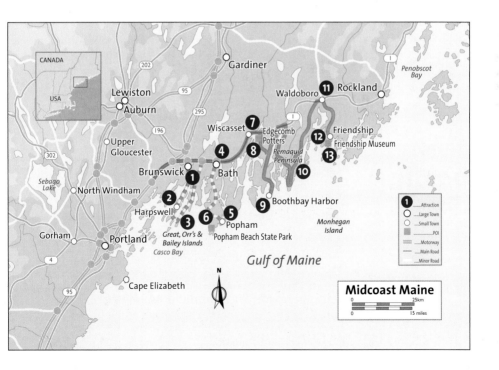

Penobscot Bay

Ratings

Nature/ scenery	●●●●●
Arts and culture	●●●●○
History	●●●●○
Museums	●●●○○
Children	●●○○○
Shopping	●●○○○
Beaches	●○○○○
Food and drink	●○○○○

The deep cleft of Penobscot Bay divides the Maine coast in two. The march of hills from inland Maine suddenly snaps off into deep harbours on the western shore, where the little towns demonstrate that good things come in small packages. From the hard-working commercial port of Rockland, with its fleet of cruising schooners, to Searsport, the last shipmasters' capital of the age of sail, the high road on the western shore offers nearly uninterrupted vistas of the bay's spruce-tufted islands. Striking Federal, Greek Revival and Italianate homes in every town attest to the 19th-century wealth of these communities. Most travellers overlook the eastern shore, formed by Cape Rosier, Deer Isle and the Blue Hill Peninsula. But its labyrinth of twisting rural roads leading past long hay fields and blueberry barrens delivers the patient traveller into picturesque yachting and lobstering harbours.

BELFAST

ⓘ Belfast Area Chamber of Commerce *12 Main St; tel: (207) 338-5900; www.belfastmaine.org. Open Mon–Fri 0900–1600; late May–mid-Oct also Sat and Sun 0900–1600.*

Ⓜ Belfast Farmers' Market *Main St; no tel; www. belfastfarmersmarket.org. Open May–mid-Nov Fri 0900–1300.*

Belfast has reclaimed its genteel elegance of a century ago, when the small city was inhabited by retired sea captains who sat in their Federal and Greek Revival manses surrounded by Oriental porcelains and counted their money. Favoured as a residence by writers, artists and craftspeople, Belfast is one of the less expensive and less crowded bases for touring the Penobscot Bay region. Not all of Belfast tries to be chic. The **Belfast Farmers' Market** is known for its range of products. In addition to fresh fruit, vegetables and flowers, vendors offer free-range duck eggs, handcrafted soaps, beeswax candles, medicinal herbs and a variety of jams, jellies and salsas.

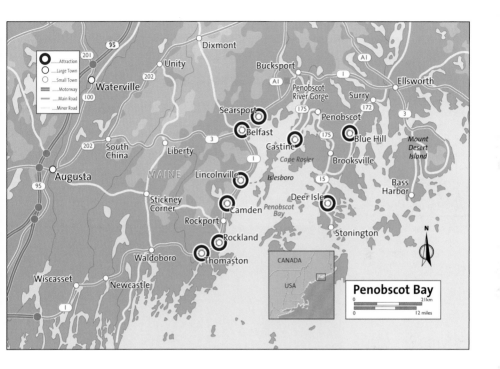

Accommodation and food in Belfast

Young's Lobster Pound $–$$ *Mitchell Ave, off Rte 1; tel: (207) 338-1160; open for lunch and dinner.* Lobster fresh off the boat or cooked to order for takeaway.

Jeweled Turret Inn $$ *40 Pearl St; tel: (800) 696-2304 or (207) 338-2304; www.jeweledturret.com.* Unique architectural features and craftsmanship set this B&B apart.

Harbor View House of 1807 $$–$$$ *213 High St; tel: (877) 393-3811 or (207) 338-3811; www.harborviewhouse.com.* Restored Federal house has great views of Penobscot Bay.

BLUE HILL

Opposite
Sightseeing boat off Penobscot
Bay at Belfast

So many New Yorkers spend the summer in Blue Hill that the *New York Times* outsells the local daily paper and the spiffy little country village has an air of Central Park West. Blue Hill is well known for its art galleries and art potters, of which **Rackcliffe Pottery** and **Rowantrees Pottery** *(tel: (207) 374-5535)* welcome visitors. For a good

Rackcliffe Pottery
132 Ellsworth Rd (Rte 172); tel: (207) 374-2297. Open Mon–Sat 0800–1600, extended summer hours. Continues the local tradition of making functional tableware with local clays and minerals.

Blue Hill Fair $
Tel: (207) 374-3701; http://bluehillfair.com. Highlights of this traditional country fair (held early September) include agricultural and livestock exhibits, a blueberry pie eating contest and the pig scramble.

take on the Blue Hill (counter-) culture, tune in to WERU at 89.9FM, a homespun radio station promulgating 'dangerous' ideas and local singer-songwriter music.

Accommodation and food in Blue Hill

Blue Hill Co-op & Cafe $ *4 Ellsworth Rd; tel: (207) 374-2165; open for breakfast, lunch and early dinner.* Health food store and casual cafe is a local favourite for soups and sandwiches.

Blue Hill Inn $$–$$$ *Union St (Rte 177), Blue Hill; tel: (800) 826-7415 or (207) 374-2844; www.bluehillinn.com.* This inn dates from 1840, Blue Hill's shipping heyday, and, while beautifully maintained, shows its age with creaky floors and walls out of plumb.

Right
Sailing ships in Camden harbour

CAMDEN

ℹ **Camden-Rockport-Lincolnville Chamber of Commerce** *Public Landing; tel: (800) 223-5459 or (207) 236-4404; www.visitcamden.com. Open summer Mon–Fri 0900–1700, Sat and Sun 1000–1600; winter Mon–Fri 0900–1700. Provides information for all three towns.*

🛥 *Lively Lady Too $$$ Public Landing; tel: (207) 236-6672. Motor yacht makes 2-hour cruises of Penobscot Bay.*

🏕 **Camden Hills State Park $** *Rte 1; tel: (207) 236-3109 or (207) 624-9950 for camping reservations. Mount Battie Auto Road open May–Oct.*

🎨 **Harbor Arts and Crafts Show** *Tel: (207) 236-4404. Outdoor exhibition held third weekend of July.*

Wedged between the tall Camden Hills and a stunning, bowl-like harbour, Camden is almost too pretty to be believed – when it can be seen through the crowds. One of the most popular destinations on the Maine coast, Camden has a bustling shopping district of boutiques, old-fashioned shops, art galleries, art supply stores and outdoors equipment shops. A few excursion schooners still operate from Camden, but the harbour is usually so thick with private motor yachts that one could walk from one shore to another on their decks. Two miles north of the village on Rte 1, **Camden Hills State Park** has 30 miles of hiking trails. Both hiking trails and a toll road ascend Mount Battie, a peak with sweeping views of Penobscot Bay all the way to the mountains of Mount Desert Island.

Accommodation and food in Camden

Camden Deli $ *37 Main St; tel: (207) 236-8343.* Serves soups, sandwiches and salads to eat on rooftop deck overlooking the harbour.

Scott's Place $–$$ *85 Elm St; tel: (207) 236-8751; lunch only.* Great lobster and crab rolls in casual digs.

High Tide Inn $–$$$ *Rte 1; tel: (800) 778-7068 or (207) 236-3724; www.hightideinn.com.* Lodging choices include motel units and lodge rooms at this 7-acre property with a private beach.

Swan House $$ *49 Mountain St; tel: (207) 236-8275 or (800) 207-8275; www.swanhouse.com.* Six-room Victorian B&B sitting at the foot of Mount Battie.

Blackberry Inn $$–$$$ *82 Elm St; tel: (800) 388-6000 or (207) 236-6060; www.blackberryinn.com.* This colourful Victorian home with 11 guest rooms is within walking distance of downtown Camden and the harbour.

CASTINE

🏛 **Maine Maritime Academy** *tel: (800) 464-6565; www.mainemaritime.edu. Call for schedule of tours of State of Maine when it is in port.*

Walking the sleepy, elm-arched streets of Castine, it's hard to believe that so many regional and world powers have fought over it since the 1600s: Castine's been under French, English, Dutch, Canadian and American flags. During the American Revolution, British sloops-of-war dealt the American Navy a humiliating defeat and occupied the town from 1779 until 1783. Following the peace treaty, British loyalists floated their homes on barges to St-Andrews-by-the-Sea, New Brunswick. As a result, most of Castine's finest houses date from the 19th century. The main action in town focuses on the **Maine Maritime Academy**, which trains merchant marine officers. Cadets conduct tours of the 499ft training vessel *State of Maine*.

Accommodation and food in Castine

Dennett's Wharf $–$$ *Sea St; tel: (207) 326-9045; open for lunch and dinner.* Seafood dinners are the speciality of this bar and restaurant right on the docks.

Pentagöet Inn $$–$$$ *26 Main St; tel: (207) 326-8616; www.pentagoet.com.* The 16 romantic rooms of this quirky Queen Anne Victorian inn are filled with antiques and collectibles.

DEER ISLE

⊘ Isle-au-Haut Boat Company $$$
Seabreeze Ave, Stonington; tel: (207) 367-5193; www.isleauhaut.com. Offers year-round ferry service to the island.

◑ Turtle Gallery Deer Isle village; tel: (207) 348-9977. Open late May–mid-Oct Mon–Sat 1000–1730, Sun 1400–1800. Excellent fine art in crafts media.

Terrell S. Lester Photography Gallery
Deer Isle village; tel: (207) 348-2676. Open Jun–late Oct Mon–Sat 1000–1700. Fine-art photography by Lester and other artists.

In just a 5-mile stretch, Deer Isle epitomises the cultural dichotomy of this region. The village of **Deer Isle** is chock-a-block full of art galleries, not surprising since the famed **Haystack Mountain School of Crafts** (*www.haystack-mtn.org*) is just outside town. At the southern end of the island in **Stonington**, lobster fishermen in gumboots rule the roost. Deer Isle is tranquil and idyllic, Stonington gritty and authentic – it remains primarily a lobster-fishing port. Stonington is also the departure point for boats to the scenic **Isle au Haut**, part of Acadia National Park and a superb spot for sighting pelagic birds.

Accommodation and food on Deer Isle

The Fisherman's Friend Restaurant $–$$ *5 Atlantic Ave, Stonington; tel: (207) 367-2442; open for lunch and dinner.* Locals favour the lobster stew, but save room for the home-made pies.

Inn on the Harbor $$ *45 Main St, Stonington; tel: (800) 942-2420 or (207) 367-2420; www.innontheharbor.com.* This casual lodging, where rooms share an excellent deck, actually juts out into Stonington harbour amid the lobster boats and scallop draggers.

Whale's Rib Tavern $$ *Pilgrim's Inn, 20 Main St, Deer Isle; tel: (207) 348-6615; dinner only.* Snug tap room features local beer, local fish, and slightly upscale local colour.

LINCOLNVILLE

⊘ Maine State Ferry $ Lincolnville Beach; tel: (207) 789-5611; www.state.me.us/mdot/opt/ferry/islesboro.php. Year-round passenger and car service to Islesboro.

Lincolnville is effectively two communities, one an inland farming village near beautiful lakes, the other a wide spot on Rte 1 where Ducktrap River flows into Penobscot Bay. **Lincolnville Beach** on Rte 1 is a surprisingly good, if tiny, ocean swimming beach where sun on brown sands creates some of Maine's warmest water when the tide comes in. A ferry service to **Islesboro** departs at its southern end. Just

1½ miles offshore, Islesboro has a year-round fishing village and a summer village of huge 'cottages' handed down in wealthy families. The island is fun to explore by bicycle. The rocky town 'beach' at Pendleton Point is often a good place to watch grey seals catching mackerel close to shore.

Accommodation and food in Lincolnville

The Mount Battie $–$$ *Rte 1, Lincolnville; tel: (800) 224-3870 or (207) 236-3870.* The decks of this 21-unit motel have great views of Penobscot Bay.

Lobster Pound Restaurant $$ *Lincolnville Beach; tel: (207) 789-5550; open for lunch and dinner.* Crack open a lobster and watch families play on the beach while ferries shuttle to Islesboro.

Below
Islesboro lighthouse

ROCKLAND

ℹ Penobscot Bay Regional Chamber of Commerce *One Park Dr; tel: (207) 596-0376 or (800) 562-2529; www.therealmaine.com. Open late May–mid-Oct Mon–Fri 0900–1700, Sat and Sun 1000–1600; rest of year Mon–Fri 0900–1700.*

🏛 Farnsworth Art Museum and Wyeth Center $$ *16 Museum St; tel: (207) 596-6457; www.farnsworthmuseum.org. Open late May–mid-Oct daily 1000–1700; call for off-season hours.*

Maine Lighthouse Museum $ *One Park Dr; tel: (207) 594-3301. Open late May–mid-Oct Mon–Fri 0900–1700, Sat and Sun 1000–1600. Closed Sun rest of year.*

⚓ Maine Lobster Festival *Tel: (800) 562-2529.* The 5-day event in early August is a New England classic, featuring a parade, boat rides, the crowning of the Lobster Queen and lobster dinners.

While not as pretty as neighbouring Camden, Rockland has more substance. Its working harbour is spiked with the masts of 'windjammer' excursion schooners and dotted with squat trawlers and lobster boats. Moreover, it has one of the finest small art museums in New England. The **Farnsworth Art Museum and Wyeth Center** emphasises Maine's place in American art with works by Fitz Henry Lane, Winslow Homer, Edward Hopper, Milton Avery, Childe Hassam, Rockwell Kent and Louise Nevelson. The Center for the Wyeth Family opened in 1998 to hold the art collection of painter Andrew and his wife Betsy. The Farnsworth also opens Olson House (where Wyeth studied and painted for over three decades) to tours late May–mid-October. Adjacent to the tourist information centre, the **Maine Lighthouse Museum** displays a huge collection of lighthouse artefacts, including foghorns, bells and glass lenses. The gift shop stocks postcards and other memorabilia. Windjammer cruises must be booked at least 6 months in advance, but boats can be viewed at the public landing Saturday evenings and Sunday mornings.

Accommodation and food in Rockland

Old Granite Inn $–$$$ *546 Main St; tel: (800) 386-9036 or (207) 594-9036; www.oldgraniteinn.com.* Smoke-free lodging with eight guest rooms near downtown and adjacent to the ferry dock.

Primo $$$ *2 S Main St; tel: (207) 596-0770; open for dinner.* Gourmets drive hundreds of miles to dine at this gracious restaurant in a Victorian farmhouse where the chef has been acclaimed for her inventive, light cuisine.

Windjammer cruises

The excursion boats sailing from Rockland, Camden and Rockport, known generically as 'windjammers', are typically old three-masted coasting schooners built for the unglamorous trade of hauling stone and timber along the Atlantic seaboard. Because their cargoes were not time-sensitive and the boats were cheap to run, these old schooners stayed afloat when larger sailing ships were cut down to serve as barges. Accommodation on the windjammers varies, especially between the historic boats and some of the newly constructed ones. Few offer many luxuries; most have very tight sleeping quarters and rather crude toilet facilities. But they make up in romance what they lack in comfort, and most week-long sails are fully booked six to eight months in advance. Non-sailors can glimpse the beauty of the windjammers when several of them converge in Castine Harbour or gather together to spend the night in the lee of Sears Island, visible south of Searsport from Rte 1.

Opposite
Sunset over Penobscot Bay

SEARSPORT

ℹ️ **Searsport &
Stockton Springs
Chamber of Commerce**
Main St; tel: (207) 548-6510.

🏛️ **Penobscot Marine
Museum $$** Church
St and Rte 1; tel: (207) 548-
2529; www.
penobscotmarinemuseum.org.
Open late May–mid-Oct
Mon–Sat 1000–1700, Sun
1200–1700.

🏺 **Searsport Antique
Mall** Rte 1; tel: (207)
548-2640. Open Jun–Sept
daily 0900–1700; Oct–May
daily 1000–1700. The best
group shop in the 'antiques
capital' of Maine. Other
shops to be found along
Rte 1.

Between its antiques dealers and its maritime memories, Searsport dwells almost entirely in the past. During the last third of the 19th century, nearly one American deepwater sea captain in ten called Searsport home, and its behemoth 'Downeasters', the largest wooden sailing vessels ever built, dominated transoceanic trade. The bold adventure of that last great Age of Sail reverberates at the **Penobscot Marine Museum**. Nine historic buildings display paintings, photographs, ship models (and even some small craft), along with China Trade art and artefacts. One wall features portraits of nearly 300 Searsport overseas trading captains. Many of the captains' capacious mansions now serve as B&Bs, making it a handsome town to tour.

Accommodation and food in Searsport

Searsport Shores $ 216 W Main St, Searsport; tel: (207) 548-6059. Campsite with private beach organises daytrips and other activities for guests.

Anglers Restaurant $–$$ *215 E Main St; tel: (207) 548-2405; open for lunch and dinner.* A reliable spot for steamed lobster, fried clams and fish and chips.

Colonial Gables $–$$ *7 Eagle Lane, Belfast; tel: (207) 338-4000 or (800) 937-6246.* Motel and self-catering cottages from the 1940s with private beach overlooking Penobscot Bay between Searsport and Belfast.

The Mariner $–$$ *23 W Main St; tel: (207) 548-6600; open year round.* Local favourite for fried seafood, grilled steaks and vegetables.

Carriage House Inn $$–$$$ *120 E Main St; tel: (207) 548-2167; www.carriagehouseinmaine.com.* Gracious 1874 sea captain's house (and former home of a painter) serves as a luxurious B&B.

THOMASTON

General Henry Knox Museum $$
30 High St; tel: (207) 354-8062; www. generalknoxmuseum.org. Open late May–mid-Oct Tue–Sat 1000–1500.

Thomaston Cafe $
154 Main St; tel: (207) 354-8589; www.thomastoncafe.com. Open daily for breakfast and lunch, also Fri and Sat for dinner. Great breakfast, baked goods, and fresh seafood lunches and dinners.

First founded in 1630 and re-established in 1736, Thomaston is the oldest community for many miles around. Its era of vast wealth (circa 1800) is long gone, and the town has returned to its roots as a fishing and boat-building centre. Thomaston is easily bypassed, but is worth driving through to view some of the stateliest Colonial homes north of Newburyport. Perhaps most impressive is **Montpelier**, a reconstruction of the mansion built by General Henry Knox, the country's first Secretary of War, who retired to Maine in 1795.

Suggested tour

Total distance: 135 miles, 155 miles with detours.

Time: 4 hours' driving. Allow 2–3 days.

Links: Connects via Rte 1 to Midcoast Maine Route (*see page 252*) at southern end, via Rtes 72 and 3 to Mount Desert Island Route (*see page 270*) at northern end.

Route: Begin on Rte 1 in **THOMASTON** ❶, where the bluffs on the east side of town mark the southwest opening of Penobscot Bay. A 46-mile drive of striking beauty begins 4 miles north in **ROCKLAND** ❷. The high hills on one side of Rte 1 and the long meadows reaching to the sea on the other make even the worst summer traffic bearable. From Rockland continue 6 miles to duck into the one-cove village of **Rockport** ❸, an artists' town with a good gallery and pretty harbour, then 2 miles into the solid wall of excited humanity on the streets of **CAMDEN** ❹. Rte 1 rises and turns to the right as it leaves Camden, passing handsome 19th-century inns and a stone castle before reaching open country with long views in the 6 miles to **LINCOLNVILLE** beach ❺.

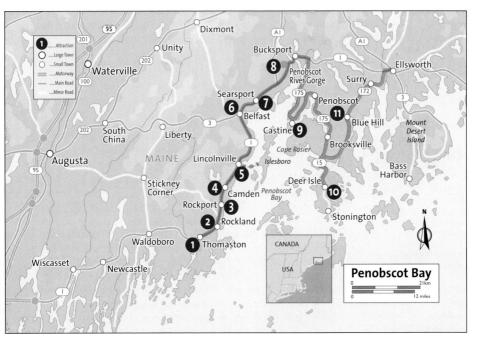

Penobscot Narrows Bridge Observatory $ *Rte 3; tel: (207) 469-6553. Open May–Jun and Sept–Oct 0900–1700; Jul–Aug 0900–1900.* Panoramic views from 420ft above the river.

Detour: The 15-minute ferry crossing to Islesboro is a scenic (if short) trip, well rewarded by the views from points all around the island.

Route 1 climbs a long hill past modest homes as it leaves Lincolnville beach and rises to a high ridge above the sea that continues 13 miles north to **BELFAST** ❻. After crossing the Passagassawaukeag River (the view of Belfast harbour from the bridge is spectacular), Rte 1 continues north 7 miles to **SEARSPORT** ❼ with views of ledges and cliffs along the way. The landscape begins to change further north as it approaches the **Penobscot River Gorge** ❽. Just before the bridge, pull into the scenic turnoff to view this deep gorge where eagles and ospreys are often seen fishing and where the Royal Navy obliterated the rebellious Americans in 1779. Cross into Bucksport and drive 2 miles to a right turn on to Rte 175. When 175 splits left in 7¾ miles, continue straight on Rte 166 into **CASTINE** ❾. Leave Castine by Rte 166N, turning right on Rte 199, then right again on Rte 175S, which is shortly joined by Rte 15S after a total of 17 miles. The high point of the road reveals a classic panorama: a foreground of blueberry barrens, a mid-ground of Penobscot Bay and its islands, and a background of the Camden Hills. In 8 miles, Rte 15 leads across the Eggemoggin Reach to **DEER ISLE** ❿. After crossing back to the mainland, turn right on to Rte 175 (Reach Rd) and follow it generally north and east approximately 25 miles to **BLUE HILL** ⓫. Route 172 from the centre of the village extends 10 miles northeast to Rts 1 and 3 at Ellsworth.

Mount Desert Island

Ratings

Nature/scenery	●●●●●
Children	●●●●○
Food and drink	●●●●○
Beaches	●●●○○
Shopping	●●●○○
History	●●○○○
Museums	●●○○○
Arts and culture	●○○○○

At 108 square miles, Mount Desert (pronounced 'dessert' by the locals) is the third largest island on the US Atlantic coast and the most dramatic. Its landscape consists of deep glacial valleys and over 15 rocky-topped granite mountains rising straight up from the sea. Nearly half the island is devoted to Acadia National Park, which draws 2.5 million visitors a year to this part of New England. Shaped like a lobster claw with its pincers divided by the fiord of Somes Sound, Mount Desert's awe-inspiring rough beauty is punctuated with small pockets of intense human activity. Bar Harbor functions as the principal shopping, lodging and dining town, its human bustle a counterpoint to the park's natural idylls. The boat-building centre of Southwest Harbor and the fishing village of Bass Harbor are less inundated with crowds but no less beautiful.

ACADIA NATIONAL PARK

> ❶ **Hulls Cove Visitor Center** *Off Rte 3 at Park Loop Rd; tel: (207) 288-3338; www.nps.gov/ acad. Open mid-Apr–Oct daily 0800–1630; Jul and Aug until 1800; Sept until 1700.*
>
> **Acadia National Park Headquarters** *PO Box 177, Bar Harbor; tel: (207) 288-3338. Open Nov–Apr daily 0800–1630. Day-use fee $$ per car. Ranger-led activities are available June–September.*

Dedicated fans of the outdoors can (and do) spend entire seasons in Acadia without exhausting its attractions. More than 120 miles of hiking trails ascend every summit and traverse every valley, and the gladed woods are penetrated by nearly 56 miles of carriage roads ideally suited to walking, bicycling, horse riding and cross-country skiing.

The easiest, and therefore the most travelled, way to sample the coast and the interior of Acadia is by driving the **Park Loop Rd**. In the course of its 27 hilly miles, the road passes virtually all the better-known highlights of the park. The entrance to the one-way circuit lies off Rte 3 at the **Hulls Cove Visitor Center**, an essential stop to learn about ranger-led mountain hikes, campfire talks and nature walks. Highlights include **Sieur de Monts Spring**, where a nature centre and wildflower gardens offer a good introduction to some of Acadia's more obvious but diverse flora. Sharing the parking area, the

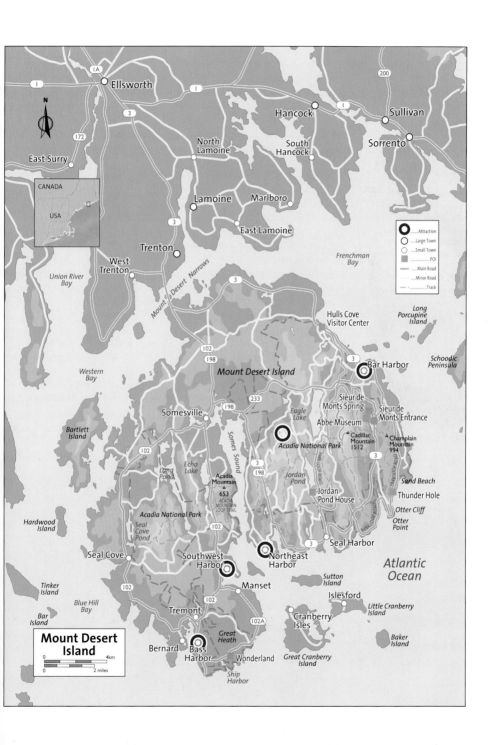

Mount Desert Island

Ellsworth

1A

1

3

172

East Surry

North Lamoine

Hancock

South Hancock

Sullivan

Sorrento

200

1

CANADA

USA

Lamoine

Marlboro

3

East Lamoine

Trenton

West Trenton

Union River Bay

Mount Desert Narrows

Frenchman Bay

3

	....Attraction
	....Large Town
	....Small Town
	....POI
	....Main Road
	....Minor Road
	....Track

Hulls Cove Visitor Center

Long Porcupine Island

Western Bay

102
198

Mount Desert Island

3

Bar Harbor

Schoodic Peninsula

Somesville

233

198

Eagle Lake

Sieur de Monts Spring

Abbe Museum

Sieur de Monts Entrance

Bartlett Island

Somes Sound

Cadillac Mountain 1512

Champlain Mountain 994

102

Echo Lake

Long Pond

Acadia National Park

3
198

Jordan Pond

PARK LOOP ROAD

Sand Beach

Thunder Hole

Acadia Mountain 653
ACADIA MOUNTAIN LOOP TRAIL

Jordan Pond House

Otter Cliff

Hardwood Island

Acadia National Park

Seal Cove Pond

102

3

Seal Harbor

Otter Point

Seal Cove

Southwest Harbor

Northeast Harbor

Atlantic Ocean

Tinker Island

102

Manset

Sutton Island

Bar Island

Blue Hill Bay

Tremont

102A

Islesford

Little Cranberry Island

Cranberry Isles

Baker Island

Bernard

Bass Harbor

Great Heath

Wonderland

Great Cranberry Island

Ship Harbor

Mount Desert Island

0   4km

0   2 miles

Tour buses $$
Several bus tour companies departing from Agarmont Park in Bar Harbor offer narrated tours of Acadia that last 2–3 hours. Stops are limited and sightseeing is rushed, but they save the frustrations of driving in park traffic.

Acadia Tape Tour $$$
available for purchase at Hulls Cove Visitor Center, provides detailed, narrated directions on CD or cassette tape for a 56-mile driving tour through the park. The tape tour is extremely well researched and presented.

Below
Acadia's granite ledges make for scenic hiking

Abbe Museum ($ *Sieur de Monts Spring; tel: (207) 288-2179; open late May to mid-Oct daily 0900–1600*) chronicles the Abenaki Indian culture and history of the region over the past 2000 years, with particularly strong coverage of the interactions of Native and European peoples since 1750.

Park Loop Rd passes **Champlain Mountain**, where peregrine falcons nest from May to August, and quickly reaches seaside cliffs and **Sand Beach**, a broad bathing beach with coarse brown sand and waters that rarely rise above 12°C (54°F).

Although famous, **Thunder Hole** lives up to its name only when the three-quarter rising tide coincides with rough seas. Under those conditions, wave motion creates smashing thunderclaps inside hollow rocks at the shore. Nearby **Otter Cliff**, pounded by relentless surf, and **Otter Point** are ultimately more interesting. Careful observers are rewarded by an astonishing variety of life forms in the low-tide pools of Otter Point.

Park Loop Rd turns inland and passes the entry to the **Jordan Pond House**, a former farm converted to a tea house with beautiful gardens. Close by are the trails to **Jordan Pond** itself, a glacial kettle hole with striking views of the twin monadnocks (steep-sided isolated hills) called the 'Bubbles'. One difficult ascent of the Bubbles departs from the pond's shore, but a trailhead that begins on the shoulders of the Bubbles can be accessed from the Loop Rd. Watch for the sign to 'Bubble Erratics', a reference to massive boulders deposited in precarious balance on the mountains during the last glaciation.

The 3½-mile winding road to the 1530-ft summit of **Cadillac Mountain** begins near the end of Park Loop Rd. Very popular at dawn and dusk, Cadillac's peak offers 360-degree views of all of Mount

Noblesse Oblige

When Acadia was created in 1919 as the first national park east of the Mississippi River, its lands were donated by some of the country's richest businessmen, especially the petroleum billionaire John D. Rockefeller Jr. He gave almost one-third of the park and constructed more than 50 miles of carriage roads to make the interior accessible to all.

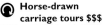

Horse-drawn carriage tours $$$
Wildwood Stable; tel: (207) 276-3622. Open mid-Jun–mid-Oct. The most luxurious way to see the park along the carriage roads built for John D Rockefeller, Jr.

Desert Island, Frenchman Bay and its string of Porcupine Islands, and the Blue Hill Peninsula. The most spectacular sunset views are not at the summit, but from the west-facing Blue Hill parking turnoff, at an elevation of about 1000ft.

Acadia's territories on the western lobe of the island are far less visited. The finest sandy swimming beach of the region is at **Echo Lake**, off Rte 102 south of Somesville village. Directly across the highway from the lake's car park is the trailhead for the **Acadia Mountain Loop Trail**, an easy hike up 2½ miles of uncrowded trails to viewpoints with broad vistas of Somes Sound and many small islands.

The portion of the park adjacent to Seawall campsite south of Southwest Harbor includes three naturalist highlights. **Great Heath**, also known as Seawall Bog, abounds with carnivorous plants and native orchids and also functions as a nesting habitat for palm warblers and yellowthroats. The nature trails of **Wonderland** and **Ship Harbor** pass through woodlands inhabited by virtually all the warblers found in the northern US and emerge on a coast where harbour seals and porpoises gather and bald eagles are frequently observed plucking fish from the waters.

Accommodation and food in Acadia National Park

Blackwoods Campground $ *Rte 3.* Reservations are required May–October for 300 woodland tent pitches. For reservations, contact National Recreation Reservations Service, *tel: (877) 444-6777 or (518) 885-3639 (international).*

Seawall Campground $ *Rte 102A; no tel.* More than 200 tent pitches are available on a first-come, first-served basis. Many pitches require that you carry your gear from a central car park.

Jordan Pond House $–$$ *Park Loop Rd; tel: (207) 276-3316.* Although the restaurant also serves lunch and dinner, the classic experience of the Pond House is taking afternoon tea and popovers (muffin-shaped bread made from batter), seated at tables on the lawn.

BAR HARBOR

Bar Harbor Chamber of Commerce *1201 Bar Harbor Rd, Trenton; tel: (207) 288-5103; www.barharbormaine.com. Open Mon–Fri 0800–1700; seasonal booth in Bar Harbor late May–mid-Oct daily 0900–1700.*

Bar Harbor is almost inescapable, as it contains the lion's share of lodging, dining and services for the entire island. Until a devastating fire scorched half of Mount Desert Island in 1947, Bar Harbor was a resort filled with the summer homes of wealthy New Yorkers. Some of the houses remain, mostly as B&Bs, but the town is more diverse these days, filled with travellers from around the world between June and October, then nearly deserted across the winter. Main and Mount Desert Sts function as the primary shopping district, with boutiques,

**Downeast
Transportation**
*Tel: (207) 667-5796;
www.exploreacadia.com.*
Free shuttle bus late
June–mid-October to
Acadia National Park,
Southwest Harbor and
Schoodic Peninsula.

In-town parking is
scarce June–October
but free on most streets
and at the town pier.
Recreational vehicle
parking is permitted only
in designated areas on the
outskirts of town.

Above
Bar Harbor

food shops and galleries jammed side by side. A delightful 1-mile scenic walk, the **Shore Path**, stretches from Agarmont Park by the town landing past many oceanfront manses. During the four hours surrounding low tide, it is possible to walk across the sand bar (from which the town took its name) at the end of Bridge St to Bar Island. From the town pier, several companies operate sightseeing cruises with an emphasis on viewing wildlife.

Accommodation and food in Bar Harbor

Route 3 north of Bar Harbor is lined with motel after motel, while the side streets of town are filled with B&Bs. Even so, most establishments are booked solid in July–August. Reservations are essential. Although most visitors satisfy their hunger with hand-held food while walking about, Bar Harbor also has many good seafood and pasta restaurants as well as the inevitable resort taverns with bar food.

Bar Harbor KOA Campground $ *136 County Rd; tel: (207) 288-3520; http://koa.com.* The 200 pitches, some oceanfront, some ocean view,

Acadia Bike & Coastal Kayaking $$$ *48 Cottage St; tel: (207) 288-9605; www.acadiafun.com.* Rents mountain bikes and kayaks and offers a variety of kayak trips including a harbour sunset tour.

Bar Harbor Bicycle Shop $$$ *141 Cottage St; tel: (207) 288-3886.* Rents mountain bikes for independent exploring.

Bar Harbor Whale Watch Co $$$ *Town Pier; tel: (888) 942-5374 or (207) 288-2386.* Motor cruises search for whales, puffins, seals, porpoises, eagles and other wildlife.

share a private beach for fishing and boating. Shuttle service to Bar Harbor.

Jordan's $ *80 Cottage St; tel: (207) 288-3586; serving breakfast 0500–1400, but closed for dinner.* Local gossip passes up and down the counter in the early hours before most tourists rise for the day.

Edenbrook Motel $–$$ *96 Eden St; tel: (800) 323-7819 or (207) 288-4975.* Bar Harbor's first motel, about a 15-minute walk from town, is lovingly maintained.

The Atlantic Eyrie $–$$$ *Rte 3, 6 Norman Rd; tel: (800) 422-2883 or (207) 288-9786.* Located north of town on a high hill, the aptly named Eyrie has stunning views of Frenchman Bay. Some suites are fully self-catering.

West Street Café $$ *West and Rodick Sts; tel: (207) 288-5242; open for lunch and dinner.* This old-fashioned restaurant offers the traditional Downeast meal of fish chowder, french fries (chips), steamed lobster and blueberry pie.

Holbrook House $$–$$$ *74 Mount Desert St; tel: (800) 860-7430 or (207) 288-4970; www.holbrookhouse.com.* One of the surviving late 19th-century 'cottages', Holbrook House has ten guest rooms and a wide front porch where breakfast is sometimes served.

Havana $$$ *318 Main St; tel: (207) 288-2822; www.havanamaine.com.* American fine dining with a Latin accent warms up the cold-water seafood of Maine with tropical spices and fruits. Dinner nightly.

Bass Harbor

Maine State Ferry Service $$ *Bass Harbor dock; tel: (207) 244-3254; www.state.me.us/mdot/opt/ferry/maine-ferry-service.php.* Year-round service to Swan's Island and to Frenchboro on Long Island.

With its lobster boats and striking lighthouse, scenic little Bass Harbor is the most tranquil of Mount Desert's seaside villages. A good and inexpensive way to appreciate the coastal scenery is to take a return trip on one of the state-run ferries from the town landing out to Frenchboro or Swan's Island.

Accommodation and food in Bass Harbor

Bass Harbor Campground $ *Rte 102A, PO Box 122; tel: (800) 327-5857 or (207) 244-5857; www.bassharbor.com.* Only a 10-minute walk from the ocean, this facility has separate areas for tents and RVs.

Bass Harbor Inn $–$$ *Shore Rd; tel: (207) 244-5157.* This 1870 house turned B&B offers rooms with harbour or mountain views.

Maine-ly Delights $–$$ *Grandville Rd; tel: (207) 244-3656; open for lunch and dinner.* Unpretentious local seafood is tops at this casual spot across from Swan's Island ferry dock.

NORTHEAST HARBOR

Beal & Bunker $$$ *Municipal Pier; tel: (207) 244-3575.* Carries mail year-round to the Cranberry Isles with stops at Great Cranberry, Little Cranberry (Islesford) and Sutton (summer only).

Sea Princess Cruises $$$ *Town Marina; tel: (207) 276-5352.* Choices include cruise of the Great Harbor and Somes Sound with stop on Little Cranberry Island, sunset cruise in Somes Sound and a dinner cruise.

Kimball Terrace Inn and Main Sail Restaurant $–$$ *Huntington Rd; tel: (207) 276-3383 or (800) 454-6225; www.kimballterraceinn.com.* Large motel overlooking Municipal Pier, literally steps from the village centre. Casual restaurant serves both seafood and meat dishes.

This principally residential, upmarket village is the preserve of such families as the Rockefellers and Pulitzers. The village centre contains an excellent cluster of boutiques as well as art and photo galleries, but most visitors come to gawk at the sleek craft moored at the yacht club or to board one of the excursion boats to the **Cranberry Isles** fishing communities located on Great Cranberry, Little Cranberry and Sutton islands south of Mount Desert Island. Islesford, on Little Cranberry, has developed as a summer retreat for many artists and craftspeople and is actually set up to receive visitors curious about island life. The National Park Service operates a small local history museum here during the summer.

SOUTHWEST HARBOR

Cranberry Cove Ferry $$$ *Town dock; tel: (207) 244-5882.* Operates ferries to Great Cranberry and Little Cranberry (Islesford).

Above
Quiet Northeast Harbor is a pleasure-boat haven

Until about 1980, Southwest Harbor was a quiet fishing and boat-building village where tourists passed through to soak up a little local colour and moved on. Now several of its fine old houses have been transformed into B&Bs and the central village is chock-a-block with boutiques, souvenir shops and cafés. But craftsmanship is still a byword in Southwest Harbor. The **Wendell Gilley Museum of Birdcarving** features the exquisite carved bird sculptures of Gilley as well as other wildlife art. The **Hinckley Company**, south of the village centre in Manset, is one of America's leading builders of luxury yachts. Visitors can walk the docks and the boatyard to admire these craft, but cannot board them. Across the street, the **Hinckley Ship Store** is a nautical paradise of charts and boating paraphernalia.

Wendell Gilley Museum of Birdcarving $ *Main St and Herrick Rd; tel: (207) 244-7555. Open Jun–Oct Tue–Sun 1000–1600 (open until 1700 Jul and Aug), May, Nov & Dec Fri–Sun 1000–1600.*

Hinckley Company *Shore Rd, Manset (1 mile south of Southwest Harbor centre); tel: (207) 244-5531.*

Accommodation and food in Southwest Harbor

Smugglers Den Campground $ *Rte 102, PO Box 787; tel: (207) 244-3944.* This facility has oceanfront camping and a heated pool and is close to a freshwater swimming beach.

Beal's Lobster Pier $–$$ *Clark Point Rd; tel: (207) 244-3202; open for lunch and dinner.* No-frills lobster shore dinners in one of the region's principal lobster-fishing ports.

The Claremont $$–$$$ *Claremont Rd, PO Box 137; tel: (800) 244-5036 or (207) 244-5036; www.theclaremonthotel.com.* The oldest summer resort hotel on Mount Desert Island affects a delightfully genteel air.

The Inn at Southwest $$–$$$ *371 Main St, PO Box 93; tel: (207) 244-3835; www.innatsouthwest.com.* Downtown Victorian home with wrap-around porch has seven guest rooms.

Fiddler's Green Restaurant $$$ *411 Main St; tel: (207) 244-9416; www.fiddlersgreenrestaurant.com; dinner only, closed Mon.* Mediterranean-inspired American menu emphasises local seafood, pastas and homemade sausages.

Suggested tour

Total distance: 90 miles.

Time: 3 hours' driving, but not recommended as a single-day tour. Stops will stretch tour to 3–4 days.

Links: Connects via Rte 3 to Penobscot Bay Route (*see page 260*).

Route: Enter Mount Desert Island on Rte 3 from Ellsworth, following signs for 7 miles to **Hulls Cove Visitor Center ❶** of ACADIA NATIONAL PARK. Follow the 27-mile circuit of the Park Loop Rd, making the 7-mile return-trip journey up Cadillac Mountain. On the last leg of Park Loop Rd, watch for signs to **Eagle Lake ❷**, reached 1 mile west on Rte 233. Boats can be rented at the lake, which also offers good fishing. Continue 3½ miles west to the junction with Rte 198, bearing right toward Somesville, the small village at the head of Somes Sound. Turn left and follow Rtes 102 and 198 south for 1 mile, then turn right on to well-named Pretty Marsh Rd, the northwest piece of Rte 102's loop around the western lobe of Mount Desert. **Long Pond ❸**, which appears on the left in 1 mile, is the main body of water in this marshy countryside, and canoes and kayaks can be rented here to explore the marshland ecosystem. Route 102 passes through marshes favoured by herons and grebes for the next 2 miles before turning inland through Boreal forest to emerge in 4 miles at scenic **Seal Cove ❹** on the coast. The road alternates between coastal views and forest as it winds 5 miles to Tremont, where

Picture Perfect

Although workshops with professional photographers are no longer part of the programme offerings at Acadia National Park, the varied but inevitably dramatic landscape seems to bring out the best in even the most casual picture snapper. The western summit car park offers spectacular sunset photo opportunities, especially when clouds appear on the horizon to reflect the light after sunset. Joedan Pond, by contrast, offers long vistas of nearby shoreline branches, a long smooth pond, and the rounded humps of North and South Bubble in the distance. Bar Island, accessible from Bar Harbor village at low tide, is most picturesque if photographers remember to place the horizon either very high or very low in the frame.

National Park Canoe $$$ *Long Pond's End; tel: (207) 244-5854. Open mid-May–Oct daily 0800–1700, until dusk Jul and Aug.* Rents canoes and sea kayaks and provides free instruction.

Above
Mount Desert Island, Acadia National Park

a right turn on to Rte 102A leads 1 mile into **BASS HARBOR ❺**. Rte 102A continues around the southernmost tip of Mount Desert as Seawall Rd, re-entering Acadia National Park. Along Seawall Rd are **Ship Harbor ❻**, **Wonderland ❼** and **Great Heath nature trails ❽**. In 6 miles the road enters Manset, the boat-building village on a cove of **SOUTHWEST HARBOR ❾**, and rejoins Rte 102 just south of the Southwest Harbor village. Follow Rte 102 north for 3 miles to Echo Lake and the Acadia Mountain Loop Trail, then another 3 miles to Somesville. Turn right on to Rte 198, retracing old ground and bearing right down the eastern shore of Somes Sound (where Rtes 198 and 3 share the roadway), following signs for 8 miles to **NORTHEAST HARBOR ❿**. Retrace Rte 198 for 1 mile north to rejoin Rte 3 and bear right, following the coastline with relentlessly scenic ocean views for 3 miles to the tiny village of **Seal Harbor ⓫**, then 7 miles through hilly woodlands into **BAR HARBOR ⓬**.

Also worth exploring

Schoodic Peninsula is part of Acadia National Park, but lies on the mainland across Frenchman Bay from Bar Harbor. Although only an hour's drive from Bar Harbor (passing through the village of Winter Harbor), the peninsula is rarely crowded. A park road off Rte 186 circles the perimeter. The 400ft-high granite outcrop of **Schoodic Point** is pounded by the sea, and the surrounding forests of spruce and jack pine are deep and wild.

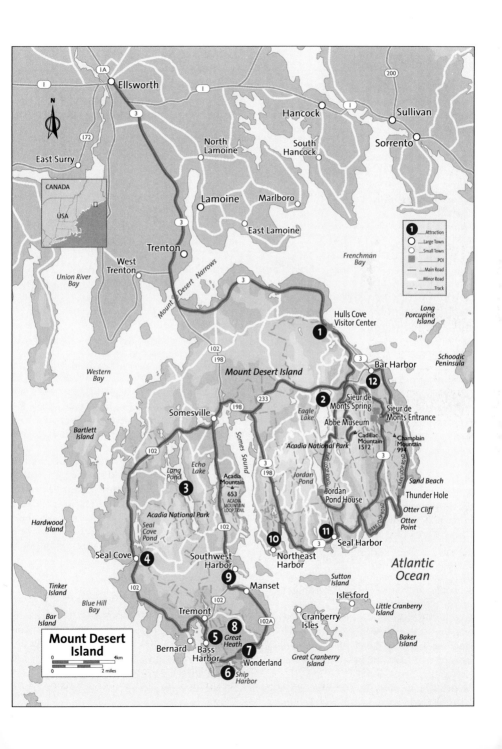

Language

How to talk New England:

Bubbler: Boston-speak for a water fountain

Buffalo Wings: Chicken wings, usually fried and served with a spicy sauce as an appetiser or as bar food

Chili dog or chili burger: Hot dog or hamburger disguised with chili, onions and cheese

Chips: Crisps

Clam roll: Fried clams, usually served on a hot-dog roll

Clam strips: Thin pieces of clam without the 'bellies'; a cheaper form of fried clams

Down East: Originally applied to Maine's coastal winds; now it's a place – either Maine or a part of its coast – and a practical attitude

Downtown: City or town centre

Frappé (pronounced frap): Boston-speak for a milk shake (milk blended with ice cream and flavouring)

Fries or french fries: Chips

Holiday: A public holiday, such as Labor Day, not a private holiday, which is a vacation

Ivy League: A group of eight prestigious universities in the northeastern US, including Harvard, Yale, Dartmouth and Brown in New England, where members of the US 'establishment' are educated

Microbrewery or brew-pub: A tavern that brews its own beer

Nor'easter: A coastal storm or gale blowing from the northeast (ie off the ocean), usually bringing heavy rain or snow

Outlet stores: Large stores specialising in factory overruns at reduced prices. Often, they are simply discount stores

Prep School: Preparatory school, a private High School for affluent adolescents heading for college (university)

Preppie: A student who attends prep school or who dresses like one who does

Quahog: An edible clam with a hard round shell (pronounced 'kwo-hog' or 'ko-hog' from the Narragansett *poqua'hock*)

Resort: A fancy hotel that specialises in leisure activities, such as golf, tennis and swimming

Road kill: Literally, animals killed by passing cars, but usually used to describe bad food

Soda: A soft drink, such as cola, anywhere but Boston

Tonic: A cola or other soft drink, but only around Boston, where it's pronounced TAW-nick; anywhere else, tonic (pronounced normally) is Quinine (as in 'Gin & Tonic') water

Yankee: An old-fashioned New Englander, usually of WASP (White Anglo-Saxon Protestant) heritage, marked by a taciturn expression, frugal ways and stern character

Some New England driving terms:

Big rig or 18-wheeler: A large lorry, usually a tractor pulling one or more trailers

Boston stop: Slowing at a stop sign, but not stopping

Bumper-to-bumper: Slow-moving, heavy traffic with little space between cars

Connector: A minor road connecting two highways

Divided highway: Dual carriageway

DUI or DWI: Driving Under the Influence (of alcohol or drugs), or Driving While Intoxicated, aka Drunken Driving; the blood alcohol limit in New England states varies from 0.08% to 0.10% and is very strictly enforced

Garage or parking garage: Car park

Gas(oline): Petrol

Grade: Gradient, hill

Highway: Motorway

Hit-and-run: Illegally leaving the scene after being involved in a collision

Motor home: Motor caravan

Ramp: Slip road

RV: Motor caravan

Shoulder: Verge

Sidewalk: Pavement

Speed bump: A road hump intended to make motorists slow down

(Stick)shift: Gear lever

Yield: Give way

Index

Acknowledgements

Project management: Cambridge Publishing Management Ltd
Project editor: Karen Beaulah
Series design: Fox Design
Cover design: Liz Lyons Design
Layout: Cambridge Publishing Management Ltd
Mapwork: PCGraphics (UK) Ltd
Repro and image setting: PDQ Reprographics/Cambridge Publishing Management Ltd
Printed and bound in India by: Ajanta Offset & Packaging Ltd

We would like to thank the following photographers and organisations for the photographs used in this book, to whom the copyright in the photograph belongs:

Karen Beaulah (pages 68 and 85).

Tom Bross (pages 1A, 34, 40A, 49, 56, 57, 62, 66, 122, 124, 134, 135, 145, 148, 158A, 158B, 163, 164, 234A, 234B, 236, 239, 244, 247 and 249).

Ethel Davies (pages 4, 10, 11, 22, 24, 26, 44, 45, 46, 50, 52, 64B, 70, 71, 76, 112, 114, 130B, 138, 144, 146, 151, 152, 154, 173, 202 and 211).

Ken Gallager (page 198).

David Lyon (pages 16, 19, 54, 59, 60, 64A, 67, 74, 77, 79, 82, 84, 87, 88, 91, 92, 102, 104, 105, 106, 108, 228A, 228B, 230, 252A, 252B, 254, 257, 260A, 260B, 262, 267, 270, 272 and 276).

Kyle MacLea (page 15, 265).

Pictures Colour Library (page 58).

Providence Warwick Convention & Visitors Bureau (page 160).

Stillman Rogers (pages 1B, 6, 12, 18, 23, 28, 29, 30, 33, 37, 39, 40B, 42, 94, 97, 98, 130A, 132, 141, 168, 170, 172, 175, 178, 180, 182, 184, 188, 190, 191, 196, 200, 206, 208, 214, 216, 218, 220, 223, 224 and 226).

Travel Ink/Ken Gibson (page 14).

Wikimedia Commons (page 61).

World Pictures/Photoshot (pages 80, 274 and 278).

Feedback form

We're committed to providing the very best up-to-date information in our travel guides and constantly strive to make them as useful as they can be. You can help us to improve future editions by letting us have your feedback. Just take a few minutes to complete and return this form to us.

When did you buy this book? ....
....

Where did you buy it? (Please give town/city and, if possible, name of retailer)
....
....

When did you/do you intend to travel in New England? ....
....

For how long (approx)? ....

How many people in your party? ....

Which cities, national parks and other locations did you/do you intend mainly to visit?
....
....
....
....

Did you/will you:
❏ Make all your travel arrangements independently?
❏ Travel on a fly-drive package?
Please give brief details: ....
....

Did you/do you intend to use this book:
❏ For planning your trip?   ❏ Both?
❏ During the trip itself?

Did you/do you intend also to purchase any of the following travel publications for your trip?
Thomas Cook *traveller guides Boston & New England* ....
A road map/atlas (please specify) ....
Other guidebooks (please specify) ....

Have you used any other Thomas Cook guidebooks in the past? If so, which?

....

....

Please rate the following features of *driving guides New England* for their value to you (Circle VU for 'very useful', U for 'useful', NU for 'little or no use'):

The *Travel facts* section on pages 12–21	VU	U	NU
The *Driver's guide* section on pages 22–27	VU	U	NU
The recommended driving routes throughout the book	VU	U	NU
Information on towns and cities, National Parks, etc	VU	U	NU
The maps of towns and cities, parks, etc	VU	U	NU

Please use this space to tell us about any features that in your opinion could be changed, improved, or added in future editions of the book, or any other comments you would like to make concerning the book:

....

....

....

....

....

....

....

....

....

Your age category: ❏ 21–30   ❏ 31–40   ❏ 41–50   ❏ over 50

Your name: Mr/Mrs/Miss/Ms ....

(First name or initials) ....

(Last name) ....

Your full address: (Please include postal or zip code)

....

....

....

....

....

Your daytime telephone number: ....

Please detach this page and send it to: driving guides Series Editor,
Thomas Cook Publishing, PO Box 227, Coningsby Road, Peterborough PE3 8SB.

Alternatively, you can e-mail us at: *books@thomascook.com*